JOURNEY
AFTER
MIDNIGHT

UJJAL DOSANJH

India, Canada

JOURNEY

and the

AFTER

Road Beyond

MIDNIGHT

Cataloguing data available from Library and Archives Canada
ISBN 978-1-927958-56-8 (hbk.)
ISBN 978-1-927958-57-5 (ebook)
ISBN 978-1-927958-58-2 (pdf)

Editing by Barbara Pulling
Copy editing by Melanie Little
Indexing by Stephen Ullstrom
Map by Eric Leinberger
Design by Natalie Olsen
Front cover photograph by Kevin Clark
Printed and bound in Canada by Friesens
Distributed in the U.S. by Publishers Group West

Figure 1 Publishing Inc.
Vancouver BC Canada
www.figure1pub.com

To Rami, who has unflinchingly stood with me; to my brother, sisters, cousins, aunts and uncles; to my children, who love me despite the long periods of neglect I visited upon them; to my six grandchildren, Solaina, Alexie, Suhani, Iyla, Mila and Damon, for whom I continue my fight and pen my life's story; and to the countless friends and supporters who have helped me stand up, speak out and fight on.

CONTENTS

*Photographs
following pages
104 and 275*

I was born in Dosanjh Kalan, a dusty village in rural Punjab. I exited my first home, the womb, on October 14, 1946 — exactly ten months before Pakistan was tragically partitioned from India, its mother, on August 15, 1947 — making me a child of midnight.

I spent the first eighteen years of my life in India, fled briefly to Britain and then came to Canada, where I have remained for close to five decades. I am indebted to India for giving me its ancient civilization as a birth gift and for nurturing me before I fled as a fugitive from its battles. I am grateful to England — which I despised as a former colonial power, until I landed in London — for what it taught me during my short sojourn in its embrace, though I felt like an interloper there. Afraid to go back to India as a failure, I embarked for Canada, where I was able to drop anchor. Together, these three countries have given me a life filled with more victories than defeats, more joys than sorrows. The world has done much to help make me a better man, and some may say I haven't done too badly.

Why should my story matter? It does not seem important in the larger scheme of things. But our own stories always matter to us, and to the generations that follow. Merging with the stories of so many others, they give meaning to our lives and to the lives of nations.

Everything may not have happened exactly as I recall it in these pages. Memory is a magician that plays tricks on us. We remember the mundane but often forget the profound. Memory saves pleasures past but deletes many episodes of pain. Nonetheless, I have remained faithful to the truth as I see it and have done my best to make this a fair accounting.

As I approach my final years, I am impatient with life, but also at peace. I am content, but still in search of the next challenge. I come by my activism honestly. My inner determination is fuelled by what I learned from my heroes, the fighters for freedom I most admired: my father, Master Pritam Singh Dosanjh; my maternal grandfather, Jathedar/Jarnail Moola Singh Bains; and Mahatma Gandhi, the father of the nation I deserted to make Canada my home.

My father used to say, "One may walk fewer steps in life, but one must always walk with dignity." His personal credo has sustained me on this journey after midnight, from the dusty roads of rural India I so vividly remember to the full life I continue to enjoy. The inspiration I draw from my heroes is responsible for any good I may have done. For the mistakes in my life, more than a few, I alone am responsible.

PART 1

INDIA

Early Years

1 I WAS BROUGHT INTO A WORLD in turmoil. The Allies had decisively defeated the Fascist/Axis armies, but the world had witnessed the first atom bombs fall on Hiroshima and Nagasaki. Several million Jews, half a million Roma and innumerable others had been killed by Hitler. The League of Nations was consigned to the history books, and the United Nations had been launched. A victorious but weakened Britain was in the midst of leaving India.

Dosanjh Kalan, the dusty village in Punjab where I was born, had been settled by my ancestors about five hundred years earlier. Dosanjhes, like most Punjabis, are believed to have travelled initially from Rajasthan. My ancestors lived a few miles away in Puadhra before moving to a new spot to create Dosanjh Kalan. From a recent study of last names published in a major Punjabi daily, I discovered that a minor princeling in Rajasthan had five sons: Dosanjh, Malhi, Dhindsa, Sangha and Dhaliwal. Since then, we Dosanjhes have grown to number several thousand in India and across the world. Of course, "Dosanjh" was a first name at a time when people in India usually had single names, so perhaps princelings were not the only fathers to name their sons Dosanjh. So though some of us lay claim to a "royal" lineage, I make no such claim. I have no doubt I come from untainted peasant stock: people of the soil who through the centuries worked their small plots of earth to eke out the most meagre of livings.

My father, Pritam Singh, along with his only surviving sibling, Joginder Singh, our Tayaji (father's elder brother), owned a mere five-acre parcel of land. We lived together as one household; my cousins, my siblings and I were cared for by our Taeeji (father's elder brother's wife), Bhagwant Kaur, and our mother, Surjit Kaur, whom we called

Biji (a family term for mother or grandmother). Even now, our ancestral land is owned jointly by the extended family. The bond between the Dosanjh cousins and our children and grandchildren is still strong.

My paternal great-great-grandfather, Dunna Singh, had two sons, Nand Singh and Bhola Singh. His brother had two sons as well. One was Jamait Singh; the other's name remains unknown to me. Jamait's brother married and had two sons. Eventually the sons married, and both of them died without issue.

One of the widows left behind by those sons was Bachint Kaur. Her husband died before *muklava*, the time when a new bride returns from staying with her parents for a short period following the wedding — a custom that likely arose because girls were married so young and needed to grow up a bit more before being *muklavaed* to their in-laws. Because Bachint's husband died during this period, his family, the Dosanjhes, rebuffed her as a bringer of bad luck. From then on, she lived the life of a rejected widow, with no prospect of remarrying. I am unable to fathom the depths of pain and despair she must have gone through, sitting in her parents' home. Once they too had died, she was dependent for her basic needs on her brothers and their wives. In her village, she would never have been able to escape the hungry eyes of the men, yet she was forbidden from sleeping with a man for the rest of her life.

When my brother Kamal had occasion to see Bachint late in life, she happily relinquished any right or title to the ancestral property in Dosanjh Kalan. She was a Dosanjh, and she wanted the Dosanjhes to prosper, she told my brother. She wanted to do this last "good deed" for the family that had rejected her. There was no question Dosanjhes were every bit as backward as their contemporaries.

The other widow, Basant Kaur, lived a long life and was an important part of my childhood. She was my father's Taeeji, and we mimicked him by calling her Taeeji, too. The contours of her face were a reminder of the beauty of her youth. Her deep wrinkles were evidence of her years of struggle. She lived alone, directly across from us, in a several-hundred-year-old brick house with intricately carved wooden doors.

On either side of the entrance, indented spaces had been created for *divas*, earthen lamps fuelled by mustard oil. I would stand in front of those doors and try to understand their place in our family's history. Why were the doors of our household not as ancient or as expensive-looking as Taeeji's?

My Pardada (paternal great-grandfather), Nand Singh, had two sons. The younger son died at an early age. The surviving son, Harnam, my paternal grandfather, or Dada, married Bishan Kaur, one of six children from Virkaan, a village about three miles from Dosanjh Kalan. The historic Grand Trunk Road that traverses the subcontinent from Peshawar to Delhi, built by King Sher Shah Suri in the sixteenth century, runs less than a mile away from Virkaan and connects the village with the nearby industrial and educational centre of Phagwara. Being near such a centre, and perhaps thus more aware of the rest of the world, may have inspired my Dada to go to Singapore, looking for work. Before he left, he and Bishan, my Dadi (paternal grandmother), had three sons: Pritam, my father; his elder brother Joginder, my Tayaji; and their brother, Raju, in between. My Dada stayed in Singapore for some time before falling ill and returning to India. The details are sketchy, but this much is known: he died in 1910, when my father was just four and Tayaji was twelve years old; Raju too had died by this point.

Bhola Singh, my great-grandfather's brother, had two children: one named Budh Singh and the other a girl whose name, sadly, no one seems to remember. Budh was a handsome, lanky man with a turban and a flowing beard. Since we had no photographs of anyone in the family prior to my father's generation, watching Budh as a boy I used to try and imagine what his first cousin, my Dada, would have looked like. From all accounts Dada had been tall, handsome and very strong. His father, Nand, had been nicknamed Ghora (horse), for being so tall, strong and handsome himself.

Tayaji, by contrast, was short, and so was my father (whom my siblings and I, following our cousins, always called Chachaji — father's younger brother). We all blamed our Dadi Bishan for the deficit in this department, because she was a few inches shy of five feet.

But what she lacked in height she more than made up for in courage and toughness. Dadi ran a tight ship. She had to, in order to raise Chachaji and Tayaji on her own. She managed it by dispatching Tayaji into her family's care in Virkaan, and Chachaji into the care of her sister, who lived a few miles away at Badala. Chachaji finished four years of primary school there. Free of child-rearing duties, Dadi managed what little land Dada had owned. It was mere subsistence.

After some years, Chachaji and Tayaji reunited with Dadi at Dosanjh. Tayaji started working on the land, helping Dadi, and Chachaji was enrolled at J.J. Government High School in Phagwara. He would wake early in the morning to feed and water the cattle, then swing his cloth book bag over his shoulder, run the few miles to school and make it to class on time. My father was a bright child, learning English, Urdu, Punjabi and math, among other subjects. He was particularly interested in history and in the ongoing political drama of India's struggle for independence.

Mahatma Gandhi returned from South Africa in 1915. The First World War was underway, and the *Komagata Maru*, a Japanese steamship taking prospective Indian immigrants to Canada in defiance of the Canadian government's exclusionary direct passage law, had been turned back in July 1914 under the menacing shadow of the Canadian warship HMS *Rainbow*. An Indian patriot named Baba Bir Singh, who had been living in Canada, sailed for India on August 22, 1914, at the head of a group of revolutionaries from the North American Ghadar Party, determined to overthrow British rule in India. The news of their departure for India to create "trouble" was duly cabled to the British colonial government in Lahore, which captured and hanged Bir Singh and forty-two others in March 1916, in the so-called Lahore Conspiracy Case. Bir Singh's older brother's son, Moola Singh Bains, in his early twenties at the time and working as a security guard in Shanghai, was my maternal grandfather, Nanaji.

To my impressionable and impoverished father, still a student, the world must have seemed full of turmoil. His own small world of Dosanjh Kalan was certainly no haven of stability or financial security.

It did not help that Tayaji, though he worked hard on the land, began to squander the family's savings on oxen, which he occasionally showed off as they outperformed and outran the oxen of the neighbours.

Dosanjh Kalan had no mechanized agriculture in the 1950s. Oxen and water buffalos were used to plough and sow our land holdings. To irrigate the soil, farmers used a Persian wheel — a chain of buckets mounted on a large wheel rotated by oxen. The buckets emptied water into a trough, from which it flowed into a network of channels.

Our lives revolved around the seasons and festivals. Some of the festivals included Persian wheel races; the largest of these was Vaisakhi, a harvest festival celebrated in northern India that has long held a special meaning for Sikhs. It was in 1699 at the Vaisakhi festival in Anandpur (now referred to as Anandpur Sahib as a sign of reverence) that the last Guru, Gobind Singh, created the Khalsa, an army of followers with strict rules for a simple life. From then on, Sikh men wore a sword, a steel bracelet, special utilitarian underwear, a comb, and turbans over unshorn hair. (The words for these five requirements all started with K; hence, they are known as "the five Ks.") My ancestors, too, became part of the Khalsa.

When I was a child, we occasionally attended the month-end Sangrand celebrations, and we almost always attended the Vaisakhi *mela*, or fair, at Baba Sung Gurdwara, the temple built at the site where Baba Sung, a prominent religious figure of his time, lived and died in the service of the people of the area. The gurdwara was about six miles from our village, and we would usually walk there, pay our respects, and then eat and rejoice with the crowds before returning. At Baba Sung, the Dosanjhes were treated royally, because we were believed to be the descendants of Baba Sung's daughter from the time of Guru Arjun Dev, fifth in a line started by the first Guru, Nanak Dev, a great poet and philosopher. The line ended with the tenth Guru, Gobind Singh, creator of the Khalsa and a great poet-warrior in his own right. Baba Sung's importance in the annals of Sikh history is evident from the reference made to him as a contemporary and revered follower of Guru Arjun in the works of Bhai Gurdas, perhaps the greatest chronicler of the Sikh Gurus.

BY THE LATE FIFTIES, our family's economic condition was better than it had been in the 1940s. As Chachaji was finishing his education, my cousin Harbans, born in 1919, was growing up. The family was in debt, and Tayaji had mortgaged most of the ancestral lands. That meant there was almost no land the family could farm for subsistence; under the land laws and customs of the time, the lender would take possession of the land until the debt was cleared. Together, Chachaji and Biraji (older brother, as we called Harbans) turned the family circumstances around. Tayaji had never let Biraji go to school. Chachaji would enrol him, but Tayaji would go to the school and physically yank him out, insisting that Biraji help him full time on the land. He claimed that Chachaji had been "corrupted" by education.

Biraji left for the U.K. in 1956. By then Chachaji was teaching at the Dosanjh School, which he and some friends had founded in 1932. Its official name was Guru Har Rai Khalsa High School, named after the seventh Sikh Guru but open to people of all faiths without conversion. Siso, the eldest of my other three cousins, was married and had settled in Ghaziabad, near Delhi. Her husband, Sardara Singh Johal, was a mechanic who ran a successful machine shop out of their home, which also served as the resting stop for family members on their way to England.

My first clear memory is of getting a brass *kalmandal* of water filled by someone at our neighbourhood well and carrying it home to my mother, Biji. From it she would have made a fresh lemon drink or perhaps the delicious white concoction called *shardayee*, made of ground seeds, water and milk, which she served in small brass glasses. In my mind's eye, I recall that I was naked except for a thread around my waist, perhaps to ward off evil spirits. At that age for children, if you were simply running around the neighbourhood, no one worried about clothing you. Nakedness had its advantages: the calls of nature were easier to contend with. I remember defecating in the nearest open space and rubbing my bottom on a grassy patch of earth before I resumed playing with the other kids.

I don't know whether Biji tied that thread around my waist because she was truly superstitious. Chachaji wasn't. And I do know that while my mother was growing up, her father, my Nanaji, used to run astrologers and palmists right out of the village if he spotted them plying their useless trade door to door. But my mother may not have been as liberated as I like to imagine she was.

There was a well beyond the compound behind our home where our neighbourhood got its drinking water. The families of the caste of water bearers, *jhirs*, serviced different areas of the village. Twice a day, my Dosanjh School classmate Balbir and his family would manually draw water from the well, fill two earthen pitchers and leave them at our home. In the morning and the evening, the well's busiest times, *jhirs* competed among themselves to be the first ones to draw water for the households they were responsible for.

In my early years, I did not realize the *jhir* caste was one of many that Indian society had divided itself into. The caste system is one of the most pernicious and sinister divisions of people on earth. The Sikh religion evolved partly to fight its insidious inequality. The Muslim faith also espouses egalitarianism. But even today, most Muslims and Sikhs continue to fall prey to caste divisions. When I first learned the word *jhir*, I thought it described someone's occupation, just as my father was called Master for being a teacher. I knew nothing of the prison of caste that existed in India or of the pain and injustice it perpetrated.

I played with the neighbourhood children in the *vehda* — the compound — behind our home. We fashioned our toys out of broken or discarded bricks or made small *guddian* (carts) and oxen from simple mud. Sometimes the village *tarkhan* (carpenter) made a few toys out of leftover wood, but wood was expensive and in short supply. Feeding your family, using any surplus to buy food you could not grow on your own land, was everyone's primary goal.

Our family was helped by Chachaji's teaching salary, though it was not huge. Our joint family had eleven mouths to feed from our five acres, and several school-going children to support. Being educated himself, my father realized the value of education, and he made sure that my Bhaji (brother) Kamal, my sisters Nimmy and Hartirath and I, as well as our Bhenjis (female cousins) — Bakhshish (the cousin we called Siso), Gurmit, and Harbans Kaur (whom we called Banso) — all went off to school.

Dosanjh was a caste of agriculturalists. The village consisted of five big families that had settled there several hundred years earlier. Each of the five was known as a *patti,* in the name of one of the five settler elders. Our home and the buildings on our land had mud walls and mud roofs, with wood from local trees holding up ceilings made of dried long grass. The roads were dusty, and the streets in our village were mostly covered by kiln-baked bricks. Sewage from homes flowed down *naalian* (channels) in the middle of the street, or on either side, out to two big ponds. The *naalian* were regularly dredged, with raw solid sewage piled up at various points on the street to dry. It was then carried away by the *choohdays* — the lowest group in the caste hierarchy — to be used as compost.

The stench from the *naalian* was bad. The monsoons were both a blessing and a curse: they washed the sewage out of the *naalian* into the ponds, but the stench from the ponds and other bodies of polluted rainwater was terrible in the extreme humidity. As young children, though, we were as one with our surroundings. One of our favourite pastimes was making paper boats and floating them in *naalian* full of gushing rain water. In the long rainy days of the monsoons, there wasn't much else to do.

People went to the lands adjoining the villages to relieve themselves of their morning solid waste. That was a headache for those of us who worked that land every day. Quite often, hay-cutting or other chores would land our bare hands and feet in fresh human droppings.

We were told the earth was a great disinfectant, so we would rub our soiled hands with dirt, and if any water was around, we would wash them. Failing that, we would wipe our hands on the hay or any other crop we were cutting.

We recycled everything. The village grew and spun its own cotton and wove it into cloth. We made our own unrefined sugar from homegrown sugarcane. The non-sugary upper leaves of the cane went to feed milk-producing cattle as well as the working oxen we used to help extract the juice. The cane's skin, pulp and lower leaves were dried in the sun and then used as fuel to boil the juice to make sugar. Any leaves or pulp left over fuelled the home fires that fed our family. Once the cotton was picked, the plants were pulled out to be used as fuel, and the land was irrigated to prepare it for the next crop. Some of the ashes from this fuel were used for cleaning our metal dishes, and the remainder was mixed with animal excrement and composted, along with any greens left over from our farm or the household. Whenever we seeded a new crop, that compost was scattered and ploughed into the land.

The partition of India in 1947 affected Punjab and Bengal more than other parts of the country. Both were divided, creating East Pakistan — now Bangladesh — and West Pakistan, which included the large western portion of Punjab, with East Punjab becoming the Indian Punjab. From these divided regions, most Hindus and Sikhs migrated to what is now India, and Muslims migrated to what are now Pakistan and Bangladesh. Land consolidation was needed to accommodate the fourteen million people who had been uprooted. Before the partition, our family's land was at Billayhana, half a mile from our home; it included a well with lots of trees around it and two Persian wheels, allowing two families to irrigate their land parcels at the same time.

Mangu, a handsome Dalit man from my mother's village of Bahowal, was compensated with food, clothing, shelter and monthly pay to help out on our family farm. He lived at Billayhana with our uncle Tayaji. Their three meals a day were sent to them there. When the farm did not require Tayaji and Mangu to be there in the evenings, they joined the rest of our family at home for the meals, sharing stories and the gossip of the day. Then Tayaji would carry goodies for his beloved oxen back to Billayhana while Mangu would carry the human cargo, me, atop his shoulders. During the winter, I slept most nights on Tayaji's bed. In the next room, the cattle were given respite from the noon heat on summer days, and shelter on cold winter nights and during the rains. On a cold night the warmth of the animals' bodies and the sound of their breathing came through the door in the common wall, keeping us warm and comfortable; the smell of their urine and dung came in too. For centuries, peasants and their cattle lived cheek by jowl; the smell of urine and dung was the scent of life.

In the mornings, as the sun rose, someone from home would arrive with Tayaji's chai. All the children in our family fought to be with him at chai time. He got special goodies, quite often *pinnies*, delicious balls made of nuts, seeds and flour that were skillet-baked in butter and raw homemade sugar.

Land consolidation after partition was a mammoth task, taking several years to accomplish. When I was four or five, the farm at Billayhana was relocated close to our village, a bare one hundred yards from our house on the other side of the *firnie*, the dusty ring road constructed around villages in ancient times for fortification — the word *firnie* meaning "one that goes around." The *firnies* of old demarcated the residential boundary for each village. Even when I was growing up, very few families lived outside them.

Our new well and the land attached to it was called the Goraywala, which means "of the *gora*" — one with a whiter complexion. The reason for the name was the colour of the old limestone platform around the well and the *chalha*, or reservoir. There was always some water in the *chalha* for the cattle to drink when the Persian wheel was not running. Until the arrival of local hand pumps in the mid-1950s, the Goraywala and its *chalha* served as the neighbourhood's communal watering and washing place.

The cleansing of the Goraywala, which had been in disuse for some time after partition, was quite an elaborate ceremony. Blessings were sought from Khwaja, the god of water. Sweets were distributed, and much fun was had by all.

The ageless Goraywala was like an ancient witness to the march of men and women on the roads and streets of our village. It had provided drinking water to unknown travellers as well as generations of Dosanjhes. Thousands of children had peered through its cool water deep into the bowels of the earth. I too wondered at the deep secrets it held. I did not know then what I know now: the Goraywala was once at the heart of life.

Yet to me the Goraywala, being just a few yards away from our home, was an extension of it. In winter, we woke up to see the Persian wheel bringing well water to the surface. Steam rose like mist, giving the surroundings an enchanted look. The occasional winter fog made the Goraywala even more mysterious to my young mind. I would not learn until later that the fog was actually smog. Many a morning, the sun toiled and failed to come through. We conveniently blamed the gods, the sun god included.

In the fall, when the corn crop was harvested at Billayhana, huge, colourful mounds of cobs lay in the middle of a circle of drying stalks. As kids, we got to sleep in that circle under the starlit sky, waking up in the morning feeling as if we were small pieces of a multi-coloured work of art, brilliantly lit by the rising red sun. That beauty helped to mask the gruelling labour the land required. It was back-breaking work — under the scorching tropical sun in May, June and July, and in the dead cold of winter mornings.

In summer, I would sleep outside, either in the yard on the farm or on top of the roof at home. The stars and the moon entertained me. I marvelled at the wonders of the universe. On the moon we saw a shadow the elders told us was an old woman with a *charkha*, the traditional spinning wheel. She looked distinctly Indian, sitting motionless with both her hands in spinning mode, connecting us to the moon. In the world of my childhood, the moon and the earth were siblings, as they have been to Indians from time immemorial. The earth was our mother and the moon our Chandamama, or maternal uncle.

ONE MORNING BEFORE DAYBREAK, my mother woke me up. It was a cold winter morning, and still dark out. She dressed me up in warm clothes. The milk that had been cultured overnight was ready for churning. Biji placed the *madhani*, a churning rod with a lid, in the *chaati*, the baked clay pot containing the cultured milk, and spun the *madhani* repeatedly with a rope, stopping periodically to check whether the cream had risen to the top. The room was dim, lit only by the oil and cotton wick in a *diva*.

3

My mother was beautiful and still very young. She had given birth to five children in a short span of time. One child, Hartirath, died within six months, a brother I never had the opportunity to know. Chachaji and Biji missed him so much that they named their next-born child, my sister, Hartirath as well, though we called her Tirath for short.

My Biji was the eldest child of my Nanaji and my Naniji (maternal grandmother), Raj Kaur, whom we affectionately called Jajo. My mother had grown up with two sisters, Gurmit and Harjit, and a baby brother, Inderjit. Because Nanaji spent most of his adult life fighting for India's freedom — nine of those years in British Indian jails and the rest organizing and agitating, often while in hiding — Naniji and Biji, unlike other women from the *jat* (agriculturalist) caste, had to work the land in his absence. Fending for themselves was a necessity for the Bains women, not an option; either they worked the land or they went hungry.

Now Nanaji was back in Bahowal with Jajo, where they lived with my aunts. But unlike on our family farm in Dosanjh, there were no little children to care for and delight in. And so a decision had been made to send me to Bahowal to live with my grandparents, for my primary education.

That morning of my departure, Biji fed me freshly churned *makhni* (butter) with *behi* roti (stale chapati). It is the ultimate expression of the legendary Punjabi/Indian motherly love to be fed *makhni* with *behi* roti in the dark of an early morning, and it is done before mothers send their sons away. But I was too young to be sad that I was leaving home; my excitement was boundless.

A new wooden *gudda*, a cart on two wheels, had been built by our family *tarkhan* at Dosanjh for Nanaji. Sawing, planing and joining the wood had all been done by hand. Chachaji had also helped Nanaji purchase a chaff cutter to prepare green cattle feed, something that all farmers needed. The new chaff cutter was loaded on the *gudda* and the oxen were harnessed at the front, ready to pull it away the moment their master, Nanaji, ordered.

Biji hugged me, and Chachaji and Bhaji walked me out. Tayaji stood waiting near the *gudda* too. An extra *jhull* — a blanket for cattle, made of discarded human clothing — had been placed on the *gudda* for me to sit or sleep on, and a homemade cotton *khais*, or blanket, was wrapped around me. The sun was still not up when the *gudda* started moving. Gradually, my home and the Goraywala became but points in the distance. Nanaji and the *gudda* were taking me to another world, though it was only twenty miles away. The hooves of the oxen and the creaking of the wheels made music on that still morning. The singing birds greeted us as they awoke.

We stopped several times on the way to Bahowal to feed ourselves and the oxen. We had brought along some fresh green cattle food for the journey. At our first stop, we fed the oxen and gave them some water before eating our *pranthas*, the tasty rotis skillet-fried in butter that Biji had made for us. We washed them down with tea from a tea shop. As we rode, Nanaji told me stories about his life to entertain me. They sounded like fairy tales, but they were nothing of the kind, as I would discover later on. I eventually dozed off, but Nanaji woke me up for more tea and delicious *burfi* he had ordered from another shop after feeding the oxen once again. Even today, my mouth waters thinking about the dense sweetness of that *burfi*.

The *kuchi sarak*, or dirt road, we travelled was punctuated by asphalt for a few short stretches. From Mahilpur to Bahowal, trees lined the *pucki sarak*, the asphalted road, on either side, forming a beautiful canopy that protected travellers from the hot summer sun.

The crimson rays of evening greeted us as we reached Bahowal, a village smaller than Dosanjh. Most homes here were either *pucka* (of brick) or *kucha* (of mud); *pucka* denoted affluence, and *kucha* spoke of poverty. Nanaji's home was a mix of both. Like Nanaji's family itself, it straddled the divide, betraying the relative poverty into which the once-prosperous family had slipped. Nanaji had been either imprisoned or in hiding for three decades; in his absence, it had been difficult for Naniji and her children to make a go of their lives. Next door, however, stood a grand *pucka* home, built by Nanaji's older brother, Beant, for his wife upon his return from Canada, where he had emigrated. It was a daily reminder of how different a path my grandfather had chosen.

In fact, Nanaji had nearly followed his brother to Canada himself. He had been working in Shanghai for four years when, in 1919, Beant invited him to join him on Vancouver Island. Nanaji returned to India to say goodbye to his mother — his passport had been obtained, and he had arranged to accompany his sister-in-law, Beant's wife, to British Columbia. Instead, he jumped headlong into the Indian independence movement; Beant's wife never made it to Canada.

In February 1921, close to a hundred Sikhs were killed by the *mahant* who controlled the gurdwara built at Guru Nanak's birthplace, Nankana Sahib (now in Pakistan). The unarmed Sikhs sought to wrest control of the temple from the *mahant* because of the sexual abuse and debauchery that he allowed there. Nanaji led a group of volunteers to Nankana Sahib to help in the aftermath of the massacre, which became known as Saka Nankana Sahib.

In the following month, a conference was organized at Nankana Sahib. Nanaji was asked by the Shiromani Gurdwara Parbandhak Committee to be responsible for the security of the venue, as many stalwarts of the freedom movement, including Mahatma Gandhi, Pandit

Madan Mohan Malviya, and Dr. Saifuddin Kitchlew, would be present. From his district, Nanaji led a *jatha* (group) of seventy-five men. As part of his duties, he also arranged the safe passage of Gurdit Singh, the hero of the *Komagata Maru* incident, to the conference.

Gandhi told those assembled that he had come to share their anguish and grief. He stated that the non-violence of the Sikhs had "greatly added to the prestige and glory of India." The "cruel and barbaric action" at Nankana Sahib, Gandhi said, was "more evil and more invidious than even Jallianwala." He was referring to the notorious incident at the Jallianwala Bagh (public gardens) on April 13, 1919, where several hundred unarmed Indians were gunned down by the British, led by General Reginald Dyer, while attending a peaceful assembly.

Nanaji's uncle, Bir Singh, who had returned from Canada to India as a member of the Ghadar Party and who fought for independence under the Ghadar banner, had been sent to the gallows by the British in 1916. Young Moola was deeply touched by his uncle's bravery. After Saka Nankana drew him in, there was no turning back. My grandfather's passport was confiscated by the government, and he gave himself entirely to the freedom movement. When the other of his two older brothers died, leaving a widow behind, Nanaji's progressive spiritual friend Jianwaley Sant urged him to marry the woman. He did, and she became our Jajo.

The Gurdwara Sudhar Lehar, the Sikh Temple Reform Movement, aimed to wrest control of all historic temples from the pro-British *mahants*. After the Saka Nankana, the Lehar gained momentum. Nanaji was appointed *jathedar* (leader) of sixty Sikhs sent from Hoshiarpur to Amritsar to take over the Golden Temple there. This was accomplished peacefully, and the charge of the Sikhs' holiest place was turned over to the prominent activist Kharak Singh in November 1921. Shortly thereafter, the Sikhs of the Hoshiarpur and Jalandhar districts, under Nanaji's leadership, took possession of Takht Keshgarh Sahib (Anandpur Sahib, where the last Sikh Guru, Gobind Singh, had created the Khalsa) and Kiratpur Sahib. The liberation of the Sis-Ganj Sahib

Gurdwara at Anandpur followed — and there again Nanaji showed his trademark courage, wisdom and tact in leading the victory.

At the Hola Mohalla celebrations at Anandpur Sahib that year, in appreciation for his service and his commitment to the cause of the country and the Panth (the community of Sikhs), Nanaji was given the title "General of Akali Army," decorated with a general's uniform and provided with a horse. (The Akali Dal was a Sikh religious and political party with strong anti-colonialist leanings.) The Hola Mohalla festival has deep religious and cultural meaning for Sikhs. It started in February 1701, shortly after the founding of the Khalsa, when Guru Gobind Singh organized a day of war exercises, sports and poetry for training and recreational purposes. The tradition continues, with a festival held in or close to March every year.

In 1924, the Gurdwara Sudhar Lehar and the *jathedars* of all thirty-six districts of the then-united Punjab appointed Nanaji the Jathedar of Jathedars to lead the Lehar. Over time, he evolved from a Sikh political activist into a Marxist who learned to read and write Hindi as a political prisoner in the British jails. He spent nine years behind bars before India achieved independence. That is a big chunk of anyone's life, but he was sentenced to many more years than he actually served. On top of that, my grandfather spent years under house arrest or being confined to his village of Bahowal. He also had to face sanctions if he violated the strict terms of his release. Add to all this the number of years of illegal and undocumented detention that he suffered, and it can be safely argued that between his return from China in 1919 and the independence of India in 1947, Nanaji was under partial or complete political detention for at least twenty years. After Independence, there were still periodic jail visits, house arrests, mandatory reporting to police and other restrictions, as Nanaji continued agitating for better economic and social conditions for the common folk in free India.

Nanaji was not perfect. After India was freed but divided, he, like millions of others, felt betrayed. He rejected the division of the country. The pace of change, too, was slow and disheartening, and, settled back in Bahowal, he came face to face with his own material poverty. He could not even provide enough wheat flour for daily rotis for his small family. Nanaji and his comrades felt that the India of their dreams was daily becoming more elusive, and one night some colleagues from the leftist underground in the region came to see him. They wanted him to do political work somewhere far away. It pained Nanaji to turn them down, but the hunger stalking his family kept him at home. He forever afterwards regretted that decision. This was the first time he had ever said no to his colleagues, and it felt selfish to do so in order to feed his family. Although he remained active in the Communist Party of India till he came to Canada in 1975, his failure to be perfect in that moment remained with him till he died.

Before his death in Canada in 1982, Nanaji regularly spoke out against inequality, religious hatred and the harebrained idea of Khalistan, the imagined homeland that Canadian Sikh separatists even then wanted to carve out of India. Alienated from the mainstream and guilty about leaving India, the separatists in the Sikh diaspora had fallen into a stupor of fanaticism.

MY MOTHER AND FATHER were married in 1942, amid
the anti-British turmoil of the Quit India Movement launched
by Mahatma Gandhi. Indians wanted a quick overthrow of
the British regime. Nanaji, of course, was at the forefront of Quit India
in his region. He was imprisoned once again — this time under the
Defence of India Act, a law deceptively named, since its only purpose
was the defence of British rule. Biji's marriage, like most other family
events, happened without her father's participation. Nanaji's friends
on the outside pitched in, as did, remarkably, the groom-to-be.

4

Sometime before 1942, when he was not constrained by royal edict,
Nanaji had asked a friend to suggest a good boy, if he knew one, for Biji,
his eldest daughter. It so happened that the friend had spotted my father
taking a bath at the Dosanjh family's Persian wheel. My grandfather
hesitated at first. Chachaji was quite a bit older than Biji, and although
the economic condition of the Dosanjhes had improved, they were still
quite poor. But Nanaji also had his other two daughters, Gurmit and
Harjit, to worry about. They, too, would be of marriageable age soon.

After some discreet inquiries, contact with Chachaji was made.
Nanaji was underground and on the run, but one day he showed up
unannounced at the Dosanjh School. He gave Chachaji a one-rupee note,
signifying that he and Biji were now engaged. That one rupee, exchanged
in an unorthodox setting, sealed the tone for the kind of marriage ceremony Chachaji and Biji would have. Usually an Indian wedding lasted
several days, but theirs would set a new record for brevity and simplicity.

Biji was only fifteen at the time of her marriage. Chachaji visited
Bahowal to help Naniji and her family make arrangements for the
wedding. It was unheard of for a prospective groom to visit his
in-laws' village at the time, let alone help with the preparations. Couples

were forbidden from meeting one another before their weddings. How Chachaji and Biji navigated such a unique situation remains a mystery; Naniji's small three-room house had few places to hide.

On the appointed day, Chachaji cycled to Bahowal, where he was met by his brother, my Tayaji; Baba Budh Singh, Dada Harnam's cousin; and the family *naai* (barber). Any wrinkles to be ironed out at a wedding usually fell to the *naai* caste, who acted as go-betweens for the bride and groom's families. Generally, *jhirs* and others attached to a family were paid seasonally, in kind with grains, hay and other farm products. On special occasions such as weddings, they, like the *naai*, would receive cash. After the wedding, as the others from his family returned to Dosanjh by train, Chachaji bicycled home, with Biji sitting behind him.

Biji had completed grade six before her marriage. Even afterwards, she attended regular classes at the high school for girls in Dosanjh, successfully completing grade eight. In 1942, it was revolutionary for a new young wife to be attending school in her husband's village. Most rural girls and women never attended school at all. That Dosanjh Kalan had one of only two girls' schools in the whole of the pre-partition rural Punjab certainly helped. Still, the people of Dosanjh must have thought Chachaji insane to send his young and exceptionally beautiful wife to school. She wanted to continue, but Bhaji came along, followed by the rest of us in quick succession. The family could not afford to look after Chachaji and Biji's children without Biji's presence at home.

While their father roamed all over India agitating for independence, Biji's sisters had come to live with us in Dosanjh. Masiji (mother's sister) Gurmit lived with us for two years while she finished her grade ten, and Masiji Harjit (whom we called Heeti) came to finish grades six to ten. Later, my sister Hartirath would attend secondary and post-secondary institutions thirty miles away at Hoshiarpur, living with Masiji Gurmit. And now I was taking my primary education at Bahowal. These "exchanges" were typical of the interdependence that's still prevalent in traditional societies, without which life would be much more difficult. And the bonds we developed in those days in our extended family endure.

AS THE ONLY CHILD at Bahowal during my first two primary school years, I had the undivided affection and attention of all. Naniji and Masiji Heeti dressed me in clean bright clothes for school, then combed my hair and tied it in a *gutta*, the knotted dome of long hair worn by male Sikh children.

The three-room Bahowal School had been established by Nanaji in a home abandoned by a Muslim family during partition. The rooms had no windows, just a small opening in each of the outside walls close to the ceiling. The yard around the school had several mango and *tahli* trees, which provided shade. In winter, classes were held in the unshaded compound; in summer we sat under the trees. On cold or wet days, our classes moved indoors. Our teachers perched on a chair at the front of the class, and we students sat on mats that were rolled up at the end of each day and stored away for the next morning. When we reached grade two, the school asked each of us to buy a two-inch-high pine pedestal to sit on. The smooth, unvarnished pine looked so clean and beautiful compared to our mats and the teachers' old chairs and tables. During recess there was time to run home, have a bite, then run back and play in the yard before classes resumed.

Masiji Heeti taught us for a few months. Mamaji (as we called him maternal uncle) Sohan Sangha also did so for a while. His father, Makhan Singh, and Nanaji were comrades in India's independence movement, and the best of friends; like brothers, in fact. Makhan Singh had stood in for Nanaji at Biji's wedding. Ours was a government school, and both teachers and funds were in short supply in a colony recently turned independent. At first, Urdu was taught along with Punjabi, so I learned the Urdu alphabet. Each letter seemed a work of art. To my dismay, schools in Punjab stopped teaching Urdu at the end of my first grade.

After a while, an older teacher named Husan (meaning "beauty") arrived at our school. Clean-shaven Husan dressed in sleeveless shirts and pants, his feet in sandals. The traditional turban he wore in spring made it seem as if he had just returned from a royal soirée. Smoking incessantly on his chair as we sat cross-legged on our mats, he looked like a Mogul emperor holding court. His word was law on the school premises. Corporal punishment was common at the time, and parents expected teachers not to spare the rod. All of us dreaded being caned on our knuckles or bums in front of the class; it was considered weak and cowardly to wince. With Husan on the throne, his subjects usually behaved.

When Husan retired from teaching, he was replaced by two beautiful women, both recent graduates. Kamala Bhenji hailed from Hoshiarpur; Kaushalya Bhenji belonged to the village Bombeli, a mile and a half away. Both had attended a training school, and the urban influence set them apart from most of the village folk of Bahowal. Our new Bhenjis, as we called our female teachers, descended upon us like the fairies in magical tales. Kaushalya rode a bicycle to school from Bombeli every day. Kamala now lived in Bahowal, boarding with Beant's wife at her palatial house next door to us. Almost everyone considered Nanaji the village elder. In that small world, as his *dohta* (daughter's son), I could do no wrong.

I had always looked forward to school, and after Kamala and Kaushalya arrived, it became even more thrilling. When Kamala spoke to me, I felt special. I looked for any opportunity to be physically close to her, and since she lived next door, I got to be with her often. She would hug me often as I played with her younger brother, who also attended our school. My childhood crush remained a concealed embarrassment until I discovered how common such childhood crushes were. My fixation ended when Kamala transferred to another school.

The school was a microcosm of Nanaji's village: rich and poor, big landholders and peasants, untouchables and Brahmins all enrolled their children. Private schools for the wealthy and the upper middle class had not yet sucked the life out of primary education. The egalitarian élan of the freedom movement was still alive. My classmates Seeto, Sutto and Mindo — bright young girls ready to challenge the world — came from the so-called lower castes. There was Gholi, the son of a relatively affluent family, and Jinder, who loved singing along with the *toomba*, a single-stringed instrument popular in the folk music of the time, which was dominated by artists like Ramta and Yamala. Bakhshish, the tallest and oldest boy at school, was my best friend. We spent a lot of time together. He was a *harijan*, Gandhi's word for untouchables — the Dalits of today. Luckily, because Bahowal was home to many independence activists, nobody worried about caste in my home or at school. Bakhshish helped Nanaji and me tend to the cattle, and occasionally slept over. I went to his home too, sharing food with him and his family and spending the night.

Bakhshish told me stories about Indian history and mythology. Lord Krishna was warrior Arjuna's guide and teacher in the grand Indian epic *The Mahabharata*. Lord Krishna and Lord Rama, of the epic *The Ramayana*, were an integral part of the Indian story, evident from the fact that there were several thousand references to them in the Guru Granth Sahib, the Sikh holy scriptures.

Bakhshish, more mature than I, may have been more aware of caste and class divisions in India. He wanted our friendship to be like that of Krishna and Sudama — Krishna being from royalty and Sudama a poor kid. Their friendship was tested when the pauper Sudama took simple beaten rice, Krishna's childhood favourite, to the adult king Krishna to seek material help. He was greeted by the king with love and affection, despite the distance of years, caste and class. Since I was not from an affluent family, Bakhshish may have had caste in his mind when talking about our friendship, which continues to this day.

Life at Bahowal revolved around school and helping Nanaji on the few acres of land he owned. He would take me with him to the fields to keep a watch on the family cattle. Often the animals, unimpressed by my tiny stature and the big stick I carried with difficulty, would wade into forbidden fields, crops or water. In Nanaji's presence, however, they never failed to behave. When he ploughed a field, readying it for the next crop, I followed the plough and picked up weed roots to be dried and used as household fuel.

The older folk could tell time by looking at the position of the sun. Time for them wasn't about what the clock struck. When I took the cattle out to graze, crossing a dry, sandy rivulet that flowed swiftly during the monsoons, I often ended up back at home too soon. Quickly, though, I developed my own way of telling time. I would stand under the sun out in the pasture, and if my shadow was almost nonexistent, it was time to go home for the noon meal. In the evening, I knew it wasn't time to leave until my shadow was at its longest. The cattle no longer returned with stomachs half-empty.

The sandy rivulet was beautiful, with trees and other vegetation on both sides. About a mile away, a gurdwara stood on the edge of the rivulet, surrounded by trees and plants of different varieties. The *bunhianwala*, literally "of the forest," was peaceful except on special days, when people flocked to it for praying and celebrations. On rainy days, the runoff in the rivulet prevented people from crossing over to the gurdwara, adding a certain mystique to the *bunhianwala* for me. When taking cattle to the pasture, I was ever afraid of being alone in the jungle. Jajo, my grandmother, told me to invoke the *bunhianwala* and my fear would vanish; it never completely did, but the invocation fortified me.

In Bahowal, a religious man distributed Sikh *gutkas*, booklets with excerpts from the scriptures, free of charge. The only conditions were that you demonstrate fluency in Punjabi, promise to treat the *gutka* with respect and cover your head when reading it. Fluency proven and promises made, I was a proud recipient of my own *gutka*, which I read several times. I only partially understood the words, but the poetry was mesmerizing. The new-book smell of the *gutka* rushed like a storm at my nostrils. Nostrils do not discriminate between the sacred and the profane.

Reading was something I was good at. Nanaji would get me to read the Punjabi newspaper of the Communist Party of India, *Nawan Zamana (New Age)*, to his many visitors. He took great pride in having this "reading machine" read (or broadcast) the news while he and his guests had lunch or tea. The two guests who came most often were Dr. Bhag Singh and Darshan Singh Canadian (he had adopted that surname after returning to India from Canada). In time, they were both elected to the Punjab legislature, representing the Communist

Party of India (CPI); both were spellbinding orators. Dr. Bhag Singh had gone as a student to the U.S., completing his PhD there before returning to India. While in the U.S., he was influenced by the secular Ghadarites of the West Coast of North America and joined the CPI. Darshan, on the other hand, was an immigrant to Canada who returned to India shortly after Independence. In Canada, he had been a member of the Communist League and was one of the founders of the International Woodworkers of America. In India, Darshan was assassinated by Khalistani extremists in 1986.

Little things made big impressions in those days, be they *gutkas*, *shinjhs* (a series of wrestling matches in the villages), or a new toy, which was rare. Our lives were definitely poor, but we were without discontent or self-pity. There were no televisions, only the village radio, the battery for which was stored with Nanaji. People listened collectively to the *Dihati*, a program that Chacha Kumaydaan and Thuniaram, the hosts, aimed at rural folk and broadcast from Jullundur in an inimitable comic style. The hosts felt like members of our family; we laughed and cried with them. I carried the heavy battery on my head five evenings a week to the gurdwara so that the radio could function for that one *Dihati* hour. Despite often tumbling to the ground with me, the battery never failed to function.

If something went wrong in my slow, contented world, I brooded over it forever. One day a group of us took a trip to Barian Kalan, a mid-sized town equidistant from Bahowal and Mahilpur. At the bazaar, Jasso, Naniji's older sister, bought some household stuff. I had eight annas (half a rupee) in my pocket, and I bought a toy wheel with a handle. When I walked, pushing the wheel in front of me, it made a noise like a bicycle bell. On our way home I was so excited that I got far ahead of others. I kept running as I looked over my shoulder at them, and I stumbled on the uneven dirt road, twisting and breaking my toy. I can feel the pain of that loss even now.

Chachaji came to visit Bahowal every couple of months. After the half day at school on a Saturday, he would bicycle to Mahilpur, briefly stopping there to pick up bananas, dates or other seasonal fruit, and then head for Bahowal, reaching us in the late afternoon. He would teach me English during his visits, preparing me for my return to the Dosanjh School for the high school grades.

Chachaji, with his white clothes and turban against his dark, sun-tanned skin, cut an imposing figure. During the school holiday he would take me from Bahowal to Dosanjh on his bike, and at break's end he would bring me back again. Our trips back and forth sometimes meant new clothes or shoes, and certainly a special treat of sweet lassi along the way. Chachaji would ask Jajo to make special dishes like *masur dal* — lentil curry — for his dinner and mango pickle for him to take back to Dosanjh for Biji and others in our family to enjoy. My grandmother was a wonderful cook, and like most women of her era, was expert at making elaborate dishes at home and packing them up into neat, travel-worthy packages for loved ones elsewhere.

Biji did not come to Bahowal as often as Chachaji did, and her stays with us were all too brief. But I remember one visit with great clarity. I was in grade two; my sister Tirath had joined me at Bahowal School. Chachaji brought my mother and my sister Nimmy to Bahowal on his bicycle, and they stayed behind for a few more days. Biji seemed thinner than I remembered, and I clung to her, dreading the moment when she would have to leave. I begged her to stay and insisted upon going with her if she couldn't. But of course she had a household to contend with back in Dosanjh, and I needed to stay at school.

Naniji, Masiji Heeti, Tirath and I all went to see Biji off at the bus stop on the Hoshiarpur–Garhshankar road. From Garhshankar, she planned to catch the train to Kultham, then walk the last mile and a half to Dosanjh. I kept hoping out loud that the buses to Garhshankar would be full and not stop for her. Sure enough, several buses packed with passengers passed by. It was getting too late to make the train connection at Garhshankar, so we turned and walked back home. At least for the day, I had won. The next morning Biji got ready early. When I woke up, she was already gone.

That visit was the last time Tirath and I saw our mother. Even today, the story is hard to tell. It was spring, the season of happiness and hope. On a beautiful day a few weeks later, sunny but not hot, Tirath and I stood with Nanaji at the place where the path from home to school crossed the *kuchisarak*. Nanaji was watching and waiting, his gaze fixed on the spot where the Garhshankar–Hoshiarpur road crossed the road that came to Bahowal. He seemed to be searching for something. For the first time in my life I did not perceive Nanaji as a giant; he seemed shrunken and shrivelled.

Suddenly, we saw two women in white walking toward us. I did not know then that white was the colour one wore in mourning. I had never experienced the death of anyone close to me, and nobody had told Tirath or me that our mother had fallen seriously ill. As the white figures drew closer, I realized it was Jajo and Masiji Gurmit, and they were crying. Nanaji's eyes were also full of tears. "Why are you sad?" I asked. "Your Biji has gone to heaven," he said, using the word *swaragvas*, meaning from then on she would reside in heaven. Jajo and Masiji were still crying as they hugged Tirath and me.

Many people came to Nanaji and Jajo's home over the next few days. The women would weep and shriek. The men sat silently, occasionally talking about Biji or, as if to offer solace, telling stories of other young mothers who had left their families too soon.

My mother's death had been cruelly sudden. In the days preceding her death, Biji had been weaving a cot for the dowry of a young woman in the neighbourhood who was about to get married. She cut herself accidentally but continued her chores, which included making half-moon cakes from wet cattle dung, to be dried in the sun for fuel. She developed a fever, and the cut filled with puss. Chachaji gave her some quinine, thinking the fever meant malaria, and he cleaned the infected wound using alcohol. When there was no break in the fever, Biji was taken to Dayanand Hospital, in the industrial city of Ludhiana. The doctors there told Chachaji that blood poisoning had spread to much of her body. They gave her a very expensive injection — five hundred rupees — but said her condition was most likely irreversible. It turned out to be so. She died of tetanus on March 13, 1954, the day Tirath turned four. Bhaji was nine, I was seven, and Nimmy was just two years old.

At the time, I didn't understand that living in heaven meant death. If Biji was living somewhere else, why? How could she do this to her children? If heaven was such a good place, why had she not taken everyone with her? Jajo found it hard to satisfy my inquisitive nature. She told me that Biji had gone to another *des* (country), to return another day. At other times she said Biji had gone to Chandamama, Uncle Moon. The implied promise was reincarnation, reappearance, a concept central to my Indian heritage, but I took her words literally and lived in hope that I would see Biji again.

Biji was cremated. Her body must have been placed on a pile of wood on the land that had witnessed generations of Dosanjhes go from ashes to ashes. Draped in white, she would have been covered with pieces of wood before burning. Bhaji had been told, as I was, that our mother hadn't really died. He found that difficult to reconcile with the sparks flying from the lit pyre. He told me years later that he stood there watching the cinders and embers in the waning fire glow late into the night.

I am told our whole Dosanjh village was in mourning at the death of our young mother. Everyone must have wondered how Chachaji, as a widower, would care for and bring up my siblings and me. They didn't yet know about the complete commitment our uncle and his wife, our Tayaji and Taeeji, would make to our nurturing and well-being when we returned to Dosanjh Kalan.

While it is true that it takes a village to raise a child, villages can be cruel and parochial places. Dosanjh Kalan was no exception. Once, while Tirath and I were on a school break and visiting home, my cousin Banso Bhenji was washing our clothes; she gave me a worn-out shirt to wear while my other clothes dried in the sun. As I played in the *vehda* behind our home, I overheard a neighbourhood busybody lamenting my torn shirt and connecting it to the absence of Biji. I told the woman off — we loved our Bhenji.

Biji's death changed our lives forever. It created a larger sense of family, and we drew even closer to our Dosanjh cousins. It taught me that the collective is important; sharing makes us stronger. Many years have come and gone since Biji went to *swaragvas*, but she has remained a compelling figure for us. When my siblings and I get together, the talk often turns to our facial features: who looks most like our mother? Our search for Biji continues in the faces of her grandchildren and great-grandchildren: her smile, her lips, her eyebrows, her cheekbones, an expression in the eyes here and there.

5 BACK AT BAHOWAL, life continued pretty much as before, though Tirath and I got some special attention. Everyone tried to ensure we did not miss Biji, at least not too much. I got my yearly new pair of leather shoes made by the shoemaker at Mahilpur. We did not wear shoes all the time, only on special occasions such as weddings or trips to other villages, but our feet outgrew the shoes much faster than we could wear them out. Once, while I was playing in the school yard on a holiday, I took my new shoes off to play, and I came home shoeless. Walking by the school yard, Nanaji had recognized my new shoes lying under a cart; he picked them up, hid them in a bag, and then, when I got home, asked me about their whereabouts. When I couldn't remember where I'd left them, he thrust the bag at me and slapped my face. I was shocked, since he had rarely punished me physically. When he later caught me wearing a new pair to play football, using a brick as a ball, Jajo's timely intervention may have saved me from another licking.

Nanaji owned four mango trees and had access to many others. During the summer break, Jasso, Jajo's older sister, would accompany Tirath and me to the *bagh*, where we'd sit in the garden's shade, ensuring that no one stole our family's mangoes. We'd eat some of the ripe mangoes that dropped to the ground, leaving the skin and the pits behind to compost, and take the bulk home with us at night, to be eaten later or made into *shisha*, a concoction of mango, salt and pepper that we ate with rotis.

During mango season, our Bahowal home had the feel of a festive inn. Jajo and Jasso's extended family and relatives all came for the mangoes, as did the Dosanjhes. Gurmit Bhenji was teaching by now, and her colleagues and friends joined us. So did many of Chachaji's teaching colleagues and friends. Our three-room home was noisy late into the evening. People slept anywhere they could find a spot, including on the roof and in the compound. We always hoped for clear skies, but when it rained, Beant's big house next door with its veranda came in handy.

One year during mango season, when my mother was still alive, Bhaji and I were in the mango groves when a buffalo came charging us. Bhaji climbed a tree, trying to pull me up behind him. I was too slow, though, and I couldn't escape the angry animal. It lifted me up and threw me several feet. The buffalo was beaten off me by its apologetic owner, but the mauling left me bleeding and unable to walk. Bhaji broke off a branch of a mango tree, placed me on it and dragged me home to Nanaji's. Our mother had come to Bahowal from Dosanjh for the mango season. Brandishing Nanaji's *khoonda*, a bamboo walking stick with a sharp steel point, she set off like an angry lioness to confront the bad buffalo's owner, who apologized profusely once again.

Mangoes were a source of income for some families, since contractors bought their fruit to take to market. The government owned the mango trees on either side of the Garhshankar–Hoshiarpur road. One day, as Jasso and I were returning from Mahilpur on foot, a ripe mango dropped onto the road in front of me. Without Jasso noticing, I picked up the mango and started sucking on it. Suddenly, someone ran up from behind, catching hold of my neck and hurling abuse at me. I thought I was going to die. Jasso screamed at the man. It turned out he was guarding the mangoes for a contractor who had bought the season's crop from the government. I put the mango back on the road, tears rolling down my cheeks. Hunger or no hunger, I'd learned that the mangoes on the public road did not belong to the public.

MY MATERNAL UNCLE, who was a good student in grade ten at Mahilpur, started missing class and staying away from home for days at a time. Mamaji had been showing signs of opiate addiction, and it turned out his absences from school were spent learning to drive a truck and indulging in drinking, smoking and taking either opium or *doday*, ground poppy husk. One evening Mamaji came home drunk and started arguing with Nanaji. Holding an unsheathed sword in his hand, he threatened to behead himself. Nanaji demanded the sword, promising to do the deed himself if Mamaji really wanted to die. Mamaji quickly dropped both the sword and the argument and ran for his life.

Jasso, Jajo, Nanaji, Tirath and I had been eating our evening meal of *saag* (mustard leaves boiled, ground and spiced with home-made butter) and *makki* (corn roti, my favourite winter staple). We were traumatized by the incident. Jajo comforted us, assuring us no harm would come to Mamaji or anybody else, but Mamaji went away after that and did not come back for a long time. Nanaji heard from acquaintances that he had become a long-distance trucker. Jajo missed him very much, though she rarely said anything about him. Occasionally, she would ask me whether I missed my Mamaji. Of course, I would say. With a smile that betrayed her sadness, she would reassure me he was safe and would come back one day. It must have helped her to voice that hope aloud, stilling her turbulent mind.

A few days after Biji's death, Mamaji arrived home in his truck in the middle of the night. In those days, very few trucks came to the villages. Most of what the villagers needed came on the *guddas*. Bahowal had no electricity or street lighting, and the truck woke up half the village. Many people came out of their homes in the dark as they heard first the truck and then Mamaji crying, overcome by grief at the loss of his older sister. As he hugged and kissed each family member, his cries became louder. Nanaji sat him down, and Jajo gave him a glass of water. When he spotted Tirath and me, tears rolled down his cheeks again. He covered his face with his huge hands and cried uncontrollably. He was a tall, strong man, but at that moment he was a child who had just lost his *bibi*.

The next time I saw Mamaji was under much happier circumstances: Bhaji and I were the best men at his wedding. Mamaji beamed with pride and happiness, and his bride, Jagtar (now my Mamiji, or aunt), looked stunning. Mamiji and I became fast friends. For the rest of my time in Bahowal, the responsibility for my care fell on her. One of her chores, an activity I didn't relish, was the washing of my long hair. It was difficult to wash and even more difficult to comb. But Mamiji was patient. She seemed a perfect match for my impetuous, but loving, uncle.

Soon after their wedding, my four years at the Bahowal primary school were complete. With my shirts, shorts and turban neatly packed into a cloth bag hanging from the handlebars, Chachaji and I travelled on his bicycle to Dosanjh Kalan. From now on I would be attending the Dosanjh School along with Bhaji, who had already been enrolled there for two years and was entering grade seven. My father would now have two sons among his pupils.

Our ancestral village had changed while I was gone. Around the circular path the oxen travelled to power the Persian wheel, the trees had grown taller, providing more shade from the sun. We called Goraywala well, the land irrigated by it, and the small building on the land close to the well the *khooh*. The *khooh* was now more inviting, since it had more vegetation. The five acres of land we owned lay in a jagged row, with Baba Budh Singh's portion contiguous to ours. In the middle, as if to demarcate the division, ran an *aard*, a channel constructed of mud that carried water from the well to the fields.

At home Bhaji and I shared a portion of one room. In the other portion were two *sandooks*, traditional wooden cabinets carved and decorated with brass. These had been part of Biji and Aunt Taeeji's dowries. Our two-storey home, with its several small rooms, now housed at least eleven of us, including our older cousin Biraji's wife and children. My uncle Tayaji slept at the *khooh*. That brought the family to twelve. According to the seasons and special holidays, the number could swell to nineteen or twenty. Gurmit Bhenji would come back from school; Siso Bhenji would bring her children to visit. Silence was hard to come by. Some people can read or study even with the radios blaring, but I had a hard time concentrating if someone so much as whispered close by.

The search for silence led me out of the house to the *khooh*. It offered more possibilities for quiet, but not always. If the Persian wheel was running, there was the constant noise made by the *kutta*, the iron brake lever that fell on each cog of the wheel as the oxen walked the circle. But the *kutta* was not as disruptive as human activity or speech. In the wee hours before daybreak, the hooves and bells of oxen being taken to plough the fields, the clanging of the *kutta* and the occasional crowing of a rooster were the only sounds. At that time of day, there was enough peace to study for our annual examinations.

When the *khooh* didn't provide enough refuge from the bustle of the village, I sought out tall crops so I could hide in their insulation. That worked only in the early spring and fall. At other times it was too cold, too hot or too wet to be outside. And even sitting in the tall plants, I couldn't escape the human presence completely; some people would be working in the fields, others were on their way there, and still others were looking for cover to satisfy the call of nature. The farther I went from the village, the better my chances of finding a clean, secluded spot. It was heavenly to hit one. Hiding in the crops, I felt like a rebel, a giant defying his pursuers by cleverly hiding.

The Dosanjh School was just under a mile away, across the canal. It was a large, E-shaped building, welcoming students east and west. There were grounds for soccer, field hockey, volleyball and basketball. Many rooms had wooden desks and benches, and all of them had blackboards. It was a definite and welcome improvement over the school in Bahowal.

Seeing the respect paid to Chachaji as, not just a master at the school, but one of its founders, made me see my father in a new light. It was the first time I realized that Chachaji was a builder of communities and institutions.

In 1923, shortly after matriculating from grade ten at J.J. Government High School in Phagwara, Chachaji had gone to Calcutta. There he obtained a driver's licence, in the process being photographed for the first time in his life. In Calcutta, he earned his living driving a truck. He did not last too long as a trucker and took off for Assam, where he became a contractor supplying labour to big and small employers. The details are sketchy, but this much is known: the employers did not pay Chachaji all of the money they owed him. He used his savings to pay the labourers who were due their wages and was about to set off for home when he received a letter from his friend Maula Singh, who asked Chachaji to help him establish a school in Dosanjh. Chachaji jumped headlong into the process, personally borrowing some money for it. Some land was donated by the villagers, but the rest had to be bought. Until the school building was complete, classes were housed in the village *diwankhana*, or communal hall. Chachaji went door to door in Dosanjh and other villages, encouraging parents to enrol their children in the new school. He also set about persuading the parents of those enrolled at places such as Phagwara to educate their children closer to home. Dr. Bikkar Lalli, a retired Canadian professor of mathematics who now lives in Surrey, British Columbia, remembers Chachaji approaching his father in the field where he was busy ploughing and convincing him to transfer Bikkar to the Dosanjh School. Obviously, the switch did not hurt Bikkar's prospects in life.

The school was not conceived as a profit-making venture. The founders who taught there received a salary if the school could afford it, based on the very reasonable fees for students. Chachaji was the only founder still teaching there when I came back to the school for grade five. His friends Maula, Mehnga and Davindra had left for England, and Thakar Singh and Chanan Singh had gone on to do other things, but these young men of the 1920s and 1930s had a special bond that would last till the end of their lives.

Chachaji too had made plans to go to England, but Biji persuaded him otherwise. After her death, he again thought of leaving for England, but Jajo dissuaded him, worried that abroad he would marry a "white woman" and our lives would be neglected and ruined.

Chachaji continued his studies privately while he taught at the school. He wrote and passed his FA (Faculty of Arts) examination for English. Next he turned his mind to writing the Punjabi examination for the certificate of *giani* (literally, "the knowledgeable one"), and passed that. He was preparing to write the BA papers for English when Biji got ill. My father's dream of a BA died with her.

Chachaji's political involvement also took a hit, as he needed to pay more attention to us. Whenever elections came around, though, Chachaji organized and canvassed for the Congress party. He was a "Congresswala," and like most of his contemporaries, he was an impeccably honest man. He had participated in the freedom movement in his country, and its ideals still glowed in his heart.

Chachaji made sure Bhaji and I were up by 4:30 AM, the kerosene lamp illuminating our books as we studied for an hour before doing our morning chores. Then it was time to run to the *khooh* to help Tayaji tend to the cattle and cut and chop fodder for the day. Bhaji and I barely had time to dip in the *chalha* for a bath, run home, dress, tie our turbans and get to school on time. Combing our long hair posed a perennial problem. Overnight, and as we worked on the farm in the mornings, it would become knotted, so on the days we were running late, combing got a miss. Chachaji kept a keen eye on his students. Some days at the end of the school assembly he would ask those who had not had a bath or combed their hair before coming to school to stand up. On the days Bhaji and I had not combed our hair, he would never fail to ask. And if we did not stand up to confess and then run the obligatory four rounds of the grounds, our father would call us out as liars. My brother and I took the punishment, in our hearts blaming Chachaji because he worked us too long and hard on the farm.

Chachaji himself wore homegrown and homespun cotton clothes. Dressed all in white with a white turban, he looked angelic, yet he was merciless to all slackers. Our family was poor, yet our father exuded richness through his appearance. Many believed we had high status and did not need to work in the fields, or work at all. Physical labour had little value in Indian culture. Some people would rather starve than be seen to labour manually.

I have always wondered why so many of my countrymen felt shame doing physical labour. Despite India's indisputable riches, a history of poverty and hunger in the country could stretch to several volumes. At one time, I put the shame down to the slavery practised by British colonialists. They hired servants to do everything for them and did no manual work themselves. More recently, I have speculated about the lighter-skinned Aryans who are alleged to have invaded India from the north and conquered it, subjugating the darker-skinned original Indians and assigning them the most menial labour, eventually creating the caste system. No matter what its origin, the problem persists.

Mahatma Gandhi's efforts to promote self-help through manual chores had a great influence on Chachaji, though, as did the teachings of the first Sikh Guru, Nanak, who, after many years of preaching and teaching, returned to his native village to eke out a living by subsistence farming.

Chachaji's honesty and simplicity were also reflected in his politics. During the independence movement and afterwards, he worked with many men who became politicians, including the first defence minister of independent India, Baldev Singh. Swaran Singh went on to hold many positions in India's central cabinet, including that of minister of external affairs. Darbara Singh's last public office was that of the chief minister of Punjab. Chachaji did not befriend these men because they were in government. Power held no allure for him, and India was already slipping into ways he felt wouldn't lead to Gandhi's *Ram Raj,* or just society.

I once asked Chachaji why he didn't run for state or Indian Parliament, because I knew he had been approached. "If one wants to befriend camels, one needs tall doors," he said. The reference, which I did not understand then, was to the corruption that was beginning to take root in India. My father was not prepared to use crooked methods to amass the wealth necessary to run in an election. He was not prepared to make the moral and ethical compromises Indian politics demanded. The country of his and Mahatma Gandhi's dreams was fast becoming a cesspool.

Chachaji had risked his life many times for his principles. After partition, he organized men in our village and the surrounding area to gather Muslims and safely escort them to the camps from which they could leave for Pakistan under proper protection. Some people in the region wanted to rob and massacre the assembled Muslims in revenge for the killings of Sikhs and Hindus across the border. When Chachaji got wind of it, he gathered a group of strong young friends. Somehow he located some liquor and handed it to his comrades-against-crime to fortify their courage. The group begged and borrowed some weapons, and at nightfall they started the journey with their charges to the nearest camp at Behram, some six miles away. Chachaji walked his bike along with the caravan. Rumours had spread about him — that Master, the teacher, was carrying bombs and a pistol in the cloth bag slung over his handlebars while in actual fact it was only his food and air pump for the bicycle tires.

Chachaji and his group continued to help Muslims escape the avengers and robbers. In a futile attempt to dissuade him from his work, some of his enemies threatened to kill my siblings and me. One day he was returning from Neehr, a predominantly Muslim village, when a gunshot rang through the air. A bullet whizzed past, missing Chachaji by inches.

India was turning its back on the collective dream of the freedom fighters. The English sahibs departed, leaving sahibdom behind. Elected and unelected officials alike began to behave like the rulers of old. Instead of a healthy challenge to authority, sycophancy gained currency. Chachaji's rebellious streak remained, and he showed it often. One day the chief minister of Punjab, Chachaji's old friend Darbara Singh, decided to visit our village school unannounced. One of his functionaries showed up at our *khooh* looking for Chachaji, who was working with us in the fields. The chief minister wanted to see Chachaji at the school, the functionary said. Chachaji thought for a moment and said to the functionary, "Tell my friend I am busy making a living. I am not a rich man. I need to finish this work today. But I am happy to receive him here." So the chief minister came by to see Chachaji on his way to his next destination. The green wheat crop, less than a foot tall, was turning and twisting in the cool breeze. After the minister left, we got right back to weeding it. I learned from Chachaji that freedom and equality are like crops: they must be diligently weeded, watered and fertilized.

Chachaji was also a voracious reader of Punjabi and Urdu books and of the *Tribune,* the prominent English daily that Mahatma Gandhi had once called the most important newspaper in North India. Our father had a small library at home that included English titles such as Shakespeare's *Hamlet* and many Urdu titles I could never make out. His Punjabi books, of which there were many, included works by the premier Punjabi novelist, Nanak Singh, and the Punjabi translation of Gorky's *The Mother.* By the end of grade six, I had devoured most of the Punjabi titles in Chachaji's collection. My facility with the language was recognized when I received the award of a book of Punjabi plays at a public function in the Dosanjh School, in the presence of hundreds of people from the surrounding villages. I still needed to work on my Hindi, however.

6

ONCE BHAJI AND I got home from school, we would eat quickly, change into our *khooh* clothes and walk over to help with the work. I did all the chores except ploughing and levelling the land, for which I was considered too young. As the sugarcane grew taller, we tied it together in bunches, using the semi-green leaves in the middle as rope. Our constant sweating cooled us down in the windless confines of the tall crop. In the evening, when we took a bath in the *chalha*, the water would sting the numerous cuts the sugarcane leaves had made in our skin.

Tying up the sugarcane was difficult, but nothing compared to harvesting the wheat or weeding the corn crop — the weeds were needed for cattle fodder — on hot, humid days. The difficulty of these tasks was, in fact, the stuff of legend. Folklore had it that, afraid of these very chores, the sons of small landholders would leave home to become *sadhus*, ascetics who renounce worldly relationships and possessions, meditate, and live on alms.

We harvested the wheat manually, squatting with a sickle in one hand. Chachaji, Tayaji, Bhaji and I raced against each other to finish our rows. I was no slouch, but I was the youngest of the four; I won only occasionally, thanks to the others letting me do so. Once harvested and dried, the wheat was strewn over a flattened surface in the field, specially prepared for separating the husk from the grains. The oxen were hitched to a *falha*, a rectangular flatbed made of branches from thorny hardwood trees covered with dried wheat stems, held together by dried bamboo and rope. The oxen dragged the *falha* over the harvested wheat, crushing it. New bales were continually added, and over a couple of days the wheat under the *falha* and the hooves of the oxen would turn into silky golden shreds. We took turns following the *falha* to ensure the oxen remained on the circular path. The wheat circle also had to be dug up and turned over constantly, to ensure no long stalks remained uncrushed.

Once the wheat was completely shredded, we piled it into a long, straight mound. It was now ready for the husks to be separated. We accomplished that by raking the shreds and throwing them into the air. The wind carried the husks a few feet away while the grains fell back on the mound. The work continued until the husks were completely isolated. Following that, cattle and buffalo were walked over any uncrushed ears until all we had left was grain. The grain went into jute bags that were sewn up and taken home.

Any surplus we took to the grain market at Phagwara. Most years we had enough for market even after the portions that went to the Dalits, the *naais* and the *jhirs* who helped our family throughout the year. The husks were added to cattle fodder and then stored in a *koop*, a dome built from dried cotton and wheat stalks. The *koop* kept the husks dry and was strong enough to withstand strong winds.

Farming work claimed much of Bhaji's and my time. Every now and then I would disappear into the village to play marbles with the other kids, but Chachaji would send my brother to find me and bring me back to the *khooh*. I never wanted Chachaji to come searching himself, as that meant punishment. Many kids, even from families poorer than ours, got more time to play. Bhaji and I did steal ourselves some fun, though, at the *samadh* (mausoleum) of a Muslim *saneen*, or saint. At the end of the wheat harvest, the *mela* was held near the mosque for three days. *Qawwals* who sang like the late Nusrat Fateh Ali Khan came from all over India and Pakistan, and their performances filled the nights. Bhaji sometimes attended the *mela* with Biraji. They would watch wrestling matches and jugglers, take in some *qawwali* and then buy sweet *jalebi* with the eight annas Biraji usually carried in his pocket. By the time they got home they would be happy and full, with lots of *jalebi* left over for the rest of the family to enjoy.

If Bhaji and I made the school field hockey teams, we were allowed time for that as well. I made the team twice, though mine was a mediocre performance on the ground. Those days, cricket was the big sport for the affluent. Field hockey was for the masses; that made us like it even more. We had another reason to like hockey too. A player named Balbir Singh Dosanjh had captained the Indian field hockey team to a gold medal in the 1948 Olympics. (It would be the team's first of three consecutive Olympic golds.) Balbir was from Puadhra, the village from which our ancestors had moved over four centuries earlier. His face adorned the cover of many a magazine and the front page of many newspapers, and Chachaji would buy these and show them to us with genuine pride. These days, Balbir makes his home in the Greater Vancouver area.

WE BOTH LOVED and feared Chachaji. One day he returned early from Phagwara and found Bhaji and me at the *khooh*, fighting and calling each other names. I had filled my brother's shoes with fresh cattle dung, and he had rubbed it into my long, knotted hair. Chachaji flew into a rage. Picking up a stick, he unleashed a barrage of blows. Bhaji got the first one, but I got most of what came next. An eternity seemed to pass before the beating stopped. Sobbing, I set about washing the dung off my clothes and out of my hair. Chachaji headed home without looking back.

Chachaji could never bring himself to say he was sorry, except for once, after he'd slapped me. I was angry at the slap, because I felt I had done nothing wrong. In protest, I refused to eat or drink anything all day — a hunger strike of sorts. Chachaji came to my room before I went to bed, embraced me and asked me to eat my meal. All was forgiven. That was the only time I remember him hugging me. He was an Indian peasant who had grown up in the early twentieth century: not the hugging sort.

During my days at the Dosanjh School, there was a short-lived scheme to provide powdered milk to students. The milk was poured into big containers of boiling water and sugar. Each of us had to stand in a queue, drink a glass of lukewarm milk, run to the water pump, wash the glass and carry it back for use by other students. Rumour had it the U.S. had surplus powdered milk, and when that ran out the scheme came to an end.

We did not miss the powdered milk. It could not compare to the thick, creamy buffalo milk most of us got at home. Chachaji would take unchurned milk that had been cultured overnight to make butter and mix it with raw milk directly from the udder; then he would sweeten it with homemade sugar. We drank this *dhrerhka* at the *khooh* several mornings a week. Quite often we left cleaned sugarcane out in the open on cold nights. In the mornings we crushed the juice from the canes by hitching oxen onto the *vailna*, a machine with vertical steel rollers, and mixed that with the cultured unchurned milk before drinking it. In years past, boys challenging each other to fights would boast of having been reared on *dhrerhka*, and many folk songs make reference to it. Such was its place in our daily lives in the Punjab.

One afternoon, having been left to tend the fire, I was sitting in front of the *bhatthi*, the round hearth where sugarcane juice was being heated to turn it into *shucker*, and pushing dried sugarcane leaves into the *bhatthi* with a wooden stick. I was oblivious to the danger of what I was doing, but the stick caught fire, lighting up the dried sugarcane leaves next to me, and suddenly the whole place went up in flames. The fire spread instantly to the other piles of fuel nearby, then to the leafy cover on top of the *bhatthi*, and then to the roof of our only *khooh* room for the cattle and men. People came running with buckets and whatever else fell into their hands to draw water from the well with the Persian wheel. The fire was brought under control before it could do much damage, but I was frozen in shock, not saying a word for many hours. The family saw that I was a scared soul, and Banso Bhenji took me in her arms. The making of *shucker* resumed the next day, though I dared not go near the furnace for a long time. The incident changed me forever; silence became my way of absorbing shock in the years to come.

At school, things were not going all that well. The math teacher, a Dosanjh, would explain a new concept or a formula in writing on the blackboard only once before asking us to complete the related exercises in our textbook. Others would be busy writing in their notebooks while I stared at the ceiling, the walls, or the pages of my book. The teacher didn't notice, since he slept through each period after the first few minutes of instruction. He probably worked late at night and early in the morning on his own farm. But he must have told Chachaji I'd failed the mid-year test, because when Bhaji and I sat down after supper to do our homework, my father told me how embarrassed he was by my math results. He was a mathematics teacher himself, so silence, I thought, would be the best policy.

The kerosene lamp had been cleaned and lit. Chachaji opened my text to the chapters covered in the mid-year test, explained how to solve the "simple" algebra questions, and then asked me to do so. Soon Bhaji and Chachaji slept. The night passed into early morning. The roosters began crowing, and I could hear the sounds of footsteps on the street. A Persian wheel *kutta* was also piercing the morning quiet. Seated at the table, I had solved the assigned problems. That night I learned self-reliance and math.

Education in India was becoming tainted by fraud and corruption as early as 1960. In the middle of writing the external grade eight Middle Standard mathematics examinations, a three-hour closed-book test, I was excused to go to the washroom. As I relieved myself in the urinal, a roofless brick enclosure, I saw a hand reach over the wall holding out a piece of paper. I looked at the paper and got the shock of my life. On it were purported solutions for some of the most difficult test questions, though the first and only answer I saw was wrong. Scared, I threw the paper back over the wall and returned quickly to my seat. Later on, I heard stories of students in high schools and colleges having their tests written by complete strangers who had guns resting on their desks and of teachers, principals and invigilators facilitating fraud.

IN THE CULTURE of India in the 1950s and 1960s, a person with one eye was called *kana*, a person who limped was called *langaan*, and a person missing a hand or part of one was called *tunda*: all extremely derogatory terms. My eye muscles were weak, and when I was tired, my eyes wandered. As a child I was called *teera* (cross-eyed), which made me ashamed and angry. India was, and unfortunately still is, a very status-conscious country. At school or college, if you wore pants and a shirt in place of an Indian pyjama kurta (the traditional long pants and short shirt), you were considered hip. If you were poor and rural, you were the lowest of the low in the eyes of the urban rich and the middle class. My family was both rural and poor: we were peasants.

Once, during summer break when I was visiting Bahowal, Nanaji hung a bag of fresh ripe mangoes on his bicycle and sat me behind. We rode off to see my new first cousin Aman Sara, the first-born of my aunt Masiji Gurmit, at Hoshiarpur. On the way it rained hard, and we had to cross several fast-moving rivulets filled waist-high with the runoff from the nearby Siwalik mountain range.

It took us several hours to reach Masiji's home, Harbax Mansion, a palace-like house built by her late father-in-law. It had two large gates and a covered patio for a car. Aman's great-grandfather had been a sup-porter of the British Raj and had served it in the capacity of honorary magistrate. His son, Masiji's late father-in-law, was a London-trained barrister, also prominent and wealthy during the British Raj. His young-est son, Harnaunihal — a teacher by training — and Masiji, who also was a teacher, had fallen in love. Nanaji was not happy about the idea of his daughter marrying the son and grandson of supporters of the colonial-ists he had fought all his life. But Chachaji persuaded him, saying what could an enlightened family do if Masiji simply decided to run away with the boy? Nanaji overcame his politics to allow the marriage to go ahead. And so Harnaunihal became my Masarji (mother's sister's husband).

One evening during our visit, somebody told a joke that had me clutching my belly with laughter. Then I heard Masarji Harnaunihal yell out what he probably thought was a light-hearted remark about me: "Look at that *paindubandar* laughing so loud." He had just called me a village monkey, and I shut up in a split second. I was a kid, and one did not confront one's elders. In the morning we got up, got ready, ate a meal and left for Bahowal. Although I never held it against Masarji, that *paindubandar* comment never left me. It was a reminder of the deeply status-conscious, class- and caste-laden Indian ethos.

As I got older, I started to connect the various dots of history, sci-ence and politics. Our mid-year English examination in the ninth class included an essay question. I chose to write on "A Street Quarrel," one of the essays in the texts prescribed for our class. We tried to commit all of the essays we read to memory so we could regurgitate them on the exam paper, but learning by rote was not one of my strengths, and my memory failed me every time I tried. However, my English lessons from Chachaji had given me the ability to think and compose. My essay on "A Street Quarrel" allowed me to plunge into history and to connect the backwardness of a village and its people to the neglect and impoverishment visited upon them by uncaring British rulers. India had become independent only fourteen years earlier. One could not blame the British forever, but it was an entirely plausible argument then. None of this was in the essay in our prescribed text, but I added my own thoughts to what little I remembered from the original.

A couple of days later, at the morning assembly, my English teacher stepped forward. He wanted to share with the whole school what he thought was the best essay of the ninth-grade test, he said, as an example of what an essay should be. He had read only the first two sentences when I realized it was my essay. With difficulty, I sat motionless through it all. Not being able to commit things to memory had been a blessing in disguise. Over the years, it has forced me to find my own voice to express myself.

There was no sex education at school or at home. All we ever heard as boys was that we were to think about and treat each young woman from the village as if she were our sister. Every cell in a fourteen-year-old's body militates against that, and I was no different. But the whole notion of good character was wrapped up in sexual strictures and mores, and violating them had very serious consequences. Boys and girls who breached those strictures were killed if they were caught, or maimed to send a message to others. Our problems were compounded when the school decided that the class a year behind us would go co-ed as part of a new secondary system. The girls were beautiful, bright and mostly local. I did succeed in treating them like sisters. But did anyone except their actual siblings succeed in *thinking* of them as sisters? The honest but dangerous answer was no.

CHACHAJI WAS A RESTLESS SOUL who liked change and improvement. For him, these two things were synonymous. After some potential robbers tried to yank out the window from the mud walls of our home, my father decided to replace the exterior walls. We demolished them ourselves, carrying the dry mud and debris on our heads to the *khooh* as fill. A bricklayer was hired, and Bhaji and I, then fourteen and twelve, prepared the mud and cement as needed. The interior walls were still made of mud, but Chachaji innovated by mixing small amounts of sand and cement into the mud and using that to plaster the interior surfaces. They turned out as smooth as the drywall would be years later in my Canadian home. The floors of our house were resurfaced with bricks, as was the roof. The spaces between the bricks were filled with cement. All the work was done by the same skilled bricklayer, with Bhaji and me mixing the cement and mud, carrying it and cleaning.

Chachaji was also part-owner of a flour mill in Dosanjh that had been built on our land. People brought their grains to be crushed and ground in a machine powered by a generator. The machine was faster and more efficient than *kharaas*, the grinding stones powered by oxen, and one by-product of the water-cooling system used by the machine was the almost-hot water that poured into a cement tank where, on cold winter days, children from the neighbourhood bathed and women washed clothes. The water was laced with streaks of engine oil, but as far as I know it did not occur to anyone that it might be injurious to our health or the health of our land.

Then one day the mill was moved from our land: the partnership had ended. Soon we were demolishing the structure that had housed it. Chachaji, Bhaji and I took it apart brick by brick, carrying

7

the wood and bricks to the *khooh* for storage. That kept us busy for days. Once the bricks and wood were stored and the area around the well levelled, Chachaji was ready for his next venture: a new three-room building at the *khooh,* with a veranda. Once again Bhaji and I did the heavy lifting — moving the bricks and preparing the mud, carrying it in containers on our heads and pouring it as directed by the bricklayer. Preparing the mud was the messiest and most difficult chore. We dug up soil from a field, piled it on a hard surface near the construction site, fetched water and then began the work of mixing water with the dirt. As the mud became heavy and harder to turn with our shovels, we crushed it with our bare feet, moving in a circle in the knee-deep mound until the soil was totally soft, smooth, and capable of flowing out of a container. The process was not unlike dragging the *falha* over dry wheat, except in this case we were both the *falha* and the oxen. (Often the mud used for bricklaying actually had wheat husk added to it; the theory was that the husk prevented the mud from dissolving quickly in the monsoons.) After we'd prepared the mud, our skinny legs would be bruised and battered below the knees.

It took many months, but finally we had a new building at the *khooh.* In keeping with the rural Indian ethos, Chachaji was a recycler par excellence. We'd incorporated every usable piece of iron, wood and brick into the new building. The bigger room became a storage room. One of the two smaller rooms became a bedroom and the other a sitting room — although the sitting room had a cot in it so that in a pinch it could accommodate guests overnight.

Another of Chachaji's ventures, a small poultry farm, meant that more structures were built a few feet from the three-room building. Eventually, the chicken moved into the original structure's big room. The stench was terrible, and the work of feeding and watering the chickens and cleaning the big room fell to Bhaji and me. Some days he bicycled to the nearby town of Kultham to hand the eggs over to someone to market. I wasn't allowed to go, since the one time I had, I'd lost control of the bike, and the eggs fell off and broke. After a couple of years, it became obvious that for the amount of energy and resources invested in the poultry, the return was minimal at best. Thankfully, the stench cleared upon the farm's closure.

CHACHAJI'S EXAMPLE made my later transition into British and Canadian life easier. His legacy, along with Nanaji's, helped me a great deal in politics as well. I inherited from them the art of being able to differ on important issues with someone and still remain friends.

My father and grandfather were always courteous and friendly with each other. They would sit up late into the night to discuss the state of the world as they saw it. Following Independence, they belonged to different parties, though their common enemy, the British, were gone. Once, just as a public meeting in Dosanjh organized by Chachaji and his Congress party was ending, Nanaji showed up with a friend. Both were members of the Communist Party of India. A few members of the audience were still milling around when Nanaji and his companion took the stage to expound the virtues of a socialist society and the ills of the Congress rule. Chachaji had already left the venue, but I caught most of their speeches as I was returning from school. That night Nanaji and his friend stayed with us. I wondered whether angry arguments would ensue, but Chachaji simply registered an objection about what had happened, and a friendly discussion followed as usual.

Dosanjh Kalan had strong contingents of Congress supporters, Communists, and members of the anti-colonialist Akali Dal. From time to time, the *panchayat* (village council) was controlled by one or the other of them. The area produced men such as Bhagwan Singh Dosanjh of Jaito Morcha fame, who led a group of Indians from Canada into the freedom movement; the Jaito Morcha was aimed at the restoration to power of the raja of Nabha, a state seen as anti-British. Amar Singh Dosanjh was another well-known figure of his time. A one-time MLA in Punjab, legendary orator and prominent Akali leader, he co-founded and edited for many years the leading Punjabi daily, *Akali Patrika*. Coming from such a politically active place, it was natural for Dosanjhes to hold strong opinions.

Poetry readings, mainly in Punjabi with an occasional Urdu intervention, were held in our village several times a year, with poets from around the region — the great majority of them, at that time, male — invited to participate. The writer could either sing his poetry or read it. The two best-known poets of Dosanjh, Nazar Singh Taras and Kashmira Singh Mahee, always participated. They wrote about the lives of the common people in simple language. I started writing verse myself, and by the time Chachaji discovered my secret, I had two mid-sized notebooks filled with poetry. My father thought pursuing poetry as a lifelong passion would keep me poor — even the vaunted Taras and Mahee had to earn their livings as a carpenter and the village postman respectively. So Chachaji took my poetry and burned it, and I can still see my words and emotions going up in flames. Ironically, even such a lover of language as Chachaji could not bear to see his son become a poet, such was his fear of poverty. Over the years, haltingly, I have tried to reconnect with the poet in me. Perhaps Chachaji was right, and the world is better off without long torrents of words from me.

Naqlaan — travelling performances by comedians, mimics, singers and dancers — also kept us entertained. In the villages of India at that time, there were only male performers in any *naqlaan*. Rural humour and folk songs would fill the air. Quite often, however, petty but violent scuffles between drunks in the village would spoil the show, and when that happened, no one was safe in the dark: you could be a mistaken target. There were no street lights; normally, as people came upon each other, they would identify themselves. We always told the truth about who we were; the political differences between fathers were not yet reason for violence to be visited upon sons.

A few young Dosanjh men once organized an evening play in the village. Ten minutes into it, the hanging kerosene lamps on stage were smashed with iron-bound *lathis*, and a fight in the dark ensued. I ran home and told Chachaji what was happening. Flashlight in hand, we returned to the scene. The actors, all from our village, had locked themselves in a room, and the attackers were challenging them to come out. A crowd of onlookers stood at a distance. With the nearest police post about five miles away and without any way of contacting it, Chachaji identified himself and told the attackers to go home. In the morning, he promised, he would be happy to talk to them about the issue that had generated such anger. Chachaji had no special powers, just physical courage and a belief that the young attackers would have respect for the schoolmaster. It could have gone wrong, but the attackers left, and the actors were escorted to their homes by Chachaji and a few other men. We never did learn the reason for the violent disruption. Some said it was because the play challenged gender and caste taboos. Others put it down to personal animosities.

Each political party had drama troupes that made the rounds as well, touring plays that were totally partisan. News about the upcoming performances travelled by word of mouth. The Communist Party of India had the best shows. Two great actors and singers, Joginder Bahrla and Narinder Dosanjh, were particularly devastating in their mockery of the ruling Congress party and its crony subservience. At the time, the Congress party controlled the government of India. It had such a monopoly and grip on power that it and the Indian government were barely distinguishable. The Congress troupes, for their part, traded on the still-fresh victory of the independence struggle.

8 THE YEAR WAS 1962; I was sixteen years old. My matriculation examinations were followed by two months of *khooh* work and visits to the school library to read up on everything I could find about medical education. Chachaji, like most educated parents of the time, wanted me to become a doctor. He took me to Phagwara to buy me an Atlas bicycle and had it assembled while we waited at the bike shop. Suddenly, I had entered adulthood.

Meeto Bhenji, my cousin and a classmate of the college principal's wife, agreed to accompany me to Phagwara so I could enrol at Ramgarhia College. I had not been out of the villages much, and the family felt I needed my hand held on my first real outing into the larger world. But as Bhenji and I wheeled our bicycles out to the road, we saw Chachaji running along behind us, motioning for us to wait. He had been talking to some friends in the village who warned him that a doctor could be woken up in the middle of the night and asked to travel to all sorts of places at the most ungodly hours. No son of his would have a life like that, he said. His new goal for me was a degree in engineering.

I enrolled in the college's non-medical science courses, but this sudden change in direction had a domino effect: I began to lose my interest in sciences and math, and I became a mediocre student. Newspapers and the world of politics had held an attraction for me since my days of reading aloud for Nanaji and listening to his stories of the freedom movement, and my interest in them grew. As time went on, I paid less and less attention to my textbooks.

Still, I rode to Phagwara and back every day to attend the college. Bhaji was taking an auto mechanics course at Jullundur, and he made the daily return trip by bike and train, so on weekdays Chachaji and

Tayaji were on their own at the *khooh*. Occasionally I returned later than usual because of a trip to Paradise, the movie theatre in Phagwara. Out of my one-rupee-a-day allowance, I had to buy the *Tribune* for Chachaji. The newspaper cost twenty-five paisa, and the cheapest cinema ticket was fifty paisa, leaving me with twenty-five paisa for a cup of tea. Yet Chachaji thought anything more than an occasional trip to the cinema meant you were wasteful and spoiled, so added to the interest of the movies themselves was the allure of youthful rebellion.

One afternoon I was on my way home from Phagwara with my friend Verinder Sharma when two men on bikes passed us, riding quickly. As they caught up with the *gudda* on the road ahead of us, one of them reached into the back of the cart. The men sped on. Verinder and I smelled a rat.

From the looks of it, the man and boy riding the oxen were poor subsistence farmers. At the *chungi*, a place where toll was collected for commercial traffic, two uniformed police officers questioned the *gudda* owner in the presence of the two "civilians" Verinder and I had seen earlier. The two "civilians" turned out to be police officers too. One of them reached into the *gudda* and brought out the thing they had clearly pushed in themselves, a bottle of hooch. As they brandished the bottle in front of the farmer, his son started to cry. The police turned the *gudda* back, hurling insults at the driver.

Realizing this was a plot to extract some cash from the farmer, Verinder and I told the police what we had witnessed and asked them to let the farmer go home. The police then turned their abuse on us, threatening to teach us a lesson if we didn't mind our own business. Persistent, Verinder and I accompanied the *gudda* to the police station half a mile back in Phagwara, where we demanded to see the officer in charge. He told us to get lost.

Verinder's father was a former member of the Punjab Legislative Council, and Verinder also knew the current Phagwara MLA, Om Parkash Agnihotri. A few minutes later we were sitting in front of a man dressed in simple Indian clothes as he wrote up our complaint in his one-room office: an image of a public official scarce in India today.

The MLA would mail our complaint to the superintendent of police at the district headquarters, he assured us. When Verinder and I passed by the police station on our way back to the main road, the *gudda* was no longer there; the farmer and his young son had either been released or been sent elsewhere for holding overnight.

This was my first real experience of dealing directly with the world. The faces of the crying son and his scared father haunted me. Their family must have been worried for their safety when they did not return to their village at the expected hour. The father probably feared that all of his proceeds from the family's produce sales would go to line the pockets of scheming policemen, causing his children to go without shoes or school books. All the way home from Mr. Agnihotri's office, I thought about Mahatma Gandhi's dream of a free and just India. He believed if Indians changed for the better, so would India. Some of my hope for my country died that day, and I have remained alive to that feeling, a fear that sustains me in my daily pursuit of social justice.

The incident continued to haunt my thoughts. Then one day Verinder and I were called to the principal's office and instructed to ride our bikes to the Phagwara Rest House, about a mile away. The place exuded authority and order. We were ushered in to see the superintendent of police, who showed us a row of uniformed men and asked us to identify the four involved in our complaint. We did, and their badges and belts were stripped off. They were being suspended, we were told, pending an inquiry. The suspended men later approached Chachaji and asked him to persuade me to withdraw the complaint. He refused, leaving me to decide the matter. Verinder and I decided to stand by our complaint. We knew the cops were not rich, and there was a possibility they would lose their jobs. On the other hand, the farmer and his son deserved justice. In the end, we never learned what became of our complaint.

A COUPLE OF MY rich friends from school spent much of their time travelling by train to cinemas in different cities. What little money my family had sat quite often on the shelf above our study table.

One day the shelf held two hundred rupees. To my father's horror, both that money and his young son went missing for two nights. I travelled to Jullundur, watched several movies, ate out and then slept at a friend's. Thanks to Taeeji's intervention, Chachaji let me off with only a warning when I returned, my wallet empty and remorse written all over my shamed face.

Until high school I had worn Indian clothes. Sweaters in the winter, yes, but even our blankets were cotton or cotton and wool mixed, homespun and woven. Chachaji did not suffer from a lack of self-esteem, and he did not need to dress his children in Western attire. That was not how I felt — I wanted to wear pants and jackets. But I did not complain. At college, the divide was even more pronounced. Many poor students pretended to be from rich families. I had not yet learned to be comfortable in my own skin. I started wearing cheap versions of Western clothes, tight pants with a well-defined crease or, even better, a stitched one. My desire to fit in was overwhelming. The pride I would later feel in my heritage eluded me at that age.

Chachaji never failed to lead by example in doing physical work. For him, work was like worship, and there was no shame in worshipping the labour that fed his children. But at college, even the students from the poorest backgrounds, who knew the need and value of physical work, denigrated friends caught working in the fields, carrying loads on their heads or tending to cattle. If one was seen by fellow students doing physical labour, there were always excuses: it was just for that day, the family servant had fallen ill, and so on and so forth.

My family was making an effort to educate me without constantly reminding me of our poverty. I was deluding myself that a new bicycle, cleaner clothes and the neater environs of the college had somehow changed our status. As I wrestled with growing up in a jungle of influences, the college offered new vistas and friends. Jagtar Sihota and Bharat Bhushan Maini, both of whom had more experience with urban India, took me under their wing, and I started paying attention again to my books and to what our teachers taught in the classroom. But their guidance came too late. I failed the final chemistry exam, receiving a compartment — a chance to rewrite it and thus avoid failing the year.

Chachaji had pinned on me his hopes of a child with a university degree. In later years, I felt like a criminal for putting him through what transpired for me at college. My brother and I never talked about it, but when a documentary about my life was made in 2009, Bhaji blurted out tearfully that in 1963, when Chachaji learned of my wretched compartment, he had cried, something my brother had never seen before. On learning that, I was justly cut down to size.

Writing the compartment exam in 1963 took me to Chandigarh, the new capital of Punjab, which was still under construction. I had been there once before, during a class trip in grade ten that took us on a bus tour of several important historical places. In Chandigarh, we had seen the Punjab Assembly, the Government Secretariat, the High Court buildings and man-made Sukhna Lake. Chandigarh had been designed in the 1950s by the French architect Le Corbusier, who was commissioned by Nehru to build his dream city for a modern India. Today it is an aging city turned into a union territory under the control of the central government.

The Punjab and Bengal were cut to pieces by the murderous partition of India in 1947, an inevitable result of pandering by politicians to religious passions and bigotry. Their lust for power could only be satisfied if the region was further divided to create a religious majority of Sikhs in the Punjab, but to shelter themselves from accusations of religious favouritism, they masked it as a campaign for a separate linguistic Punjabi-speaking state. The panderers succeeded in carving three states out of the Punjab, which had already suffered serious cuts and body blows. The central government, not to be left behind, acted like the monkey resolving the dispute between two cats over a piece of bread. Since the new states were not able to agree who should get Chandigarh, the central government appropriated it as a union territory.

The bus taking me to my compartment exam reached the city in the late afternoon. I could not afford a hotel room, so I stayed with the extended Dosanjh family of the poet Nazar Taras. They were generous hosts, making sure I had a room to myself in their three-room home, with a light for studying. On the day of the exam, I took a rickshaw to the Panjab University. The wide boulevard leading to it was freshly paved, and my nervousness perhaps made the spotless white building look even more imposing. This was no ordinary exam; a compartment meant a close brush with failing your year.

There were about two hundred other students ready to plunge into the test. Invigilators distributed the questionnaire, along with a booklet for our answers. I looked up to the ceiling, then at the door and the closed windows. By now, political battles were more exciting to me than chemical reactions. But there was no escape. For the next three hours, my head was empty of everything except chemistry.

Back at home, everyone wanted to know how the test had gone. I wasn't sure. If I'd failed, I would have to be content to be a subsistence farmer for the rest of my life. I could not bear to see Chachaji worried to death about me anymore. In a society where the honour of parent and child were so inextricably tied, I would not see him humiliated.

Luckily, I did pass the test, and I worked hard to get back into a rhythm at college. I wanted to succeed, especially for Chachaji and the rest of my family. My friends Jagtar and Bhushan were a good influence, and we all became close. When the chief minister of Punjab visited our village, Jagtar and Bhushan arrived for the day, bringing with them our new English teacher, Ranbir Singh. After the crowds dispersed, they came home with me for tea and sweets.

In a village household, a visit from college friends signalled a coming of age of sorts. My family remained silent, despite their view of the exercise as wasteful since I couldn't afford the more expensive ways of my friends. I craved the approval of my elders and my family, and I knew I would have to earn it. From then on, in spite of other temptations, my focus remained squarely on education. I had also realized that if I became self-reliant, it might mean more freedom to pursue my own goals without burdening Chachaji.

9   I KNEW MANY YOUNG PEOPLE who yearned to go abroad and leave poverty behind. Thousands of sons and daughters (mainly sons, back then) of the newly independent India were trekking west to make their fortunes. Those who returned to visit seemed happy and wealthy. In my immediate family, my cousin Biraji had made the journey when I was ten, in 1956. I had not thought of leaving India myself, but then something happened to change that.

One afternoon as I was enjoying the spring sun on the college lawn and catching up on my reading, a fellow student named Harjinder Atwal stopped to say goodbye; it was his last day at college, he said, because he was leaving for England. He had been accepted at Faraday House Engineering College in London, he told me, and he thought they were still taking applications for admission from foreign students. He gave me the address for the college and bicycled away. Call it coincidence, fate or chance — our encounter would sculpt the story of my life.

I headed home that evening with my mind racing faster than the wheels of my bicycle. The dust on the road crackled under my tires, as if to prick my conscience. Chachaji had always made it clear that I was to stay in India to study. Riding home to Dosanjh that evening with the London college address in my notebook, I felt the shame of a deceitful son. The night felt darker and lonelier than usual. Even the warm quilt on my bed later that evening failed to quell my shivering bones and trembling spirit.

The next morning, after some quick chores at the *khooh*, I set off for Phagwara as usual. The fog was slowly vanishing in the glistening rays of the morning sun. Post-compartment, I was working very hard.

But I was not happy. Chachaji would never abandon his dream of an engineer son and allow me to do a BA in history or political science instead. Those who studied humanities remained poor or under-employed: that was his logic, and it was somewhat true. Chachaji's own life of poverty dictated his choices for me.

After several days of battling my doubts and fears, I invested half my daily allowance on an aerogram. I wrote to the college in London, asking for a prospectus and an application form. Not a soul knew about it. My routine of college, home and *khooh* continued uninter-rupted for the next few weeks. Then, one Saturday, Mahee, the village poet-cum-postie, delivered an envelope from the college in London addressed to me. I quickly hid it from sight, opening it when I got back to school, in the anonymity of the college library.

As I read the prospectus and the application form, two challenges emerged. First, I would need to consult a dictionary to decipher many of the words and phrases used in the material. That would be cumber-some, but doable. The other was more difficult. The completed applica-tion had to be returned with a five-pound draft attached. At the time, getting an amount greater than three English pounds required approval from the Reserve Bank of India in Delhi. Getting that approval would be an impossibility for me. It meant travelling farther than I had ever gone and, what's more, I would need Chachaji's consent.

By now, I had made up my mind to try to get to England. I didn't have the courage to share that with Chachaji or Bhaji — not until I had the college admission in hand. Biraji, too, had to be bypassed — having been repeatedly yanked out of school by my Tayaji, he was anxious that nothing should delay my continued education. For him, as for Chachaji, that meant staying and studying in India. But Biraji had a brother-in-law, Pushkar Singh Lail, living in Nottingham. I wrote to Pushkar for the draft, impressing upon him that he was not to tell Biraji.

While I waited for his reply, I filled in the application form, except for the space for my name. As a non-Christian, I didn't know how one dealt with providing a "Christian name." I couldn't ask Chachaji since

I had not yet told him what I was up to. I asked some of my friends, without disclosing why I needed to know, but no one could help. One day the thought of asking our Dosanjh School headmaster, Dharam Singh, crossed my mind. I broached the subject when I found him alone at his home. He had a bachelor's degree in English himself, and he agreed to help. A few days later, Mahee delivered the draft from Pushkar, and my application with the draft was on its way to London.

On the day the reply came from England, the college at Phagwara was closed for a few days. After finishing work at the *khooh*, I went over to the school grounds to play field hockey with some other village boys. The movement of the ball was hard to control on the uneven ground, making the game both more interesting and more trying. The deserted school buildings looked forlorn as we played on into the dusk, delaying the walk home. There were no road lights. On a pitch-black night, you had only your wits and your knowledge of the road to guide you.

This night, unknown to me, there awaited a challenge at home. Mahee had delivered the reply from London to our home, and Chachaji was restlessly waiting for my return. As a father in the India of the early sixties, when sons dared not disobey their fathers, he must have wondered why this was happening to him. Did he feel lonely having to deal with an errant child without his wife, my Biji? There must have been many moments in his life when he felt her absence keenly.

As I entered our home, I was met with Chachaji's anger: "Why did you do this? How could you do this without telling me?" He showed me the letter: I had been accepted. But instead of elation, I felt all the pain of my father's disappointment. My tongue felt frozen. Taeeji took me into her embrace and then went away to get my dinner.

There was no studying that night, only an uneasy sleep. From his bed beside mine, Bhaji said, in a wounded voice, "you could have told *me!*" I had no answer for him, but when we woke the next morning, Bhaji asked what we were going to do. He was always responsible in family matters, and still is to this day. As we busied ourselves in the *khooh*, we discussed it. I knew Bhaji wanted to go abroad himself.

If I went first, it might be easier for him to follow, I said, and he agreed to speak to Chachaji on my behalf.

Bhaji triumphed; a couple of days later Chachaji handed me a bunch of papers. It was an application for a passport. I had a photograph taken, my first ever in a studio.

The completed passport application had to go from the official district town of Jullundur to Phillaur, one of several *tehsils*, or sub-districts. When the papers did not reach Phillaur, Chachaji, now fully on board, accompanied me to Jullundur in an attempt to speed up the process. There was a deadline: I had to be in London before the first week of January, and it was now mid-November. The following week, the papers arrived in Phillaur. They had been gathering dust somewhere, and someone advised me nothing would happen unless I greased a palm or two. It was getting late in the day, so I decided I should make the trip to Phillaur as well.

I bicycled with a college friend Hargurdeep Dosanjh, nicknamed Chand. At the passport office, I was told I needed to fill out a special form that cost fifteen rupees. When we asked whether the form was available elsewhere, the official said yes — I could get it from another office in town. Chand and I got the form, filled it in and handed it to the original clerk. But the form seemed to have no relevance to my application, and next the clerk wanted to sell us some tickets for an upcoming hockey match in Jullundur, the proceeds from which, he said, were to go to a charity. Chand lost his temper. It was a scam. The clerk wanted a bribe. And if we were to get to Dosanjh at a reasonable hour, we needed to leave right away. We decided to try a different strategy. The residence of the sub-divisional magistrate, the administrative head of Phillaur, was nearby. But like many other residences of the rich and powerful, the SDM's had a high wall around it, with a sentry stationed at the tall gate. The guard said "sahib" was not home.

The next day at 9:00 AM, Chand and I were standing outside the unwelcoming gate again. We had left Dosanjh early in the hope of catching the SDM at home. "Sahib is not in," the sentry informed us. (I detest with a passion this colonial term of "sahib." In India today it is almost mandatorily uttered by subordinates addressing seniors, the poor addressing the rich, and the weak addressing the mighty. Not coincidentally, the same word is often used to invoke or allude to the Almighty in religious discourses in India.) I peeped through the narrow spaces between the wooden planks of the gate and saw a middle-aged man in a nightgown walking around the yard. I immediately decided he must be the SDM. I called out, "SDM-*ji*, we are two young men. We would like to see you. Your subordinates are asking for money to do their work." The man opened the gate, heard our story and sent his guard back with us to the passport office, where we overheard the guard telling the clerk to do what we were asking. Moments like this reaffirmed my failing faith in the new India.

Before long we received confirmation that the Punjab State had forwarded my application to the nation's capital for the issuance of my passport. Delhi was only about two hundred miles from Dosanjh, but to us it seemed like a million. The train took ten hours to get there. Undaunted, Chachaji set out immediately, taking the train to Ghaziabad, where he stayed with my cousin Siso, and then bicycling the rest of the way into Delhi. He must have had to push his way through crowds in various offices. And he might have had to find some "people of influence" in Delhi to return with my passport in hand so quickly.

It all reminded me of a time one winter when Chachaji had left home on his bike with a woollen blanket and a change of clothes in a cloth bag. I saw him leave, but I repressed my curiosity; it was considered a bad omen to ask a departing person where they were going, just as it was to call out after a person already on their way. A week later, Chachaji had returned with exhaustion writ large on his crumpled clothes and ashen face. His dishevelled beard and turban spoke to the tense moments he must have endured on his trip. Years later, I learned that Chachaji had been in Chandigarh that week, successfully securing the reversal of a decision by corrupt officials that had seen an acre of our land illegally registered in someone else's name.

IT WAS MID-DECEMBER 1964, almost ten months since Harjinder Atwal had bidden me farewell on the college lawn in Phagwara. The bumps along the way had thrust me into deep despair, but the Punjabi equivalent of "this too shall pass" — "*darvuttzamaana cut bhalay din avangay* (gird up, persevere, good days shall come)" — always came to my rescue.

I had started to grow up, and I needed more practice in doing important things without Chachaji or Bhaji holding my hand. That was probably what prompted Chachaji to send me, rather than Bhaji, to Hoshiarpur to get some money from Masiji Gurmit. The money was needed for my ticket to England. Maybe Masiji owed Chachaji money, or maybe he had asked her for a loan. I didn't know. Either way, I made the journey from the bus depot in Phagwara to Hoshiarpur and received the money from Masiji; it was also my chance to say goodbye to my sister Tirath, who was still living there to attend school. Nothing was said between us about my planned departure for England, however; I do not believe Tirath had been told I was leaving.

For reasons I cannot remember, I arrived by bus back at Phagwara late at night. I was carrying over two thousand rupees: not a small sum in those days, especially for the Dosanjhes.

From Phagwara, the direct road that followed the canal and passed by the Dosanjh School was not well travelled at night. The Banga road was much busier; late-night truckers, motorcyclists, cyclists and farmers on *guddas* ensured the night did not provide easy cover for robbers or the infamous bandits known as *dacoits*. Still, the *rickshawalas* wanted forty rupees for the trip on the Banga road at night. I could not afford that kind of money, and anyway, what robbers there were would think me rich if they saw me on a rickshaw. But I could not think of a safe place to spend the night at Phagwara, and I was hungry too. I bought half a dozen bananas and some peanuts for the walk back to Dosanjh and set off on the Banga road.

It was 10:30 PM. Phagwara was an industrial town, but not yet a big urban centre. In the roadside establishments, things were coming to a halt. The road lights stood as if fighting off the night. I was less successful in fighting off my fears. I ate some bananas as I walked, which helped assuage my anxiety. As I passed by the *chungi* where the police had stopped the farmer, in my mind's eye I saw again the poor farmer's son crying on the *gudda*. My eyes scanned every tree, caught every fleeting ray of light. The moon occasionally pierced through the canopy of branches overhead. The shadows wove a pantomime punctuated by the sounds and speed of traffic. A nightingale sang from the banyan trees.

After a while, I found myself in Mehli, at the turnoff to Mandhali, where the paved road ended. No canopy of trees here, and almost no traffic. In Mehli's poor homes, *divas* were mounted in makeshift windows. Those better off had electric bulbs affixed to their plastered gates. The two kinds of homes sat next to each other, framing the chasm between wealth and poverty. On my left was the primary school where, during the monsoons, I had sometimes taken shelter from the pelting rain on my way to or from college. Silent and solitary, the school seemed to be calling to me for company, even for just a moment, in return for the comfort and reprieve it had offered me.

Even bricks and mortar can speak, I believe. To hear them, you need to let the voices enter your being. It had happened to me once before, at the Jallianwala Bagh at Amritsar, where Meeto Bhenji took me to have my wandering eyes corrected at the Medical College. My family knew an ophthalmology student, who arranged it; the surgery was done by visiting professors in private practice as part of the student's practicum. (Only the surgery to my right eye was successful; the left one still wanders when I'm tired.) Walking through the narrow passage that served as both entry and exit from the Jallianwala Bagh, I imagined General Dyer ordering his riflemen to gun down the peaceful and unarmed protestors listening to speeches for the freedom of India in 1919. Having just visited the Golden Temple and the Durgiana Mandir, both abodes of Indian spirituality, might have rendered me susceptible to the power of suggestion. The sound of gunfire, the screams of men, women and children, and the sight of General Dyer frothing at the mouth with hate and imperial arrogance vividly entered my soul that day.

Lost in these memories, I finally crossed the railway tracks that led on one side to Saila and on the other to Phagwara and beyond. A cyclist rode by, noticing me, and quickly stopped. "Who are you, and what are you doing here this late at night?" the rider asked. I told him who I was, giving my father's name and village. The man was Comrade Harbans Singh of Mandhali, and he ordered me to hop behind him on his bike, promising to drop me within Dosanjh village limits, where I would be safe. He left me no more than a mile away from our *khooh* building.

All danger past, I began to dread explaining to Chachaji why I was this late at night. Why had I not waited overnight at Masiji's place in Hoshiarpur, rather than taking such a big risk with so much money? Bhaji would have been smarter about it, I was sure.

Soon I was passing by the land on which we toiled. Gobs of cattle dung, with its distinct, fresh smell, lay on the road. Mixed and composted with household garbage of ash and greens, then allowed to mature for a few months in a heap at the *khooh*, the dung was a potent organic fertilizer. Whenever we needed manure, we dug some from the composted mound, piled it on a *gudda* and carried it to the field. From there, Chachaji or Bhaji filled up the *tokras*, wide-rimmed buckets made of cotton stems or tree branches that were lifted for carrying onto the spreaders' heads. When we stopped for lunch and siesta on hot days, we would have to stand outside the *chalha* and use pots to pour water over our bodies to wash away the coats of manure.

Chachaji was still awake when I got home. I had once again disappointed him, and he got out of bed, filled with rage. He stood before me, and I felt his hand strike my cheek. It was not my cheek but my heart that was hurt. It was not until years later, when my own sons were in their teens, that I was able to understand the full anguish of a parent not knowing where a child might be.

10 I HAD LITTLE WINTER CLOTHING to speak of, so I packed one sweater, a couple of shirts and some shorts to take with me to London. And of course there was my *rajaee*, the cotton-filled quilt that travellers from the villages carried as a bundle tied with rope, belongings wrapped inside, to obviate the need for a suitcase.

On those last days in Dosanjh, I observed my surroundings with a sense of impending loss, storing away scenes of my family and the sights and sounds of village life. I had no camera, so my eyes were the aperture, my brain the recording device. The dust and beauty of my little world, including the faces of the men, women and children, began to feel special, since I would no longer be able to see them at will. I would miss friends like Bakhshish from Bahowal, Sardul, Hari and Gunga from Dosanjh, Jagtar and Bhushan from college. I had no photographs of them, so I tried to keep their images strong in my mind.

I took a quick visit to Bahowal to see Nanaji and family. Who knew when we next would meet? Air travel was very expensive. Punjabis who left for England returned rarely, and only after long periods away. I also went to Bakhshish's home, only to learn he had enlisted in the army. A sadness came upon me, but soon other friends from school heard that I was visiting and showed up at Bakhshish's house. Soon we were reminiscing about the rote sequential chanting of multiplication tables our teachers had forced us through, and our game of blindfolding a boy and then milling around him, chattering continuously, to see if he could follow the voices and footsteps and manage to touch one of us. Our talk also turned to a play we had once performed; I had played the newlywed wife, dressed in bright red clothes, and Bakhshish had played the husband who was going away to earn a living. The duet,

66

which I still remember, was "*Kahnoo pavaaiyan kothian vay kahnoo Chhattia a Vehra*": if her husband was planning to go away, the wife asks him, why did he have this big house and yard built?

On my way back to Dosanjh, I rode along the route that Nanaji and I had travelled by *gudda* twelve years earlier. In a culture where things had remained the same for thousands of years, this road had certainly been on the move. The spotless mud hut where Nanaji and I had enjoyed such memorable *burfi*, tea and milk was no longer there, and in its place stood a row of grimy brick shopfronts whose owners obviously lacked pride in their establishments. Inside the new tea and sweet shop, the walls were blackened with soot, and a single sooty electric bulb hung from the ceiling. But the chai was exquisite and the *burfi* delicious. The present had merged with the past.

It was getting dark as I entered the Dosanjh village limits. I tried to imagine what awaited me in England: the roads there were paved with gold and life was easy, people said. I knew that was a myth; yet I had no knowledge of my own to replace it. The darkness was a sanctuary for my ignorance. Bhaji had always been a fellow of few words, but that evening, in the room we shared, he and I talked late into the night.

The morning of December 28, 1964, brought mist and fog. As the sun burned through, I walked the five acres of land our extended peasant family jointly owned. Most of the hay had been ploughed and the ground prepared for sowing the next crop. By mid-February, the wheat would be lush green for miles across Punjab. The sugarcane would be ready for making *shucker* in a month or so. From the spot where our land ended, I could see the Saneen da Rauda of Mandhali, the site of the *mela* where *qawwals* from Pakistan used to sing. I was voluntarily leaving my motherland, and how painful it was! What must have gone through the minds of the millions who were forced to abandon their birthplaces and move hundreds of miles away after partition? Their lives lay in ruins.

My sister Nimmy, an irrepressible spirit, still lived in Dosanjh. Like my sister Tirath, she hadn't been told of my departure — perhaps my father thought her too young, though she was considered responsible enough to help make roti for the family and to wash the family clothes, all while attending school full time. Within a year of my departure for England, Biraji's wife, Kuldip, and their three children, Kulbir, Parveen and Jasmine, would leave India to join Biraji in England. Most of the household work of cooking and cleaning for family and for the hired help on the *khooh* would fall on Nimmy. She was forced to grow up fast. Years later, she told me that when she saw a photograph of me from Derby with my friend Resham, whose family tree connected with ours several generations back, she could not believe that clean-shaven boy was her brother.

Not many people outside the family were privy to my plans, either. Hurdles to emigration could be easily created by people who did not like you: a false police report here and a malicious prosecution there, spurred by petty jealousies or perceived offences.

I planned to catch the evening train, a milk run that would reach Delhi early the next morning. The tightly bundled and roped quilt holding my belongings had to be carried as well, so we took several bicycles. Outside our home, I was surrounded by neighbours and my family. Taeeji's moist eyes kept looking down, as if she couldn't bear the sight of me leaving. Tayaji stood watching and waiting near the Goraywala. He blessed me with his hand on my head, patting me on the back to launch me into the unknown. He must have been thinking of Biraji, the son in England he had not seen for eight long years. I have always cried easily, and tears rolled down my cheeks as we walked with the bikes to the *khooh*. Behind our home we passed the clay hearth of our water-drawer, Bachni. In the evenings she would light a fire in the *bhatthi* and roast corn for anyone who wanted it. You brought your own corn for that purpose, and Bachni kept a portion of it as payment for her labour of roasting the rest. I turned to take one last look at the home where I had been born and raised.

We took the less-travelled canal road to Phagwara. It was early afternoon, and the canal was filled with water that flowed from a much deeper, wider canal irrigating the land in Dosanjh and beyond. I still remembered when this canal was freshly dug and the bridge over it that connected our school to the village was brand new. One morning the students gathered to watch the new canal fill, and as the water sped into it we saw a human corpse floating toward us: the decayed, bloated body of a man. It had the look of a huge sculpted statue perched on the surface of the moving water. The swollen limbs, the penis — the "statue" looked grotesque, and a strong stench emanated from it. I felt it should be taken out of the water, and I said so to the adults in the crowd. They shut me up, saying, "Let others downstream worry about it." Anomie in India was already in full bloom.

Now the canal looked so much smaller than it had appeared to that grade-six child. Its banks were overgrown with tall grass. As we rode past Virkaan, the noise of a *chuckee*, a flour-mill engine, filled the air. Once, during the monsoons when the cattle-pulled *kharaas* was inoperable, Jajo milled our *atta* by hand for seven days straight. I tried to help her, but I couldn't even budge the stone. But I poured grain into the *chuckee* as she rotated the grindstone holding the handle, first with one hand and then the other as her arms got tired. The work was so difficult that, historically, it was part of the sentence of hard labour endured by convicts. Guru Nanak had once offended the Mughal emperor Babar, and as a consequence was sentenced to hard labour of the *chuckee* in prison. Offending is the fate of all great reformers, of course. Men like Nanak and Gandhi viewed it as their dharma to offend against the evils of their time. Perhaps Jajo's own husband, my Nanaji, had felt the same about the hard labour he endured in the British prisons of colonial India.

By now, we were on the Grand Trunk Road that passed through Phagwara, taking travellers on to Delhi on one side and to Amritsar and Lahore on the other. The textile mill by the railroad tracks was the largest year-round employer in Phagwara. The sugar mill farther down the road provided seasonal employment. Some men from Dosanjh worked in these mills, cycling to and from work every day. Finally we reached the intersection of the Grand Trunk and Banga roads. Turning right would take us back to Dosanjh. We turned left instead, arriving at the rail station a stone's throw away. Chachaji's cousins from Virkaan had come to see me off. Bhaji went to purchase train tickets for Chachaji and me while others carried my bundled quilt to the platform.

11 THE POWERFUL STEAM ENGINE sounded ominous. Its noise lent an air of finality to my fate. There was no turning back now. Those who had gathered offered me hugs and words of reassurance. It was one of the few times I have ever witnessed my brother cry. Chachaji and I boarded the train, and the engine spewed steam as the train pulled away. Bhaji waved one last time, and then I could see him no more.

As the train found its rhythm, the fields alongside appeared to be dancing to it. Acre upon acre of hay, sugarcane and other vegetation glowed green in the dusk. Farmers were ploughing and levelling the earth, and the dust from the hooves of their oxen seemed to touch the heavens. As night fell, sounds took over: the steam engine and the wheels clacking along the steel tracks. Most of the passengers were dozing by now. As the train slowed at various stations, lights from homes and from tea and peanut stands punctuated the sleepy darkness. Dogs barked, disturbed by the activity. Inside lit-up factories, I could see people working away. Cities and towns never completely rested, I was learning. Chachaji slept on and off, every now and then glancing at me. He was worried, no doubt, about whether I would be able to make a go of it out there in the world.

It was still dark when we got off at Ghaziabad. The station was in need of repair and a thorough cleaning. Probably not much had changed in the city since the British left it in 1947. Dosanjh had its own share of filth, with raw sewage accumulating in puddles and ponds, but at least it had open fields one could escape to. In Ghaziabad, I soon saw, there was no escaping the crowds, the filth or the general pollution. Chachaji and I took a rickshaw to Siso Bhenji's home, which had a big enclosed yard with a machine shed on one side.

In one corner of the yard was a four-room house with a kitchen and a bath. Scattered everywhere were the machines and parts worked on by my Bhaji Sardara Singh, an expert machinist. Everybody managed to find a place to sleep.

The next morning we went shopping. Chachaji selected the fabric for my suits, which would be made by the fabric store's tailor. I would soon be the proud owner of two woollen suits, my first ever. I also bought some toothpaste and a toothbrush, another first; I'd been told England did not have thorny *kikar*, acacia karroo, or cockspur thorn, trees whose thin branches had served as toothbrushes and tooth cleaners all my life.

Chachaji also bought me a small suitcase to put my clothes and toiletries in. I didn't have much in the way of toiletries. I was a turbaned Sikh boy with virgin whiskers — nothing you could call a beard yet. I had never heard of deodorants. Natural body odour was fine as long as one was clean, we thought. And instead of body creams and lotions, we had mustard oil.

It had rained a little, and the puddles gave the paved roads an ugly, pitiful look. Traffic splashed the muddy water around, with bus, car and truck passengers avoiding the airborne mud only if their windows were shut. Travelling around as we were — in rickshaws, by bike and on foot — made us prime targets for mud's fury. Chachaji's outfit of naturally white *khadi* — homespun cotton — did not retain its pure whiteness for long.

That evening, Chachaji, Bhaji Sardara Singh and I visited Connaught Place, perhaps the poshest commercial section of Delhi at the time. The rain-washed marble on the buildings, floors and pavement shone whiter than ever. Shops and stalls were full of the merchandise the elite of Delhi splurged on. The area was filled with expensive restaurants and emporiums; beautiful, colourfully bedecked women accompanied "kaala sahibs" in their London-style suits and boots. It appeared as if many of these "Mahatmas" had just returned to India after completing their dinners at the inns of the court in England. Certainly they had not gone to South Africa to be thrown out of first-class train compartments as coolies. This was the Indian idea of England. I wondered what the actual England would be like. Did the English people there hate doing their own chores, polishing their own shoes, cooking their own meals and doing their own laundry?

My mind was racing. A part of me longed to be like the rich of Connaught Place, though I knew intellectually that it was wrong to be consumed by the lust for wealth. I was travelling to greener pastures, and like all beating hearts, mine was a battlefield of competing influences. How would I navigate those influences to figure out what and who I would be? At that moment I had no business passing judgement on kaala sahibs. At least they were not abandoning India.

As the hour of my departure drew nearer, my fear of the unknown grew stronger. But Chachaji did not need to be burdened with the knowledge that his soon-to-fly son was ill prepared for the journey and beyond. The next morning was filled with love, food and laughter. Siso Bhenji made delicious *pranthas*, mango *achaar* (pickle) and home-made yogurt. As usual, I overate. Most human beings are blessed with a satiety mechanism. Within a few minutes of beginning a meal this mechanism sends signals to their brains to slow down and eventually to stop eating. I have never received such signals. We are all related to animals, and in this trait I am definitely related to dogs.

An old-model Ambassador taxi waited outside the front of Siso Bhenji's house. Baggage tucked away in the trunk, our goodbyes said, Chachaji and I sped away in the cab through the descending fog. The turbaned *sardarji* driver artfully negotiated the traffic, offering a running commentary as we drove past places of historical interest. A mosque here and a fort there; he regaled us with stories of kings, queens, courtiers and intrigue from centuries long past. My head was spinning. My ancestors had struggled along with millions of others to free India from British rule. Now I was going to the home of our former colonial rulers in search of something better. It did not occur to me at the time that I was running away.

The Delhi airport was a building with a few high-ceilinged rooms. After I checked in, Chachaji and I sat down in the waiting area. I had three British pounds with me — all the money a person was allowed to take. That and the very restrictive controls on passports were Nehru's way of encouraging Indians to stay in India. My leaving would be no loss to India, I was sure, but Nehru did have a point. He wanted Indians to stay and build their own country instead of providing cheap labour to the world. He was acutely aware of the history of indentured and other Indian labourers working on sugar plantations or building railways in other countries under exploitative conditions. In purely personal terms, though, I felt India was lucky not to have to expend any more resources on me. There were millions of others who were abler, keener and more useful for the future of the country than I was. I was not good at sciences or calculus, and I was more interested in politics than in engineering. India already had too many people interested in politics, not as a noble calling but as a means to power and influence for personal profit and glory. Had I stayed, the same fate might have befallen me.

At two hours past midnight, my fellow passengers began filing out to the airplane on the tarmac. "Get up, Bhai Ghunattha Singh, time to go," Chachaji said. When he was feeling tender and affectionate, that was his favourite name for me: Mr. Ghunattha Singh. He hugged me tightly, then motioned for me to leave. Overcome with emotion, I focussed on climbing the mobile stairs reaching into the plane. But as I lifted my foot to the first step, a voice rang out, "Bhai Ghunattha Singh, come here." It was Chachaji, a few feet away on the other side of the rope divider, standing among the relatives and friends of other passengers. "If you want to cut your hair, you may," he told me. "When in Rome, do as Romans do." He enunciated the latter in crisp English, employing the Indian accent later made notorious by the inimitable British actor Peter Sellers. "If you feel like drinking," he continued, "it is all right. But don't drink too much. And if you ever smoke I'll kill you. Go. Run now. You are going to be late."

Looking back, I am amazed at these words of wisdom from a father to his going-away son. Chachaji's advice was at once liberating and arresting. He who had cherished his unshorn hair all his life and would have preferred me to follow his example had freed me from this Sikh religious stricture in an instant of foresight. He had never been out of India, but he had the wisdom of a seasoned world traveller. All those days as I was getting ready to leave, he must have been pondering the life and the challenges in store for me in England.

I settled in my seat. My feet were no longer touching the soil of my forefathers, and the plane was readying for takeoff. I had not even seen an airplane before. Once, a plane had landed in the fields near a village a few miles from Dosanjh, and the kids who saw it said it was larger than many *guddas* put together. Now I was not only seeing one for myself, I was sitting in one. By the old stored in our brain's magic box of memory, we measure the new.

The plane's interior was spotless white with a blue tone. The contrast with the earthy homes and streets, the dusty roads and fields of Dosanjh, was stark. It was as if I had entered an uninhabited and sterile part of the universe. I paid full attention to the flight attendant's seatbelt and life jacket demonstration, struggling with her Aussie accent.

Though there weren't many other passengers on board, they were all, as far as I could see, *goray* (white). I had seen few *gorays* in my life to date, and no *gorian* (white women) at all. Miss Jacob, the Anglo-Indian headmistress at our Dosanjh Girls' School, was the first white-looking person I had ever met. There were a few Dosanjh girls who looked white as well.

The awareness of being among strangers now coursed through my head. To my left, across the aisle, sat the only other Indian passenger on the plane. He was deep in conversation with the *gora* beside him, and every now and then they would turn to look at me.

When the plane took off, my eardrums were ready to explode. I'd felt a similar but much less painful sensation when I'd played on the swings tied to a tall old banyan tree at Bahowal. This was no mere swing, however, and the skies no banyan tree. We were in a colossal machine ascending to float in the air. There was no rope to hold onto, just the armrests of my seat.

To distract myself, I tried to memorize the features of each of the white people on the plane, including the hostesses, as they were called then. All the hostesses had pinkish skin, some paler than others. In the hormonal department, the sexual repression and prudery drummed into my young head were in full control; nothing to worry about there. When my gaze fell upon an English newspaper in the seat pocket in front of the Indian man across from me, I asked in my broken and previously untested English if I could borrow it. He smiled and handed me the paper. I was still looking through it when the Indian asked if he could sit next to me for a while.

He turned out to be a professor at the University of London. His *gora* friend in the seat next to him was also a professor, and he soon joined our conversation. The Indian quickly realized I was more linguistically challenged than my request for his newspaper might have led him to believe. We spoke in Hindi until the *gora* joined us, then we switched to English. The two men were returning from a conference in Australia, they told me. I wish I could recall their names, because I have never forgotten the kindness they showed me during that flight and all the way past immigration and customs at London's Heathrow Airport. It was undoubtedly clear to them that I hailed straight from the village and was untouched by the sophistication of big-city life.

The Indian man took me to the back of the plane to show me how to use a flush toilet. One could not squat on it, Indian-village style, he told me. That aspect of my education completed, the men turned their attention to my table manners. Breakfast had just arrived, and they sat me between them to explain the use of a knife and fork. I had never come across these utensils, and my natural inclination was to hold the fork in my right hand to convey the food to my mouth. To my amazement, however, the fork was to be held in the left hand. Both men showed me on their own plates repeatedly how to cut a piece of meat and then carry the pieces to your mouth. Finally, a light went on in my head, and it was smooth sailing thereafter. (Years later, when my wife-to-be, Rami, had to tutor me in the art of chopsticks, I found my apprenticeship with the professors on the plane had lit the path.

She was an army major's daughter, and good table manners were considered a prerequisite for marrying into many a military family.)

Our flight made two stops: Karachi and Paris. At each airport, we were allowed to get off the plane. (Security was essentially nonexistent then; the hijacking or bombing of planes to make political points came much later.) Landing in Karachi reminded me that the city had once been an important and integral part of an undivided India. I recalled stories of the conferences Karachi had hosted during the freedom movement. Nanaji's favourite had been the conference of the Indian youth society Naujwan Baharat Sabha on March 27, 1931, timed to coincide with the opening of the Indian National Congress the next day. The hanging of Bhagat Singh and his associates, on March 23, 1931, had galvanized the country. There were fissures in Congress, with Subhas Bose, a prominent Congress leader who became the party's president in 1938, arguing for more aggressive action than Gandhi was willing to take. On both days, Nanaji was in charge of security around the perimeter of the conference and for Subhas Bose personally. Inside the Karachi airport, I looked into Pakistani faces for signs of longing — for what could have been rather than what was now. To be fair, many Indians had gone about their lives, oblivious to the larger questions of fate and history. Why should the Pakistanis be any different? We were one people by history, blood, culture and our place on earth, though we were taught the hate that stands now between us.

Back on the plane, the welcome instruction of the two professors continued. The Indian man even touched on the issue of how one viewed women in British culture. He himself had been an immigrant, and he told me in no uncertain terms that just because British women dressed differently and spoke with men freely, it did not mean they were promiscuous. He also advised me that spitting and littering in public places were regarded as horrible behaviours.

As we flew into Paris what came instantly to mind was the oft-repeated myth that Nehru's clothes had regularly been sent to Paris for washing and dry cleaning. There was no question his family was rich, but in the twenties and thirties, the frequency of air traffic would have made that impossible. As the inhabitants of a former colony, though, many Indians had an exaggerated sense of Paris and London's splendour. Perhaps that was why the Indian professor made a point of reminding me that the ancient civilizations of India had gone through periods of splendour still evident in the classical literature and the monuments of the various eras. He did not want me to drown in the vicissitudes of history and disown my Indianness.

I did not buy anything on my stops at Karachi or Paris lest I exhaust my three pounds before I got to London; if Biraji did not show up to get me, I might need those three pounds and more. The *gora*, though, bought a small box of chocolates at the Paris airport and offered some to me and the Indian professor. The chocolate had a very different taste from anything I had ever eaten.

It was now the last leg of our trip. We flew over clouds that looked pure white in the sun. At first I mistook them for snowy mountains. The plane pierced the clouds as we descended to land at Heathrow. We fastened our seatbelts.

PART 2

ENGLAND

12 AS WE DISEMBARKED in London, the *gora* professor planted himself in front of me, and the Indian behind. A customs and immigration officer stood at the only open wicket. The professor was cleared in an instant, and he moved aside to make room for me. The customs officer was polite to a fault, looking first at my passport and my acceptance letter from the college in London, then at me, a five-foot-seven, 120-pound turbaned Indian. "For what purpose have you come to the U.K.?" he asked. To date, my answer rings in my ears: "For higher studies." The *gora* professor and I then waited for the Indian professor to clear. We had to wait for our baggage for a few more minutes, the professors bemoaning the time it was taking. I listened with the ears of my own experience; the slow turning of the wheels of government in India, in matters small or large, bred in people an unhealthy degree of patience.

While we waited, I noticed two neatly uniformed janitors in neckties mopping the floor in a corner of the large baggage area. What in the world? Men doing the jobs of the "lowest of the low," the most untouchable of the untouchables, in ties and uniforms? I now understood the criticism that Mahatma's effort to rebrand Dalits as *harijans* — "God's children" — was a good beginning, but too feeble. The sight of these janitors had another life-altering effect on me. The Western suit, I realized, was just a form of dress, no better or worse than any other, including traditional Indian clothing. It wasn't meant to be worn by "sahibs" only. Even the janitors could wear it. They were people too, dignified, as was their labour. It taught me the dignity of labour and the irrelevance in life of how one dressed, as long as one's clothes were neat.

I was feeling the fatigue of my long trip and the newness of everything. I was worried, too, about Biraji not being there to meet me.

But as we exited the baggage area, there he was in the huge crowd, smiling in response to my wave. Once the professors saw that I was safe, we shook hands and they said goodbye.

Biraji had arrived in England nearly a decade earlier, in 1956, successfully entering the U.K. on his second attempt. The first time around, he was stranded in Pakistan and had to return home. But within six months he had secured a passport to go to Indonesia, and from there he found his way to Britain.

My cousin had maintained his beard and turban; details I was surprised by, since I knew him to be a very secular man and regular reader of *Nawan Zamana,* the Punjabi-language daily of the Communist Party of India. He told me that although he had had difficulty finding jobs in factories and foundries because his turban and beard were considered a "safety hazard," he refused to give in to racial and religious discrimination and cut his hair. He had settled into a job in a brick kiln a few miles from the northern city of Bedford; he would work there, in fact, until his retirement.

Despite Biraji's secular outlook, I learned, in England he had become more involved in matters of faith. In 1965, there was still no gurdwara in Bedford, despite a sizeable Sikh population. The community had begun to gather and pray every Sunday in one of the large rooms in Biraji's home. Later, from that beginning, a gurdwara was indeed established in Bedford, with Biraji as its first president. In preparation for the centenary of Guru Nanak's birth in 1469, to be held at the Royal Albert Hall in London in 1969, the more than thirty-five gurdwaras of the U.K. set up a committee of which Biraji was elected chair.

Leaving India on December 31, 1964, and arriving in England in the early evening of the same day has always made it easy for me to remember the date. As Biraji and I walked to the nearest entrance of the London Underground, he told me he'd been worried about me being denied entry into the U.K. A planeload of Indians trying to enter the country as students had been sent back earlier that day.

Unsurprisingly, Biraji's English consisted of a few words supplemented by gestures. He had not been to school in India, and he'd had no opportunity to go to school in England, either. In the tube station, he asked me to get directions to King's Cross. I tried my luck with a couple of people, but the rudimentary English that had enabled me to converse with the professors and the immigration officer failed here. Finally we succeeded, and we boarded the train. I surveyed the flood of white faces around me. My eyes were slow to register the differences, so they all looked the same.

At King's Cross, we boarded a bus for Bedford, and soon we were on the freeway. It was dark by now, and snowing. The headlights of the coach illuminated the falling flakes, and the snow was already piled up on both sides of the freeway. I had never seen snow, and Biraji explained it to me using the only Punjabi word there is for snow or ice: *burf*. (There is also a word for hail: *ahan*.) The coach picked up and dropped off passengers along the way, and when it came to a stop in front of a barber shop, Biraji and I got off. It was still snowing, and standing there under the lamppost, I felt as if we were in a scene from a movie. Fortunately for my numb feet, Biraji's house was less than fifty yards away.

Two of Biraji's friends, who were also his tenants, were waiting up for us. So was Meeto Bhenji, my cousin, who had come to England a month earlier to be married. The coal in the fireplace in the front room was red hot. I was famished and cold, but soon, with a plate of food on my lap and my feet stuck out close to the fire, I started to unwind. My physical journey to England was over.

The next morning, I learned more about my surroundings. Biraji's home, at 2 St. Leonard's Avenue in Bedford, was a two-storey brick house with a detached two-car garage. A nearby subsidiary rail line used electric trains to connect to several smaller towns, including Stewartby, the location of the brick kiln where Biraji worked. Biraji had only recently bought this house. He had a substantial mortgage on it, which his tenants were helping him to pay off. While establishing himself in England and carrying this large debt load, he had still been sending significant funds to Chachaji, which were used to buy several more acres of land for our family. Biraji's wife and children were still in Dosanjh, but Biraji was hoping to save enough to have them join him in Bedford soon.

The British economy was strong in 1965, but every place I went looking for work I was turned away. The recently elected Labour government of Harold Wilson was dealing with the large trade deficit left by the previous Conservative government. Wilson had tightened the country's fiscal policy. He did not want Labour to be known as the party of devaluation — a previous Labour administration had devalued the pound once before — so the economy was feeling the effects. Unfortunately, while I may have been accepted into Faraday House Engineering College, as yet, I had no money to enrol there. Biraji could not support me, given all his other obligations.

Meanwhile, Meeto Bhenji married Jarnail Singh Klair of Birmingham. Since there was no gurdwara in Bedford, the holy Sikh scriptures, the Guru Granth, were brought to Biraji's home for the ceremony, and after her marriage Bhenji left for Birmingham. I continued my job search. I consulted Biraji's friends, young and old, and made lists of the employers they said I should approach. Every evening Biraji would cook a meal, eat his supper early, and then bike to the brick kiln, where he worked the evening shift. All of his tenants were men whose wives were still in India. They had no leisure time, and there was no radio or TV at the house. I would pick up the local evening paper to scour the Help Wanted section. Each morning, I would dress in one of my woollen suits from Delhi and the long woollen overcoat Biraji had bought me the day after I got to Bedford, and hit the road to look for work. Some days I walked many miles. Other days I went a little farther on the bus. But there were no jobs to be had.

Finally, Biraji suggested I try my luck at finding a job in Derby, a city about seventy miles away. Packing for Derby was easy. I simply bundled all my clothes and whatever else I needed in my quilt, tying a rope around it; my Indian experience still dictated my behaviour in most matters. But things were to become more difficult.

Nobody in Bedford had taken me aside to explain the dos and the don'ts of English life. I learned by trial and error. My English reading level was probably the equivalent of grade four in Britain, and my spoken English was much worse. If I knew I had to speak with someone in English, I would prepare by imagining the conversation and translating it in my mind. If the actual conversation veered even slightly from the anticipated course, I would get stuck. Luckily, most people laughed with me, rather than at me, especially upon learning I was a brand-new immigrant.

I had been a shy child, and had even stuttered a little. There were no speech therapists to help, of course; only the anxious stares of my father. I was left to figure it out on my own, along with Nanaji's somewhat idiosyncratic advice: Pretend that the person you're speaking to is blind, deaf and mute. Fear of elders, teachers and authority figures brought on the bouts of stuttering, and in England the stutter threatened to reinvade. The people here were British: the former rulers of India. Whites were considered "superior" in my Indian experience. But my love for reading and Indian history came to my aid; proudly I recalled the stories of Ashoka the Great, who became a Buddhist and a votary of non-violence at the height of his power, and Mahatma Gandhi, who non-violently stood up to the might of the British Empire. Kautilya, who lived from 370 to 283 BCE, had written The Arthashastra, his advice for kings, 1,800 years before Machiavelli wrote his, and his treatise put Machiavelli's to shame with its bluntness and clarity. My pride in India's past gave me the strength not to stutter. I was no less a person than any other, regardless of colour or heritage. I did not have to defer to anyone. Deference must be mutual; otherwise, it is servitude.

In 1965, the British Indian community was still small, except in the London suburb of Southall, which was often called "Turban Town." The Indian Workers' Association was a left-leaning immigrant organization that spearheaded efforts for integration and equality. Bedford had no local chapter, but some Bedford men were active in the national organization; they spoke better English than most other Indians and acted as social, political and language interpreters. These men were also called upon by the English political parties who wanted to connect with the Indians. Their role as the go-to people for Indians on the one hand and the larger society on the other mirrored the way the British had depended on a certain class of people in India to control and govern the country. That colonial experience is fortunately a far cry from the more integrated and assertive British Indians of today.

Dev Badhan, one of Biraji's young Indian friends, was studying full time at Mander College in Bedford. Dev, who lived a block away with his parents, was a bundle of energy, always smiling, always impatiently ready to ride off on his bike with his bag of books.

On a sunny winter morning, Dev put my bundled quilt on the carrier at the rear of his bike, and we walked together to the railway station. Dev was doing his A levels, after having completed several years of schooling in Bedford. A year older than me, he spoke English reasonably fluently, and we hit it off from the moment we met. Dev's mother doted on him to the point of possessiveness, which irritated him. His mother's lack of schooling made him rude to her, and he was justifiably angry with the Indian world. A Dalit, he carried centuries of oppression in his soul, and now he was competing with the children of the erstwhile rulers of India in his daily intellectual labours.

The Bedford railway station reminded me of the major Indian rail stations, which of course had been built by the British too. It was a lot cleaner, though. On the wall opposite the solitary bench in the station's waiting room was a regional map of the railway routes. I spotted Derby on it. The year was not 1893. This was not Durban, South Africa. I was not a barrister; I was looking for a job without any skills for one. I was no Mohandas Karamchand Gandhi, but his story played through my mind nonetheless. He had boarded the train on a first-class ticket at Durban, and partway through his journey he had been thrown off the train. He waited in the bitter cold of the station at Pietermaritzburg, pondering whether to stay and fight racial injustice in South Africa or to return to India to make a living as a lawyer in the colonial courts. So far, Gandhi had not been known as a fighter, but being thrown off a train because he was not white shook him to the core and steeled his soul.

My economy-class ticket had no seat or compartment specified. I tried to push my bundled quilt through the door of the compartment nearest to where I stood on the platform, but the door was too narrow for the bundle to pass. As I stood on the platform wrestling with it, the train guard called out, motioning for me to come over to his compartment, which had a much larger sliding door. He signalled. The train moved. Then, in Punjabi, he asked me where I was heading. I looked at him in surprise as I answered. "I thought you were a *gora*," I said. He took his cap off, and his pitch-black hair and his dark eyes shouted "Indian" then.

As it turned out, Jasbir Mann was an immigrant from Banga, the town ten miles from Dosanjh. He had been to our village and school during a hockey tournament, and he knew my father. He lived in London, he told me, and had worked for some years for British Rail. Our conversation stretched all the way to Derby, interrupted by station stops along the way. Jasbir reminisced about his early life and his time in Britain. The more he talked, the brighter his face glowed. He clearly missed India. As we spoke, I imagined what lay ahead for me. Finally, the train slowed, creaking, and stopped at Derby.

Many people were milling about at the station. Taxis waited in line for fares. Already the region seemed more vibrant than what I had seen in Bedford. I hoped it meant I would find work soon.

I TOOK A CAB to Chacha Chain Singh's house on Depot Street. It was early afternoon on a Sunday, and Chacha and his sons Resham and Ajaib were at home. Theirs was a typical row house of five rooms, with the toilet outside at the end of a small walled backyard. Each of the two bedrooms had two single beds. I was given the only unoccupied bed in the house. There was no bathroom; instead, my new housemates went to the nearby public baths once a week. Chacha was a foundry worker. Workers in the foundries and factories, where work was physical and hard, had bathing facilities at work, I would soon learn. In Chacha's household, people occasionally heated up water on the stove and took a quick bath in the kitchen, which had a brick floor with a drain under the sink that carried water to the sewer.

13

Chacha was a member of Chachaji's generation, and he belonged to the same *patti* as we did of the five there were in our village, which made him closer to us genealogically than many other Dosanjhes were. He was a tall, heavy man who had been in the U.K. for more than ten years. He had returned to India to visit in the late fifties bearing Terylene shirts, shiny suits and a reel-to-reel tape recorder deck that looked like a small suitcase. Ajaib and Resham had not yet immigrated to the U.K. with their father, and we had a whale of a time with that tape recorder. We would borrow an *iktara*, an Indian one-string instrument, to accompany ourselves. I sang my own poems, and I loved hearing myself replayed. Others laughed at my lousy performances.

In those days, when you went job searching or even shopping in a city centre, you dressed in your Sunday best. But there was a problem. There was no facility that starched turbans in Derby — nor had there been in Bedford. In Punjab, in the bazaars and along the roadside, there were countless places that did this for a price.

A starched turban is like a crown that you can take off and put away to wear the next day and the day after. A starchless turban usually loses its shape once it is taken off — and that, indeed, is what had happened to mine. In desperation, I tried to starch the turban myself, but the visible gobs of starch destroyed its beauty. There was only one solution. I thanked Chachaji in absentia for allowing me the choice to cut my hair, and one Saturday afternoon the deed was done.

It took me a couple of long weeks to land a job with British Rail. The railway had a large goods yard in Derby and they provided on-the-job training. The job was twelve hours a day, six days a week, starting at 2:00 PM. Sundays we had off. I made good money: twenty-two pounds a week after taxes.

I had been introduced to two neighbourhood pubs with names ending in "Arms." I did not see any arms of the dangerous kind there, only the warmth of family-owned establishments. They served great draft beer, and everyone told me a beer a day did not hurt anybody. I learned it was in the pubs where working-class people met and entertained themselves in the evenings. But on weekdays I didn't get home from the railway until three in the morning, so I visited the pub for a beer at lunchtime, walking to work afterwards with the food I'd packed for the night. On the way I would pick up a newspaper, which kept me busy in the intervals between trains being shunted.

For me at that time, everything was new: new country, new language, new culture — and now, the totally new experience of working for an employer in an industrialized country. I wanted to learn everything quickly, and the walk to and from work gave me time to be alone with my impatient thoughts. I hungered for knowledge.

My co-workers at the rail yard came from Pakistan, India and the West Indies. We worked on the grounds, coupling, uncoupling, slowing or stopping the wagons. All the other jobs were held by whites. Chanan, a teacher from Punjab, was the longest-working person at the yard at our level. Another worker, Aslam, was from Azad Kashmir, as he called it. (I called it Pakistan-occupied Kashmir.) Aslam always exchanged good-natured repartee with Bhatti, a Pakistani from Lahore, who claimed he had a BA from the University of the Punjab in Lahore and walked around with an air of superiority. The India-Pakistan War of 1965 happened during the time we were all working together, but we kept our passions inside us.

Shunting was not always safe work. One day a Pakistani co-worker not much older than I was fell while slowing down a wagon as his wedged bat slipped. He lost his right ankle and foot when they were crushed by the wagon. Chanan Singh had made sure I bought a pair of steel-toed work boots, but even those, I knew, would not prevent a leg from being chopped off.

The coal-burning stoves in the cabins in the yards were handy for warming our Indian food or for frying eggs and heating beans. The cabins served as lunchrooms and resting places when there were no trains to shunt. I read as much as I could when there was quiet: newspapers, books and magazines. There were heated debates among the men as well. For the West Indians, cricket was the thing. For Indians and Pakistanis, it was field hockey; cricket had not yet assumed the gigantic role in the life of these former colonies that it has today. The West Indians talked sports; we of the Indian subcontinent talked mostly politics. Religion in Pakistan had not yet poisoned minds, and there was no resurgent Hindu or Sikh militancy in India. We all knew stories of families maimed and butchered during partition on either side of the border.

One temperamental West Indian co-worker, though, often picked quarrels with others. Everyone tried to avoid him, but one day, when I had the misfortune of being in his company, the man made a vulgar remark about my sisters. I had not yet dealt in my mind with the question of violence, but I let the man know my culture didn't appreciate that kind of talk. He flew into a rage and lunged at me with a knife he was using to peel an apple. The third person in the cabin intervened, and when the foreman heard the commotion, he ran into the cabin and led me away. It took me some time to learn that walking away from a principle is wrong, but walking away from an idiot is not.

Derby was not far from Nottingham, where Biraji's brother-in-law Pushkar lived. He had helped me with the draft of five pounds I'd needed for my British college application, and now I was hoping he could provide some advice. I was questioning where my life was heading and why I had come to England. Pushkar had been to college in India. He might help me find some answers.

It was early evening, cold and getting darker. As I waited for the bus to Nottingham, anxiety engulfed me. (I'd experienced the same feeling on Indian winter evenings, and many years later I self-diagnosed my condition as seasonal affective disorder.) Seeing me waiting alone on this dark and dingy evening, a motorcyclist stopped and, hearing my destination, offered to drop me directly at Pushkar's in Nottingham, since he was going that way. I accepted the ride, but the resulting wind chill made the miserable cold much worse. My hands and ears felt ready to fall off. But as we passed through Nottinghamshire, I remembered that Sherwood Forest had been the hideout of the legendary Robin Hood, known for plundering the rich to give to the poor. The Englishmen who came later colonized, plundered and divided India. I thanked the biker when we reached my destination, and he waited until Pushkar's door opened.

Pushkar, in his forties and balding, had an endearing smile. He welcomed me in and turned on a heater, and the warmth gradually brought my limbs back from the dead. I thanked him for the draft he had sent me and told him of my dilemma. His advice was to find a way of going to college as I worked. Being a bus driver and active in the trade union movement, he supported the Wilson government. We talked late into the night.

The Britain of the sixties was a class-conscious and rigidly stratified society. There were working-class areas in most cities, as well as posh enclaves where the rich lived. In between lived the middle class and a small number of nouveau riche who mimicked the aristocracy, hungering for entry into their ranks. Indians, like the other visible minorities, were on the outside looking in. I was an alien in every sense of the word in Britain, an interloper. But giving up and running back to Daddy just wasn't an option.

And truth be told, I, too, was trying to rise. Though I didn't realize it at the time, I was an economic immigrant, in that it was the very affluence of the West that had attracted me here. Our poverty had not pushed me out of India; though poor, we still had more than most. I had succumbed to the greed for more: an ambition to be pursued elsewhere. Economic immigration is about opting out of one's own society. It is about not wanting to face the pain in your native country, about choosing to flee to greener pastures.

On the bus back to Derby, I found a seat beside an older white woman who slid over to make room for me, smiling. She worked as a packer in a nearby plant, she told me — the kind of person sociologists said was likely to be incorrigibly racist. She got off the bus near her work, and a middle-aged black man got on. I smiled and moved over, but he hesitated for a moment before taking the seat. He was an educated man, originally from Kenya, and we made small talk. I was curious about his hesitation in sitting next to me, and gingerly I asked. His answer was shocking. In his experience, he said, Indians were more racist than whites.

My eighteen-year-old self was taken completely aback. I had never before thought of Indians as racist. I had not yet fully understood my ancient heritage. Now I know too well that racism, colourism and casteism all have a long history in India, predating the arrival of the British. Colourism and racism arrived with the Aryan assault on India around 2500 BCE, and the Aryans married caste to colour to produce the despicable social hierarchy that still bedevils Indian society. Many in the Indian diaspora continue to perpetuate colour, caste, racial and religious divisions.

WORKING FOR BRITISH RAIL allowed me free travel, and Blackpool was one of the places I visited with colleagues from work. I had never seen the ocean, except in books or on holiday posters, and I was struck by its wondrous beauty. The rays of the early afternoon sun seemed to be dancing on the waves. It was an experience as unforgettable as seeing a beautiful woman's naked body for the first time and hearing her soul speak to yours. I wondered about the ocean's depth, about the beauty below the surface deep in the core, in the bowels of the earth.

Some in our group had brought swimming shorts and towels. I just took off my socks and shoes, rolled up my pants and stood knee deep in the water. There were plenty of people on the beach. By the standards of my rural Indian roots, many of them were almost nude. I felt the sting of shame as my eyes fell upon female body after female body. In all of my years, I had never seen a grown-up female woman who wasn't fully dressed. It was a shock for an eighteen-year-old immigrant from the villages of India to be in Britain in 1965.

Life in Derby also allowed a few pleasures. There was a weekly Indian movie shown at one of the local cinemas. Almost every Indian in the area came out to see it, dressed in their Sunday best. But apart from the weekly movie and pubbing, there was little else to do in Derby besides work. I felt stalled, and my earlier restlessness returned.

IN GRADE SEVEN I had complained to Chachaji about my eyesight being poor, but he laughed it off, teasing that I only wanted to wear glasses in order to look smart. When I insisted, he took me to his friend, Verinder's father Dr. Lekh Raj Sharma — a qualified denturist. I stood in front of Dr. Sharma, who held open each of my eyes in turn, looked into them and pronounced my vision twenty/twenty. I dared not disagree. Now, in Derby, I had my eyes tested by an ophthalmologist — who verified that I needed glasses. My eyesight improved and stabilized thereafter for many years.

For some time I had been thinking about taking classes at the Derby Technical College. Due to the hours required for my job at British Rail, however, part-time or evening courses were out of the question. Some employers allowed their employees one paid day off a week to study at an approved institution. I knew that wouldn't be possible in my case, since my studies would not relate to my work. Still, I reasoned, even a day release without pay would be worthwhile if it meant I could attend school. Before I could register for classes, however, a formal letter was required from British Rail authorizing the arrangement. Despite the efforts of my foremen, no such letter was forthcoming.

I was determined to go to school, so I decided to return to Bedford to try my chances there. Chacha Chain Singh advised me against it; in Bedford I would not make the kind of money I was making in Derby, he said. Education did not matter much in relation to making money, argued others in the Derby community. Some even claimed that spending years at college or university would make it impossible for me to compete with those of my contemporaries who stayed out in the "real world," amassing wealth.

14

This was an "immigrant syndrome," as I saw it: poverty and scarcity led to an obsession with economic security to the exclusion of all other pursuits. Nonetheless, on the train to Bedford, anxiety overwhelmed my heart. My bundled quilt still hid within its embrace all my worldly goods, but I had tied it much more tightly this time so it would fit through the door of the train. I found a compartment with only an older white man sitting in it. He was reading the day's *London Times*, but a few minutes into the journey he put his paper aside to ask where I was heading.

From my accent, the man could tell I had not been in England for long. He was a sociology teacher at a college in the Midlands, he told me, and he was researching the integration of immigrants into British society. How was I finding the new country? he inquired. Did I miss India?

Of course I missed India, the place that had nurtured me and was the only home I'd known until six months before. Everything in England was new, and I felt I was under scrutiny all the time. The hardest part of it was not understanding the nuances of the language — not being able to understand, for example, whether someone calling you "blue blood" was a put-down or a good-natured joke. The unease was less about the amount of money I carried in my pocket than about whether I could converse with people with ease as an equal.

The sociologist sensed tensions building up in the country with the influx of new people, he said, and I could see he was genuinely concerned about race relations. The television comedy *Till Death Do Us Part* had begun airing on BBC One, portraying the working-class life in a realistic way. The main character, Alf Garnett, had become a cultural icon, despite his being a racist and a reactionary. Millions of people watched the show.

When I got off at the Bedford station, I looked for a cab to no avail. So, Indian peasant style, bundle on my head, I walked home. When Biraji opened the door, the expression on his face conveyed a silent question: why had I returned to Bedford with all my worldly belongings? Promising to explain in the morning, I went off to bed.

LEAVING DERBY had been the right thing to do. I had to live among people who did not mock education, and Biraji agreed with that. During the day I went looking for work, and evenings I spent with Dev and his wide network of friends. Bedford had a smaller Indian community, though it was a younger one, with many professional and educated Indians among them.

This time my search for work bore fruit more quickly. I found a job on the shop floor at Cosmic Crayon Company, a five-minute bike ride from Biraji's home on St. Leonard's Avenue. The factory ran just a day shift, which appealed to me; on the other hand, working eight hours a day, five days a week, I'd be making half the money I'd made at Derby.

My job required a couple hours' training from Joe, a West Indian. He loved talking as we waited for the crayons to form. Solid wax was melted with the required colour, and the concoction was stirred until the mixture was evenly hued. The hot, coloured wax was then poured into the crayon-making machine, a tray with holes in it. Cold water was used to cool the machine, and the excess wax was scraped off. The crayons came out standing straight on their bases. They had to be picked up and piled in special boxes, ready for packing. I repeated the process ad infinitum, and I was soon bored out of my wits.

The workers on the shop floor were mostly young men and women, almost all of them high school dropouts. They seemed like bright kids, happy doing their work, and I envied them that. At lunch time there was talk of soccer, cricket and sex. Such blunt sexual expression I had never heard before. I was pretty well versed in the Indian profanity department, and I'd heard many new British and West Indian swear words as well. But until then, I had never heard that kind of language used in mixed company, and some young women expressed themselves as boldly as the men.

As a child of Indian peasantry, I was a new entrant to the working class; in Marxist terms, I had taken a revolutionary step from the land to a cash nexus. I eagerly awaited my weekly pay envelope, my only source of sustenance. I think I was the youngest and most inexperienced worker at Cosmic, and that was probably the reason for everyone's generosity toward me; even the lab staff stopped by to chat whenever they were on the shop floor. The lab staff spoke slowly and clearly, so I could easily converse with them. The shop floor workers spoke more quickly, and their earthy colloquiality was often Greek to me, but they were equally caring in their own way. Every time I needed a new sack of solid wax for my work area, someone was always there to help, and I often joined in on the Friday pub crawls.

Robert Symes, the personnel officer who had hired me at Cosmic, walked the shop floor a couple of times a day, talking to workers. The company had started a monthly newsletter shortly after I began working there, and Robert asked me to contribute something. I put together a hodgepodge of words about India, stealing an idea here and a word there, and a few days later Robert stood with me for a few minutes on the shop floor talking about his life at university. Before he went back to his office, he asked if I would like to join him sometime for a drink.

After that, Robert and I went pubbing every two to three weeks, visiting a different country pub each time. Robert would pick me up in his beige, two-door Italian Fiat. Our conversations ranged from English literature, about which I knew very little, to the politics and economy of Britain, India and the rest of the world. Robert and I differed on many things, and we argued our positions. My limited vocabulary encumbered our conversation, but he would correct me, suggesting words and expressions for what he thought I was trying to say. I looked forward to those pub outings with Robert, and he became a tutor of sorts.

A few months into my time at Cosmic, some of the office and lab staff, including Robert, planned a pleasure trip to Wales, and I was invited to go along. We set off in a rented multi-passenger van in the morning, arriving at our destination just as the sun set. Along the way, people played music, and the conversation traversed the mundaneness and profundity of the world. The Beatles were the craze at the time, though I could not make out all the words to any of their songs.

We put up at a bed and breakfast for three nights near the base of the Snowdon Summit, one of the highest peaks in the United Kingdom.

The first day we climbed a steep mountain; I sat down halfway up and waited for the others to return. That evening we had reservations at a restaurant popular among the locals. It was walking distance from our lodgings, and since I was a bit late getting ready, I made my way alone, dressed in a suit and tie under my long coat. The doorman would not allow me in, despite my explanation that I was joining friends already in the restaurant. "We have no friends of yours here" was his reply. Stubbornly, I stuck my head into the restaurant and spotted Brian, the tall, curly-haired head of the Cosmic lab. I yelled out for him, and I was let in. That was my first experience with overt exclusion, and it rattled my soul.

The next morning we drove to the base of the Snowdon Summit and walked up rather than taking the train. The view from the top was astounding; we could see for miles, a new experience for a boy from the prairie of India. The Shivalik range of the outer Himalayas could occasionally be glimpsed from the plains of Punjab, but I had never seen the mountains up close. Now I was atop one. Spreading my arms, I made several 360-degree turns, for those few seconds feeling as though I was flying high above the world. I lost my balance, falling and rolling down to the railway tracks. I was lucky. Had I fallen off in the other direction, I would have plunged several thousand feet to a certain death.

AROUND THIS TIME, the Vietnam War was intensifying. Under President Lyndon Johnson, the U.S. had increased to four hundred thousand the number of its troops in Vietnam, and the dreaded napalm bombs were falling from the skies. There was huge anti-war sentiment throughout the Western world, which drew my sympathies, and I started hanging out with the Labour party activists in Bedford. Christopher Soames, a son-in-law of Winston Churchill, had been a conservative MP for Bedford since 1950, but he was defeated by Brian Parkyn of the Labour party in March of 1966. Along with some friends, I had volunteered in Parkyn's campaign.

Dismayed that the Indians in Bedfordshire were by and large not civically active, Dev and I called a meeting of all the young men we knew. We met at Dev's home, and there we founded the Young Indians Association (YIA) of Bedford. One of the group's first public functions was to commemorate the anniversary of Bhagat Singh's hanging by the British thirty-five years earlier for carrying on a violent campaign against British rule in India. I made the introductory remarks and managed the stage, and it was a proud day. But I soon realized it was easy to celebrate what we already knew; it was much more difficult to think about the problems Indian immigrants faced in our new societies. The YIA became a vehicle for representing our concerns and challenges to Bedford's civic administrators. We also got immigrant youth involved in sports. Some YIA activists veered left over the years, and others started paying more attention to matters of faith and business, but the organization continued into the 1980s.

County and public libraries were the holy temples of my weekends. I checked out a book or two every Saturday after a couple of hours of reviewing the *London Times*, the *Guardian*, the *Daily Telegraph* and the *Christian Science Monitor* in the library's reading room. Books in hand, I would meet up with Biraji to help him carry the week's groceries. At home, the books and BBC Radio 1 were my constant companions. I also stayed out late with friends, talking about our lives and the world. My options continued to seem severely limited, not just because I was penniless but because my English was still so poor. Hanging out and talking felt better than my lonely, desperate wanderings.

I was still seeking a job that would allow me a day release to attend college, and I ended up as a laboratory assistant for a science teacher named Mr. Tyler at the then Elstow Abbey Secondary School, a half-hour walk from St. Leonard's Avenue. Mr. Tyler was keen to teach me what I needed to learn to do the job, and I took a course on operating a sixteen-millimetre projector in the evenings. I was soon responsible for setting up films on various subjects for the students. The fish in my care in the school's fish tank did not fare as well; they died of too much food at the hands of someone afraid of scarcity.

The teachers at Elstow were kind and eager to teach a young immigrant the skills necessary to get on in the world. I was invited to their get-togethers on weekends, and the students too were anxious to make me feel included. The female students at Elstow had a cooking class that prepared a delicious lunch once a week, and I was often invited to share it. The school's young chemistry teacher, William Jefferies, was interested in politics and history. He took Dev, our friend Jeet and me to London to see the Parliament Buildings and 10 Downing Street. The London bobby, a permanent fixture in front of the prime minister's residence, obligingly moved over so we could snap a picture.

I had applied to several universities on the off chance one would grant me admission as a mature student, and only the University of Keele at Newcastle-under-Lyme, which offered a four-year degree in politics and law, showed interest and invited me for an interview. The interview, with the dean and two others, lasted an hour. Initially our conversation focussed on British politics, including constitutional conventions dating back to the Magna Carta, the "Great Charter" of liberties England had introduced in 1215. I felt I answered their questions fairly well, but then they narrowed in on further specifics of British history, which in truth I had not studied at all.

Following the interview, the university offered me provisional admission for the following year if I passed the British history O level in the interim. I had huge doubts about being able to fulfill this requirement, and I spent every available minute studying history, reading nothing else for the next two to three months. A new teacher at Elstow even gave me his history notes from high school, and I studied those, too. In the end, though, I still could not distinguish one Queen Elizabeth or one King George from another. I decided not to sit for the history O level after all.

I was not making much money at Elstow School, and my education appeared to be going nowhere. So I found a job with Armco, a company that made auto parts in Letchworth, a few miles from Bedford. Malkiat Rai, a dear friend of mine, worked there too. Another Armco employee drove us there and back, and we contributed to his petrol expenses for the week. The job was physically demanding. I was making more money, but my body ached from the hard physical labour, and my heart ached at my failure to find a way to educate myself. I spent the weekends with my friends.

A friend of Biraji's, a man from Taeeji's village, had a daughter who was barely twenty, a school dropout and clueless about life. Her father floated the idea of my marriage to her, and Biraji, thinking like many Indian parents of his time, felt marriage might give direction to my life. Malkiat ridiculed the idea among our friends, and the man never forgot the insult he perceived Malkiat's remarks to be. A few years later, after I had left for Canada, Malkiat was severely beaten by the man's friends. Malkiat was an orthodox Sikh, and his beard was also forcibly shaved. He was humiliated in this way because he was a Dalit; in the minds of his abusers, he was a lesser human being.

Caste, in all its ugliness, was alive and well in Britain. Another Dalit in Bedford, Meehan Singh, a handsome elderly man, was assaulted because someone's relative had lied about some money he had already paid them. Nobody in the community stood with Meehan Singh. Because of caste's millennia-long spell, the spectators and perpetrator alike were numb to Meehan's humanity and his suffering.

Malkiat and a friend named Gurdial Ryat had been discussing the idea of launching a news and literary weekly. It was to be named *Mamta*, a term evoking a mother's love for her child. When their plan firmed up, Malkiat asked if I was interested in helping put the weekly out. I would receive a salary equivalent to what I made at Armco, and I would have free room and board at Gurdial's home in London. I accepted. Whatever the uncertainties, it would be an environment of letters. I was named the assistant editor of *Mamta Weekly*, and once more I bundled my belongings, this time for a move to the capital.

For the next twelve weeks I lived as a member of the Ryat household, which included Gurdial's wife and two young children. Malkiat and I spent several weekends travelling in his brother's car to different parts of England, signing up subscribers and ensuring that Punjabi shops and other establishments displayed and sold *Mamta*.

Many details about *Mamta* now escape me, but I do remember writing an editorial on the death in March 1968 of the first man to enter outer space, Russian cosmonaut Yuri Gagarin. My view was that we should use the resources on earth to improve the human condition instead of "conquering" space. I have not changed my mind about that; the space race for most countries is one of those "nice to haves." For most people, more earthly needs beckon.

The other big news story of 1968 that I wrote about was the execution of five black prisoners on death row by the regime of Ian Smith in what was then called Rhodesia. I have followed with keen interest the developments in that country over the years, from Ian Smith's white regime to Robert Mugabe's corrupt brutal dictatorship in what is now Zimbabwe. I still remember the hopes the world cherished of a resurgent Africa throwing off the yoke of colonialism and of Africans taking their rightful place among the peoples of the world. With some exceptions, the dream has turned into a nightmare. In South Africa, Nelson Mandela's successors are small men not up to the task of building a prosperous, compassionate and inclusive country.

At the time *Mamta* was launched, there were already two well-established Punjabi newsweeklies in the English market: *Des Pardes* and *Punjab Times.* That made ours an uphill struggle. Tarsem Purewal, the editor and publisher of *Des Pardes,* made a scathing attack on *Mamta*'s quality. I telephoned him to suggest we could disagree without engaging in personal attacks, but I should have known that the man who'd invented abusive and extortive Punjabi journalism would not be receptive to reason. Purewal was known to warn men about upcoming negative stories, offering the suggestion that there was nothing a little hush money could not suppress.

Every week I took the original proof of *Mamta* to the printers in central London to have several thousand copies made and then carried the printed paper home on the tube. The Ryats and I would fold the papers and prepare them for mailing. But the paper's narrow focus and limited readership, along with the suffocating nature of the Punjabi news culture of the day, soon made me lose interest. The crowds of people on the underground seemed to move purposefully, in sharp contrast to the meaningless drift of my days.

The state of British race relations also made me angry and discouraged. During the Notting Hill riots of 1958 in London, white youths had attacked immigrants from the Caribbean. In 1963, the Bristol Omnibus Company imposed a colour bar, refusing to employ West Indian or Asian crews; only after a lengthy boycott did the company agree to hire people of colour. Britain's Race Relations Act, passed in 1965, made discrimination in public places on grounds of colour, race or ethnic or national origin against the law. A Race Relations Board was set up to handle complaints the following year. But the act was weak, and it did not deal with employment. The lack of jobs in immigrant communities brought colour prejudice into their homes, and unemployment pitted white workers against workers of colour. During the Bristol boycott, the Transport and General Workers' Union had threatened that all wheels would stop if one black man stepped onto the platform; the union opposed apartheid in South Africa while supporting the colour bar at home. That's how ugly and schizophrenic the response of even the so-called progressive Left was to discrimination at the time. Activists among the minorities and a significant section of the political class realized things had to change. The housing issue was also rearing its racist head. Blacks were at the bottom of the heap. Asians weren't treated much better, but some Indian immigrants considered themselves "superior" to the black people anyway (I was finding that my companion on the bus had been right). Few recognized that equality for blacks would bring equality for us all.

The soot-darkened buildings of London in 1968 seemed to mirror my soul. Escape seemed the only option, but how and where to?

On one of my trips to central London, I noticed the office of the Canadian High Commission as I was passing through Trafalgar Square. In that split second, I paused. My Masiji Heeti was now in Canada: why not join her there? I entered the building, deciding then and there to apply for a visa. I returned a few days later with the additional documentation the High Commission required, along with a medical certificate and my passport.

ENOCH POWELL, a Tory cabinet member, was a vocal opponent of the recent amendments his party had proposed to the Race Relations Act. Powell had already made many speeches against immigration, and on April 20, 1968, he made the speech for which he would become infamous. In it, he quoted the sybil's prophesy from *the Aeneid,* saying, "As I look ahead, I am filled with foreboding; like the Roman, I seem to see 'the river Tiber foaming with much blood.'" As a solution, Powell proposed compensating immigrants and repatriating them to the countries they had come from.

Powell's speech was followed by a rash of violent incidents against people of colour. In one incident, fourteen youths attacked their victims while chanting "Powell, Powell." Overnight, Powell became a pariah among the political class. His was "an evil speech," roared the *London Times.* Britain's ruling class, however reluctantly, made a united front in condemning such outright racism.

I too had experienced firsthand the indignity of racial violence in Britain. I had been to Marks & Spencer, looking for something to buy for a friend, and was now a block away from the public library. It was a Saturday, and I was looking forward to reading the newspapers.

By the mid-sixties, skinheads were a phenomenon among working-class youth in London and other parts of England. A group of skinheads walked by on the opposite side of the street. I heard the sound of their metal-heeled shoes as they shouted at me, "Go back, Paki." I picked up a piece of paper that was lying on the ground, pressed it into a ball and threw it in their direction. The group crossed the street and pounced on me, punching and kicking me repeatedly with their sharp-toed boots. They left quickly once people started shouting at them and running to help me. In that moment of total humiliation, lying on the ground, I was brown and "Paki." Ironically, what Mohammed Ali Jinnah, the chief proponent of partition of India, could not accept, the skinheads fathomed and promoted: that a "Paki" and I were one and the same.

It was during the chaotic aftermath of Powell's "Rivers of Blood" speech that I received my immigrant's visa for Canada. As I prepared to leave, I felt a certain amount of foreboding myself. At this point, there was no going back to India; my classmates and friends would have moved on, and Chachaji could no longer support me. He had no means other than the piece of land I had already left behind.

Biraji was dismayed to learn I was leaving the U.K. to go to Canada. He had hoped I would educate myself in England, living close to him. He was afraid that if I hung around with politicos without further educating myself, I would always be a *chamcha*, a hanger-on. In Indian political culture, *chamchas* are in abundance. They are like the flies piled on the mounds of solid sewage found on many city streets. If one sewage mound is removed, the flies find another. As power moves, so do the *chamchas*. Corruption is the currency that feeds the trade.

I was leaving behind some good friends in England, with a lot of sadness. I did not know much about Canada, and yet I was uprooting again. I needed to find somewhere to belong, somewhere that in turn would belong to me. The footprints of my ancestors linked me inexorably and eternally with India, yet at that moment I was leaving my home country behind as well.

Tarsem Purewal wrote a sarcastic story in *Des Pardes* about me flying off to Canada and deserting *Mamta* in its infancy. Except for that brief mention, my departure from England was uneventful.

My father, Pritam Singh Dosanjh, circa 1925. This photograph may have been taken for his driver's licence.

My mother, Surjit Kaur, in 1944. She completed grade eight at the school in Dosanjh Kalan after marrying my father.

ABOVE: *My mother, Surjit, flanked on the left by my cousin Biraji's wife, Kuldip, and on the right by my cousin Bakhshish Siso. My brother, Kamal Bhaji, stands in front holding a garland.*

OPPOSITE FRONT ROW, LEFT TO RIGHT: *My sister Nimmy; Manjit, a member of our extended family; me; Biraji's son Kulbir; and my brother, Kamal Bhaji.* BACK: *My cousin Gurmit Meeto Bhenji.*

A 1956 family photo. BACK ROW, LEFT TO RIGHT: *Mamiji, the wife of my maternal uncle; my mother's sister Masiji Gurmit; Jasso, the older sister of my maternal grandmother, Naniji; and Naniji.* MIDDLE ROW, LEFT TO RIGHT: *My maternal uncle, Inderjit Mamaji; Masarji Harnaunihal, Masiji Gurmit's husband; my father; and Nanaji, my maternal grandfather.* FRONT ROW, LEFT TO RIGHT: *The siblings: me, my sisters Tirath and Nimmy, and my brother, Kamal Bhaji.*

OPPOSITE: *My aunt Taeeji, who helped raise my siblings and me, stands on the far right in this photo taken in the mid-1950s. My youngest sister, Nimmy, is the small girl on the left. Behind her, LEFT TO RIGHT, are my cousin Siso Bhenji; Bhajan Kaur, Derby Chacha Chain Singh's wife; and Biraji's wife Kuldip, holding their son Kulbir.*

Kamal Bhaji, Nimmy, my father, our cousin Biraji, Biraji's son Kulbir, and my uncle Tayaji posing just before Biraji left for England in 1956.

ABOVE: *Raminder Sandhu (Rami) and her family in 1967. FROM LEFT: Rami's sister Raj; her mother, Biji; her father, Papa; her brother Harwant; her cousin Iqbal; her brother Jasbir; and Rami holding her baby sister, Mani.*

ABOVE: *My passport photo, November 1964. I left for England one month later.*

OPPOSITE: *This photo of me was taken in the spring of 1965 while I was living in Derby. Photo: W.W. Winter Ltd.*

My friends William Jefferies (FAR LEFT) and Jeet Ram with me in front of London's most famous address, No. 10 Downing Street, in 1967.

OPPOSITE: *Rami and
me at home after our
wedding ceremony
in 1972.*

ABOVE: *Rami on the ferry to
Victoria in fall 1972. We had
decided to take our fathers on
a trip to Vancouver Island.*

*Rami and me in front of our
home on September 13, 1977,
the day I was called to the bar.*

113

TOP LEFT: *This photo was taken in Dosanjh Kalan when Rami and I travelled to India in 1977.* LEFT TO RIGHT: *My father in his work clothes, my cousin Banso Bhenji and Rami.*

TOP CENTRE: *Our sons at a home in Punjab during their first-ever trip to India in December 1983.* LEFT TO RIGHT: *Pavel, Umber and Aseem.*

TOP RIGHT: *My maternal grandparents, Nanaji and Naniji, on the day I was called to the bar.*

OPPOSITE: *My father with Kamal Bhaji's children and our three sons in Vancouver in 1979.*

PART 3

ARRIVING

IN

CANADA

15 LEAVING ONE COUNTRY for another is never done lightly. I had left India in search of the almighty pound in 1964. Now I was leaving England, the country I had called home for more than three years, in pursuit of the almighty dollar.

I landed in Toronto on May 12, 1968. Going through Customs and Immigration took only a few minutes, and my form was stamped "Landed Immigrant." I collected my baggage and checked in for my flight to Vancouver. The Toronto-to-Vancouver leg of the trip seemed never-ending, bringing home to me the vastness of this new country. As the plane descended for the landing in Vancouver, the waves of the Pacific Ocean sparkled under a bright sun. The land was lush green. Vancouver and Richmond together were a small metropolis at the time, with only a few high-rises. What is now the south terminal was the airport in its entirety. Having come from London, it felt as if I were arriving in a beautiful village.

I took a cab to Masiji Heeti's home in South Vancouver. A fresh, cool breeze bathed my face. The beauty and natural splendour of Vancouver seemed not of this world. The wide boulevards were vast compared to the narrow roads of the English Midlands. I pledged to no longer be a nomad. In that moment, I vowed to live nowhere in the world besides one of two places: the city of Vancouver or my ancestral village of Dosanjh Kalan. I have kept that promise.

The warmth inside Masiji's home, with its southern exposure, matched the fresh invitation outside. Four generations of Dhillons lived under one roof. Masiji's husband, Manjit Dhillon, was a lumber grader, one of three brothers who had come to Canada in the late forties. Their father, Gurdev, was also a lumber mill worker, and he was a progressive Indian patriot who dabbled in poetry. Their grandfather, Babaji Naranjan Singh, had been in Canada for a long time. He had been an active member and at one point secretary of the Ghadar Party, to which Nanaji's uncle Bir Singh had also belonged. This was a CCF/NDP household, with most male members of the extended family working in unionized lumber mills. The household also included Masarji's mother and my adolescent cousins Aman, Sital and Karan.

The Dhillons had stacks of political literature, dating back to the 1930s. This was not the history one found in the textbooks in Canadian schools. It was a much more painful history, covering the treatment of aboriginal Canadians, the persecution of Japanese Canadians during the Second World War, the Chinese head tax, the *Komagata Maru* episode, and the 1907 B.C. law that disenfranchised Indian immigrants. There was lots of literature about how the CCF/NDP had fought for equal rights for minorities, but no reference to how organized labour had sought restrictions on the entry of Chinese and Indian workers into Canada. By the time I came to Canada the unions had been for some time playing a more progressive role. The IWA, the International Woodworkers of America, represented many East Indians, as we called ourselves then. I knew that Darshan Canadian, the friend of Nanaji's I had met in India, was one of the founding members of the IWA.

When I was unsuccessful at finding work in Vancouver as an audio-visual technician, Masarji got me a temporary job in the mill where he worked, as the night clean-up man during its two-week summer shut-down. Every hour on the hour for the duration of my eight-hour shift, I made the rounds of the mill, punching the security clocks to ensure no one stole anything during the shut-down or set fire to the mill or the lumber around it. In between patrols, I cleaned the areas around the conveyor belts, separating wood from sawdust with a shovel.

My senses were overwhelmed by the smells of lumber and saw-dust, the Fraser River and the Pacific Ocean. I walked to and from the mill, carrying my lunch billie. By morning, the fatigue in my muscles and joints was great, and my life ran through my brain like a movie. With every step I took toward Masiji's home, I would ask myself if I had blundered by moving first to Britain and now to Canada.

I continued to search for other work. I applied for a lab technician's job, the category that had enabled me to come to Canada, at the British Columbia Institute of Technology in Burnaby. I didn't feel I was sufficiently qualified for the job, but I was ready to plunge into new learning for work that was even remotely challenging. The interviewer told me I was "overqualified" instead.

I spotted an opportunity in the Help Wanted columns in the *Vancouver Sun:* Encyclopaedia Britannica needed door-to-door salespeople. They paid no salary, only commission, but I rode the bus downtown for the training on the appointed day. The trainers took turns showing us how to ensnare unsuspecting customers. We were supposed to show beautiful colour pictures to the parents of preschool and school-aged children to impress them with the ease with which school projects could be done using the encyclopaedia. If the young children were at the presentation, all the better. I spent an entire day experiencing a visual and verbal bombardment, only to decide the company's sales pitch wasn't for me.

When Masarji told me that an opening was about to come up at Burke Lumber for an industrial first-aid attendant, I took the course offered by St. John Ambulance near the old Woodward's store in Oakridge. For several weeks, I walked twenty blocks to the St. John Ambulance building in the morning and twenty blocks back after a few hours of instruction. Walking that distance every day kept me in shape, despite overindulging in Masiji's great cooking. Chachaji had written to me, repeating Biraji's refrain about educating myself so I wouldn't end up as a potboy in someone else's tavern. His words echoed loud in my mind during those walks.

The overwhelming majority of South Asians living in the Lower Mainland were Indians. People called us all Hindus regardless of religion, since "Hindustan" was one of the names by which India was known. The gurdwara on West 2nd Avenue, managed by the Khalsa Diwan Society since 1908, was still the heart of the community. It had been built by Indians of all faiths — Hindus, Sikhs, Muslims and Christians — and in it the community worshipped together. It was a gurdwara in the truest sense of the term.

The gurdwara, as an institution, had been at the centre of the activities of the Ghadar Party in North America during the first three decades of the twentieth century. The Ghadar movement radicalized the gurdwara's membership, and the Canadian government became worried about the anti-British activities of the Indian patriots. The government hoped its spies and informants in the community would be able to gain support for the proposal it was floating — to resettle Indians living in Canada to British Honduras.

When the committee it had appointed recommended rejection of the proposal, one particular government informant, William Charles Hopkinson, stood exposed. Hopkinson had been born and raised in India. A former police officer in Calcutta, he had travelled to Canada to spy on anti-British activities on behalf of the British Indian Government. In 1914, Hopkinson was shot and killed by Vancouver resident Mewa Singh as he entered court to testify on behalf of Bela Singh, a man who had killed and injured several people at the gurdwara. Mewa Singh accepted responsibility for Hopkinson's death. He was hanged in New Westminster, B.C., and is still revered among Indians for being associated with the Indian freedom fighters. Bela Singh, detested in the community as an informant, was later killed upon his return to India.

The gurdwara on 2nd Avenue had also played a significant role in helping the *Komagata Maru* passengers when they were stranded offshore during their unsuccessful attempt to land in Canada in 1914, challenging the direct passage laws aimed at excluding immigrants from India. When Jawaharlal Nehru, India's first prime minister, visited North America in 1949, he made a point of coming to the 2nd Avenue Temple in Vancouver. In his remarks to the Khalsa Diwan Society, Nehru praised the struggles of Indians on Canada's West Coast both for equality there and for the freedom of India. Vancouver was the place in Canada where most of his *humwatan*, compatriots, lived. He recognized the loyalty Indian immigrants continued to feel for India, but he urged Canadians with roots in India to be "loyal" to Canada too and become fully "integrated" into its life. Nehru saw absolutely no conflict in this dual loyalty, he said.

Nehru's message resonates even today, in view of the ethnic enclaves still found all over Canada. It is ironic that fifty-five years after Nehru's assertion of the separation of church and state, some men and women born and raised in Canada, a secular country, are agitating to dismember India with their dream of establishing Khalistan, an independent theistic country, in place of the current state of Punjab.

During my first week in Canada, Masarji introduced me to some prominent men in the Indian community, such as Mohinder Gill and Dr. Gurdev Gill. In 1968, the community was in the grip of a crisis. The *Granthi*, or ceremonial reader, at the gurdwara was the bone of contention. With a few exceptions, opinions divided along regional lines. Not regional in the Canadian sense; it was much remoter than that. The conflict arose between those hailing from Doaba, the region between the Sutlej and Beas Rivers in India, and those from Malwa, the region south of Sutlej. North of Beas was Majha, the region that extended to the border with Pakistan, though it was not in the mix yet.

Until then, I had not heard even a mention of regional tensions in Punjab or among Punjabis in Britain. The leadership of the Khalsa Diwan Society had worked with all Indians in the fight for a free, egalitarian India. Now, however, members who had jeopardized their lives for the freedom of all were arguing over petty regional differences. Regional and religious identities can become distortedly pronounced among immigrants. Perhaps it is the combination of feeling distant from your roots and alienated from your new country that creates a space in people for these sub-identities to emerge so strongly.

In the chaos of the speeches and endless heckling in the gurdwara, one man stood up and spoke about the need for rational, democratic debate. He was Hazara Singh Garcha, the first Indian graduate from UBC; he had earned a master's in agriculture but remained a lumber grader in a sawmill all his life because the governments and private employers of the 1930s refused to employ him. Inspired, I asked for time to say my own piece. I reiterated Hazara's point and denounced regional prejudices. My words struck home, angering a few while pleasing many others.

At the temple, I also met Gurcharan Rampuri. A renowned poet, my senior in years and wisdom, he had been well known in Punjab before migrating to Canada. Gurcharan would be severely assaulted in the mid-1980s on his way to work in downtown Vancouver by extremist Khalistani followers after writing an article critical of their leader, Sant Jarnail Singh Bhindranwale. Gurcharan himself was a gentle man, and never one to miss a chance to crack a joke. Many years later, when I was bedridden with a bad back after bending down to leash one of my dogs, he asked, referring to the legions of political enemies I'd amassed, "Why have you not learned from your life experiences not to want to leash all dogs?" We were in stitches.

After I had completed the first-aid course, Masarji got me a job at Burke Lumber sorting lumber, pulling it off the "green chain" as it rumbled by. It was tough work. From seven in the morning till the end of our shift at 3:30 PM, my co-workers and I perspired rivers. I eagerly looked forward to the fifteen-minute breaks before and after lunch. I also relished the few minutes I got away from the chain to ensure that the first-aid room was clean and stocked with the necessary supplies. I was paid ten cents an hour more than the other workers for serving as the first-aid attendant on top of my other duties.

One day, early in my time at the mill, I was asked to untangle the junk wood on the conveyor that fed the chipper. It was impossible to stand up straight and do the work, so I struggled the whole day bent over at a seventy-five-degree angle. That day, my coffee and lunch breaks felt like breaks from hell. That evening as I got up from the sofa to eat dinner, my back refused to straighten. Now I knew the meaning of back-breaking work.

I did not want to admit defeat, so I returned to the conveyor belt the next morning like a lamb to slaughter, in pain but defiant. Thankfully, that was the last day I was assigned to work near the chipper. My brother, Kamal Bhaji, had arrived in Vancouver by then, and he was also working on the chain at the mill. He passed the test at Lumber Mill University more elegantly than I did.

16 I HAD BEEN A NEWS JUNKIE since 1962, the year I started college in India and bought the daily *Tribune* for Chachaji. On the night of June 5, 1968, I was watching TV coverage of the Democratic primaries in California when Robert Kennedy was assassinated. Kennedy had just turned from the podium, and in the next moment the commentator announced in total shock that the senator had been shot. I remembered the speech Kennedy had made in Indianapolis on learning of Martin Luther King, Jr.'s death just two months before. King had viewed Gandhi as his guide and teacher in the struggle for equality, and Bobby Kennedy had taken inspiration from King. Now these two giants who had symbolized hope and social justice had been snuffed out in the land of the Statue of Liberty.

BHAJI AND I purchased a small home on East 44th Avenue, half a block west of Main Street, for $22,000, borrowing from our family and the bank. We lived in the two-bedroom basement suite, renting out the upstairs to help pay the mortgage. As members of the Vancouver local of the IWA, we were both making a union wage of over three dollars per hour. My life was finally stabilizing after the chaos and initial regret of moving from one country to another.

Masiji found a bride for Bhaji; that was one way of staying in Canada as a permanent resident. Masiji's friend Amar Sihota had been the matchmaker for the arranged marriage. Amar knew our family from India, and she knew the family of the prospective bride, Manjit, too. The wedding took place on a snowy day in January 1969 at the 2nd Avenue Temple. Since then, Bhabiji has been the communal nurturer of the Dosanjhes.

As Bhaji's immigration application proceeded, I went to Dr. D.P. Pandya's office in an attempt to speed up the application. D.P. had been instrumental in arguing that wives and children be allowed to join Indian men in Canada during the thirties and forties. He was always very kind to me, and it is one of my lasting regrets that his tremendous historic contribution to the community was later overshadowed by his unfortunate tax evasion.

Chachaji and my sisters Tirath and Nimmy came as permanent residents to Canada in November 1969. Though I was only twenty-three, I had applied for them as my dependents, and in those days dependents were quickly processed. It was the beginning of the Trudeau era's policy of family reunification. But as I sat before the white immigration officer submitting our application, I thought about the passengers on the *Komagata Maru* and all the men who had paid the Chinese head tax, suffering in loneliness for years before their families were allowed to come to Canada. The right to vote in Canada for my kind was a recent thing, as was the ability to practise professions such as medicine and law. I was standing on the shoulders of the many who had come before me.

Our family was beginning to feel like an extended Indian family again, only this time on Canadian soil. My maternal uncle Mamaji was here also — he had quit truck driving and moved to Canada some years before I arrived. He worked at Burke Lumber too. There he was a kind of jack of all trades. Being a quick study, he had picked up the work rather quickly and did everything from driving the load carrier and the fork lift to working the barker and the booms. His wife, Mamiji, and my cousins Gogan and Palay had recently joined Mamaji in Vancouver at his cozy Lanark Street home. Mamiji gave birth to my youngest first cousin, Ranbir, in 1969, shortly after Bhaji's wedding.

Mamaji was a loving brother, uncle, father and husband. But once again, addiction got the better of him. None of us knew how to deal with it when Mamaji's addictions, this time to alcohol and non-prescription drugs, began taking over his life. Arguing with him about it drove him deeper into the depths of whatever was eating at him.

We needed to get help, but we did not know it then. Sadly, our ignorance hastened his estrangement from his nuclear family; even the patient Mamiji couldn't help him. There was not a mean bone in Mamaji's body. He would drink and quietly wrestle with his demons. Then, one day, suddenly, he was no longer in this world.

During my time at Burke Lumber, the IWA local attempted to organize some non-union plants. Many workers in those plants were Punjabi speakers with little or no knowledge of English. A union rep and I visited many of these men at their homes. Subsequently, the union delegated me to vote in a by-election for the Vancouver South provincial NDP nomination. Norm Levi and John Laxton contested the nomination. Although I would develop a lot of respect and admiration for Levi, that day I voted for Laxton, because I found him a superior orator. Levi won the nomination, however, as well as the subsequent election. Dave Barrett led the NDP to its first-ever victory in B.C. in that election, and Norm Levi served in cabinet for the duration of the Barrett government. In both the 1969 and the 1972 elections, I volunteered as a canvasser for the NDP.

I had been exposed to left-wing politics in India during my formative years, of course. My grandfather Nanaji was an active member of the Communist Party of India, and his political involvement had run the gamut — from challenging conservative controllers of the historic Sikh temples, to singing freedom songs on religious and political stages, to helping the struggles of the peasants and workers, to fighting the Raj and spending years in British jails. Chachaji was an educator and reformer who had joined the Akali Dal for its anti-colonialism. Over time, it became more important for my father to be both anti-colonialist and secular, and he joined the movement of Mahatma Gandhi, whose follower he remained to the last. The NDP, with its social democratic outlook, was a natural home for me in the political landscape of British Columbia.

During the Vancouver South campaigns of 1968 and 1969, I got to know Kehar Sekhon. He had immigrated to Canada from Punjab long before and he was completing his teaching degree while working in a lumber mill. Growing up in India, Kehar had known Chachaji, as had his older relative Ram Singh Dhillon, a one-time priest at the 2nd Avenue Temple. Through Kehar, I met Hardial Bains, the Punjab-born founder and leader of the CPC-ML— the Communist Party of Canada (Marxist-Leninist). Hardial was a tall, articulate man given to bombast. He supported the uprising of violent Maoists at Naxalbari in India and argued for a violent revolution in Canada as well. It was clear to me that Hardial's prescription for Canada was outrageously stupid. As for India, though, I had yet to be convinced that it could democratically bring about the drastic reforms it needed. In a nutshell, I had not yet been persuaded that democracy was inherently important in bringing about lasting change. Nor had I absorbed completely the Gandhian view that the means invariably dictate and often skew the end. For the next few months, I hung around Hardial's Indian associates in Vancouver.

The 1968 federal election had been in full swing when I landed in Canada. Trudeaumania had already reached across the Atlantic, so I already knew something of the Liberal contender for prime minister when I arrived. Masarji took me to a rally for NDP leader Tommy Douglas, who was a spellbinding orator. But the images of Trudeau at Montreal's Saint-Jean-Baptiste Day parade the night before the election, standing firm in the face of the rocks and bottles thrown at him by supporters of Quebec's independence, sealed the election for the Liberals. Since then, balanced by how decisively he dealt with the FLQ Crisis and the Quebec referendum of 1980, Trudeau has remained my favourite Canadian.

The Hardial Bains narrative was simple: the government of India did not represent the people of India. Bains argued for overthrowing the government of the day by force, to replace it with a government of the proletariat. He was to lead the revolution initially from Canada. Mahatma Gandhi was the villain of the piece. For a while, I bought his nonsense.

In the spring of 1970, at a gathering in Vancouver, Gurpuran Gill and Pralad Gill, two of Hardial's classmates from India, questioned him about the embezzlement of funds from their school's students' association. Bains incited his followers to physically attack the Gills, which, like robots, they readily did. I too became embroiled in the incident and was dumb enough to manhandle Gurpuran. My actions were reprehensible, and I realized the enormity of my blunder immediately afterwards. I had come face to face with an extremist movement that blinded its adherents to their common humanity. Fortunately for me, later the same day the Gills happened to visit Masiji, and I was able to apologize for my stupidity. The incident prompted my political and ideological departure from the Bains outfit.

By then, I had started attending night school at Vancouver Community College. Not long before, I'd written an English proficiency test at the University of British Columbia with the intention of seeking admission there. On my test, I'd chosen to respond in the affirmative to a question on whether or not we should ban nuclear weapons and work toward a nuclear-free world. Once the test results were in, the successful prospective students were invited to an interview at UBC. When I walked into the room, I encountered a huge man in a suit and tie sporting a crew cut. He looked as if he had just changed out of military uniform. He told me I had passed the test with flying colours. But clearly, my stance on nuclear weapons didn't sit well with him. At least I assumed that's what led him to say it was people like me who went on to become guerrillas in the third world. I was offended, which led me to enrol at VCC instead.

I enrolled in a journalism course initially, but after attending a couple of classes, I decided I would need better English and a better understanding of Canadian society before I could succeed as a journalist. The teacher felt otherwise, reading one of my assignments out loud to the class as an example of a story with an attention-grabbing beginning. But I followed my inner voice. I tried my hand at English 101, a prerequisite for doing a BA in humanities, then withdrew from it, enrolling next in a sociology course. My sociology teacher was Kogila Adam-Moodley, the first South African Indian I had ever met. She was a great teacher, and the Indian clothing she wore reminded me of my heritage. By that time, I had started using the name "Dave" in non-Indian circles, anglicizing my middle name, Dev. In Kogila's class, though, five of the twenty or so students were named Dave. In the entire country of Canada at that time, there was probably no other Ujjal: Ujjal meaning bright light, Ujjal meaning clean, Ujjal connoting purity. I knew my name was difficult to pronounce. Were the Canadian names from all over the world I was learning any easier to pronounce, though? Shouldn't I expect in return that people do me the same simple courtesy? I had a beautiful Indian sub-continental name, and while I was in Kogila's class, I decided to claim it again.

After coming home from work, I would quickly shower, snack, finish my homework and take a bus to the college for my evening classes, returning just before 11:00 PM. My sisters and sometimes Bhabiji were still up. I was fed and pampered like a little child.

IN EARLY 1970, I injured my back while handling big pieces of yellow cedar at the mill. I was reluctant at first to report my injury to the Workers' Compensation Board. Some months earlier, a heavy piece of lumber had fallen on my right foot, causing a hairline fracture. Despite the pain and my inability to walk without a painful limp, the WCB kept harassing me to go back to work. So this time around, despite my stiff back, I reported to work the next day. The pain went from bad to worse, however, and that turned out to be my last day at Burke Lumber.

An orthopaedic surgeon monitored me for several months while I went for physiotherapy treatment at the WCB headquarters. Nothing helped, however. My slipped disc caused shooting pain from my left hip all the way down to my foot. The surgeon decided I needed to have surgery, and I was put on a waiting list.

That summer, the High Commissioner of India visited Vancouver. Outside the Cecil Arms in Marpole, I attended a peaceful demonstration for the release of political prisoners languishing in Indian jails without being charged or given trials. Some of the Indians going into the reception for the High Commissioner stopped to talk to us.

One of them told me angrily that I would no longer be welcome at the Ross Street Temple.

The Ross Street Temple was brand-new. I had been present at the sod-turning ceremony the previous April, since Bhaji, like others in the community, had donated money toward its construction on behalf of our family. Designed by the late Arthur Erickson as a successor to the 2nd Avenue Temple, the Ross Street Temple was one of the architectural wonders of its time, and it was on the itineraries of many foreign and Canadian tourists.

The following month, I went to the Ross Street Temple to hear the renowned Punjabi poet and former chief minister of Punjab, Gurmukh Singh Musafir, at the Indian Independence Day celebration. Natural light travelled through the temple's domed skylights and fell on the lush red carpet. Men and women in sparkling clean clothes sat on the floor, divided by gender by the aisle that worshippers walked up to pay obeisance to the Guru Granth. I paid my respects to the scriptures and then took my seat with Chachaji, Bhaji and Masarji. There is an age-old tradition of people sharing their views from temple stages, and a member of the temple executive asked if I would like to speak. When I nodded, he came back and told me I could speak before Musafir gave his address. The man returned a few minutes later and asked me to instead speak after Musafir. I agreed, but I could tell there was something not quite right behind the scenes. The man returned again to tell me I'd be speaking before Musafir spoke after all. At the very moment I was deciding to decline his invitation altogether, the man asked me to accompany him to an area behind the wall next to the Guru Granth. Chachaji and a few others came with me.

There were four or five men waiting to see me. I recognized them all. "Why are you here?" demanded one, one of two brothers there whose family nickname I knew to be Mohlay. "We warned you not to come to the temple." Karnail Johal and Jagir Johal, the president of the society, pounced on me, tearing my shirt collar and breaking my glasses. The muscles I'd built up in the mill came in handy. I held both of them off for the fraction of a second it took Chachaji and others to intervene.

Everyone present knew there had been an altercation behind the wall. But the orchestrators, a man named Sabu Singh chief among them, felt they had not succeeded in putting God's fear into me. They decided to regroup outside the temple to attack me again. Masarji and Chachaji advised everyone they knew to be a friend against leaving, and Masarji received updates about the brewing threat outside. The Mohlays, we learned, were organizing a posse of their relatives and friends outside the temple. Many had weapons in their cars or hidden in their jackets.

I steeled myself, and I let the temple executive know that after all that had transpired, I was not leaving without speaking. I have never brooked interference in exercising my right to speak. Nor would I hinder anyone else, no matter how disagreeable their message.

Musafir spoke without incident, and then the executive reluctantly allowed me to speak. My shirt collar was torn for all to see, and my broken glasses barely rested on my face. I spoke about freedom from slavery and the freedom to be and express yourself. The legacy of the Khalsa Diwan Society was one of dedication to both freedom and fearlessness, I reminded those present.

Afterwards, our friends and relatives placed themselves on both sides of the route that Masarji had charted for me to his car, forming a protective cordon. The posse froze in their places, eventually melting away. In my heart I had already forgiven them. I was going home free from anger and hate.

17 A FEW WEEKS AFTER the Ross Street episode, I went under the surgeon's knife at St. Vincent's Hospital. Two of my lower discs were fused, using bone from my hip, and secured in place with screws.

The day after the surgery, Chachaji and I were deep in father-son conversation when a Vancouver police officer entered the room and asked if I was Ujjal Dosanjh. I was shocked to receive a summons for allegedly committing common assault against the Mohlay brothers at the Ross Street Temple the day of the Musafir visit. The Mohlays had done what even today happens hundreds of times every day in India: they had falsely accused me of something I hadn't done.

The Vancouver police were being used as tools, some in the community said, to ensure I got a criminal record. Kehar Sekhon suggested I contact Thomas Berger to see if he would take my case. I remembered Berger from his short stint as the B.C. NDP leader; he'd resigned after the NDP lost the snap election former premier W.A.C. Bennett called in 1969. While he was campaigning, Berger had spoken at the 2nd Avenue Temple, and I had served as his interpreter. Berger agreed to represent me, and his articling student Harry Boyle attended court with me at 312 Main Street to fix a trial date. Boyle came to law late in life, but justice was richer for it: he became a provincial court judge and a Master of the Supreme Court of British Columbia. I was to have many occasions later on to appear before him as a lawyer myself.

Once my trial got underway, it was clear that the Mohlays' testimony was full of contradictions. Dr. Gurdev Gill, who was subpoenaed by Berger, testified to the truth of what had happened; that I was in fact the victim of an assault. Dr. Gill told the court about the tradition of the temple, which was to allow anyone who wished to do so to speak respectfully from the stage. My testimony was simple and direct: I maintained my right to be at the temple and to speak there. The judge acquitted me of the assault charge and admonished the Mohlays for bringing false and frivolous matters to court. Justice and freedom of expression had triumphed, at least for the time being.

I WOULD NEVER be able to do hard physical labour again because of my back. But after my surgery I did heavy lifting of a different kind, carrying a burden of uncertainty and anxiety until events intervened to take me in an unanticipated direction. My life, perhaps more than most, has been moulded by chance.

In October of 1970, the October Crisis erupted with the Montreal kidnappings of British diplomat James Cross and Quebec government minister Pierre Laporte by members of the FLQ, the *Front de Libération du Québec*. Quebec premier Robert Bourassa called for the deployment of the Canadian Army "in aid of the civil power." The federal government obliged with the country's only peacetime invocation of the War Measures Act, suspending civil liberties. Prime Minister Pierre Trudeau called in the army to patrol the streets of Ottawa and parts of Quebec. Shocked at the sight of boots on the ground, a reporter asked Trudeau how far he would go. Trudeau made his now historic response: "Just watch me."

I watched events unfolding on TV and remained glued to the radio. I had been hanging around "communists" myself and had a great deal of leftist literature at home, including some of Lenin's writings and Mao's infamous *Little Red Book*. McCarthyism's terrible shadow still hung over North America. W.A.C. Bennett had successfully used the "Red Menace" tactic in the 1969 election in B.C. to defeat the NDP, and now, once again, governmental dread of the so-called radicals was rearing its head. Several hundred people across Canada, mainly in Quebec, were arrested, and more people involved in "insurrectional" or "seditious" activities were being rounded up. I packed up my "revolutionary" literature and hid it at Masiji's place.

My image of a modern and peaceful Canada stood shattered. The extreme fragility and vulnerability of our freedoms, even in a country like this one, became obvious. I'd learned that I could not take for granted my right to freedom of expression in the Ross Street Temple. I'd seen that religious despots and political terrorists could rob anyone of their lives or their liberty. And it was clear in the aftermath of the War Measures Act that police did not always act in an exemplary manner. In the grip of terror, the protectors of freedom can unwittingly become freedom's enemies.

The October Crisis helped me complete my journey to rejecting violence as means of political and social change and to embracing non-violence. I saw the "annihilation of class enemies in India" advocated by Bains and the Naxalites for the absurdity it was. Acting in service of a just cause, such as ending poverty, injustice or corruption, is forever tainted once violence is employed.

The question of violence versus non-violence is a recurring theme in Indian history. Buddha's tremendous influence turned the victorious warrior king Ashoka into a permanent devotee and advocate of non-violence. Guru Nanak spread his message of peace, while Guru Gobind was prepared to shed blood to achieve justice. Gandhi was committed to non-violence, whereas Subhas Bose raised an army and accepted help from the fascists in his desire to free India. Some Indian revolutionaries praise Bhagat Singh and speak derisively of the Mahatma. I stand with Buddha, Nanak and Gandhi in the means I have chosen to effect change. The means unalterably define the ends, even if we are not always able to see that in our own time on earth.

By the end of the October Crisis, my differences with the Bains outfit were permanent and irreconcilable. I saw the group as a cult. I was branded a traitor, but I was happy to be a traitor to an agenda of violence.

BEFORE I WENT UNDER the surgeon's scalpel, I had **18** completed half a year's worth of credits at night school toward a BA. The time had come to make the decision — to find a job or to commit to the classroom. Bhaji was working full time. Nimmy and Tirath had completed their English classes at Vancouver Community College and were ready to enter the job market. My family had saved enough money to purchase another house in South Vancouver. We moved there and rented out our first home. That helped to pay our mortgages, and I felt freer to embark on my schooling uninterrupted.

My wage-loss benefits had ended, but the Workers' Compensation Board eventually agreed to pay my fees and cover the cost of course materials for two full-time semesters at the Vancouver Community College.

In addition, the WCB had finally assessed the "permanent partial disability" caused by my injury and offered me a disability pension of nineteen dollars a month. I was furious at such brutal minimizing of my permanent disability. I had been making a top union wage while I was injured, and I would never be able to do that kind of work again. I began to hear similar stories from other badly treated workers. The WCB, an institution supposedly set up to assist injured workers, was simply a cover to protect employers from litigation. I wrote a sarcastic letter to Premier Bennett, asking him to take my pension away and use the money to buy candies for his grandchildren. An angry missive was better than a rock thrown through the windows of the WCB offices. With the cost of living increases, my disability pension has risen since 1971 to the grand sum of just over $100 a month. The WCB tried to buy me out in the 1980s for a lump sum payment of just under $6,000, but I rudely told them where to go.

135

Years later, when I became B.C.'s Attorney General, I was interviewed by someone on behalf of injured workers. I remarked that the WCB as an institution needed to be "blown up" and replaced by something more fairly disposed toward injured workers. If that was not possible, I said, the insurance requirements for employers should be changed so that workers had a right to sue over their injuries. I still believe this. If we can provide public auto insurance where the right to sue in tort is preserved, we should be able to ensure that workers in this province do not continue to get a rotten deal.

I was on the third continent of my short life, trying to complete my schooling, and I immersed myself in my studies. I had decided to major in political science. VCC Langara was a relatively small campus, and I had some wonderful teachers. Barry Brill taught history with the enthusiasm of a sports announcer. Peter Broomhall, a towering presence in the classroom, made English fun. Russ Johnston taught political science as actual politics, and for Phyllis Atwell and a teacher named Mr. Robertson, sociology was a way of changing the world. Sam Pagee, an Indian from the West Indies, taught philosophy with his eyes closed, like Buddha's, as he steered us through Hermann Hesse's *Siddhartha*. John McBryde, an Aussie, enjoyed teaching math as much as the field hockey he played.

The October Crisis had electrified Canadian campuses. Hallways, classrooms and cafeterias were arenas for a multitude of political discussions. The FLQ Crisis was just the latest in a series of events that were unalterably changing the political landscape. Martin Luther King's 1963 "I Have A Dream" speech had made the world believe in his dream of equality. JFK's assassination had seemed to dim that hope. King's own assassination followed, and then Robert Kennedy's. The Paris strikes by students and workers in May of 1968 had unleashed hopes of liberation worldwide but also dread of anarchy among the political classes. The May 1970 killing, by National Guard troops, of four Kent State University students demonstrating against the Cambodian campaign shocked and shook America. In the midst of all of this, and in spite of the FLQ Crisis, Canada felt like an oasis of hope and peace.

Under Pierre Trudeau, Canada was becoming a more just and open society. But the events in Quebec were a rude reminder that even liberal democratic societies were vulnerable to terrorism and that our response, while needing to be firm and fearless, could easily become overzealous.

Like most of my classmates, I challenged everything. Many social and cultural norms came under attack. The movement for gender equality, the pursuit of racial equality and the fight for gays and lesbians to live as who they were captured the essence of the era. Being on campus allowed me to observe and participate in these debates, and my political, social and linguistic development got a huge boost that year.

The discussions also drove home for me that disagreement is as natural as agreement, and that it is criminal to remain silent on matters of fundamental public interest. In the free flow and fierce exchange of ideas at Langara, I learned the importance of everyone's right to speak, and that reaffirmed for me the need to hear opposing views with respect. I was still young and brash, but I knew right from wrong, at least most of the time. The chasm between the state of the world and what it could be drove me to search for alternatives. The Left held great appeal, but Marxist ideology appeared rigid, uncompromising and foreign to mainstream Canadian political culture. I was learning that real and permanent change is slow and comes only through hard work.

Langara gave me some lifelong friendships, too. Doug Wellbanks, an "immigrant" to B.C. from Ontario, was a fellow sociology student. He became quite an expert on Max Weber, in contrast to my interest in Marx, and we had some interesting discussions. Doug went on to find rewarding work with St. James Community Services before joining the B.C. public service. Phillip Rankin, later to become a senior lawyer in Vancouver, was in some of my classes, always arguing for progressive change. I later learned Phil was the son of Harry Rankin, an immensely powerful presence for many years on the Vancouver political scene.

My old friend Harjinder Atwal from Ramgarhia College, Phagwara, was now in B.C., working in a bank while finishing his CGA.

In 1971 Harjinder and I drove all the way to Yuba City, California, in my Austin 1100. Yuba is a small town that has figured prominently in the early history of Indians, many of them Punjabis, settling on the West Coast, and we were curious to see this part of our people's history for ourselves. The wealth of the U.S. was evident everywhere on our journey, yet poverty was there to see if you looked. In Yuba City, a town of farms and farmers, the many new immigrant families from the Punjab who worked the fields were only marginally better off than their Mexican counterparts. Harjinder and I spent a night with a Punjabi family, and before the evening meal we took a shower in a tin enclosure that looked like one of the shanty dwellings near the Mumbai airport that you can spot in the thousands from a descending plane. The cold shower water flowed into, not a sewer, but a small man-made pond outside. The family's sleeping quarters, too, cried endemic poverty, though they had been in the U.S. for over fifteen years.

I WAS PLEASANTLY surprised to see my name on the honour roll after my first semester. I headed straight to the notice board at the college for information pertaining to scholarships and bursaries, since I was now eligible to apply.

As I turned away from the notice board, ready to drive home to share the honour-roll news with my family, I saw a strikingly beautiful woman in a sari sitting on a chair opposite me. She looked exquisitely Indian and about my age. She had an air of self-confidence, refinement and sophistication about her; she seemed sure of herself and her place in the world. She sat thumbing through a thick anthology called *Theories of Society*. I had taken a course in which parts of the book were required reading, and I had found it heavy going, keeping a dictionary in hand as I read. The woman was turning the pages rather quickly, so I assumed she was sizing the book up for consumption.

I turned back toward the notice board. I wanted to talk to her. There were so few Indians in Vancouver at the time that it was considered rude not to at least say hello to a compatriot. That she was a beautiful woman made me hesitant, lest I be misunderstood. In a remote village in India I could have been killed for speaking to her directly. We were in college in Canada now, I reassured myself. Still, I stood pondering the cultural minefield for what felt like a painful eternity.

Finally, I screwed up my courage. The customary hello from me was greeted with a barely perceptible smile. I shared my assumption that she was Indian, to which she nodded. I asked her name. Raminder, she said. Realizing she was a Punjabi, I did what most Punjabis in Vancouver did at the time: I asked, "What village are you from?" "That is none of your business," came her reply. It fell on my ears like a public slap for a simpleton.

Trying to recover from the humiliation of her unexpected belligerence, I steered the conversation toward the book in her hand. But I do not remember much more of that first encounter. It was almost like a hit and run: she had lashed out, and I ran.

Over time, I would learn that she was Raminder Sandhu, a daughter of Balram Singh Sandhu, a major in the Indian Army, and Charanjit Kaur Shergill, from Majitha. Majitha was the home of many *sardars*, Sikh chieftains, during the time of the founder of the Sikh empire, Maharaja Ranjit Singh. Rami was the great-great-granddaughter of the Maharaja's general, Mehtab Singh. Her father and his family had migrated to India from their village of Ghaniainke in what is now Pakistan, after partition. They'd settled in Atari, the village of her father's mother, who belonged to the family of the Maharaja's most legendary general, Sham Singh Atariwala.

Rami was the second of six siblings. Her father was posted all over India as she was growing up, and she travelled with him, living and studying all over the country. She had a BA from St. John's College, Agra, the city of the famed Taj Mahal, and a Bachelor of Education from Khalsa College, Amritsar. She had taught for a year at Dagshai Public School, a private school in the hills near Simla, and then her father had cashed his life insurance policy to buy his second child a ticket to Canada. She arrived in October 1970.

Rami had been advised by credentialing officials in Victoria to take a few refresher courses at VCC so she would qualify for a teaching licence in B.C. After her rebuff, we continued to bump into each other at the college. Rami worked in the college library a few hours a week, at a medical clinic as a switchboard operator after school, and as a typing/filing clerk in the evenings. After class, she would take the bus to the medical clinic, near Broadway and Granville. Once her work there was finished, she took another bus to go to her uncle Surajjit Sandhu's house on East 13th Avenue near Commercial Drive.

I loved being around Rami, but I had already decided that this beautiful woman deserved someone more sophisticated than I. I was still not sure where I was heading. Any prospects for a meaningful life had so far eluded my grasp.

During the summer semester of 1971, I invited Rami to join a group of us on a day trip to Alice Lake Provincial Park, north of Squamish. I had thought she and Harjinder might be a good match, but later Harjinder told me Rami was too headstrong a woman for his liking.

In August 1971, Rami received landed immigrant status as a clerk typist. Immigration in Canada has always had its weird ways. The country at the time did not need teachers. Rami's kindly immigration officer openly lamented that he was approving scores of immigrants barely able to put together a sentence in English, while here was an applicant, fully conversant in English, whom he might have to reject because her teaching skills were not needed at the time. When the man asked if Rami had any other skills, she started digging through her certificates, and he noticed a certificate for typing, though her typing speed was poor. The man wrote down the address of the Pitman School on Broadway and Granville and asked Rami to come back and see him in a couple of months, once she had acquired a certain typing speed. She did exactly that, and her landed immigrant status was granted.

During the fall semester, Rami took fewer courses at VCC. By now, she had received her teaching licence, and VCC's education department had agreed to her taking upper-level courses at UBC in special education and teaching English as a Second Language. She also started volunteering at the Ross Street Temple and in schools.

By now, Rami was feeling comfortable enough with me to ask for my help on term papers in history and sociology. One paper in particular had to do with the historic Winnipeg Strike. A day in the library hid my relative ignorance, and she completed her assignment. She was carrying a heavy academic load while working at the college library and the medical clinic, so I often drove her to the clinic. I had grown fond of her. She had the strength and determination to make a go of life, as well as an impressive ability to organize things and events. Once she had made up her mind, she was not easily swayed. There was none of the mild-mannered meekness about her that many Indian men of that era preferred in a woman. If I were to marry, I felt, I could not find anyone better suited to the kind of life I wanted to have.

By the late fall of 1971, Rami and I had come to know each other well. When I shared my thoughts with her, she told me she already had someone she loved and would like to marry, a man from her days at St. John's College in Agra. They had fallen madly in love, and then her parents had found out. Rami was a Sikh, the man a Hindu, and Rami's mother wanted the man to convert. He agreed, but her mother's resistance did not dissipate. Rami was taken out of college and finished her studies at home. The man quit college and joined the Indian Army. Rami was hoping in time to reunite with him in Canada or in India. Now I understood why there lurked an unmistakable sadness behind her beautiful, infectious smile.

The fog of pre-examination preparations at VCC in late November deepened when a new India-Pakistan War broke out on December 3, 1971. West Pakistani rulers, opposed to the incoming majority government of an East Pakistani party, tried to sabotage things by arresting the prime minister elect, Mujibur Rahman. The indigenous rebel movement gained strength, and the Pakistani Army, consisting mainly of West Pakistani Punjabis, was accused of killing and raping East Pakistanis. When Pakistan made pre-emptive strikes against eleven Indian air bases, over eight million refugees poured into India. India responded, and the war ended thirteen days later with the surrender of the Eastern Command of the Pakistan Armed Forces. Out of East Pakistan was born the new country of Bangladesh.

I had finished my term-end examinations at Langara, and I was planning to enrol at Simon Fraser University to complete my undergraduate degree. I was still in touch with Rami, though not every day, as when she had been at Langara. I learned that tragedy had knocked on her door. The man she loved had perished in the Indo-Pak War. One of his sisters had written Rami with the tragic news. His Indian family had lost the only male in a household composed of a mother and two sisters, and they were as heartbroken as Rami was. In his last letter, Rami would later tell me, the man had urged Rami to make a life for herself and said he had decided to devote his to the army. Rami had taken that to mean it was best if they did not marry. The man was probably being a good Indian kid, not wanting to marry against her parents' wishes, and Rami had still held out hope that he would change his mind. But for the Indo-Pak War and his untimely death, life may have taken Rami and me in different directions.

IN 1971, Simon Fraser University was still relatively new and small. The student population was about 6,500, as opposed to UBC's 40,000. SFU is situated atop Burnaby Mountain, and my old car had a hard time getting up there. My whole body would tense driving up that steep hill, as if I was pushing the car along. It would have been more convenient to go to UBC to do my BA, but SFU exuded subversion. Two years before, I had followed the upheaval in the Department of Political Science, Sociology and Anthropology (PSA) at SFU. Students and faculty were demanding more say in the awarding of tenure and other issues, and in November of 1969 several hundred students had demonstrated, disrupting classes. Over a hundred of them were arrested and fined. Matters cooled down, but I felt drawn to the energy at SFU.

19

I had an uncomfortable memory of SFU, too, which concerned the installation in 1970 of a bust of Gandhi on campus. Officials from the Indian High Commission and many local dignitaries had been on hand for it. At the time, I lacked any real appreciation of Gandhi's legacy, and like a slumbering idiot I went along with Hardial Bains's cronies. As the bust was unveiled, we erupted in mindless slogans. I have made some moronic decisions in my life, and that is up there with the rest of them.

There were some interesting teachers at SFU. The internationally renowned constitutional law scholar Edward McWhinney regaled us with stories of his discussions with famous political and legal people around the world. Professor A.H. Somjee had researched and written about life in a Gujarati village. Hari Sharma, a perpetual pipe smoker with a beard, dressed like Castro and plotted radical change in India from his office in the Quadrangle. And there was Professor Cassidy, who called my paper comparing Marx, Lenin and Mao's concepts of class "banal."

The hill campus had the feel of being in another world; though not an ivory tower, it certainly was an uphill climb. Most weekends Doug Wellbanks and I went up to the hill to study, getting far away from the social scene. Some weekends Rami and her friends would accompany us. Rami was still taking courses, although she was now substitute teaching more regularly. She still worked evenings at the clinic.

While no one ever fully recovers from a first love lost to mortality, it is human nature to heal and persevere. Rami and I drew closer, and we became fixtures on South Vancouver's civic scene. We went together to public meetings and seminars at temples, churches and community centres. We partied together, too. At one of those parties, I had my first experience of being drunk out of my mind, at the ripe old age of twenty-five. At that party I also heard, to my utter surprise, my Chinese friend Moira from VCC speak fluent Bollywood Hindi for the first time. It turned out she was an Indian Chinese from Calcutta!

As our community became aware of my friendship with Rami, Masiji got quizzed about her rebel of a nephew's relationship with Rami by the busybodies, the concerned and the merely curious alike. The Indian community was still small, and male-female friendships challenged traditional mores.

Rami had moved out of her uncle's home to a basement apartment near VCC Langara early in 1971. It was unheard of at the time in the Indian community for a young, unmarried woman to live on her own. Her landlady was a retired nurse who was always telling Rami how things were done in Canada and looking out for her. Visiting Rami meant being subjected to her landlady's matronly gaze. Undeterred, we continued to see each other. I usually had no money, other than the bare minimum for gas, school supplies and fast food, so for any outing, Rami paid. There was not much that was conventional about our relationship.

Finally, we announced to our families that we were getting married. Rami wrote to her parents about me and my village in Punjab, neglecting to mention that I had not even finished my BA. She projected into the future, claiming I would soon be starting my master's degree — which at the time I fully intended to do. Her father and mother likely wondered what caste the Dosanjhes belonged to, but they decided not to stand in Rami's way.

Her uncle Surajjit knew me quite well, and to hear Rami tell it, he had raved about me being one of the best young men in the community. But he had also warned Rami privately to watch out, because if I followed my "Marxist leanings into the fields and forests of India," he said, she would have to fend for herself. Then, upon hearing our plans to wed, Rami's uncle went ballistic. How could she, a Mujhail belonging to the Majha region of Punjab north of the River Beas, ever think of marrying a lowly Doabia from the region of Doaba south of Majha? Here again was a regional prejudice similar to the one that had erupted at the 2nd Avenue Temple in the fight over a *Granthi* in 1968.

Undeterred, we set a date for our wedding at the Ross Street Temple, with a reception to follow at Rio Hall on Kingsway near Joyce Street. We sent a plane ticket to Rami's parents so that at least one of them could come for the wedding; Chachaji had since returned to India, so we sent him a ticket as well.

My family was not altogether happy with my choice of life partner, either. They did not mind that Rami's roots in India lay on the opposite side of the River Beas. Their problem was more mundane: because she had grown up in urban centres in India, and they were a rural lot, they worried they would find it difficult to get along with her. As a city dweller, she might be snobbish and arrogant.

Unknown to Rami, her uncle sent a telegram to her father, asking him to not travel to Vancouver for the wedding. Rami's father and Chachaji were booked for the same flight out of Delhi, so her father decided to travel at least as far as Delhi to see if meeting Chachaji might shed some light on her uncle's message. They hit it off; they were both decent, honest human beings. Our two fathers ended up travelling together and were received at the airport by all of us, including Rami's uncle.

We had settled sending one invitation card from both families to our invited guests, rather than having a different card for each. There was nothing given or taken between families. A friend made Rami's wedding dress and her evening wear for the reception. I owned just one suit at the time, which I wore sparingly — I bought most of my clothes at Honest Nat's at Fraser Street and 48th. Nat's had clothes at prices that a new immigrant could afford. For the wedding, however, Mamaji wanted to buy me a new suit, as is the tradition for the mother's brother. Fortunately for the penniless groom-to-be, a store called Asher's was having a sale: buy one suit, get a second one for fifty dollars. Mamaji paid for the first, and those two suits carried me through my life for many years, until calories rudely took their toll.

Rami and I sat in front of the Guru Granth for the ceremony, but I did not sit cross-legged on the carpet. In Indian culture, at work or at home, squatting and sitting cross-legged play a central role. My injury at Burke Lumber, however, had forever put a stop to that for me. The wedding ceremony proceeded with my right leg and foot extended toward the scriptures. Despite Guru Nanak's dictum of God being everywhere, and the direction in which one's feet are pointing meaning no disrespect to the holiness of the place or the scriptures, Rami's father asked me to turn my leg inwards. I obliged. Sitting in pain was a small price to pay for a peaceful wedding.

I had not bought a ring for Rami. I would not have done so even if I'd had the money, and it did not matter to Rami at all. But one of Rami's friends was upset when she realized this, and she asked me about it as we sat in the *langar* eating after the wedding ceremony. I explained to her that in Indian culture a ring had no marital meaning, but she quickly removed a ring from Rami's hand and thrust it into mine, suggesting I put it on Rami's finger. I did the needful, as some Indians still say.

In those days in the small Indian community, wedding receptions were rare, and there were no Indian caterers. For our reception, some of the food had been prepared at the temple. Bhabiji, Nimmy, Tirath, Mamiji, Masiji Heeti and other members of my family had made chicken curry and the rest. Rami's landlady and friends had prepared sandwiches. We had decorated the Rio ourselves, with the help of our friends. My Austin 1100 did not pass the family's standards for the wedding, so we borrowed a friend's car, and another friend took photos and shot eight-millimetre film of our wedding and the reception.

I had never been schooled in the ways of receptions. Since it was our reception, I should be there welcoming the guests, I thought. When I noticed people standing around because of a shortage of tables and chairs, I eased myself away from Rami's arm to address it. Despite the limited invitations we had sent out for the reception, people kept arriving. The party had just begun!

As the night wore on, the music and dancing continued, but the food ran out. The nearest Kentucky Fried Chicken outlet came to the rescue; the Rio kitchen hummed again. There were no speeches that night, although Rami remembers me thanking everyone. Rami's friend Hasmig sang an Armenian song as a solo and performed a duet with her brother. At Hasmig's insistence, I sang my favourite song from the Bollywood movie *Aaj Aur Kal*, "*itni huseen itni jwan raat kya karain, jagay hain kuchh ajeeb se jazbaat kya karain*" (It is a beautiful night/ Strange emotions have welled up/What should I do?). Rami was called to the microphone to join me in singing "*Aap ki nazron ne samjha pyar ke kabul mujhey...Jee humain manzoor hai aap ka yeh Faisla...*" (Your eyes have judged me worthy of you...I accept your decision...). The witnesses to our performance still tease us about it.

Honeymoons were foreign to village cultures, and there was no money or time for one anyway. Rami and I went to my home at the end of the evening, and on Monday it was business as usual. Rami went off to do her substitute teaching, and I went to SFU. That was the beginning of our married life. After our wedding, we were sometimes amused to hear our marriage described as a love marriage. All the marriages in Canada were love marriages, were they not? It was still rather novel for Indians, however, particularly immigrant Indians, to find their own partners.

The 1972 B.C. election had been in full swing while Rami and I were preparing for the wedding. Since I was a full-time student at the end of my semester, I hadn't been able to volunteer much, but I did do some literature drops at doorsteps. The "socialist hordes" under Dave Barrett won the election nine days before our marriage.

Someone had suggested that if I wanted to enrol for a master's degree at UBC, it might be better to complete my BA there. Transcripts from Langara and SFU in hand, I showed up at the UBC Admissions office. I hesitated in front of a wicket marked "Foreign Documents" then chose the one marked "Canadian Documents" instead. The friendly staff person who got up to help me directed me with a gesture back to the "Foreign" wicket. Obediently, I moved over, though I was pretty sure she had slipped into an easy stereotype of those days: coloured is foreign. (A few years later, CTV's FW5 program would fall victim to this stereotype, showing footage of Chinese-looking students while talking about "foreign students" at UBC. Some of those shown turned out to be second- or third-generation Canadians.) I understood the phenomenon myself; when I first arrived in Britain, I had presumed every white person I saw to be fluent in English until I met Italians in Bedford who could hardly utter a word of the language. So I had forgiven the UBC staff member even before she saw my documents. She apologized profusely, however, and insisted on walking me over to the wicket for Canadian documents before explaining the transfer process at length. UBC required a student to complete at least two years of course work there before granting a degree; that would mean redoing almost a year of work. I decided to complete my Honours BA at SFU.

I had made up my mind to enrol in the master's program in international relations at Carleton University in Ottawa, and I was offered a teaching assistantship and other financial assistance there. Then one day, at the end of a friendly argument, Rami declared, "You could never be a lawyer." Her mocking challenge, coupled with the latest figures on the unemployment front — 3,200 PhDs without jobs in Canada — sparked a change in direction. Without abandoning the idea of a master's in international relations, I started applying to law schools as well and quickly wrote the LSAT, the Law School Admission Test.

To my surprise, both Osgoode Hall in Toronto and Dalhousie Law School in Halifax sent me letters of admission. I had not heard anything yet from UBC. I did not really want to leave the West Coast, and I remembered the promise I had made to myself when I landed in Vancouver in 1968: from then on, I would live in either Vancouver or Dosanjh Kalan. Rami was now a full-time ESL instructor at Vancouver Community College, and another happy complication had arisen. Rami was pregnant with our first child. My extended family did not want me to leave, either, and with Bhaji standing beside me, I phoned the law admissions clerk at UBC. I was overjoyed to learn that a letter of admission had been mailed to me that morning. Another of the defining events in my life had occurred.

The Dosanjh family sold our 61st Avenue home and bought a home farther east, on College Street. And on December 1, 1973, the family had another mouth to feed and mind to nurture: Pavel Dosanjh came into this world at Vancouver's Grace Hospital. Pavel arrived late in the afternoon; there was still time for me to attend a meeting that evening about the community centre that was proposed to be built near the Ross Street Temple. Some days later a public meeting took place at the temple, but the centre never materialized. Even today, Indians do not have a community centre in British Columbia. We have countless gurdwaras, *mandirs*, *masjids*, and *girjas*, but no secular space to call home.

During my BA and law school years, I worked nights during the Christmas breaks at Burke Lumber. I had completed the same UBC course on teaching ESL that Rami had done, so I taught at VCC during the 1974 and 1975 summer breaks while at law school as well. My mill work and teaching supplemented Rami's salary, but money was certainly not in abundance. One day a fellow law student, Yoke Lam, asked me to participate in a program funded by the Legal Services Commission of B.C. to disseminate basic legal information to the province's growing immigrant communities. The work involved translating legal information into different languages, in my case into Punjabi and later Hindi, and then reading it aloud on CJVB, a multilingual radio station, in short segments every week. The topics ranged over many areas of law, including wills and estates, landlord and tenant relationships, and real estate. The program reached most Indians and Pakistanis, and my work supplemented our meagre monthly income by a couple of hundred dollars.

The radio program won many admirers for me, though it also made me some enemies among the unthinking and the narrow-minded. Because I provided information on divorce, custody, maintenance and property division in family law, I sometimes received abusive phone calls from irate husbands accusing me of "spoiling" what they called "their women" with information that made the women powerful and "gave them ideas." I was happy, even remotely, to help women find a way out if they faced hell at home.

Soon after our marriage, Rami had started thinking about establishing a women's organization. She spoke to many women, and in 1973 she, Masiji Heeti and Premchit Siripawa became the founding members of the India Mahila (Women's) Association, soon to be joined by Roda Pavri and Baljinder Sidhu. The IMA rallied against violence against women, female feticide and much more. In a socially conservative immigrant community, the organization invited the wrath of many, including some men in the Indian journalistic fraternity. After our three sons were born, Rami was often accused of advocating women's empowerment because she did not have to live with the "curse" of daughters herself. Once I was a practising lawyer, some made the ridiculous allegation that Rami encouraged divorces so that I would get more legal business. Undeterred by such nonsense, she has continued advocating for gender equality over the years. Today, she has added incentive. She is fighting for a more egalitarian world for our four granddaughters and two grandsons.

In 1973, there were several incidents of racial violence against Indians in the Greater Vancouver area. A community meeting held at David Thompson School in East Vancouver was attended by B.C.

Attorney General Alex Macdonald and Vancouver alderman Setty Pendakur. The meeting went fine until it was disrupted by Hardial Bains's outfit. It was almost as if the group had a stake in causing violence and instability in the community. Finally, the meeting was brought under control, and I was able to say my piece from a mike placed in the aisle to enable audience participation. Later, the disruptors denounced me as a traitor in their free, widely distributed rag. A few days afterwards, a few of them came to see me to ask why I had not responded to their slanderous attack. "Not every piece of trash deserves a reply," I told them. Days later, the group penned another attack on me, asking, "How could a person in possession of a *gudda* of books in his library be so stupid?"

Our happy life was going fast and furious. Rami could not always share the family responsibilities as she wished, however, and Bhaji and I did not like the discordant notes in our family conversations. In traditional Indian society, there is tremendous pressure for everyone to live in a joint extended family, but ultimately families must and do go their own ways. Rami and I and Pavel moved back to the family home on 44th Avenue, where I had once lived in the basement with Bhaji, Bhabiji, Nimmy, Tirath and Chachaji. The family bond survives today as strong as ever, because we understood that all of us needed freedom to grow.

20 IN THE SUMMER OF 1974, I taught part time at VCC while working for the B.C. Human Rights Branch to educate minority groups about their rights. I made arrangements with the Immigrant Services Centre on Main Street, Mosaic on Commercial Drive and the Mount Pleasant Community Centre to use their premises to provide information and advice to people. I wrote in various ethnic and community newspapers about rights and procedures under B.C. legislation. Community radio and newspapers helped spread the word. During this time I learned more about the plight of farm workers and the extreme exploitation of janitorial workers by unscrupulous and fraudulent contractors.

I had met Gayle Gavin, a bright and left-leaning student, in a sociology class at VCC, and she was now at law school, a year ahead of me. In the summer of 1974, Gayle had a job with the B.C. Attorney General's ministry, researching the jurisdictional issues around fisheries. She worked closely with the deputy Attorney General. The project needed a few more first- or second-year students, and Gayle told the deputy Attorney General she had a friend who would be a good candidate. She and I took the ferry to Victoria early in the summer break to meet with him. We had to wait for a few minutes before being ushered into his office. As Gayle entered, he had a huge smile on his face. Once his gaze turned to me, his infectious smile disappeared. I shook his hand and then he sank into his chair, barely mustering a cursory question or two to ask me. I punctured the tension in the air with some information about my academic background, and then Gayle took over. The meeting was over in less than five minutes. Gayle was colour-blind. The world wasn't. Luckily, I had other work that summer.

Late in 1974, I met with two students who were keen to research the feasibility of unionizing farm workers in B.C. The NDP had amended the labour laws, giving farm workers the right to organize, and the question the students sought to answer was whether a traditional union model could work, given the role of contractors and the farmers' dependence on them. Or would a hiring hall model, where the union manages the supply of labour to the employers, be more feasible? It was my firm view that if anything could work in the long run, it would be the hiring hall model. Seasonal farm work, which the overwhelming majority of the workers were engaged in, did not lend itself to anything else.

In 1975, I met John Borst, a fellow NDPer who had worked on the farm workers' unionizing campaigns led by Cesar Chavez in California. John's wife, Gail, who at the time worked for the B.C. Federation of Labour, knew of my interest in the farm work conditions in B.C. The farm workers here were mainly recent Indian immigrants, most of whom were picked up daily in big industrial vans by contractors and paid on a piece rate: the more they picked, the more they made. People worked long hours without any overtime pay, and existing health and safety regulations did not apply to them. The province's minimum wage laws now covered farm workers, but only if they didn't work on a piece rate. At the end of each season, moreover, many workers remained unpaid or only partially paid. Often, they were given unemployment insurance contributions by contractors for work done in lieu of full payment. Contractors also charged a fee for making unemployment contributions for people who had not done even a day's work so that they could qualify for unemployment insurance benefits. The contractors were perpetrating a fraud upon the government as well as the workers.

In the summer of 1975, John and I decided to experience the workers' conditions for ourselves. By now, mine was a reasonably well-recognized face in the Indian community, so I grew five days' worth of stubble, took off my glasses and put on grubby clothes and a cap. We called up Gurbakhash Rai, one of the more notorious farm contractors, and my friend Sukhwant and Rami's brother Jasbir joined John and me in Rai's van in South Vancouver. We were herded in like cattle. The back of the van was windowless and suffocating, and the narrow wooden benches that had been installed left barely enough space for the workers' legs and feet. I felt as if I was in the world of the dead already as we set out for the hour-long drive to a farm in Abbotsford.

At the farm, the workers were divided into two groups. Buckets in hand, the four of us advanced toward the rows of ripe blueberries. Because we were not getting an hourly wage, neither the contractor nor the farmer supervised us, except to make periodic checks to ensure we didn't drop any berries on the ground or leave any ripe ones on the plants. The four of us settled in, picking less and observing more as we asked simple questions of our fellow pickers. How many hours did they work? Where were the proper toilets? We learned that there were no proper toilets on the site, either portable or permanent. No regular water was provided to the workers in the rows as they picked, and the only usable source of drinking water was quite a distance away. Some workers had not been paid for several weeks. They continued to work for Rai, they said, because if they switched to someone else, Rai might never pay them what they were owed.

John came close to dehydrating in the scorching heat, and he retired to the shade with lots of water. As we continued to probe the workers, someone among them must have recognized me, because Rai started hovering around us, and the workers grew quieter. I took off several times, pretending to go for water or to relieve myself; while walking to and fro, I stole some moments to talk freely with workers. My unpredictable movements sent the farmer, Rai, and his cronies scurrying.

It was a very long day for us, but it was even longer for Rai. The workers who had been sweating all day looked tired. But instead of over-benched, windowless vans, a big, new-looking bus awaited our fatigued bodies. There was some triumph in this, even though we knew it was a temporary gambit. But we were dismayed, too; once our cover had been blown, we'd failed to get much further information from the workers. I understood the fear gripping them. For their livelihood, they had to deal with Rai or others like him. They wanted to ensure he picked them up the next morning and paid them as well.

The four of us were dropped near the spot where we had been picked up in the morning, with a promise from Rai that he'd be there again the next day. But nobody came the next morning to pick us up. I called Rai several times to collect our hard-earned money, with no success.

During this time, some contractors threatened harm against me. I received phone threats, and a close friend warned me he'd heard there was a contract out to kill or maim me. The murder of a Fraser Valley Punjabi realtor added a ring of plausibility to the information.

John Borst spoke to some union activists. We arranged a meeting with leaders of the International Woodworkers of America, since many of their members, like most of the farm workers, were Indian. We met as well with Harinder Mahil, the Indian editor of *The Chipper*, the newspaper of the IWA's New Westminster local. The response was less than overwhelming. It was my view that if we were to succeed in a hiring hall drive, we would have to call for an industry-wide strike in the province just before picking season. If we could successfully sustain a strike, keeping workers away from the contractors' vans for a couple of weeks, the farmers and the contractors would be forced to come to us. We could then negotiate wages and working conditions. Workers could register and be dispatched under this standardized agreement.

John was committed to the cause, but the unions were not biting. In the meantime, the Labour Advocacy and Research Association (LARA) had been established. Cheryl Dahl, Rachel Epstein, John and I were its first board members. LARA successfully applied for funding from the Law Foundation, a non-profit entity run with interest from the trust accounts of the members of the Law Society of British Columbia. We opened an office near the offices of the Vancouver Community Legal Assistance Society, and the VCLAS lawyers helped John do legal advocacy for the workers. LARA focussed on helping farm workers collect their wages, pursuing small claims actions as necessary for that purpose. Nashatter Dhahan, a young woman raised in Britain who was fluent in Punjabi, joined John at LARA, and soon the organization had several active claims on behalf of workers underway. LARA worked on creating public awareness in preparation for a unionizing drive, and it widely distributed a bilingual Punjabi and English leaflet outlining farm, domestic and janitorial worker's rights.

I BUMPED INTO Anthony Fraser, who became a lifelong friend, on my first day at UBC Law School. He stood out as the only one in the class wearing a suit and tie. A son of English immigrants, born and bred in Victoria, B.C., Anthony spoke with an Oxonian accent, as if he had just landed in Vancouver from Britain. We hit it off, and whenever we found time between classes we walked over to the Graduate Centre to eat, sip tea and study.

The library on the top floor of the Graduate Centre was exquisite. A former Canadian general had donated his complete collection of books, which contained some gems on India. We did our law research in the law school library and of course went to the law school classes, but we studied, fed our bodies and nurtured our souls at the Graduate Centre. The Grad Centre library was a refuge and a retreat. It contained books on the great debates of the Indian independence movement about partition, the Indian constitution, and the nature and history of Indian civilization. The centre reminded me that the law regulates worldly human relationships and guarantees fairness, equality and justice for all. But even more importantly, it is a tool to mould and change the world.

In the Grad Centre library, I also came face to face with Gandhi's writings and those of his nemesis in the Indian National Congress, Subhas Bose. In Bose's *The Indian Struggle 1920–1934*, published in 1935, he argues at length that certain elements of fascism can be useful as organizing principles. Bose may not have known about the creeping, officially promoted and sanctioned isolation and hatred of Jews and Roma that soon turned into genocide. Britain, as the imperial power in India, was considered the enemy. But "the enemy of my enemy is my friend" can't be a principle in every human endeavour.

My real tryst with Mahatma occurred during the Christmas break of 1974. I was nursing a stomach problem that doctors could not diagnose. At home, in front of the fireplace in our almost-bare living room, one-year-old Pavel played in Rami's lap while I read Gandhi's autobiography, *The Story of My Experiments with Truth*. That was the beginning of both an unending journey of self-discovery and a lifelong affair with both my Indianness and Gandhi's philosophy. His life's work lent Gangetic sacredness and Himalayan nobility to politics.

Living happily ever after is a mirage pursued in many marriages. Rami and I knew from the beginning that uninterrupted happiness occurs only in the fantasies churned out by Bollywood and Hollywood. I also had told Rami that "divorce" was not a word in my dictionary, though we were free to agree, disagree and even argue endlessly. Once, however, after some forgettable argument, Rami told me she wanted to move out. She started packing, but she wanted to wait until the weekend to find a place to rent. I hated the thought, but, hurt, I told her to leave that day. I started putting her packed items out in the front yard. She would bring a package back into the house as I was putting another out. This continued for a few minutes, until Rami had an epiphany. "It is my home too. Why should I move out?" said she. "Well, then, I'll bring all the packages back in," I said. I did, as she laughed uproariously. Our non-divorce pact was cemented forever.

Our second son, Aseem, was born in May 1975. He was a happy, irrepressible baby, and his arrival made our household busier. Rami was breastfeeding him one afternoon when she noticed an infection on one of her fingernails. We got to the doctor just in the nick of time: her arm showed the beginnings of potentially serious blood poisoning. I was scared — my mother had died of tetanus — but thankful for the quick medical attention Rami received.

One of the more interesting experiences at law school was the first-year moot. The students teamed up in pairs. We were given the facts on which a lower court had based an actual decision, and the moot was the appeal. I can't remember whether my partner, Jill Terheide, and I acted for the appellants or the respondents. I can't recall the facts of the case, either. But I do remember the outcome and the cast of characters.

Two third-year students sat as judges. Acting for the other side were fellow students Jack Webster, son of the famous journalist Jack Webster, and Sue Ruttan, daughter of the supernumerary B.C. Supreme Court judge, Hon. Mr. Justice Ruttan. We had been required to cite our authorities on the factums we exchanged with the opposing counsel some days before arguing the appeal. It so happened that on the day of the argument, just a few hours before it was to be held, Jack and Sue found an unreported decision by Mr. Justice Ruttan they thought would clinch the case for them. Jill and I pored over the decision, but the case was not on point at all. After the arguments were heard, the judges deliberated for a few minutes and announced their decision. The young working-class woman from the interior of B.C. and the ESL kid from the east end of Vancouver had won. Jack and Sue had been brilliant, but the facts were what they were, and the law prevailed.

RAMI AND I MANAGED with one vehicle, an old Ford Comet, until 1975, when I bought a used Datsun station wagon for $1,100. We had two sons to feed and care for, and money was tight. I did not have the money to cover my law school tuition for the year to come. I was about to ask Bhaji for help when a cheque from the B.C. government bursary program arrived in the mail.

Rami and I have never let financial hard times stand in the way of our activism. If anything, they have brought home the reality of the poverty faced by many people in Canada and around the world. India made me and has kept me humble. My experience and my station in life have allowed no room for arrogance. Some may mistake my anger for arrogance, and there have been lapses on my part — some public, others private. But anger at the way things are provides fuel for changing them. Only the dead are never angry.

The year 1975 saw turmoil at the Ross Street Temple once again. After a gathering at the temple in late spring, I heard from Biraji's son Kulbir, who had immigrated to Canada a couple of years earlier, that there had been a serious physical brawl and that some of Bains's followers had been hospitalized. A few days later, Father Jim Roberts, a teacher of religion at Langara, invited me onto his weekly radio program to comment. Father Roberts and I talked for a while and then took calls. It had been alleged that the group that controlled the temple's executive was unfairly skewing the election process. I argued for more open and democratic elections at the temple, offering only a fair commentary.

Religious institutions in the Indian community in Canada play a much larger role than they ever did in India, partly because secular institutions in the Indian community here are few. The pandering by Canadian politicians to faith groups at their places of worship has further exaggerated their importance.

Two weeks after the initial violence, there was another attempt at elections at the Ross Street Temple, using a show of hands. I had publicly disapproved of the methods and tactics of stasists, supporters of the status quo, and I should have known they would retaliate. But curiosity got the better of me; Rami and I attended and sat at the back of the hall against the wall, she on the women's side and I on the men's. Hands rose for and against a matter before the assembly. I sat motionless, one hand clutching the other. There were raised voices, and I realized a physical altercation was not far away. Rami and I and some others, including the writer Sadhu Binning, left though the door farthest from the looming fracas. Back at home, we received news of severe violence at the temple. Again the police had to attend.

The retaliation for my perceived impudence on the radio with Father Roberts came in the form of another summons to appear in court. Once again, I was falsely charged. This time the dispute was all in the family, literally. Masarji's older brother, Daljit Dhillon, had sworn that in the second bout of violence at the temple, Mamiji's brother Sohan Mann and I had assaulted him. Ironically, I had seen neither Daljit nor Sohan that day. As I saw it, Daljit was angry that his son Marshal was still a Bains crony, and he held me responsible for that. He and his fellow stasists were also angry at my radio rebuke.

By now Nanaji and Naniji were in Canada, having immigrated to be with their large extended family earlier in 1975. Nanaji and Masarji suggested I apologize to Daljit for my radio analysis and commentary, so that he might consider dropping the charges. They worried about a possible conviction standing in the way of my legal career. They also knew I was a poor university student, and that we had two babies to feed on Rami's lone salary. I was outraged at the suggestion. I would not apologize for commentary that was innocuous even by Canadian standards. Apologizing to ward off evil simply invites more of it, and in substantial measure. The real problem was that in ghettos of values different from those of mainstream society, even a hint of weakness can mean a lifetime of humiliation. I was not about to allow free speech to be suffocated by the tools of criminal justice. Prosecution or not, criminal record or not, I wasn't for apologizing.

I retained Peter Leask, a well-known member of the criminal defence bar and part-time law professor who was later appointed a B.C. Supreme Court justice. Don Rosenbloom acted for Sohan. The trial was based on a lie, an assault that never was, yet it lasted several days, spread over several months, and involved various witnesses. At the end, Judge Jerry Paradis dismissed the charges. My stubbornness in refusing to talk to Nanaji or Masarji for several months afterwards was the saddest part of the whole ordeal. Family warmth and affection, once dimmed, can be difficult to restore. Shortly after the trial, Jajo visited Bhaji, and in my presence she sat with tears rolling down her cheeks. The tension in the family was tearing her up. Nanaji, though more of a stoic, was hurting too. When I finally apologized to them for being childish, all was forgiven.

That summer, the summer of 1975, I had spent a week at St. Vincent's Hospital undergoing tests for my stomach problems. The doctors were puzzled. They suspected some tropical bug or infection, but I had been away from India for eleven years. My stomach kept troubling me, and none of the medications I was given helped. Late one night, after studying for a law exam the next day, my stomach was bothering me so much I couldn't sleep. I got out of bed and went to the cupboard where we kept small quantities of liquor. I grabbed the bottle of vodka, poured myself a sizeable amount, mixed it with some orange juice and gulped it down. I rarely had a drink in those days, but I slept like a log, waking up to my alarm clock. My stomach pain was gone, and my insides felt smooth as silk.

Medicine isn't always an exact science. When Nanaji went into Vancouver General Hospital for cataract surgery in 1982, seven wonderful years after arriving in Canada, he was close to ninety-five and healthy as a horse. The doctors put him under a general anaesthetic, and his liver reacted badly. He died a few days later. When we asked the doctors for an explanation, they were clueless. "It was probably a dormant tropical infection," they said — the same diagnosis doctors had offered me seven years earlier at a different hospital. In this case, the true culprit was simple and obvious: their negligence in unnecessarily administering a general anaesthetic to an elderly man.

Rami's younger sister, Rajinder, had arrived as an immigrant in 1974, staying with us until her husband joined her the following year. Rami's older sister, Tripat, immigrated to Canada in 1975 and also stayed with us for a while.

OUR LIFE AT HOME was very busy during this time. This made for some interesting cultural episodes we were able to laugh about later. When our friends Bob and Leah Osterhout heard that Tripat and her family were staying with us, they phoned to say they were on their way over to visit. Tripat initially refused to come out of her room, since they had not made an appointment with her. Eventually, she joined us in our small living room. Bob and Leah greeted her but remained seated. We chatted and shared chai, but after they left, Tripat let us know that Bob and Leah had no manners, since they had not gotten up to greet her. On top of it all, Bob had had the temerity to wear worn-out socks, Tripat said, "with his big toes boldly peering out."

Rami's parents and siblings — her brothers Jasbir and Harwant and her sister Mani — immigrated to Canada in 1976. That meant Rami's family and mine were all settled in Canada except for my father, who came and went every year. Chachaji enjoyed life in the village, where many of his lifelong friends were still alive and well, and he hated the Canadian cold. Besides, there was nothing for him to do in Canada, while back in India, the land and the *khooh* beckoned. But he missed us and his grandchildren, so he came to Canada in the summers and left as the fall returned.

By April of 1976 I had graduated from law school and was looking for a place to article. I sent more than a hundred handwritten applications to law firms in Greater Vancouver and beyond, attaching a typed resume. I got two interviews, but no articling placement. Was it my "weird" name, my middling marks or my handwritten cover letters?

The Law Union, a collective of left-leaning Lower Mainland lawyers, invited me to a meeting where they were discussing the conditions and the state of law regarding seasonal farm work. Many present knew I was looking for articles. At the end of the meeting, Ted Holekamp, whom I didn't know at the time, came over to talk to me. Ted's articles with lawyer John Motiuk were concluding in a couple of weeks, he told me. John had offices in Vancouver and Burnaby, and he was a litigator with a thriving civil, criminal, wills and estate, and real estate practice. I was more than interested in taking Ted's place at the firm.

It was John Motiuk's manager, his father-in-law Vern Bigelow, who interviewed me for the position. Vern asked less about my qualifications than about my background in India. We talked about Hardial Bains and his followers, too. Finally, Vern asked if I knew Phil Rankin, a friend of mine from Langara and SFU, though I suspected he had already spoken to Phil. At the end of the interview, Vern told me I was hired and could begin work after the Labour Day weekend. John Motiuk came out of his office to introduce himself. He would pay me $1,000 a month, he said, as well as covering the fees for my call to the bar and bar exams, the cost of my barrister's gown, and mileage for my car. I suddenly felt rich.

At 9:00 AM on my first day on the job, John handed me two files containing applications for New Westminster County Court at 10:00 AM. I hadn't the foggiest idea what to do, but John said they were routine motions, briefly explaining each one. I drove to the old red brick court house in New Westminster; in chambers, Judge McTaggart was presiding. This was my first time in court, other than my two stints as a falsely accused defendant in 1970 and 1975. That experience in the dock made me less apprehensive than I might have been otherwise, though it would not be true to say I was completely at ease.

The first application went like a breeze. On the second application, clearly pegging me as a brand-new articling student, Judge McTaggart asked for my authority for the relief sought under the then B.C. Execution Act. When I couldn't cite the specific section in the Act, the judge granted the order but put me on notice that I needed to have all my ducks in a row before entering the court again. (I knew that anyway.) McTaggart was quite aware of the situation new articling students faced. I would appear before McTaggart many other times, during my articles and afterwards. Once I appeared before him representing an Indian woman petitioner for divorce who had been born and bred in England. After McTaggart granted the decree nisi — an interim order before the decree absolute would finally dissolve the marriage — he told her, "Madam, you have a wonderful accent." Without batting an eye, she asked, "What accent?" He was stumped.

I worked from John Motiuk's Kingsgate Mall office. It was open on Saturdays for half a day, since Motiuk wanted to ensure his working-class clientele was able to see him. Personal injury, family law, and criminal and civil litigation remained my focus throughout my articles. I argued several cases and appeared in court several times a week on behalf of Motiuk. My experience belied the claim that articling students were merely hired as researchers or photocopiers.

One of the most memorable cases I handled during this period was that of a farm worker charged with assaulting Rai, the contractor who had never paid me for my day of berry-picking in Abbotsford. The impoverished worker was owed money by Rai. When Rai's mother died, the accused went with some friends to pay a condolence visit. He had called Rai several times about his unpaid wages in the days preceding that. Unbeknownst to the accused, Rai had taken offence to the calls, and after shouting abuse at the accused in front of a house full of mourners, he pulled out a gun. The accused ran to his car, Rai followed and a scuffle ensued. Police charged the wrong guy.

We drew Judge Moffatt, who was considered unfriendly to the defence. The Crown presented its case, and Rai's story bore no resemblance to what had actually happened. I called the accused to the stand, attempting to lay a foundation for his calls and his visit to the Rai home. The judge instructed me to go directly to the assault, but I pleaded that assault usually did not occur in a vacuum. When I repeated my question to the accused, the judge forbade the accused from answering, then turned to me, asking if I understood English.

He threatened to hold me in contempt if I repeated my question. I assured him I'd understood his ruling, and told him I planned to ask the question once more, even though he might again direct the witness not to answer. That happened, but in the end Moffatt surprised us all by acquitting my client.

Another memorable episode stemmed from the case of Leonard Peltier, a prominent member of the American Indian Movement who had allegedly been involved in a shootout at the Lakota Pine Ridge Indian Reservation in South Dakota the year before, in 1976, where two FBI agents died. The saga had begun with the seventy-one-day occupation by the AIM of the town of Wounded Knee, on the Pine Ridge reservation. Peltier was arrested in early 1976 in Canada. As the Canadian courts deliberated on his case and the Canadian government deliberated on his extradition, the B.C. Law Union called for people to picket the courthouses. The day of the pickets, I was set to appear on a criminal matter in the County Court at New Westminster. I decided to not cross the picket line, and I called the prosecutor to ask if he could resolve the matter in my absence, since it was a simple question of fixing a date for trial. The Crown agreed, but presiding Judge McMorran ordered me to appear before him the following morning to explain why I should not be held in contempt.

As a new kid on the block, the order put the fear of God into me. John Motiuk attended McMorran's court the next morning in my place. I do not know exactly what he said to McMorran, but the matter was resolved, and judicial tempers cooled. Unfortunately, after being extradited to the U.S., Peltier was convicted of killing the FBI agents — unfairly, I believe. He remains in jail to this day.

In September of 1976, not long after I began my articles with John Motiuk, Tara Singh Hayer, who had not yet started his weekly *Indo-Canadian Times,* told me about a bad experience he had had with unscrupulous operators in the janitorial industry. I met with him, Amarjit Bains and Raj Bains (who were not related to one another, but were close lifelong friends), along with several other janitorial workers in a borrowed room on Victoria Drive. They were all victims of D&V

Janitorial Services, a limited company doing business in Greater Vancouver. D&V entered into janitorial contracts with office building owners, and then subcontracted the work at a higher price without the knowledge or consent of the owners. The subcontract gave D&V many arbitrary powers, including the ability to cancel the contract for minor infractions or to penalize subcontractors by not paying for work done. D&V refused to pay janitors for months, and then cancelled their contracts for spurious reasons. The same contracts were subsequently sublet to others from the large pool of unsuspecting and unemployed immigrants. By the time of our meeting, subcontractor janitors were owed thousands of dollars by D&V and similar companies. The victims had no recourse but to sue D&V under the Trade Practices Act that had been passed by the NDP government. Following this complaint, the Director of Trade Practices retained my principal, John Motiuk, and we successfully sued D&V in the Supreme Court of British Columbia. D&V had no assets, but it was a moral victory.

In February 1979, the Farm Workers Organizing Committee would be established by Harinder Mahil and others. LARA, the Labour Advocacy and Research Association, extended its full support to the committee, and when the Canadian Farmworkers Union (CFU) was founded that April, LARA turned over all its records, files and contacts. Years later, when I was a member of the NDP government benches in B.C., we extended health and safety regulations to the farm workers. But the CFU did not survive, unfortunately, and today most farm workers remain unorganized and at the mercy of contractors and farmers. The old master/servant relationship has barely changed.

IT WAS A GREAT HELP having Rami's parents in Vancouver. Her mother who, as we had mine, we called Biji — was now the caregiver for Aseem and Pavel when Rami and I were not around. And on most working days, both Biji and Papa minded our sons from nine to four. One day just before Christmas, Biji was working away at the stove when Aseem snuck up behind her and pulled a boiling pot of dal over himself. He suffered serious burns to his neck and chest and was scalded in other areas as well. Rami spent the entire Christmas break with Aseem at the Children's Hospital. Even after coming home, he needed extra care. For the next couple of years, Aseem had to contend with elastic braces around his neck and chest to stem the keloidal scars in the area of his deeper burns.

During those years, Biji and Papa anchored our home life, giving Rami and me the freedom to pursue political work. It was Biji's nature to have the kitchen always going, so we never ran out of food. No one visiting our home was allowed to leave without food or tea. Biji and Papa recreated in Vancouver the atmosphere of any thriving village household in India.

I had not attended the graduation ceremonies for my BA or LLB, but the call to the bar was mandatory in order to be able to practise law. My full extended family accompanied me to the occasion on September 13, 1977.

In my early years as a lawyer, I did a lot of pro bono work for poor people and non-profit and charitable organizations. When the Ross Street Temple and others bought some land off No. 6 Road in Richmond, my office acted for them without a fee. When the Guru Nanak Sikh Gurdwara needed independent legal advice as they constructed a new temple on Scott Road in Surrey, and when the Akali Singh Sikh Society was obtaining a mortgage to build a new temple on Vancouver's Skeena Street, there was no question of charging a fee.

A fixture on the community's social scene in those days was the ponytailed, bearded and spectacled Ripudaman Malik. Malik and I met first at an evening get-together where the booze and smoke flowed freely. He and his wife subsequently visited us at home. Seeing Malik then, one could not have imagined the man later accused and prosecuted on a charge of blowing up Air India Flight 182 with its 329 passengers over the Irish Sea in 1985. Over the years, Malik changed from the long-haired hippie I'd met into a steely-eyed, orthodox man. He came to see me at my law office to register the Satnam Trust, which eventually set up the Khalsa Schools — schools combining academic instruction with Sikh religious studies — in the Lower Mainland. I did not foresee his dangerous evolution or designs. Malik was charged with terrorism in the Air India bombing, though he was acquitted when the Crown failed to prove its case beyond reasonable doubt.

PART 4

THE

FIRST TRIP

BACK

22   EVER SINCE LEAVING INDIA, I had missed its beauty and my sense of belonging to its dusty roads, searing sun and torrential monsoons. I missed the puddles on the rain-soaked roads. The tea stalls along the busy streets and thoroughfares haunted my memories. I missed the colourful peacocks roaming the empty, sundrenched fields from which golden wheat had just been harvested. I yearned for the smells, sights and sounds of India. Canada was now my country in a legal sense, but emotionally I was torn between two places and destined to remain so. Never let an immigrant tell you he does not miss the land of his birth. We have fled our countries in search of a better life, and we carry that pain in our hearts. I could rationalize my exit from India and dress it up in palatable garb, but the ugly truth was that I was a fugitive from the struggles of my motherland. To this day, I am a fugitive from India; my crime is desertion.

My call to the bar was a personal milestone, and I began to plan a trip to India for the first time since I left. Rami and I might never again be able to take a two-and-a-half-month break from our working lives. We could leave Pavel and Aseem in the care of their grandparents, surrounded by aunts and uncles from both sides of the family; Bhaji and Bhabiji now lived less than a block away from us. John Motiuk was fine with me returning to start work in January 1978 as a newly called lawyer. Rami arranged to take time off from teaching. Our friend Sohan Pooni decided to accompany us on the trip. He was returning to India for the first time, after six years in Canada, to find a wife. I was returning with my wife, after thirteen years away, to find India.

We set off in mid-September of 1977. As we settled into our seats on the plane to New York, my mind journeyed back. Prior to leaving for Britain, I had not travelled outside of Punjab, and I had left India as a young man. I wasn't sure what would await me in the country of my birth. The dark period of the country's undemocratic state of emergency had recently ended. India had again dared to dream and had defeated Indira Gandhi's Congress party. The right-winger Morarji Desai was now the prime minister. His government couldn't provide the progress and stability Indians hungered for, however, and the country was in turmoil.

The three of us spent a pleasant flight. But as the plane approached its destination, I was rudely shaken from my reveries by an incident with the flight attendant. Sohan and I had both ordered drinks; the flight attendant gave me my change, but did not give Sohan his. She reacted angrily when he asked her about it, and she accused him of lying, saying "people like you from the villages always pull this kind of stunt." We asked to see her boss, and the bursar was busily defending her when the chap in the seat in front of me chimed in, saying the flight attendant had mistakenly given him Sohan's eighty dollars. After we'd landed, I complained to the pilot, and I followed up with a letter to Air India upon returning to Vancouver. As expected, my letter received no reply.

We transferred in New York to a plane bound for London. As if we hadn't been insulted enough already, Sohan was approached at the baggage carousel after we landed at Heathrow by a man in Arabic garb clutching cash. The man tried to steer Sohan and his buggy in a particular direction. Not speaking much English, he must have mistaken the dark-skinned Sohan, dressed in jeans and a denim jacket, for a "coolie." In places like Dubai, Indian immigrants sometimes worked as baggage handlers.

Sohan had had similar experiences related to his skin colour in Punjab. The caste system also has an element of colour, and in those days Dalits from Punjab and many southern Indians went to Dubai and the other gulf states looking for work. Because Sohan was dark-skinned, people sometimes assumed he was from Dubai. Sadly, many people still think "lower caste" when they see an Indian with dark skin. The effects of caste consciousness are debilitating no matter where one fits into the sinister scheme. I do not have too many disagreements with the Mahatma, but I do disagree with his position of letting the caste system remain. Perhaps he only did so because marshalling all Indians and resources against British rule had to be his priority, but even the greatest of leaders have blind spots.

From Heathrow we took a cab to King's Cross station, and from there the train to Bedford. My happiness at seeing Biraji and other family and friends was punctured when I realized my old friend Malkiat Rai, whom I'd worked with on *Mamta*, was not among them. It was on this visit that I learned from others the indignities visited upon Malkiat during the beating in Bedford; to save me pain, he had never shared that incident with me. I sought him out during our visit to reaffirm and pay respect to our friendship.

Rami's cousin lived in Derby. Her husband, who had a taxi business, took us around England over the week that followed, including to Bradford to see my friend Jagtar Sihota from my Ramgarhia College days. In Bradford, we bought a couple of small portable tape players to bring to family and friends in India.

When we arrived back at Heathrow to continue our journey, we learned our flight would be delayed by a day. The chap at the British Airways desk exclaimed that Sohan, being a Pooni, must be from the village of Jindowal in Punjab. Upon being told of my village, he asked if I knew Master Pritam Singh Dosanjh: Chachaji. The man turned out to be the son of a prominent politician from near Jindowal and a first cousin of the railway guard Jasbir Mann, who had rescued me on the platform at the Bedford railway station. We decided to stay the night at a nearby hotel, and the British Airways fellow showed up in his car to ferry us to his home for a sumptuous dinner. These gestures of kindness and love have been extended to me scores of time throughout my life.

In those days, Indian Customs charged a high duty on most foreign clothing and electronics. As we approached Customs at the Delhi airport, we declared the tape recorders and paid 250 rupees in duty. Armed with our receipt, we walked over to the main Customs office to ask for Joginder Gill. He was the son-in-law of Rami's uncle

Gurbakhsh Atariwala, who had persuaded Rami's father to let Rami travel to Vancouver in 1970. Were it not for him, our lives might have taken a very different turn. To simplify things, I referred to Joginder as my brother-in-law, and the man asked us why we hadn't told the Customs officer about our relationship — to get the duty waived, presumably. When we met Joginder, he, too, was surprised that we had not informed him in advance of our arrival. Nevertheless, he and his family turned out to be very good hosts for our days in Delhi.

We'd borrowed a car from another friend in Delhi, and the next morning, we hired a driver to take us to Sohan's home in Jindowal, about ten miles from Dosanjh Kalan. The roads were more crowded than they had been in 1964. Cars and buses jostled with trucks so overloaded they threatened to tip over sideways. On the medianless Grand Trunk Road from Delhi to Punjab, our car and the oncoming vehicles appeared to be in a suicidal contest, giving way only in the nick of time. The big trucks were the kings of the road, the buses the queens, and cars came next. The rest of the pecking order in this suicidal road dance descended from tuk-tuk to rickshaw puller to cyclist, with pedestrians at the bottom. The ubiquitous honking added to the chaos.

At a roadside *dhaba,* a traditional eatery, we stopped to order food and chai. As we were leaving, Rami saw two young boys at a distance watching us intently. She had an unopened bottle of soda, so she walked over, gave them each a hug and handed them the soda to share. The patrons of the *dhaba* and the adjoining establishments watched her in shock. Food was offered by the rich at religious places all the time to feed the hungry, often with grotesque pomp and ceremony. What stunned people was the simplicity of this interaction between a wealthy-looking woman and the boys. We had run up against some of the sad but undeniable truths of India: so much religion, yet so little humanity; so much ritual, yet little spirituality; so much wealth, yet so much poverty too.

We spent the night at Jindowal, putting the chaos of the road behind us for the night, and in the morning, after eating my favourite Punjabi winter staple of *saag* and corn rotis, Rami and I set off on our own for Dosanjh Kalan. This was my first time driving in India. As we took the turnoff and passed by my old friend Verinder's village, Mandhali, I remembered riding my bike to Phagwara and back along that same curvy road. Often I'd be the only soul on it. I'd once known its every pothole, but my ears were no longer attuned to its rhythms. I had become a stranger.

Chachaji's face shone as we got out of the car. We put our baggage in the newly built second-floor rooms at the *khooh*. There were new sofas and beds as well, and a shower with a regular water supply. There were still no toilets, though, seated or otherwise. The memories came flooding back: working on the farm, running to school each morning after taking a dip in the *chalha*.

The ancestral home inside the *firnie*, once bubbling with life, was empty except for a solitary tenant. Even the family's dog, Deepak, less than a year old when I left for England, had died two weeks before at the ripe old age of thirteen. Life in Dosanjh, too, had changed beyond recognition. Most of my school friends had gone abroad or moved to other parts of India. Poverty had exacted its price on those who remained in the village. Their wrinkled, weather-beaten faces and hands betrayed the harshness of their lives.

It was the strangest feeling, being in my ancestral village. It was mine, yet it wasn't. I loved it, yet there was emptiness in my heart. My heart was searching for something, but I did not know what. The deserter in me felt a moment of shame.

For the first few days we remained close to Dosanjh. Chachaji showed me the land he had purchased with money sent to him by Biraji. I drove him to Virkaan, his mother's village, where we met his first cousins and their children. He and his cousin Darshan could almost have been mistaken for identical twins.

Chachaji took me to see Amar Singh Dosanjh, one of his former students, in Jullundur. The daily he'd started many years earlier, *Akali Patrika,* was still going strong. In the mid-sixties, Amar had success-fully run as a Congress candidate, and he won the seat for the state assembly from our area, but the Congress party didn't win government.

That night, Amar called the Congress party a "fading light" and offered his support to his former party, the Akali Dal, instead. The very next day, when he was not appointed to the cabinet by the Akalis, he declared his return to the Congress fold, asking, "Who will fuel the fading light, if not I?" His political career never recovered. Nonetheless, he was so well known that when Rami and I met Mrs. Indira Gandhi years later, the *sardarji* at the reception looked at my business card and asked, "Do you know Amar Singh Dosanjh?"

The Akali Dal had successfully agitated for a Punjabi-speaking state, a controversial move that saw the Greater Punjab dreamed of by Partap Singh Kairon, a former chief minister of Punjab, reduced to twelve districts and less than a third of its original post-partition size. In the old Punjab, every student was required to learn at least three languages: Punjabi, Hindi and English. In the state of Punjab today, most students neglect Punjabi, preferring instead to focus on Hindi and English as vehicles for progress. Scrawny Punjabi preteens who can hardly speak Punjabi are learning the Victorian English still being taught in many schools. Such is the disfavour Punjabi faces in the Punjab of today.

VISITING THE PLACES of Rami's heritage came next. From our base in Dosanjh, Rami and I made a trip to Amritsar, where Rami had spent several years at school and college. Amritsar is also the city of the Harimandir Sahib — literally, "God's temple" — otherwise known as the Golden Temple. By now, I was getting used to driving in India, though Canadian swear words came in handy whenever I felt that other drivers had done something stupid or unfair. To my ears, swearing in English did not sound as vulgar as it did in Punjabi, though Rami found it revolting either way.

Of all the puzzling rules, or rather non-rules, of the road in India, the one that confused me the most was blinking one's headlights while driving head on into an oncoming vehicle. In Canada, people flash their headlights at another vehicle to yield the right of way. In India, the blinking headlights were a message for the other vehicle to get out of the way. Rami and I had at least one close call before we figured this out. Might is right on the roads in India, and courtesy be damned; the same principle holds, in fact, in many human interactions in the country.

When we arrived at Amritsar, we drove to the Kandhari family residence. The Kandharis are fabric manufacturers, and the business was a partnership run by brothers Narinder and Lali. Narinder's wife Ramesh, Meshi for short, was a friend of Rami's from her school days.

Narinder's widowed mother, Jhaiji, ruled the household with an iron fist that she never had to show. Her mere presence was enough to keep order. The brothers' manufacturing facility was in an industrial area, with the showroom in a narrow lane not too far from the Golden Temple. The lane was the city's wholesale hub for fabric, most of it exclusively manufactured in Amritsar. The lane and its buildings, some of them quite ornate, were several hundred years old. They had lived through the glory of Maharaja Ranjit Singh's rule and the humiliation, blood and gore of the Jallianwala massacre at the hands of the British.

Next we visited Atari, a village near the border of Pakistan that was famous for providing the Maharaja with his most prominent general, Sham Singh Atariwala, a close ancestor of Rami's paternal grandmother. After the partition of India in 1947, Rami's Papa took his family to first settle in Atari, eventually moving on from there as his army life demanded. Rami and I saw several very old buildings made with small bricks, the kind that were used to build the house across from our ancestral home in Dosanjh. Extraordinarily ornate, palatial and tall, the buildings must have housed people of wealth and influence.

Papa's maternal home still had an ancient, fully functioning well from which the family drew its water for daily use. The nearby buildings, occupied by some of Papa's second and third cousins, had the hallmarks of having once been occupied by aristocrats or wealthy landlords. In one of them, the third-storey ceiling was entirely covered by a painting rimmed with an ancient border.

As we walked the streets of Atari, I felt embraced by the history of a secular reign that had ended a bare 136 years earlier. The bond of affection among these citizens, descendants of the warriors of Ranjit Singh, was still palpable.

Rami's maternal village of Majitha was the next place we visited. It, too, had been famous for Sikh *sardars* from the Maharaja's era. In Majitha, though, the previous glory of many households had faded into visible poverty and near-misery. The wealth and power that her Biji's family had at one time enjoyed had not survived the ravages of time. One of her maternal uncle's sons was much older than Rami was, so some of his children were her contemporaries. One of those people was Vinney, who had completed her master's in English. Vinney's parents were anxious for her to find a husband and a job, preferably in that order.

Our voyage companion Sohan had not yet found anybody compatible, so we introduced him to Vinney at Majitha. They met and talked for a while. The next day they wanted to talk some more, so Vinney and her mother came to visit at the Kandhari home in Amritsar. To Jhaiji's shock, Sohan and Vinney took off into the city for several hours together. "If Sohan elopes with Vinney, or attacks her, the Kandharis will be dishonoured," Jhaiji worried. Neither calamity came to pass, and in October, Sohan and Vinney became engaged in a traditional ceremony at Jindowal. They married on November 19 at Jullundur in a simple and dignified ceremony.

After the wedding, we joined other friends in Jindowal, including Darshan Khatkar, a well-known Naxalite who had survived the "fake encounters" — unauthorized killings by police or the armed forces — by which the government of the day killed scores of young men who were struggling to bring about a violent Maoist revolution. Darshan is a prominent Punjabi poet, and he remains an activist to this day. Fake encounters would become increasingly common during the 1980s in Punjab, and unfortunately they are still all too common in India today.

23 KASHMIR, the northwestern region of South Asia, once prompted the Mughal emperor Jahangir to say, "If there is heaven, it is here, it is here." The region has also been an undying bone of contention between Pakistan and India from the days of partition, with insurgency ebbing and flowing. But in 1977, its peace was intact and its beauty undimmed.

Rami and I took a short Indian Airlines flight from Delhi to the Kashmir Valley city of Srinagar. For the next three days we walked around Srinagar taking pictures. We saw many children working on the streets as janitors, or as helpers in stalls and shops. Grinding poverty sent these little human beings out to do adult work.

I fell in love with the Kashmiri *pharen*, the traditional full-sleeved woollen pullover worn by Kashmiris during their cold winters. In early times, Kashmiris would sometimes tie a bowl of hot coals around their waists under the *pharen*. I had a *pharen* tailored for myself. I wore it with a Kashmiri cap in Srinagar and later the rest of India, but I dared not try the hot coals. I feared self-immolation.

In the middle of Srinagar, the famous Dal Lake was an oasis of nature and divinity. In the mornings, parts of the lake and the old palace of the Maharaja of Kashmir were engulfed in fog that receded as the sun rose. On the northeast shore of the lake, the Shalimar Bagh (garden), originally built in the second century AD by a ruler of Kashmir and then added to by Emperor Jahangir in the sixteenth century, was exquisite. One night Rami and I took a trip on the lake, renting a boat with someone paddling. We witnessed the beauty of the lake and of the moon up in the heavens. The legendary beauty of Kashmir was indeed seductive. But when Rami snapped some quick photos of a boat lit by lanterns passing us, angry voices rose. We realized that the women in the boat should not have been photographed. Rami apologized, and calm descended; the men in the boat would not argue with a woman.

The next evening, when Rami and I bought tickets to a movie and entered the crowded lobby, there was not another woman in sight. A young male employee tapped my shoulder and asked that we remain with him, explaining that women usually came to the earlier shows. Inside the theatre, the young man seated us close to a couple with a young teenager in tow.

We decided to travel by bus from Srinagar to Jammu, a distance of 185 miles by road. We'd been told the bus service was safe, but once we got out of Srinagar and onto the winding road through the hills, it seemed very much touch and go. The valleys on either side were hundreds of feet deep, and there were no barriers to prevent vehicles from going over. Many times the wheels of the bus were sheer inches away from the road's eroding edges. But we did not plunge into the abyss, and once out of the hills the bus stopped at a place full of roadside *dhabas*. The bus driver selected one for us, and we gorged on the most delicious *pranthas* to our heart's content. I ate as if I had been reborn. The bus ride had felt like an eternity, during which I had suffered the indignity of floating in the purgatory of the bus; on the one side, down in the abyss, was hell, while on the other, the mountainside appeared to be ascending to the heavens. My feet once again on the ground, I had come back to earth.

We reached Jammu at nightfall. The ticket window at the railway station was crowded with people, making it total chaos. I thought we would never make our train for Amritsar. But confronted by a strong and determined woman, the crowd parted. Rami walked up to the window and returned with our tickets. We were on our way back to the plains. After staying a few days in Punjab with my father we headed to Agra, where we stayed for a few days with Rami's father's friends from the army.

Agra is known for the Taj Mahal, now a world heritage site, which was built by the Mughal Shah Jahan in memory of his favourite wife,

Mumtaz. A monument to their undying love, commissioned in 1632, it took over twenty years to complete. In 1977, Rami and I found the site in a state of significant neglect. Like most things related to India's heritage, the Taj Mahal had not escaped the notice of bureaucrats and politicians looking to line their pockets for their progeny. Rami remembered it being in a better state in the sixties, when she lived in a part of the nearby Agra Fort with her family while her father was stationed in the city with the army and she was attending college. Despite its decline, the Taj Mahal left its mark on us; its mixture of pre-Mughal and Mughal architecture makes the building an exquisite synthesis of the traditions of the day. I imagined it on a moonlit night, with the pristine Yamuna River flowing by; how its white marble must have soared in the midst of the surrounding lush green forest, its reflection dancing on the sparkling waves!

A few miles away at the Agra Fort, Rami showed me the place where, legend has it, Shah Jahan spent the last years of his life as the prisoner of his son Aurangzeb. From one spot in the tower where he'd been confined, the Taj was visible in all its majesty. The story has it that Shah Jahan was sustained by the view symbolizing the presence of Mumtaz in his life till he breathed his last.

Our next stop was Fatehpur Sikri, a city that served for some years as the capital established by the Mughal emperor Akbar, grandfather of Shah Jahan. Fatehpur Sikri was built from scratch from the red sandstone in the area, synthesizing the Islamic and the non-Islamic in its architecture and layout. Akbar even tried his hand at synthesizing religion, starting a new religion called Dīn-i Ilāhī. Like his new capital, his religion did not last long, but he became known as Akbar the Great for establishing a religiously liberal and relatively non-coercive empire.

Four years before, in 1973, a great Indian movie about the partition of India, *Garm Hawa* ("*Scorching Winds*") was released. It featured a melodious song that a worshipper is shown singing at the Sufi saint Salim Chisti's *dargah* (tomb) in Fatehpur Sikri. When Rami and I visited the *dargah*, to our pleasant surprise the very chap who had sung the song on screen was there performing it in person, busking at the *dargah.* After Fatehpur we returned to Delhi, where we visited monuments in and around the city such as the Red Fort, Qutab Minar and Humayun's Tomb, all reminiscent of the glory of India in days gone by.

Travelling back through Delhi, we caught the train to Lucknow, where some of Rami's father's army friends and their families were stationed. Lucknow is known, among other things, for the Nawabs (the regional native governors under the Mughals), the Urdu language, and the *bhulbhulayah*, or labyrinth. The labyrinth's Indian name literally means a place where one may get lost. I did, and Rami rescued me.

When we tried to buy train tickets to go from Lucknow to Bombay (now Mumbai), we were told none were available, even for the army quota the friend we'd been staying with was willing to use for us. As we stood wondering what to do, we spotted people going in and out of a door behind the ticketing window. We could see a person behind the ticket window who seemed to be exchanging tickets for money. Rami walked in through the door. She was dressed in a sharp Punjabi suit, wearing glasses, her purse over her shoulder. She has a presence I have seen rattle many men, and the man half-rose from his chair to greet her. She paid him the exact amount required for tickets to Bombay and received the tickets in return.

We boarded the train for the overnight trip, settling onto hard wooden sleepers. When dawn arrived, so did many more people, and the sleepers were folded back up into seats. The hawkers' chants of "chai *garm*" (hot tea) at rail stops along the way were interludes in the ongoing symphony of the moving train.

We conversed with the parade of passengers who got on and off the train, sitting with us on the benches. One young mother was carrying her only child, a boy who looked very much like Aseem, except not as chubby. By this point, Rami and I had been in India for a month and a half, and we were missing Pavel and Aseem. Communications then were still in the dark ages of land-line telephones, which most Indians did not have, and there were not many public phone facilities. We did not call home for the three months we were away, and every time we saw little kids we felt some measure of delinquent parents' guilt.

Somewhere between Lucknow and Bombay, we met a man who was on his way to a college to obtain his MBA. When he told me his name was J.J. Singh, I asked him for his full name. Jagat Jit Singh, he said. "The one who wins over the world?" I asked, referring to the meaning of his name. I was even blunter then than I am today. When I asked why he was hiding his beautiful name behind the initials, he looked shocked, and although I apologized for my rudeness, Rami rebuked me once he got off the train. The story did not end there. In the late nineties, when I was the Attorney General of British Columbia, I was walking through the rotunda of the legislature when a voice called my name twice in quick succession. I turned, but did not recognize the Indian man walking toward me at first. "I am Jagat Jit Singh," he said, slowly articulating his name. My face lit up, as did his; we both recalled our meeting on the train to Bombay twenty years earlier. We hugged, and he told me he had stopped using his initials.

Rami and I got off at the famous Victoria Terminus in Bombay. It was bustling with people talking loudly and walking in all directions, narrowly avoiding colliding with each other. The hawkers advertising their wares at the top of their lungs made it a perfect pandemonium. We took a cab to Rami's relatives' apartment in Koliwara, western Bombay, which was our base for the next few days.

J.P. Dixit was a professor at the renowned St. Xavier's College, and I had met this humble, likeable Indian leftist in the early seventies in Vancouver. He and his wife and young daughter accompanied us to Juhu Beach that afternoon. The beach was crowded with stalls hawking delicacies such as fried fish, fish pakoras and coconut water drunk directly from the shell through a straw. It was the first time I had ever drunk coconut juice that way, and it tasted like a revelation from the food gods. Juhu Beach is famous for the Bollywood stars who live there, but we did not spot any of them consorting with ordinary beachgoers. We did spot a man selling postcards, and we bought one with two monkeys on it to mail it to our two little "monkeys" at home. In affectionate moods, I would sometimes call Pavel and Aseem *bandar kisay thaan they*, "monkeys from someplace."

John Borst, my Vancouver friend from the farm workers' struggle, joined us in Bombay. Together, we paid a visit to the University of Bombay, Santa Cruz, where we met several teachers who were interested in the conditions of immigrants and aboriginal people in Canada. This was well before the satellite invasion and the onslaught of the internet and cell phones, and Indians were hungry for news and new ideas.

My friend Bakhshish from Bahowal, who had joined the Indian Army, was stationed not far from Bombay, in the city of Pune. As we waited at the Victoria Terminus, the first train to Pune came and went, because I could not bring myself to wrestle with all the other passengers to board it. When the next train came, the same thing happened, despite my trying to board that time. When the third train arrived, Rami and John lifted me over the other passengers, shoving me onto the train before they shoved on themselves. It was a sheer case of "if you can't beat them, join them." That asinine logic applies to most things in life in India, from corruption to the non-rules of the road.

Bakhshish was stunned to see us. It was obvious his family had not told him I had been asking after him. He now looked much older than his years; time and life had taken their toll on him. He was happy to see us, however, and he reminded me of what he used to say about our friendship during our childhood, comparing it to the true friendship of Lord Krishna and Sudama. I was neither king nor lord, and Bakhshish was no pauper, but we reminisced over chai for a long time.

John Borst returned with us to Dosanjh. John was an easygoing travel companion. He was undaunted by the clamorous Indian streets, and except for his skin colour he blended in completely. I toured him around Dosanjh, though in 1977 there were only a few shops along the canal between the village and the boys' high school, unlike the scores of them there today. One day he decided to stay behind in Dosanjh while Rami and I went on a day trip. In the company of Sarwan, one of the Dalits close to Chachaji, John explored village life, sharing meals with our Dalit friends. In the evening, he and Sarwan consumed some hooch. We had heard stories about hooch made in the villages rendering people blind, and I had forgotten to warn John to be cautious. Luckily, the next morning he could see as well as the day before.

On one of our several car trips to Amritsar, John accompanied us. The ride was uneventful until we reached Jandiala Guru. There were shops and people on either side of the road. It was a busy place. I pulled as far as I could to our side of the road to let an oncoming truck pass, but the truck took no steps to avoid a collision, and its right rear wheel scratched the rear wheel of our car. The truck carried on without stopping while I noted down its licence plate number. Several people, seeing me doing this, shouted at the truck driver that he had been caught. He slowed to a stop.

The truck driver and some other men, members of the Trucker's Union, I learned, proceeded to blame me for the accident. One of them claimed to be a union boss. Refusing to be intimidated, and noticing a police station nearby, I asked Rami to get a police officer to come to the site. As she set off, the union men changed their tune, saying, "Let's settle the matter now. If the police get involved, it may take years to settle." They must have been wondering, who is this *khadi*-clad, sandalled, bespectacled man, accompanied by a white man, who sends his wife to the police station?

The police officer who arrived also suggested we settle the matter without involving him. The driver paid me 350 rupees, and I prepared a receipt for him, signed it and handed it to the union boss along with my "Barrister and Solicitor" card from Canada. The boss yelled, "Had we known you were from Canada, we would not have given you a single *paisa*!" In hindsight, I regretted being so harsh with that poor truck driver. The affluent do not drive heavy freight trucks in India.

IN EARLY DECEMBER Rami and I saw John off for Canada before taking the train to Moradabad in Uttar Pradesh. From there we took a bus to Karanpur, where Papa had bought land just before his retirement from the military. We unlocked the empty home. The sadness that engulfs all vacant homes hung over this deserted home too. Rami looked for the clothing, china and other things her mother wanted her to carry back to Canada, but we found almost nothing she said she had left behind. Rami kept reassuring me — and herself, too, I am sure — how lively and vibrant the place had looked when she last saw it. It was now a shell that contained life only in the imagination.

My cousin, Banso Bhenji, lived in UP with her two children and her husband, who had been paralyzed in a farm accident. They owned land in the District of Lakhimpur Kheri at a place called Gaddanian Farm. It took several hours for us to reach Pilibhit by bus from Karanpur, and from there we took the train to Lakhimpur, arriving late at night. The next bit of the journey could be made only by bus, and the bus stop for Gaddanian Farm was another hour or so away. By now, we were exhausted and cold. We were travelling light. Rami, dressed in winter clothes, had a woollen shawl to help keep her warm, and I was wearing the Kashmiri cap and the *pharen* I had gotten stitched at Srinagar.

We finally reached the bus stop for Gaddanian Farm, a non-descript T-junction on the bus route. There was nothing to suggest it was a bus stop; it was on the say-so of the other passengers that we got off the bus. By now, it was almost midnight in a part of India we had never before been to; the place was no doubt rife with man-

24

eating animals. We had no flashlight or weapons, though I happened to be carrying a fancy walking stick. We walked for what seemed like a couple of miles before we saw the lights of some farmhouses. We yelled to see if there was anybody awake who could help us. Luckily, a man responded, and when he came closer, he realized we were two harmless lost souls. He knew of my cousin Banso and her family and helped get us to their home.

Banso Bhenji's husband, Sewa Singh, greeted us from his wheelchair with the same infectious smile he had worn the day he came to Dosanjh with the wedding party to marry Bhenji in 1963. Despite his disability, he and Bhenji had made a go of their lives and raised two beautiful children. Their son Bilhar still lives at Gaddanian Farm today, and their daughter has moved to England.

IN ONE OF OUR detours en route to Karanpur and Gaddanian Farm, we had visited Simla. In the parlance of the colonial rulers, it was a hill station. I had wanted to see where the *gora* sahibs had retreated during India's tropical summers. To India's shame, the rich and ruling classes of today mimic the sahibs of yore. Some of them still head to the hills with their servants, the Indian equivalent of the black slaves of the United States. These servants, who come generally from the so-called lower castes, are deprived of regular working hours, overtime pay, statutory holidays and any protection by health and safety regulations. Tragically, many of these "slaves" are also children. It is unforgivable for this situation to exist while governments continue turning a blind eye.

We persuaded Balwinder, a student of Rami's from the Dagshai school who had become a friend, along with his wife, Parmjit, to make that trek to Simla with us. Sohan and Vinney, now happily married, joined us too. We had reached Simla in a few hours, travelling in Balwinder's small Fiat. Simla turned out to be a relatively small city. The Mall, an open space with a church at one end, was tiny, and the streets were narrow. I did not see any of the splendour associated with imperial rule of years past. I was looking for the colonial glory that Simla had supposedly once been shrouded in, but my imagination failed me.

I bought a walking cane I saw in a shop window. Outside the shop, it broke the first time it hit the road. When I asked the owner to exchange it, he accused me of not knowing how to use a cane. I assured him I did, but he was not going to listen. I lost my temper and used a few choice words, accusing him of not stocking durable merchandise. Regional chauvinism got the better of me; I told him I was a Punjabi and I knew how to get a new cane out of him. The implied threat was childish on my part, but in the end he was a better man than me. Ignoring my rudeness, he agreed to sell me a more expensive cane if I paid the difference between its cost and that of the broken one. That was how I had come to have the beautiful and hardy cane I had with me as we searched for Banso Bhenji's farm that dark night. Today, I keep the cane in the entryway of our home in Vancouver. It reminds me of the smallness I am capable of.

I had had recurring thoughts of practising law in India, but three things stood in the way. First, in order to be able to practise law in Canada, I had become a Canadian citizen. (An amendment to the Charter of Rights and Freedoms would change that in 1985; now, one need not be a citizen of Canada to practise law in Canada, which I believe is wrong.) The second obstacle was my children, who were Canadians by birth. I was not sure I could give them the kind of hassle-free life in India that I could provide in Canada. Third, my legal education had been completed in Canada, and I would have to pore over Indian legal texts to become an Indian lawyer. That would affect my ability to earn a living right away. From Canada, I had corresponded with the two most prominent lawyers in India at the time, F.S. Nariman and Nani Palkhiwala, and while we were in India I spoke to both of them on the phone. Their response was very encouraging, and they both invited me to make an appointment with them once my plans were more certain. I did some research about the conditions of practice in Chandigarh, and I bought some law texts, but after thinking long and hard, I decided not to pursue the idea.

INDIA HAD BECOME more corrupt since I left, and the caste system bedevilled the country as it had for centuries. Slowly, though, the country was becoming more egalitarian. I had learned this lesson the very first week we were in Dosanjh, when Rami and I attended a girls' kabaddi tournament on the grounds of my old high school. My mother, on her wedding day, had been wrongly asked by the *naai* to do purdah from all men older than her husband, except her own siblings and close family. That meant she could literally not look older men in the eye or ever be treated as an equal of theirs. Once the practice started, it was difficult for her to change, lest she appeared arrogant. From the land of purdah, India had now become a land of schoolgirls playing the previously male contact sport of kabaddi in shorts and short-sleeved shirts in front of a predominantly male crowd.

It was time to return to Canada. I was not as sad or as torn as I had been in 1964, but as we bid goodbye to Banso Bhenji and Chachaji, I wrestled with the never-dying duality of both wanting to stay and wanting to leave. My eyes welled up, for I was once again tearing myself away from the land of my ancestors. But Pavel, Aseem and our siblings and extended families were beckoning us back to Canada. We had purchased some of the things we missed about India to take home with us: a small Kashmiri carpet, wooden and brass lamps, tables of etched and painted brass and wood, saris for Rami, and kurtas and Kashmiri caps for the children. Like most immigrants, we strove to recreate part of our lost Indian world in our home decor.

It was mid-December; Delhi was fairly cold and smoggy. On our last day in Delhi, I returned the car to my friend, and that would be the last time I ever drove in India. Some drivers like to boast of their ability to drive anywhere in the world after navigating the chaotic disorder of Indian roads, but I am not one of them.

PART 5

FIGHTING

EXTREMISM

25 BACK IN VANCOUVER, Pavel and Aseem were as happy to see us as we were to see them. Rami was scheduled to go back to work in the new year. I was in the office the day after we landed in Vancouver, even though it was a weekend. The bliss of our vacation was already fading. My desk was covered with stacked files, barely an inch of its surface visible. Life had taken over.

From then on, the work and the clients poured in. John Motiuk passed on some of his files to me, and my own cases were growing in number. I quickly became a trial lawyer, in court several times a week. Some mornings I was scheduled for two or three different courts in the Lower Mainland at the same time, and I had to juggle my appearances, asking the prosecutors and other lawyers to accommodate me. Many people who were facing discrimination and substandard working conditions came to me looking for help. Some I was able to help free of charge; others I would send to other legal colleagues with a social conscience.

The next B.C. election was expected to be called in late 1978 or early 1979. It would be the first election since the NDP had lost the government to the Social Credit party under Bill Bennett, and Dave Barrett was going to lead the party into the battle again. Since unseating Barrett, the Socreds had partially dismantled the human rights machinery in the province, in response to the demands of business. (Surprisingly, though, Bennett had not touched the Agricultural Land Reserve or public auto insurance under the Insurance Corporation of British Columbia.) The NDP had been branded by the media and the business elite as bad financial managers, and the right wing had succeeded in creating the impression that it was better at creating jobs and balancing budgets.

Rami and I were expecting our third child by now, and my law practice was still very new. We had a mortgage to pay off as well. Politics is a noble calling, but win or lose, a foray as a candidate into an election campaign is bound to have disruptive financial consequences. Running would mean being away from my law practice for three to four months. Even if I were elected, MLAs did not get great pay, and I knew it was next to impossible to be an MLA and run a law practice at the same time. Any way I looked at it, financially it was a lose-lose proposition.

Our home on 44th Avenue, purchased in 1968, was not big enough to meet the needs of our extended tribe, including Rami's parents Papa and Biji, who were now living with us. After looking around, we bought a "Vancouver Special" on East 52nd Avenue. It was architecturally mundane and aesthetically sterile, but it had lots of room and that's what we needed. It was close to the J.W. Sexsmith Elementary School for Pavel, and the Langara Golf Course, with over a mile of jogging track, was right next door. From 1978 to 2000, I would jog the Langara track almost every day.

As the election drums grew louder, some friends suggested I lend a hand in the then dual-member riding of Vancouver South. The annual general meeting of the NDP Constituency Association was coming up, and I was encouraged by some to get on the executive. I had never given any thought to that, although I had been a member of the party since 1968 and had volunteered in the 1968 by-election in Vancouver South and in the general elections of 1969, 1972 and 1975. Leading up to the federal election in 1974, Rami and I had canvassed door to door, with Pavel tucked in a backpack, for NDP candidate Denis Mulroney. Canvassing was much better than selling encyclopaedias; it meant arguing for a set of ideas and principles.

I agreed to run for the position of the secretary of the Vancouver South riding association and won without contest. Now came the hard part. The association had no money and no more than a small core of active volunteers, so I suggested we hold a low-cost fundraiser. We settled on Indian food. The ticket price was decidedly cheaper than we would have liked but the objective was not only to raise some money, but to have some fun and enhance the profile of the riding, as well. We were able to line up Dave Barrett and Grace MacInnis as the guests for the evening. Grace was a founding member of the CCF, the daughter of its founder, J.S. Woodsworth, and the first wife of its long-time MP Angus MacInnis. She was the first woman elected to the House of Commons in her own right rather than by succeeding her husband in a by-election. Our volunteers and supporters were inspired by Barrett the orator and MacInnis the legend.

My job with John Motiuk had become a question mark. I was bringing enough work into the firm to support my bid to become a partner. Motiuk was open to raising my salary and giving me a percentage of my billings, but he had a thriving practice with or without me; what he really needed was someone to simply share the load.

While I was deliberating, I received a call from Meb Pirani, a friend from law school. Meb wanted to set up a law practice and was looking for a partner. I was a trial lawyer. Meb was knowledgeable about business, and he understood corporate and commercial real estate law. We would be a natural fit for a two-lawyer firm.

We found an office on Victoria Drive near 43rd Avenue for our new law firm, Dosanjh & Pirani, Barristers & Solicitors. Telephone lines were installed with the number 604-327-6381. That number still rings today, at my sons' Dosanjh Law Group office. Our third son, Umber, was born on December 13, 1978. Once again, in our turbulent and fast-moving lives, Biji's presence lent stability and support. We opened the doors to our law office early in January 1979. At the end of the first month, after paying the overhead expenses, Meb and I each took home the princely sum of $250. But working for ourselves more than compensated for the temporary financial constraints.

John Motiuk and I parted company as good friends. We maintained contact, if somewhat irregularly, and for counsel and advice, he was always there. He also felt close enough to me to reach out in some difficult moments. When he died in 2010, I felt privileged to be able to pay him a fulsome tribute.

Our lives were soon to become even busier, if that was possible. One day a couple of old-timers from the NDP's Vancouver South riding association showed up at my office. They asked first of all that I keep our conversation confidential. I agreed, once they assured me what they wanted to propose was not illegal or unethical. What they wanted was for me to run for the NDP nomination as one of the two candidates for Vancouver South in the upcoming election. I silently wondered: Why the secrecy? Was it because so few persons of colour had ever run before, because they were ambivalent about associating themselves with my candidacy? Whatever the case, they left me to ponder the most pressing question. To run or not to run?

Rami did not want me to run, but she was prepared to help if I did. Meb would have preferred I didn't; our practice was still in its infancy. Luckily for us, Rami and Meb's wife Fariyal were both working full time, so our households would be able to survive. Among my extended family and friends, there was consensus in favour of me running. I thought about it long and hard. I felt I had experience as an immigrant activist that might be useful on the provincial stage. I would be able to give voice to the concerns of the unorganized, and of unprotected farm, domestic and janitorial workers. As well, my work with the provincial Human Rights Branch had prepared me to articulate general concerns about the need for equality.

Jim Duvall, a college instructor and long-time party activist, had decided to throw his hat into the ring for one of the two Vancouver South slots. He was not aware of any third party's interest in the nomination, and nor was I, so we decided to team up, hoping to coast to a nomination victory without a contest. The prospect of a provincial victory by the NDP did not look great, and the riding itself had been won by the CCF/NDP only twice in its history.

Jim thought he and I should sign some new people up as members in the riding even if the nomination was not contested. When we picked up the membership application forms from the NDP office at Boundary and Kingsway, we stumbled upon clear evidence that a huge sign-up campaign for Vancouver South was already underway. Leading it turned out to be my old friend Kehar Sekhon, himself a long-time NDP member and an IWA activist turned teacher. Kehar had told me he was not going to run for the nomination; I had in fact approached him to run in 1975 with the promise of my active support. The thought of contesting the nomination against him felt awkward. But by now I had told all my friends, family and supporters of my intention to run.

A large majority, though by no means all, of the long-time party activists in the area urged me to stay in the race. It was next to impossible to put the genie of my candidacy back in the bottle, and quitting would severely hurt my chances of ever running again.

I found myself between a rock and a hard place. I could not withdraw from the contest, but I hated the thought of a sign-up. Mass sign-ups have happened everywhere in Canada throughout the country's political history. In the not-too-distant past, Greeks, Italians and others had been targeted in some contested races. Now there were enough Indians in British Columbia to trigger a sign-up campaign in the Indian community. But much as I disliked the idea of a sign-up in Vancouver South, I detested the thought that a mass sign-up would be interpreted as a self-serving process of Indians joining the party merely to support other Indians. When Greeks, Italians or Indians signed up to support Anglo-Saxon or other "white" candidates, the sign-ups did not cause outrage and were not seen as "mass" at all. Sixteen years after 1979, Gordon Campbell would defeat Gordon Wilson for the leadership of the B.C. Liberal party with mass sign-ups in the Indian community. About seventeen years after that, Adrian Dix would defeat all other NDP candidates for the party's leadership with mass Indian sign-ups. No one questioned the legitimacy of their wins. "Mass" sign-ups were legitimate, in other words, unless the person running was part of that mass. In 1979, both Kehar and I were accused of "mass sign-ups" and of "herding cattle" — as if we were not signing up human beings.

Papa kept a record of the memberships and the money coming in. Rami and I went door to door to sign up people we knew personally. In 1979, Vancouver was home to the largest number of Indians in Canada, and most of them lived within the boundaries of Vancouver

South, which ran from Boundary Road to West Boulevard, with 49th Avenue as its northern boundary and the Fraser River as its southern one. Many of these people were recent immigrants and not yet citizens of Canada. That did not pose a problem for membership in the party, though they would not be eligible to vote in the election.

Party rules regarding membership for permanent residents of the country is an issue that excites passions and legitimate debate. Those in favour argue that permanent residents have made a commitment to Canada. Many of them or their dependents are taxpayers. Some may have applied for citizenship, and others may be waiting to apply once they have met the residency requirements. As such, permanent residents have a real stake in the selection of the political representative for the area. Opponents argue that, in a constitutional democracy, non-citizens should not have the right to determine the candidate citizens will be voting for.

By March, the ranks of the NDP membership in Vancouver South had swelled to over 1,100. The anti-Ujjal spin had been going on for weeks. I had been and probably still was a Maoist, argued Kehar's people, apparently not remembering that it was he who had introduced me to Hardial Bains and crew. The other charge against me was that I was a recent immigrant, and so an upstart. It was as if my eleven years in Canada, and my Canadian citizenship, did not matter; as if my advocacy of farm workers' rights, even at the risk of my own life, did not count. The fact that I lived under threats of harm from some farmers and contractors and had "contracts" out on my life seemingly did not matter. In the eyes of my critics, all of this made me "controversial." They said not a thing about Kehar. This happens in immigrant communities; we sometimes "eat our own." If someone who has my skin colour or speaks my language succeeds, there may be no room for me, goes the thought.

There is a double whammy in politics when one is unfairly targeted by one's "own community" and at the same time the political parties unofficially limit the number of candidates from particular groups, as if to say, "We already have enough of you." Nobody will admit it. It is all unofficial. But the backroom boys and political operatives of any party will admit they devise creative ways to achieve their ends without having the words "ethnicity" pass their lips. There is the green lighting of some candidates, allowing them to easily place their names in nomination. If all else fails, the signatures of the party leaders required for someone to appear on the ballot can be made an insurmountable hurdle. Political parties will claim they limit no one in this way. Recognize that for what it is: bunk.

During the seventies, many new immigrants from India treated Indians from the earlier immigration waves and their offspring with contempt. The men and women who had laboured hard in the lumber industry, doing back-breaking work at wages much less than their white colleagues earned, became the targets of derision among nouveau Canadians. The deriders were oblivious about how hard it had been for those who arrived first.

In the fight to achieve equality, the gurdwaras had served as temples of progress. Learning from their Canadian friends that to take off a hat or cap in a church meant respecting piety, many Sikhs began to pray bareheaded in front of the Guru Granth in the temples they had built. Still men of faith, most also became clean-shaven. Sikh, Hindu or Muslim, but above all Indian in their hearts, men and women adopted Canadian ways of dress as well. Women began to go to the temples wearing skirts, with scarves on their heads. When they sat down on the carpeted floor to enjoy the scriptures, they used the available clean linens to cover their legs. Most immigrants also made an effort to learn at least some English.

But all that strength and ability to integrate were seen by recent newcomers as weakness and folly. I witnessed the resulting hurt and sadness on the faces of many a pioneer. Occasionally, that hurt turned into anger and resentment. The community fractured, and a group of Sikhs abandoned the historic Ross Street Temple to build a temple on No. 5 Road in Richmond that was open to bareheaded worshippers.

The internal politics of an ethnic community are often quite ruthless. In recent electoral contests, the supporters of candidates of Indian origin have sometimes told Indian voters they should vote for candidate A or B because he or she is of a particular faith or caste or is from a particular district in India. It is disgusting. I faced similar parochialism in 1979. At one household Rami and I went to in Vancouver South, the Punjabi man who answered the door asked who else was running for the NDP nomination. I mentioned Setty Pendakur, a former TEAM (The Electors' Action Movement) city councillor, who was thinking about entering the race, as well as Kehar and Jim. The Punjabi man then gave us the rationale for his political preferences: he wouldn't consider voting for Jim when he had three Indians to pick from; he would have voted for Setty, a Maharashtrian from India, had there been no Punjabis running; he did not think Kehar good MLA material; hence his vote was mine. I did not want a vote arrived at with that reasoning, I told him point blank. When he did not comprehend my reaction, I explained I did not want his support as only the better of two Punjabi contestants; I wanted his vote only if he felt I would make a better representative than any of the others. I also let him know that if "whites" used the same yardstick that had resulted in his dismissal of Jim, no person of colour had a chance of being elected dog catcher anytime soon in Canada. The man wanted to become a member, and I signed him up. I don't know who he voted for, if he voted at all.

The nomination meeting was held a few days after the election writ was dropped. Each volunteer was asked to call the members they had signed up and get them out to the meeting. If the signers needed help with that, we drew from a pool of volunteers. Rami oversaw all this organizational work. Her job was made easier by the meticulous handwritten lists Papa had kept, showing the name, address and telephone number for each new member and each volunteer signer. I continued to meet and phone people personally to ensure they turned out to vote for me and Jim.

Kehar had asked Stan Persky, an author, journalist and teacher, to team up with him. It was a bolt from the blue to see Stan running for nomination in Vancouver South. Jim and I had no clue how Persky had come to join the race until the day of the nomination meeting in the John Oliver High School auditorium. As the auditorium filled up, I noticed a tall young man helping Kehar and guiding his effort. I was told the young man was Moe Sihota, then a UBC student. He and Kehar's family were close, I learned, and apparently Moe had promised Stan an easy run against me, a "controversial" — a term many Indians use as a negative attribute.

The auditorium was full almost to capacity, and the speaking order was determined by lots. I would be the last to speak. Persky, usually an inspiring orator, failed to connect with the crowd that evening. Kehar, an otherwise nice man, stumbled a few times; public speaking wasn't his strength. Jim spoke well, and the applause for him seemed a sign we might win the contest.

Then it was my turn to speak. John Borst had worked on my speech with me, and I had rehearsed it many times. I talked about the environment, mentioning the leak from the nuclear reactor at Three Mile Island that had happened just days before. I talked about the human rights record of the Socreds, as well as the need to do more in support of farm workers' rights. The theme of my speech, which I returned to every couple of sentences, was the need for change. From the applause that followed, I knew we had won the nomination. The balloting went off without a hitch, with the exception of one incident: Sohan Pooni noticed a known troublemaker from the Indian community grab a ballot container from a volunteer and make a run for the door. Sohan, an accomplished sprinter during his school years, caught up with him before he could bolt from the hall. His idea, I suppose, had been to invalidate the results by stealing the ballots. Despite this moment of drama, Jim and I won handsomely. Persky congratulated us on a fair win, but Kehar left abruptly.

In the adrenaline rush of our nomination victory, I had not noticed Rami looking sad. After the kids had gone to sleep and we were alone, her tears started flowing. She told me that in her heart of hearts she had been hoping I would lose the nomination, because she did not want me away from home. I assured her there was no danger of the NDP winning in Vancouver South, or in B.C. generally, in this election.

No sooner were Jim and I victorious than someone began phoning journalists to tell them that I was a closet Maoist and that the constituency would not be able to raise enough money for our campaign. Contrary to the fear-mongering, however, the money rolled in. Our friends and supporters collected over $13,000, a huge sum in those days, allowing Jim and me to run our campaign and conclude it with a healthy surplus. Since then, all my campaigns, including the NDP leadership campaign of 2000, have ended with a substantial surplus. The money has flowed in from supporters and friends all over Canada, often arriving unsolicited. I believe that if you stand up for something even in the face of fear and threats, countless others will stand with you.

Since I was one of the first people of colour to run for election in B.C., and the first to do so in Vancouver South, our campaign chair Frank Nolan suggested I should be at the doorstep canvassing the voters whenever I could. Usually I was paired with a woman, both to ensure a message of diversity and inclusion and because some people shied away from opening their doors to a man alone. People from all over the Lower Mainland supported my campaign. Terry Gidda raised funds and came in all the way from Mission to volunteer. Ajit Pooni drove his pick-up truck to the campaign office most days; in addition to raising and contributing funds, he helped put up election signs. Paul Gill, a grade twelve student from Killarney Secondary, was encouraged by his Law 12 teacher, Ron Joe, to learn about the world by volunteering in my campaign. Paul and many others worked day and night folding, mailing and delivering campaign leaflets and election day poll cards. Later, Paul became an NDP activist. We also heard from NDP campaigns elsewhere in B.C., places like Prince George and Victoria, that more Indians and people from other minorities were participating enthusiastically in their campaigns, as well.

No campaign is ever a completely happy experience. The 1979 campaign was no exception. At the doorstep, most constituents were friendly and receptive. Some doors didn't open, however, and others were opened and then rudely shut without a hello or without the resident asking why I was there. Some of it may have been my political stripe. The rest could be safely put down to my skin colour. I was ready for that. What I wasn't prepared for was the way our election signs were printed. In dual-member ridings, unless they included an incumbent, the candidates normally appeared on signs in alphabetical order, according to their last names. So when our signs arrived and read DUVALL DOSANJH, I was in a rage. We were already halfway through the campaign, so there was no time to change them. Thirty-five years later, "who done it" still remains a mystery.

A young journalist named Kevin Griffin followed the campaign in Vancouver South for *Vancouver* magazine, considering it a bellwether riding. When he interviewed me, Kevin asked about all the dirt being spread by those who hated my candidacy. But I had no proof about where most of it was coming from, only suspicions.

Jim and I ran a good campaign, even winning a couple of polls in the west side of our riding. That was a big surprise for the NDP on the otherwise barren west side. But we lost Vancouver South, and the party failed to take the province. Of his speech the night of the nomination in the John Oliver auditorium, Persky later said he felt he had been suddenly transported to India, addressing a meeting in Bombay, not Vancouver. He has always had a good-natured flair for the dramatic.

IN EARLY SEPTEMBER OF 1979 I had been trying to restore normalcy to our lives in the wake of the election. I was at the NDP convention when Bhaji had me paged from the stage. Chachaji was unwell in India, possibly having suffered a minor stroke. Immediately, my mind went back to our goodbye and the tears of December 1977 at the *khooh* in Dosanjh. After that, he had visited us in Canada, and we were awaiting his visit in the winter of '79. But now I left everything in the hands of Rami at home and Meb at the office and I took off for India the next day.

We had been told he was in a private hospital at Phagwara. I took the train from Delhi to Phagwara and went straight to the hospital. I was relieved to see him sitting up in bed, talking to his long-time politician friend Jagat Ram Soondh. I quickly made arrangements and within a few days he and I were in Vancouver, where he stayed a while. This was to be his last visit to Canada. He seemed fine and insisted on leaving for India, which he did after Christmas.

From India we received letters from him showing his handwriting to have deteriorated; his memory, too, was failing. Obviously he wasn't well, and Bhaji went to India to ensure he was properly cared for. After several weeks of hospitalization, he passed away. I went to India to attend the memorial service at Dosanjh at the *khooh*. Biraji had come from England. Chachaji's friends, including Dr. Lekh Raj and Jagat Ram Soondh, were there too. It wasn't until the service was over and the attendees had left that it sank in he was really gone. That night, on our beds under the stars at the *khooh*, Biraji, Bhaji and I reminisced for hours before dozing off.

Back in Canada law became my priority after losing the election. For the next four years, I devoted myself to my legal work, though other interests still demanded some of my energy. Law is a great tool for understanding the world, but I have never wanted to limit myself to simply searching for legal solutions to problems. Baba Bir Singh, Nanaji's uncle, was hanged by the British for rebelling. Nanaji spent years fighting the British. Chachaji rebelled against women's inequality by sending my mother to school in Dosanjh after their marriage, and my Biji revolted against Chachaji to vote for communists in our village in the early fifties. Mine is the soul of a rebel. Party discipline has been torturous on my soul; I have submitted to it only because without it, parliamentary democracy is rendered dysfunctional.

Once again, our finances were not in great shape. Bhaji and I had bought two lots next to each other in South Vancouver between Main and Fraser Streets. Our application to subdivide was turned down. It was disappointing, but we decided not to appeal to City Council. By this time, my friend Mike Harcourt was Vancouver's mayor. Another friend, Bill Yee, was a councillor, and I knew several other council members, including Darlene Marzari. Harcourt, Yee and Marzari had run on a slate, and during their campaign, in addition to donating some money, Rami and I made the basement of our house available to them as a campaign sub-office. I wanted no part of any perception that my brother or I might benefit in our zoning appeal because of whom I knew.

A friend who had moved to Winnipeg suggested we trade our two lots for an apartment block in Winnipeg, saying the building would pay for itself. The deal was made, but soon afterwards, he gave me the bad news: the apartment block was not paying for itself. Around the same time the friend sold me some lots in New Mexico. (When I became an MLA seven years later, Conflict of Interest Commissioner Ted Hughes suggested I should check before declaring these lots as assets to see whether they actually existed and were registered in my name. I discovered neither was the case.) The apartment matter was resolved by transferring the building back to its original owner. All in all, Bhaji and I lost a total of $100,000 in after-tax dollars in 1984. It took both of us some time to recover from this disaster, which was purely of my own making.

OVER THE CHRISTMAS holidays in 1982, my friend Amarjit Bains, Rami and I took a trip to California with Amarjit's daughter Kamal and our sons. Kamal was Pavel's age, and we mixed the fun of visiting Disneyland and Universal Studios in Southern California with a visit to the Yugantar Ashram in San Francisco. The ashram had been the office of the Hindustani Ghadar Party, which organized Indians on the West Coast of North America starting to fight for the independence of India. The Indian consulate in San Francisco kept the ashram closed except on certain holidays, including Republic Day and Indian Independence Day, but they agreed to open it for us. There were a few books stacked on the otherwise empty shelves, and some old artifacts lying around. It was depressing to see the neglect of this place, which ought to have been treated as a shrine to the memory of those who fought for our liberty. After B.K. Mitra, the Consul General of India in Vancouver, heard me talk about this at the temple upon my return, he was instrumental in having the ashram reopened regularly.

While we were in San Francisco, we drove to Yuba City to see Didar Bains, a Punjabi originally from Nanaji's area in the district of Hoshiarpur. Didar was now a big landholder in California, and he regularly donated large sums of money to temples around North America. I suggested he establish an endowment to fund research into the history of Indians in North America and into ways we could better integrate and succeed. Didar could have played a role in our collective success. Instead, in the mid-eighties after Operation Blue Star, he, like many others, flirted with Khalistan.

IN THE EARLY EIGHTIES, Indian cabbies were involved in a dispute with Yellow Cab, the largest taxi company in Vancouver. I had coffee with some of the drivers and attended a rally they'd organized at a small hall. I can no longer remember exactly what was said, but there were two men there I have never forgotten: Surjan Singh Gill and Talwinder Singh Parmar. I had first met Surjan Gill as a clean-shaven, suited and booted Canadian who owned a grocery store on the corner of 57th Avenue and Knight Street. Now he was a turbaned

Sikh with a flowing beard. The rally, though, was the first time I saw Talwinder. Wearing a turban and kurta, with a long, unshorn beard, he presented as an eighteenth-century Nihang, an orthodox Sikh member of a somewhat nomadic group of warriors, ever ready to fight for the guru. Talwinder made fiery comments at the hall. I can still remember his blistering zeal. The taxi dispute was soon resolved, but these two men would linger, playing a key role in events that have cast a tragic shadow over Canadian and Indian history.

Jagjit Singh Chauhan, a one-time cabinet minister in the Punjab government, made his home in the U.K. and the U.S. after 1970 but continued to visit Pakistan. Shortly after his first visit to the country in 1971, he published an advertisement in the *New York Times* calling for the establishment of an independent state for Sikhs. Chauhan founded the Council of Khalistan in the U.K., from which he issued currency, postage stamps and passports, styling himself the president of this imaginary state of Khalistan. In the late seventies, Chauhan visited Canada and preached separatism to the few who cared. At one time, both Talwinder Parmar and Surjan Gill were aligned with him. Surjan started presenting himself as an Ambassador of Khalistan in Canada.

The two men found an enthusiastic fellow traveller in Tara Hayer, who in 1978 had started publishing a Punjabi weekly, the *Indo-Canadian Times*. The paper soon became an unbridled mouthpiece of hatred and violence against India and Hindus. He fashioned the paper in language, tone and content after the acerbic and demeaning style of his acknowledged guru, Tarsem Purewal, whose *Des Pardes* was still published from London.

Tara had not always fanned the flames of hatred against Hindus and India. He had gone to the same high school I had in Dosanjh, and Chachaji was his Punjabi teacher in grade ten. In Vancouver, Tara started publishing a monthly literary magazine, *Watno Dur,* and eventually selling it to his friends. I contributed several hundred dollars to its purchase when I was a poor articling student. When satirist Sher Jang Jangali, an accomplished, left-leaning political and social satirist, visited Vancouver and expressed a desire to see me, Tara and his wife accompanied Sher to my home for dinner one evening. Sher had us in stitches with his political jokes.

As Tara was establishing the *Indo-Canadian Times,* Talwinder founded Babbar Khalsa International in Canada. It was in that capacity that Talwinder visited Pakistan and subsequently India in 1981, where he was accused of involvement in killing several police officers. Upon his return to Canada, he was hailed as a "living martyr" by Tara on the front page of his paper. Talwinder was charged in 1982 with the murders in India, but he was never extradited by Canada. Over time scores of others were glorified by Tara for perpetrating terror in Canada and India, including violent Khalistani jihadists in India.

WHILE ALL OF THIS was happening in the ranks of separatists in the seventies and eighties, something else was brewing in leftist circles. The separatists were oblivious to the racism exhibiting itself through attacks on Indo-Canadian individuals and homes. The leftists, who *were* alive to these issues, had challenges of their own with extremism. Some Indians who supported the Communist Party of India (Marxist), which had democratically elected governments in West Bengal and Kerala, established the East Indian Workers' Association (EIWA) because they did not see eye to eye with the Hardial Bains outfit or one of its offshoots, the East Indian Defence Committee (EIDC). The EIDC and its parent, the CPC-ML, by now owed allegiance to the corrupt Enver Hoxha of Albania, and they were blatantly violent and disruptive of any moderate efforts at combating racism in Canada. For them the state was the enemy, period: and anybody who worked with the state or lent it credence by participating in the mainstream was a traitor.

During the B.C. provincial election of 1979, the EIWA had called a meeting in South Vancouver, inviting me as the NDP candidate to speak on matters of equality and the farm workers' struggle. After I left, some EIDC men stormed the stage. A few people had to be taken to the hospital, and criminal charges ensued against the violent disruptors. EIWA persevered, struggling valiantly but peacefully to address the issues facing Indians, including racism and fundamentalism. The EIDC then targeted another group, the B.C. Organization to Fight Racism (BCOFR) at a rally against racism held to protest the recent murder of a young Indian man in Vancouver's Memorial South Park. The BCOFR was seen by the EIDC as a threat to its claim to secular leadership among Indians. Many in the BCOFR suffered injuries in the pitched battles that ensued.

During these years, racist incidents were increasing. The response by religious fundamentalists to the isolation and alienation in their new host countries was to look backwards to their home country, responding to both real and imagined grievances in the language of separateness. The anger and resentment they felt at their plight in Canada projected itself onto their roots in India, finding an outlet in the snake oil that was Khalistan, being sold by Jagjit Chauhan and his ilk. Chauhan was strategically and financially supported by the Inter-Services Intelligence of Pakistan, and Pakistan in turn was funded by U.S. dollars. It was a lethal mix.

The most active left-wing Indians in Canada were divided along ideological lines that originated in India. The Indians active in the BCOFR were led by Hari Sharma from SFU. Hardial Bains claimed to follow Charu Mazumdar, and Sharma claimed allegiance to Satya Narayan Singh; the men they followed were leaders of two main factions of the Naxalites in India in the sixties and seventies, whose main credo was the killing and "annihilation of class enemies." The EIWA, which had a lot more understanding of the reality in Canada, was itself prevented from playing the larger, more effective role it could have by the ideological straitjacket it had inherited from the Communist Party of India (Marxist). It is only in recent years that Indians formerly associated with the BCOFR and the EIWA have joined the mainstream NDP.

It is natural for immigrants to be influenced by what they learned in their countries of origin. And it is the luck of the draw whether immigrants arriving in a new country experience welcoming and integrative circumstances or isolationist and ghettoizing ones. Either way, it is possible for newcomers to free themselves from the shackles of inherited values and ideologies — or even to reform and mould those ideologies in order to become more effective citizens of their new countries. If one's frame of reference remains stuck in a different culture, continent or century, there is not much hope of making a positive difference.

The conditions in Canada's Indian community in the early 1980s were exacerbated by events in India, such as the murder of Gurbachan Singh Nirankari, head of the Nirankari sect and considered a heretic by orthodox Sikhs, and the arrest of Jarnail Singh Bhindranwale in relation to Lala Jagat Narain's murder. Lala, an old freedom fighter accused of fanning the flames of Hindu fanaticism and causing a communal divide in Punjab, was murdered on September 9, 1981. Bhindranwale, a fiery fundamentalist orator who urged Sikhs to revert to "pure Sikhism," was arrested in connection with the crime because he had been publicly critical of Lala. Bhindranwale was subsequently released, but within the traditional Sikh peasantry, he became a hero. All of this added fuel to the fire of separateness now burning in expatriate communities abroad, which began to be forcefully directed at India in the demand for the creation of a separate Sikh state. Alienated immigrants in the West had suddenly found an outlet for belonging and meaning.

THE 1983 B.C. ELECTION was called in the midst of severe economic woes. Premier Bill Bennett and his Social Credit government had responded to the worsening economic climate by passing a series of bills that weakened labour laws and social services and collectively came to be known as "the Restraint Program." Joyce Whitman and I were chosen by acclamation to be the NDP flagbearers in Vancouver South. The well-known NDP activist Margaret Birrell agreed to be our campaign manager. Joyce and I jumped into canvassing, going door to door, meeting people at coffee parties and attending all-candidates' meetings. Our Socred opponents were Stephen Rogers, whom I knew from the 1979 campaign, and Russ Fraser. Rogers, of B.C. Sugar fame and a trained pilot, was a witty rival. Fraser, a professional engineer, was friendly and courteous.

In the week leading up to the May 16 election, over three hundred people took the training to volunteer for us to pull the vote and scrutinize on election day. Things were going well for the party. Talk of victory was in the air. Then Dave Barrett, in an unscripted moment, promised to dismantle the Restraint Program. The Socreds took advantage of that, rebranding the NDP as the tax-and-spend party of "bad British Columbians." Our numbers started slipping, and on election day, half of our trained volunteers didn't show. The NDP lost the election, and Joyce and I were defeated.

With my personal loss in Vancouver South, I was free to pay more attention to the unhealthy tensions in the Indian community. The government in Delhi was not making it easier for secular and progressive Indians to respond to the poison regularly spewed by the likes of Tara and Talwinder. Bungling by Delhi in Punjab had turned Jarnail Singh Bhindranwale into a hero. And then there was the Foreign Exchange Regulation Act (FERA), passed in 1974 and enforced beginning in 1982, which made it mandatory for all foreign citizens to declare annually to the Reserve Bank of India their ownership of any agricultural land in India. Even hereditary land was not exempt from this requirement. People seethed with anger as they streamed into my office to sign the declarations under oath.

I helped them, but I didn't file my own declaration. It troubled me that a law intended for foreign investors was criminalizing me, an Indian by birth, for not filing an annual declaration for the land I had inherited from my father. I advised the Consul General of India in Vancouver of my view that Delhi needed to revisit the law, and I issued a call for non-compliance among the millions of Indians abroad. In Punjabi, I called the law *Naa Tameeli Lehar*, meaning Non-Compliance Movement, and I circulated a petition asking the government of India to reverse this law for Indians and our descendants abroad, at least in so far as it applied to hereditary agricultural land. Separatist elements called the legislation anti-Sikh, ignoring the glaring fact that millions of other Indians living abroad were affected just as much.

Papa and family had bought a house in South Vancouver, so Rami and I no longer needed so much space. We put our house on the market, and the older home we then purchased on East 50th Avenue had character and an ambience that exemplified *raunak*, liveliness, for me. We had it recarpeted and moved in. I did some simple renovations in the basement, turning it into a study area with desks for the kids and a library for my ever-increasing book collection. I painted different areas of the house and papered others, with the boys pitching in. Rami loved it; finally I was paying some attention to our household. We would spend six years in that old house, and it is still the one we most fondly remember.

27 DOGMA, be it political or religious, suffocates me. In an atmosphere of competing attempts to control the narrative, emotions can easily come to the boil. A poisonous cocktail of rumours, killings and political posturing was exacerbating tensions in Punjab in the early 1980s. Never before in the history of India had Sikhs and Hindus harboured hatred for each other. In places like Amritsar, particularly at the Golden Temple, Hindus worshipped alongside Sikhs, and the same was true at Hindu *mandirs* across Punjab. Sikhs had been bestowed a distinct identity by Gobind Singh, the tenth Guru, and that identity had enjoyed honour and respect among Hindus as well. Growing up in India, I had never felt excluded or devalued by other Indians. The language wars of the 1950s had less to do with faith and more to do with the pursuit of political power. Hindus and Sikhs had always intermarried, and in many Hindu families, the first-born male was ordained a Sikh so he could become part of the Khalsa — the Guru's army. And yet now the relationship between the two groups was boiling over, not just with mistrust, but with the stirrings of violence.

The predominantly Sikh party Akali Dal had started a Dharam Yudh Morcha, "Battle of Righteousness," calling for more autonomy for Punjab. The wording of the party's 1973 manifesto, the Anandpur Sahib Resolution, stressed more autonomy for Sikhs than for Hindus in Punjab. Perhaps that is why the Akalis soft-pedalled their resolution in the ensuing years, placing more emphasis on autonomy and rights for the state than on the personal and collective rights for Sikhs that had been mentioned in the Resolution. In this way, the Akali Dal had avoided being seen as separatist, which, in any event, it wasn't. When Bhindranwale was asked to be part of the *Yudh* in the early 1980s, however, he interpreted the contents of the Resolution literally. Sitting in the Nanak Niwas, a residential quarter in the Golden Temple precinct, he became the de facto leader of the *Yudh*.

The peaceful approach taken by the moderate Harchand Singh Longowal, president of the Akali Dal, was no match for Bhindranwale's fiery oratory. Bhindranwale started amassing weapons in the Harimandir Sahib, the Golden Temple, in Amritsar, along with several hundred militant followers, and violence escalated outside. There were numerous murders in Punjab, and many of the perpetrators were known to be hiding in temples across the state. The government did not move to flush them out, justly fearing a backlash from Sikhs. Bhindranwale's influence and power grew, and so did the fear of him in the minds of many, including the police. In April 1983, a senior police officer, Avtar Singh Atwal, was shot in broad daylight just outside the Harimandir. Not a soul touched his body. It took the police two hours to show up on the scene, and they came only after Bhindranwale had given his permission. In the toxic brew of fundamentalism, opportunism by the Akalis and the Congress party, and the scheming and searing incompetence of the police and intelligence personnel, no one seemed to be minding the store to maintain peace and harmony. The politicians fiddled while Punjab burned.

As if to jolt the government out of its willful stupor, unidentified gunmen, in a daring attack in broad daylight, pulled six Hindus off a bus in Punjab and shot them dead on October 6, 1983. The chief minister of Punjab, Darbara Singh, resigned. Emergency rule that would last almost a decade was imposed in Punjab. There are many theories about why things went so terribly wrong. Bhindranwale had become an international celebrity for some Sikhs, and a thorn in Indira Gandhi's side. According to Tavleen Singh, a prominent Indian journalist/columnist, Bhindranwale was seen as a prophet of hate by some and a messiah by others.

The situation in Punjab was tense, and India was facing serious challenges on the road to long-expected but still-elusive prosperity. In the stagnant aftermath of the 1960s' Green Revolution, which had attempted to increase agricultural yields in India through the use of modern methods and technology, Punjabi youth were despondent, and they were ripe for extremist influence both from the Left and religious fundamentalists. It was not surprising to see disgruntled Maoists joining the ranks of Bhindranwale's supporters inside the Harimandir.

AT THE END OF 1983, in this environment of simmering tension, rampant violence and boiling hate, Rami and I decided to visit India with our three sons. With our shorn hair, wearing neither turbans nor karas, the steel bracelets considered one of the five Ks for Sikhs, I wondered if we would simply be asking for trouble. We might be asked to get off the train or the bus to be slaughtered as Hindus. It was a tough choice even for a stubborn son of a gun like me. But Umber, our youngest, was about to turn five, and Rami felt it was as good a time as any to acquaint our boys with the country of their ancestors. When I bumped into B.K. Mitra, the Indian Consul, at a friend's home in Vancouver, he suggested I arrange a meeting with Mrs. Gandhi to share my concerns about the land declarations as well as the overall deteriorating environment in the Indo-Canadian community. I had never considered that the prime minister of India would be interested in hearing from me, but Mitra felt Mrs. Gandhi needed to hear how what was happening in India was having a deleterious impact on harmony among Indians abroad. He secured me a date and time for the meeting.

We took off for India before the Christmas break. At the Vancouver airport, we saw a sizeable crowd of Indians, Didar Bains of Yuba City among them, surging forward, bending and touching the ground in front of and behind the robed and bearded cult figure Meehan Singh. Unlike us, the proletarian riffraff, he travelled first class. The subservient prostration was a sorry scene right out of the tyrants' courts of the Middle Ages.

Sohan, Vinney and their sons Sagar and Suraj accompanied us to India, and we spent a couple of nights in London with my nephew, also named Sagar, who had two sons around the same age as ours.

As we were exiting the plane in Delhi, I spotted Indian cabinet minister Buta Singh standing with garlands in his hands and several red-beaconed Mercedes in toe. The recipient of this welcome was none other than Meehan Singh: the state welcoming the Godman. To this day in India, politicians prostrate themselves before Godmen to win the votes of their followers; the Godmen exact their price by illegally occupying public lands and exercising extralegal influence.

I would later hear a story about Meehan that made him at least momentarily endearing. After Operation Blue Star in June 1984, some hot-headed Sikh youth, angry at the government of India for the bloodshed at the Golden Temple, approached Meehan to enlist his support for the separate state of Khalistan. Apparently Meehan thought for a moment and then said, "A lion needs a large kingdom. If all the lions are confined to one cage, they will kill and devour each other." "Singh" means lion. I am told the young men left speechless. Heads held high, Sikhs continue to live all over India.

We spent some days in Delhi with the Gills, Joginder and Guddi, in the government high-rise block where they lived with their two daughters. In Delhi, the three-wheeler rickshaws and the tuk-tuks decorated with ornate paintings and phrases written in praise of gods or celebrities were a big attraction for our sons. They had never seen crowds of that size, and the noise was amplified by the chaotic traffic with its constantly honking horns. Wherever we travelled, I felt the boys taking in the scenes, the dirt and the beauty of their roots. Among the many faces of India, most looked like theirs. They no longer stood out as they did at their elementary school back home.

In Agra, we stayed with Rami's college friend Inderjit, whose father was good friends with Papa from their days in the army. Inderjit and her husband owned a pharmacy in Agra, and they had a son Pavel's age and a younger daughter. Inderjit's son took a day off from school to be the kids' very knowledgeable guide to the Taj Mahal. Next we drove to Fatehpur Sikri. It was impossible to visit the site without being first regaled by the monkeys of Sikri, trained captives who made money for their owners by playing tricks to entertain kids and adults alike. It was impossible not to see the cruelty of this to the animals, but human hunger was the alternative, given the grinding poverty of the monkeys' minders and their children. The kids were entertained. I ached. I paid the minder. I was guilty too.

Past the monkeys lay the remains of the wondrous new city the great Mughal emperor Akbar built. Though we had been here six years before, I was excited to share this place with my children. Here was the amphitheatre where classical singers must have sung, philosophers surely debated and religious scholars engaged. Sikri was the capital for the new world of unity that Akbar had wanted to create. Ashoka took a similarly bold leap toward peace after a bloody war. Two millennia after Ashoka and four centuries after Akbar, Mahatma Gandhi shared with India a similar vision and a path out of colonialism. India killed him.

Most of our trips within Punjab and our trips back to Delhi and Agra were by rail. The journeys by train were a novelty for our sons and Umber was mesmerized by the rhythmical chants of the *chaiwalas* — tea hawkers — at the railway stations along the way.

From Delhi we went to Kanpur by taxi to see Manjit Singh, one of Rami's Dagshai students. His family owned a thriving business in the city, and he had two young daughters. Theirs was a happy home, bustling with people. Manjit now lives in Australia; during the riots that followed Indira Gandhi's assassination, the family lost their business and feared for their lives.

Had he been alive, Chachaji would have been happy to see his grandchildren visit his village, his country, his ancestors' soil. Humble as it was, this was his slice of the earth.

At Amritsar, we stayed again with the Kandharis. Meshi's sons Ashu and Manu and their first cousin Salil still lived with the joint family under the watchful eye of Jhaiji. The Dosanjh and the Kandhari boys flew kites from the roof all day, descending only to eat and drink. The days were sunny and warm, while the nights were cold.

One day we decided to go to the Harimandir. Jhaiji was worried, because there had been recent violence outside and inside the complex. An *Indian Express* journalist had been stabbed in the Harimandir. With our shorn hair, somebody might harm us, believing us to be Hindus. It was sad to see fear in the hearts of this Hindu family who regularly prayed at the Harimandir before praying at the nearby Hindu temple, the Durgiana Mandir, as many non-Sikhs did in Amritsar.

On the way to the Harimandir we visited the Jallianwala Bagh. As we walked, I shared with our sons the story of how troops under Brigadier-General Reginald Dyer had shot unarmed Indians at a peaceful meeting against British rule held here on Vaisakhi in 1919. The meeting was in support of the freedom of India and the release of imprisoned leaders such as Saifuddin Kitchlew. Vaisakhi is an important day for Sikhs as well as Hindus, who also believe that Guru Gobind Singh ordained the Khalsa to protect Hindus from the tyranny of Aurangzeb. Among those attending the meeting, then, there were many pilgrims who may have visited the Harimandir that day before coming to the meeting. Dyer stationed fifty Gurkhas — Nepali soldiers — at the narrow entrance to the Bagh, and without warning ordered that they fire into the peaceful, unarmed crowd. Firing continued uninterrupted for ten minutes, after which one thousand lay dead and five hundred were injured. Shortly after the massacre, the Jallianwala Bagh was made into a shrine, and the Mahatma came to honour the memory of true martyrs killed for their peaceful devotions and political beliefs.

After our walk of respect in the Bagh, we continued on to the Harimandir. We entered the complex shoeless, our heads covered. As we made our way along the Parikrama, the marbled walkway by the water-filled *sarovar* ("pool of nectar") surrounding the sanctum sanctorum, I felt I belonged to all faiths. I could have entered through any of the four gates that invite and embrace diversity from four corners of the world. Why was this place important? one of my sons asked. I thought of my own father: the only time in my life that Chachaji ever asked me to go to gurdwara was the day before I left for Delhi. Paying my respect to the holy scriptures at the gurdwara was paying respect to my elders. "It is your ancestors' place," said I, finding no better answer than that. It was our ancestors' place as were, too, the Durgiana Mandir and the historic mosques and Christian churches of India. Our ancestors converted to different faiths; our shared genealogy, culture and history make us indivisible.

Having paid our respects in the sanctum sanctorum, we exited and stood facing the Akal Takhat, the highest of the five Sikh seats of authority for temporal decisions. The Akal Takhat was built by the sixth Guru, Hargobind. Some believed that by placing the Akal Takhat in the Harimandir complex, the Guru meant to ensure an interlocking of state and religion. Others argue that he built the Akal Takhat to be separate and distinct from the sanctum sanctorum, as were the legendary swords — Miri, the temporal, and Piri, the spiritual — that the Guru carried. The debate is endless. In the current environment in Sikh circles, the temporal and the spiritual are not seen as divisible, but the separation of religion and state is the sin qua non of a true and stable democracy.

I was eager to see Harchand Singh Longowal. A temple employee said he would probably be at the residential complex, the Nanak Niwas, at the opposite end of the Harimandir complex. I knew Bhindranwale had first set up his headquarters there too, though by now he was safely ensconced in the Akal Takhat. Every morning, with a long traditional spear in hand and his retinue in tow, Bhindranwale would walk over to the complex's Langar building, across from the Nanak Niwas. Most of the day, seated on the roof of the Langar building, he held court for visitors from far and wide, including TV and radio journalists. He was always coy about a separate country for Sikhs, saying it was up to the government to decide whether "it wants to keep us part of India" while betraying his leanings toward the alternative. He argued for Sikhs to return to their roots, the ways of living that prevailed at the time of the last Guru. In his long robe, less-than-modern Sikh turban and longish Sikh underwear, carrying the kind of spear with which the last Guru was known to have struck many enemies, Bhindranwale presented himself as the man who could return Sikhs to the purity and principles of old.

The Langar building is named for its *langar*, the free communal kitchen that is estimated to feed up to one hundred thousand people every day. After a meal there, Rami and I and our three sons had taken just a few steps toward the Nanak Niwas when we came upon three men in their late teens or early twenties carrying three rifles each: one on each shoulder and the third in hand. Aseem asked me why they had guns in the temple. We never saw those in Canada, he said. I suggested he walk up to the men and ask them. He did, in English. From a few feet away, I translated. The armed men said the tenth Guru Gobind Singh had ordained them to be armed. Of course, but only with a sword, said I. They countered that this was a different age, and the Khalsa had the right to modern arms. Shocked by their argument, I demanded, why stop at guns? Why not have tanks and AK-47s and all the modern and deadly paraphernalia of war? At that, they immediately asked where I was from. I told them I was an Indian Punjabi from a Sikh family. Did I know of Sant Bhindranwale? they asked. Had I met him? "Sant," like the English word "saint," with which it shares its Indo-Aryan roots, is an honorific title for persons known for their religiosity and spirituality. Of course I knew of Bhindranwale, I told them, but I had not met him. I was looking forward to seeing Sant Longowal instead.

At that, the young men became even more insistent that I meet Bhindranwale. I hesitated; I was no fan of Bhindranwale's fundamentalist approach. But without understanding Bhindranwale, I realized, one could not get a complete picture of the tragic tensions simmering in Punjab. I relented and climbed up the stairs to the top of the Langar building. The boys and I were frisked. Rami was allowed to keep her camera.

The image I had in my mind of Bhindranwale was of a menacing giant of a man. The media stories had worked their magic on me much as they had on other unsuspecting souls. In person, he was nothing of the kind. He was tallish, of slender build. Physically, nothing about him stood out as dangerous or frightening.

The five of us were ushered to a place in front. Bhindranwale was resting with the traditional round pillows at his back. A couple of men who had just come in bowed to touch his feet before sitting down. I had been taught never to prostrate, and to bow only in front of the sacred books and monuments of all faiths. We bid him *Sat Sri Akal* — "God is the ultimate truth" — with folded hands, as was the custom in Punjab. Rows of sandbags were piled two- and three-high around the rooftop, and many men stood behind Bhindranwale in a semi-circle, most of them armed with bayoneted guns. Standing on the periphery of the audience were more men, some also carrying guns. It seemed like a scene from another world, not from the India I knew.

Bhindranwale's rhetoric was in full flight. He was angry at the Akalis, who supported Longowal. He was unhappy he was not being given as many gun licences as the Akalis. Nirlep Kaur, a one-time Akali MP, had said that if Bhindranwale wanted to preach the ancient purity of Sikhism to the masses *outside* the Harimandir complex, she would accompany him. Her comments clearly stung him; he did not take kindly to the charge that he should remove himself from the Harimandir. For several minutes he spewed forth poison, calling her names I had never heard a public figure use in reference to a woman, let alone a former MP.

During his vitriolic tirade, Bhindranwale remained seated. Then he stood up and addressed me. I did not know why, of the more than one hundred people in the audience, he felt the need to speak to me. At that moment, I noticed my card, which I had given to the young men earlier upon being asked my name, in the hands of a man who had been whispering into Bhindranwale's ear. It felt strange to be addressed by someone who was seen by many as a messiah while he was standing and I was sitting. I urged him to sit down to talk to me. He insisted on standing. I then asked if he had any objection to me sitting as I listened to him; he said he had none.

Bhindranwale began by acknowledging my Sikh roots and then expounded on what it meant to be a Sikh disciple of Guru Gobind Singh: observing the five strictures, including unshorn hair. For him, he said, the guru-disciple relationship was like that of a parent and child. A child should not be rebelliously inquisitive about the dictates of the parent, he believed. He was promoting not just blind faith but blind submission. Since the last master had been male and I was of Sikh religious heritage, according to Bhindranwale Guru Gobind Singh was my father, and I must never ignore my father's commandments. He sought a promise from me to grow my hair and don a turban back in Canada. I politely refused.

I explained that the tension and the political conflict in Punjab were negatively affecting our lives in Canada. Extremist language directed at Hindus in the diaspora filled the pages of some Canadian newspapers; hate was in the air. If growing my hair and tying a turban would make even an iota of positive difference, I would be happy to do it, I said, but it wouldn't. We should move on to discuss the really important matters, I suggested, such as economic development in Punjab and the threatened amity between Sikhs and Hindus.

Bhindranwale remained obsessed with my hair. It symbolized my betrayal of Father Guru Gobind Singh, he said. I did not consider my Father my father; therefore, I was not his son. "What do we call one not the son of his father?" he thundered. I did not want to offer my belief that all children are legitimate, so I turned the question back to him. Bastard, he said. I replied that I was a human being in pursuit of becoming a better human being. I used the Punjabi words *insaan* and *admi*. No matter the father, none is a bastard, I told him.

By this point, I had been talking to Bhindranwale for over half an hour. I was tired of sitting with my calves curled under me, and I repositioned myself spreading my lower limbs a bit and leaning backwards. Not pleased with my earlier response, Bhindranwale threw the next question at me: "Do you know what an *admi* is?" Again, I urged him to answer his own question. To my utter shock, he said *"Aa dum, admi:* if one breathes, one is a human being. If one is no longer breathing, one is not *admi* but a corpse." There was deafening silence around us. Pointing to some of his numerous followers who clutched bayoneted guns, he added, "If one of them slashes your throat you will no longer breathe; not be an *admi*."

His men seemed to enjoy their messiah's apparent invincibility. In Punjab, no one wanted to be on his bad side. It was a common belief that anyone who argued with Bhindranwale publicly was in mortal danger; those who dared had ended up dead. His disciples stood silent as he played the lion among the sheep.

A woman sitting behind Rami cautioned her to stop me from arguing with "Babaji Bhindranwale." It could be very dangerous for Babuji, she said, using the word for a clean-shaven man to refer to me. Rami touched my hand to pass on the warning I had overheard. After a long pause for effect, Bhindranwale reasoned again that "one can only be an *admi* if one is true to one's Father and therefore is not a bastard" and reiterated his appeal for me to grow my hair. Growing one's hair was like seeding one's own land and waiting for the crop to grow, he said. I replied with a bit of a smile that the thing to do would be to take some sleeping pills and wake up after a couple of weeks with a half-decent beard and a head ready for a turban. To use the English words "sleeping pills" while talking to someone who did not understand English was terribly unthinking of me. Bhindranwale turned to the chap who held my business card, saying, "Vakil Sahib (Mr. Lawyer), what did Babuji say?" When the *vakil* explained, Bhindranwale accused me of mocking him.

Finally, I responded. Far from making fun of him, I said, I had listened to him with respect, even when he had made a threat about me being slashed with a bayonet and ending up as a corpse. I had listened to him call me a bastard. What do you know about me? I asked him. Nothing other than how I look and dress. I know a bit about religion, perhaps more than you think. I had told him repeatedly I couldn't make a false promise, I said. Despite that he had continued to press the point. Threats did not work on me, I informed him. I had a very proud heritage. My Nanaji, Jathedar Moola Singh Bains, had been the leader of the *jatha* that freed Harimandir from the *mahants* and the leader of forty Sikhs tasked with freeing the Takht Keshgarh Sahib Gurdwara from them. He had fought for the independence of the country and spent years in British jails and under severe restrictions. I was his eldest daughter's son. My father had been a practising Sikh all his life. Neither he nor my Nanaji had ever known fear. I too was never afraid, I told Bhindranwale. One cannot live a life in fear.

When I stopped, there was stunned silence. Bhindranwale stood silently, perhaps in disbelief.

To pierce the tension, I asked whether I could take his picture. He would agree, he said, if I promised to grow my hair. I argued it would not cost me anything except my conscience to make a false promise;

he would never know if I kept it. He claimed he would always know about anything going on anywhere in the world. If that was his belief, how could I argue with it? I got up, bid him *Sat Sri Akal* and turned to go. His men respectfully escorted us down to the ground floor.

It was well into the afternoon by then. I was exhausted, but we walked over to the Nanak Niwas nonetheless. Longowal was not in, but I could see him at 3:00 PM the next day. He was a public figure, and I had written to him requesting a meeting. We were only a few feet from the gate when we noticed four Sikhs, each with a six-foot spear. Rami asked me aloud what was going through my mind: were we safe? The men smiled as we approached. They were curious as to how my encounter with Bhindranwale had gone, they said, since they had left partway through. I told them it was inconclusive, and they laughed.

The Kandharis were waiting anxiously when we arrived at home later than expected. Jhaiji had warned me I would be suspect in the complex since I was not turbaned. Things had come to that! The Harimandir of the four gates welcoming all was now in the grip of the forces of exclusion. The place of spiritual ecstasy was under a siege of fear. The source of love was under threat from the hate abroad in the land of Nanak, Buddha and Gandhi. The echo of eternal bliss emanating from the Harimandir was being drowned out by cries of violence all over Punjab. The Harimandir of peace was witness to a Dharam Yudh in danger of being overrun by *adharam*, irreligiosity.

My sons' Punjabi was poor enough that they had not understood the frightening exchange between their father and Bhindranwale. They did not say much except to comment on his gun-toting disciples. The consensus was that they were a scary-looking lot.

The next day Rami and I set out to see Longowal, paying a visit first to Durgiana Mandir. Again, Jhaiji did not want us to go. People had been murdered on the buses, and even police officers were not safe. As we returned to the Harimandir that afternoon, I wondered why I was so worried about the brewing storm when the leaders in Punjab and the rest of the country did not seem to care. Who was looking out for the public and the national interest?

The Durgiana Mandir, Punjab's most important Hindu temple, is quite close to the Harimandir. It is believed that Lord Rama's spouse, Sita, and their sons Luv and Kush spent time in Amritsar, and that the Mandir was designed to be similar to the Harimandir. Historically, Guru Gobind Singh traced Guru Nanak's and his own antecedents to Luv and Kush respectively, connecting himself directly to Lord Rama, one of the two most revered deities of Hinduism, the other being Lord Krishna. Punjab had a robust legacy of Hindus, Muslims and Sikhs living in harmony; it was only during partition that it was overwhelmed by communal hatred and violence.

Sant Longowal was a short man with the aura of a devout and saintly being. Rami and I walked into his small, unadorned room in the Nanak Niwas and sat down. He was alone, attended by no hangers-on, and we talked for several hours. I told him of my upcoming meeting with Indira. He was anxious for a peaceful resolution of the demands of his Dharam Yudh Morcha, which for all practical purposes had been hijacked by Bhindranwale. Bhindranwale had at first been invited into the Nanak Niwas by Longowal to assist in the agitation, but now they were at loggerheads. Longowal disagreed with the violence unleashed by Bhindranwale's followers. There had been sporadic exchanges of gunfire between their respective supporters in the complex. There were rumours that Bhindranwale had been empowered by the Congress government to create problems in the ranks of the Akalis, and as a result Longowal did not know how much he could trust Indira. We shared our fears about the violence getting out of hand. He did not ask whether I was a Sikh or not, but as Rami and I begged leave, I told him I was from a Sikh family. "If we keep meeting like this, you may change your mind and grow your beard and hair, eventually donning a turban," he said. He truly deserved the honorific Sant.

IT WAS ALMOST TIME to return to Vancouver. The only piece of business left was the meeting with Indira Gandhi. I had never met the prime minister of any country, though I had met various premiers of B.C. and the legendary Partap Singh Kairon when he was chief minister of Punjab, as well as Darbara Singh. How did one prepare for a meeting with the prime minister of the largest democracy in the world? I realized I needed to be crystal clear about the purpose of the meeting from the outset.

Back in New Delhi, Rami and I took a cab to the South Block, the office of the prime minister. It was a bright sunny day, with no whisper of the monstrous dark clouds gathering over Punjab. The majestic South and North Blocks housed the most important departments of the government, and up ahead was the Rashtrapati Bhavan, the presidential house then occupied by the former chief minister of Punjab, Gyani Zail Singh. The sight was not reassuring; the chap whose role as president was to be the ultimate check and balance for a powerful prime minister was known to be a puppet of the Gandhi clan. When he was the minister of home affairs in Mrs. Gandhi's cabinet, the president had picked up young Sanjay Gandhi's sandals behind him, pledging to clean the family's toilets if he was ever asked. He was sycophancy personified, quietly tolerated as if he were an imbecile king and treated like a slave of yore. Not surprisingly, there were allegations that it was Zail Singh who had been instrumental in Bhindranwale's empowerment.

The Blocks and the presidential house had been built by the British Empire to strike awe into the hearts of the subjugated. The men of the empire had physically disappeared, but their legacy lived on in the colonial practices handed down to the kaala sahibs. Being received by the PM was a process that seemed no less imperious than that imposed by the British viceroys before Independence. We had to go through several layers of bureaucracy before we were ushered into her presence. The sardarji at the reception desk was pleasant enough. We were escorted past him and seated in a large room before being greeted by someone I recognized as R.K. Dhawan, one of the four or five men rumoured to guard and control access to Mrs. Gandhi. Next we were led by M.L. Fotedar, who was from the same circle of loyalists as Dhawan, into the PM's office, passing first through the office of the tall, lanky P.C. Alexander, then the prime minister's principal secretary. Mrs. Gandhi was clad in her usual sari. She rose to greet Rami and me, shaking our hands, and then we were seated across the table from her.

When Mrs. Gandhi had visited Vancouver several years earlier, I had stood alongside other demonstrators outside a reception at the Queen Elizabeth Theatre to call for the release of the several thousand political prisoners being held in India without trial, some even without formal charges, under draconian laws dating from the British days. I was no longer shouting from the sidelines. Now I was meeting the prime minister on issues that touched the very existence of India as a united and secular country.

She started by asking me about the situation in Canada. She reminisced about her father and grandfather and their role in the freedom movement, and I told her about Baba Bir Singh Bahowal and Nanaji meeting with Nehru and Gandhi on several occasions, including at the Mahilpur political conference in July 1936.

I shared my concerns about the state of affairs in Canada, relating them to what was happening in Punjab. I apprised her of my encounter with Bhindranwale, my discussion with Longowal and the extreme volatility in Punjab, urging her to work for a speedy and peaceful resolution to the Dharam Yudh Morcha. She described at some length the discussions she was having with Akali Dal representatives and some intermediaries. She was aware, she said, of the serious tensions existing between the Longowal-led Akali Dal and Bhindranwale, the de facto leader of the Morcha with his radical followers. She expressed a degree of helplessness as well; she was not able to conclusively negotiate in Punjab, she said, since no one was able to negotiate a deal and make it stick without some other group agitating for more or a new deal altogether.

She had obviously been well briefed, because she herself raised the Foreign Exchange Regulation Act and the way its skewed implementation was affecting ordinary Indians abroad who held agricultural lands in India. The Act was never intended to be applied that way, she said, and she promised that declarations would no longer be required from the Indian diaspora. She kept her promise, and the practice of seeking the hated declarations ended.

RAMI HAD DECIDED TO STAY on in India with her friend Prabha Khosla to do more travelling. She dropped us off at the airport. My sons and I checked in and waited to board our flight, which was delayed because of the smog/fog in Delhi.

28

Dilli dil hai hindustan ka ("Delhi is India's heart"), goes the saying. It is a city of legends, and indeed India's heart — but it is a most polluted heart. In winter in some parts of India, including Delhi, despite the sun being so powerful, one does not see it for days.

Finally we were told our flight would not leave until the next morning. We were bussed along with the other passengers to the newly built Centaur Hotel near the airport. Putting Pavel in charge of a sound-asleep Umber and a barely awake Aseem, I joined the line in the hotel lobby to check in. It took over forty-five minutes for the crowded counters to be cleared, but those who patiently await their turn are sometimes rewarded. The only room available was the Presidential Suite, so the four of us ascended in a shiny glass elevator to the huge, bright suite. Umber was carried in asleep. Aseem kept his eyes open just long enough to be helped into the suite by Pavel. Soon all four of us were snoring.

In the morning, my sons were in awe of our surroundings. They had not yet seen this kind of wealth in India. The Presidential Suite at the Centaur was palatial compared to the "slumming" we had enjoyed while staying with relatives and friends.

In the hotel restaurant for breakfast, the receptionist sat us at a table for four. There were not many people waiting for service when we got there, but several others came in behind us, and most of them were white. They were served while we waited. No one approached us to offer coffee or tea or to take our order. Finally I called a waiter over and asked him to get the manager. I tried to speak Hindi to the manager, but he responded in English. I reminded him the whites no longer ruled India, and we were all equal now. It was 1984, thirty-seven years after Independence, yet in my mother country I was being treated as a second-class citizen. We finally got our breakfast and left without leaving a tip on the table. On our way out, a tall *sardarji* sentry bent and saluted us, as he did to everyone. I was so embarrassed, I went and hugged him. He appeared to be in a state of shock. In his life as a sentry, he was used to being ignored. I felt my whole being in rebellion against the colonial slavery that was still so pervasive.

Our trip to India had been an eventful one, not merely because by sheer coincidence I had met the triumvirate of Bhindranwale, Longowal and Indira, but because that troika would unleash forces that would influence the fate of Punjab and India for years to come, sealing our fates in turn. As I flew back with Pavel, Aseem and Umber, I wondered what this trip would mean to them.

I had thought nothing of bringing the boys back to Canada without their mother, but I soon realized it was difficult managing them singlehandedly while getting back to my law practice. I was used to making lunches and doing dishes, but I hadn't (and still haven't) learned to cook. Biji always kept us supplied with delicious dals and rotis. A less expected obstacle was the clock radio alarm. My relationship with gadgetry is one of absolute ignorance, and it took me several tries to figure out how to set the alarm that got us up on time every morning. Once Rami returned, so did normalcy.

I WAS BUSY WITH my law practice, but still struggling for some direction in my life. Restlessness was my constant companion. Law was a way of making a living, but it didn't satisfy me on a deeper level. I thought perhaps writing fiction would give me that.

I enrolled in a typing class at Langara College, which was less than a hundred yards from our home. I struggled to master an IBM Selectric. At the office, our secretaries were agile masters of these latest machines: their machines obeyed them. Mine did not obey me.

My clumsy peasant fingers would not do the walking I willed them to. I am ordinarily a stubborn soul, but this time I readily quit. I will do my writing longhand, I told myself. But as I haltingly started writing in English, I remembered Pablo Neruda's less-than-charitable characterization of a man trying to write about matters of the heart and soul in anything other than his mother tongue. I felt rebuked. My progress was slow and unsteady. I wrote a few hundred words of prose, wondering if it was an essay or a story. I decided I needed to read more before unleashing my fiction on the world.

Perhaps my inability to write in English is simply a complex I have. It is definitely an immigrant thing. I am an ESL kid. I find it impossible to write poetry in English, though I can readily string together a few lines of it in Punjabi or Hindi. Even now, after fifty years of living, breathing and toiling in the English-speaking world, in matters of the heart and soul, I feel more at ease in Punjabi and Hindi. I find political discussions more difficult in Punjabi than in English, though. That is as it should be, after half a century of politicking in English.

I may have given up on writing fiction, but what happened next in India could scarcely have been imagined even by an accomplished war novelist. Through World War I and II, the armies had avoided bombing or attacking religious places unless they were being used as sanctuaries by the opposing army. Now, the Indian Army was storming the Harimandir complex to flush out Bhindranwale, who was holed up there with dangerous weapons. He and his supporters were not a foreign army; they were a motley crew of gun-toting fanatics and extremists. For the Congress party and the Akalis, though, Bhindranwale was Frankenstein's monster.

The internal politics of a country are rarely resolved by a violent military intervention. India, as the melding of a million minorities, is one of the least likely countries in which violence should be considered a viable response to political issues involving a religious minority. In a nutshell, the situation with Bhindranwale was not a military problem warranting or requiring a military solution.

Nonetheless, Operation Blue Star was launched by Indira Gandhi on June 1, 1984. There were several pitched battles between Bhindranwale's men and the military, and at one point the army blocked all the entrances to the Harimandir. The four gates stood silent: the gates that the boys, Rami and I had used barely five months earlier were no longer open to visitors. The army suffered heavy fire from the variety of weapons in the hands of the separatists, who were well fortified in their positions. By the time the operation was over, the army suffered eighty-three deaths and over two hundred casualties. The official tally of civilian deaths was 492, Bhindranwale among them; unofficial figures placed the number of civilian dead much higher.

The bloodshed spread throughout the state of Punjab as government forces combed the countryside for any remaining radical followers of Bhindranwale. The violence at the hands of militants would continue for several years afterwards, as would the often violent and extralegal response of the police.

As the news broke about Operation Blue Star, our visit to the temple replayed like a movie in my head. I thought especially of those young men who had taken us up to see Bhindranwale, in whom they had placed their faith and in whose hands their lives rested. Their innocence and their wasted youth haunted me, as did fears about the future of Punjab. What I had seen of Bhindranwale had not endeared him to me, but I had spent an hour of my life with him under very tense circumstances. As the depth of the tragedy sunk in, I kept seeing his face. What could have been going through his mind as the military closed in? Was he fearless? Was he afraid at all or perhaps more afraid of surrendering than of dying, especially if the former meant an unbearable loss of face? The tragedy at the temple and the loss of life brought sadness to my heart.

Alarmingly, in Canada, recent and not-so-recent immigrants from Punjab were increasingly being swept up in the virulent campaign of hate led by the likes of Talwinder Parmar. Tara Hayer was the disseminator-in-chief of their venom. In Punjab the Dharam Yudh Morcha was no war of independence. The clumsily crafted Anandpur

Resolution that formed the basis of this movement for more autonomy had become a tool for easy religious bigotry. If there had ever been any clarity in the cause, it was now lost in a cacophony of voices creating utter confusion.

In this tragic drama being played out on the soil of India and fifteen thousand miles away on the western coast of Canada, the unsuspecting Sikhs were being played for suckers. First-generation immigrants were easily exploited by unscrupulous politicians and salesmen promoting the snake oil of separatism. They were led to believe that the religion they now held even dearer than before was under attack "back home." The Indian Army going into Harimandir was a cataclysm for the Sikhs. For those living abroad, the distance and sense of helplessness they felt made it even worse. In its aftermath, fundamentalism and a sense of "religious persecution" guaranteed the damage would be long-lasting.

On June 10, thousands of angry Sikhs demonstrated in cities across the western world, including Canada. Vancouver saw a large demonstration, perhaps second only to the one in London, England. Effigies of Indira Gandhi were burned. Some men and women expressed their condemnation of her actions by shouting anti-India slogans and carrying pro-Khalistani placards.

The President of India broadcast an appeal for calm, peace and harmony among Indians, and in Vancouver that appeal was broadcast by Sushma Sardana Dutta on radio and TV. The appeal was also published by Promod Puri in his English weekly, the *Link*. Following that, unidentified callers threatened to kidnap Sushma's only child, ten-year-old Sudhir. The *Link* was forcibly removed from shops by people calling themselves by different organizational names, one being the Dashmesh Regiment. I had never seen such hate in my life. Anger I could understand. But hate? And directed against a whole faith community, the Hindus, who had never thought Sikhs were strangers to them?

I approached the committee of gurdwara executives who had started meeting on a regular basis to deal with the ongoing turmoil.

I expressed my concerns regarding the journalistic freedom of Sushma and Promod and the threats made against Sarabjit Singh Khurana, a Vancouver merchant who had displayed a newspaper at one of his outlets that the enforcers had mandated be boycotted. Most members of the committee saw sense in my arguments, but they didn't have the courage to uphold freedom. They had mortgaged their good sense and judgement to their own fears and the anger of the enforcers. Khurana had accompanied me to the meeting, and on the way home I drove him to his store in the Punjabi Market at East 49th and Main. He asked to be dropped off out back to ensure the militant enforcers of hate and conformity would not harass me. We live only once, I told him, and we couldn't afford to die every moment of every day in fear of bullies.

A few days later, several temple committees held a meeting at the Ross Street Temple. They invited me and a few others from the community who were not organizationally or otherwise involved in any temple. Some people spoke in anger, while many urged restraint. I called for a revisiting of our heritage of peace as a multi-faith community from multi-faith India in a multi-faith Canada. I deplored the threats being issued to broadcasters and individuals who should be free to express themselves; we needed to conduct ourselves within the four corners of the law and respect civil liberties, I argued. I was walking out of the meeting when Santa Singh Tatlay, who was out on parole after being convicted of murder in hiring a killer to blow up his own daughter and son-in-law, stopped me to ask, "What is illegal about what is happening in the community?" Unable to resist, I replied, "You know all about the illegal stuff," and turned to go.

I HAD BEEN WRITING a weekly column in the *Link* for several years on happenings in the community, and occasionally Promod and I played tennis at the courts in the Langara Golf Course. We spoke of our shared concern about the fanatics who were continuing to organize disruptive, violent and separatist activities in the Lower Mainland. Their reign of terror was palpable. Various groups of out-of-control, angry men lashed out at even the hint of any disagreement with them. In true Bhindranwale style, they circulated hit lists of their perceived enemies. Written and telephone threats were issued in the names of new and unheard-of groups. When Vancouver's Akali Singh Sikh Society refused to support the call for an independent Sikh state in India, separatists threatened to forcibly raise the flag of Khalistan at the Skeena Street temple. The separatists were led by Manmohan Singh of the Sikh Students' Federation — by no means to be confused with the renowned economist Manmohan Singh, who in 2004 would become India's prime minister. The Akali Singh Sikh Society obtained an injunction against the leadership of the Federation, banning them and others from hoisting the separatist flag.

Every year on August 15, the anniversary of India's independence, the Indian Consulate in Vancouver celebrated by raising the Indian flag in the morning and holding a reception in the evening. Attendance at both events was by invitation only. As in years gone by, I had been invited to both events, and as usual I was not planning to go. That summer, I was also laid up with a bad back, for the first time since my back operation in 1970. One day while I was getting ready to go to court, my back had gone into spasm, and I had fallen to the floor in pain. An ambulance took me to the hospital, where they injected painkillers. Bhaji built me a hard wooden platform for bed rest, and I

29

lived on a diet of painkillers and muscle relaxants in our small family room. I was often in a fog, losing track of the time and the days.

The morning of August 15, I was dozing off and on and thinking about Indians' struggle to achieve equality in Canada. Disenfranchisement in 1907; exclusionary legislation like the direct passage law and the requirement that all those arriving from India have $200 with them; the *Komagata Maru* tragedy, in which 376 Indians were prevented from entering Canada. After a few violent episodes and long years of lobbying, Indians in Canada had regained the right to vote in 1947; it was not until 1953 that they won the right to enter professions such as law and medicine. The Chinese in Canada faced similar, and perhaps even more draconian, measures, such as the head tax that lasted over four decades. These things had happened because of the inherent racism in the society of the time and the demands by organized labour to keep "cheap" labour out of Canada.

In the 1940s and 1950s, unions, particularly the International Woodworkers of America, had a significant membership of Indians. This provided a vehicle for political awakening and participation. When I arrived in Vancouver in 1968, the Indian community, though small, was well integrated into Canadian life. Now, with all the threats and violence, we were turning on ourselves. Even prior to June 1984, the actions of some Sikh fundamentalists were calling into question the maturity of the community.

Stuck in bed that morning, I turned on the television to keep myself occupied. The lead story on the BCTV noon news showed a group of angry Sikhs attacking the Indian tricolour-raising ceremony at the home of the Consul General of India in West Vancouver. A police helicopter could be seen circling above as the Indian flag was pulled down and set on fire; unruly demonstrators battled with police on the ground.

Prior to June 1984, some of us had written off the few members of the Babbar Khalsa in Canada as relatively harmless clowns and nincompoops. How tragically wrong we were. In the wake of the armed assault on the Harimandir complex, the angry Sikh diaspora provided unlimited recruits for the likes of the Babbar Khalsa and dozens of other violent outfits that mushroomed overnight.

Freedom of expression for those who disagreed with the extremists was already under threat. In what had metamorphosed into a religious crusade by Bhindranwale to maintain the "purity and honour" of Sikhism, some elements of the diaspora mistakenly saw parallels between the Dharam Yudh of 1984 and the 1914 call of the Ghadar movement for Indians living in North America to return home to free India from the yoke of British rule. The intention of the 1914 movement was to establish a secular, free and united India. The Ghadar movement had never been about one religion.

By burning the Indian tricolour in Canada, the 1984 demonstrators were only hurting the Sikhs' standing in India. Scores of Sikhs had struggled and died alongside other Indians to defeat the mighty British Empire. For Indians, the tricolour had a kind of sanctity; it symbolized the love of country, a love second to none. These demonstrators were distorting our position in the minds of other Canadians; they were also undermining the place the Sikhs occupied in free India. The Khalistanis were stifling free speech and wrongly claiming that the majority of Sikhs abroad supported the dismemberment of India.

I began to rethink my plan not to attend the Independence Day ceremonies. Normally, I rarely went to these events. The cocktail-circuit types populated them in large numbers, not out of support for India or the idea of India, but simply because they were something to do, and there was always good scotch. But I knew many of these same types would stay away from that evening's reception, not wanting to be seen at the residence where that morning Khalistani demonstrators had burned the tricolour. I, on the other hand, decided on principle to go. The anger of ordinary Sikhs over the assault on the Harimandir complex was understandable, but none of the temples here, nor the many militant outfits that had cropped up overnight, sought to channel that anger into constructive work for peace in Punjab. No one seemed worried about the families of the men and women who'd been killed on both sides in the Harimandir complex. Many angry men would have agreed with Ontario journalist T. Sher Singh when he said of the assault on the Harimandir complex, "If I had an atomic bomb, I would like to drop it on Delhi."

Rami and I, along with my walking stick, strode into the residence of the Consul General in full view of the placard-carrying demonstrators. There was a heavy police presence there, too. The mood of the smaller-than-usual crowd inside was sombre but determined: determined to ensure that we remained sensitive to the feelings of the Sikhs, but also determined to ensure that no one be allowed to permanently scar the close relationships among all the people of the Indian diaspora, particularly between Sikhs and Hindus at that moment. Violent demonstrations and hate speech as natural responses to religious injury were medieval; they had no place in a modern democratic state.

Above all, I did not want the desecrators of the Harimandir or the torchers of the tricolour to speak for me. The voices calling for the dismemberment of India did not represent me. If I remained silent, I would never be able to look myself in the mirror again. I was a human rights activist. I had fought for the rights of domestic, janitorial and farm workers. I had twice attempted to be elected to the legislature of B.C. How could I represent people if I did not have the courage to speak up for peace in the face of violence and intimidation? I remembered Mahatma Gandhi's dictum: An eye for an eye will make the whole world blind. Silence was no longer an option.

I talked to many friends at the reception and shared my angst with some. Rami and I also bumped into Nancy Knickerbocker, who had taught ESL with Rami and was now a journalist with the *Vancouver Sun*. Nancy wondered aloud if anyone would dare to speak out against the hate and violence the demonstrators represented. I asked for her card. As we rode home, Rami asked if I was thinking of saying something publicly. I have never been able to hide much from her.

I returned to work on August 20. By then, I had written a background statement about why I felt the need to speak out now. I had prepared a summary of it that I could hand to the press if I decided to go public, and a longer version I could read at the press conference I was now mulling over.

I had already decided that silence was not an option. I had no hesitation or second thoughts. But I wanted to be sure I was ready for the brutal assaults that I knew would follow — on my integrity, my reputation, and perhaps even my person. More importantly, I wanted to shield my sons from the negative fallout of my actions by changing the school they attended. Their current school, J.W. Sexsmith Elementary, had lots of Indian children, and some of them might take hurtful attitudes to school that would affect my sons.

I called a press conference at my law office on Victoria Drive for the early afternoon of August 23. Three reporters showed up: a journalist from radio station CKNW whose name I can't recall, Nancy Knickerbocker from the *Vancouver Sun,* and Gillian Findlay of CBC TV. My position was simple. All Sikhs had been hurt as a result of the politics in Punjab, the actions and omissions of Bhindranwale, and the government of India bringing us to the tragic spectacle of Operation Blue Star. I had had time to talk to many Sikhs, I told the reporters. Many of them wanted to speak out but remained silent out of fear. I did not blame them. I had personally witnessed the anger of the separatists and their reckless antics. What had transpired at the consular residence on the morning of Indian Independence Day worried me deeply as a Canadian and as an Indian, I said. The Indian community had come a long way during its ninety years in Canada, and the separatists threatened to take us back into the dark ages. I wanted other Canadians to know that the vast majority of the Sikhs were peaceful. That, despite their silence, most did not support the violence or the demand for Khalistan. Above all, on behalf of the silent majority of Sikhs, I wanted to reclaim the right to free expression. I no longer wanted the reign of intimidation by separatists to go unchallenged. With my comments, I wanted to shout from the rooftops: I fear not a soul. My soul has no fear.

On June 12, I had written a letter to Mrs. Gandhi, reminding her that during our meeting in January 1984, "I indicated to you that

Indians living abroad would like to see a just, reasonable and peaceful political solution to the issues of Punjab. I am deeply saddened and hurt that that was not to be. It disturbed me that the government sought a solution with guns and ignored the fact that a bullet shot into the Temple is as desecrating as one shot from inside the Temple." I further expressed the hope that one day the wounds and divisions could be healed. She replied in a letter dated June 30, saying, among other things, "Few decisions in my long political career were sadder than the one to ask our troops to clear the terrorist hideout which was misusing the refuge of the Golden Temple. It was a duty I owed to the nation and the Sikh community itself." In August, as I spoke out, I wrote an open letter to the Sikhs of the world. My letter and her reply were extensively reported in the newspapers in India and abroad at the time.

FOLLOWING MY PRESS CONFERENCE, a deluge of threats came in: telephone calls, messages left on our home answering machine, notes delivered to my law office or pushed through our mail slot at home. The oldest Sikh organization in Canada, the Khalsa Diwan Society, then controlled by Khalistanis, issued a press release branding me a "heretic." The *Vancouver Sun,* however, received a few calls commending my remarks and the *Sun*'s responsible coverage, and I got dozens of calls myself from all across Canada supporting my views and my right to express them.

The war of words kicked off by my press conference would continue into the late eighties. I did not seek to silence the separatists. They were entitled to their views, and they had the right to express them. But I made it clear I would not brook any interference with my right to express my views, and I would not let go unchallenged the Khalistani claim that most Sikhs supported their cause and their violence. I knew that was not the case.

Promod Puri wrote me a letter telling me he could no longer publish my weekly column in the *Link.* He was frightened of those who now controlled the narrative of the Sikhs. He made a flimsy excuse for his capitulation to intimidation, arguing that I expected my column to receive more prominence than he was prepared to give it. The excuse was a figment of his imagination — I had never expressed a desire for special treatment in his paper. From then on, he became my critic. Years later, one woman in the community shared with me her view that in our culture, any ethical compromises made to protect one's livelihood or family are forgivable sins. I disagreed, but if it is true, this is one more explanation for the deep-rooted and ubiquitous corruption in India.

In mid-September, Harjit Atwal, who was later charged but subsequently acquitted in the attempted assassination of the visiting Punjabi minister Malkiat Singh Sidhu near Campbell River, asked to bring some friends to meet with me. I spoke to Rami about it, and we decided to invite Joyce Whitman to be present, so that no one could distort the discussion if it were to be reported publicly.

Five or six men showed up at our home at the appointed time. I recognized most of them from the melee at the Indian Consul's home on Independence Day. A man named Amar Sandhu did most of the talking. He argued that I was wrong to oppose Khalistan and also said I should not be speaking to the mainstream English media; I should confine my views to the Punjabi media. If I did that, he said, my opponents would not be as concerned or as angry.

I was taken aback by their suggestion. I was a Canadian, I said, and no community was an island unto itself. What a few hotheads were doing in Canada under the pretext of legitimate anger at the government of India was a Canadian issue, even if the government of the day and most Canadians did not yet see it that way. Canadian politicians were not yet concerned that some brown guys were fighting each other in the streets of Vancouver over something that had happened fifteen thousand miles away in Amritsar, a word most of them could not pronounce. And yet I believed it *was* their concern.

Harjit Atwal and his friends wanted to neuter my views. In the Indian community of the time, it was easy to suffocate the voices within. The voices from outside were harder to silence through threats of violence. I told them their biggest supporter and mouthpiece, Tara Hayer, would not last a single day if he wrote in English what he so routinely did with impunity in Punjabi.

Community activist Charan Gill had publicly denounced both the harebrained idea of Khalistan and Bhindranwale's tactics. When he was inundated with threats, he issued a retraction to get the angry men to go away. The only man left standing publicly against the violence among my friends in the Indian community was Darshan Gill, who published and edited *Canada Darpan* — "*darpan*" meaning mirror — a Punjabi weekly that promoted secularism, amity among faiths, non-violence, and the integrity of India. His paper was the sole progressive voice in the Punjabi media. Darshan published *Canada Darpan* from 1982 to 1990, during the most difficult years. Even when his home was firebombed, he unwaveringly stood his ground. *Lokta*, an irregular publication put out by friends of the Communist Party of India (Marxist) in the East Indian Workers' Association, made its presence felt, too. Sadly, neither publication was enough to counter the poison spewed by Tara Hayer's *Indo-Canadian Times*.

Another courageous voice of the time belonged to my friend Gurcharan Rampuri, a renowned Punjabi poet. At the beginning of October 1984, he wrote a piece in Punjabi in *Canada Darpan* analyzing how Bhindranwale, an articulate populist perhaps mesmerized by his own rhetoric, unwittingly created the conditions that led to Operation Blue Star. Tara Hayer, already angry at Rampuri for truthfully describing Tara in an interview with a Punjabi daily as a staunch supporter of Sikh separatist militancy and violence in Canada, fanned the flames against him by distorted reporting on Gurcharan's piece. A few days later, on his way to work, Rampuri was ambushed in downtown Vancouver by unknown Sikh assailants. He escaped with minor but painful injuries. Tara Hayer gleefully reported on the attack, suggesting what had happened to Rampuri was not severe enough. Progressive Sikhs and others, however, organized a meeting to condemn the dastardly attack against Rampuri. Wearing the Charter of Rights and Freedoms as a placard, I was one of the speakers at the meeting.

THE ATTACK ON RAMPURI came just days before the next bombshell: the assassination of Indira Gandhi at the hands of her own bodyguards. I learned of the news late in the evening of October 31, 1984, in a telephone call from Sohan Pooni. I was concerned immediately about what her killers might not have anticipated: violent reactions from Indians to the killing of the prime minister. The Sikh bodyguards had served Mrs. Gandhi loyally for some time. After Operation Blue Star, her senior staff had replaced the bodyguards out of an abundance of caution, but Mrs. Gandhi had ordered them reinstated.

Her murder was not completely unexpected for those who knew of the "tradition" of revenge against "desecrators" of the holy Harimandir. In her letter to me, she had maintained that her actions were taken to protect the sanctity of Harimandir and the national interest of India. After Operation Blue Star, she had visited the Harimandir, because she recognized the anger among Sikhs and felt it important to make a gesture of atonement and reconciliation. But the flames of revenge consuming her assassins had finally engulfed her.

That night I went to bed worried to death about the fallout on the ground in India. We were woken at midnight by the noise of drums and slogans in the Punjabi Market a block and a half away. To my horror, I learned the next day that the demonstrators had been celebrating the killing of Indira Gandhi. The Himalaya Restaurant, owned by Kewal Pabla, had opened its doors to allow *laddoos*, Indian sweets, to be distributed. In television footage of the night's chaos, I spotted one of my own close relatives celebrating the death of the prime minister of the country he had left behind. In times of crisis, we are often touched, even if not directly overcome, by insanity.

The killing of Indira Gandhi made sense only to those swirling in the vortex of revenge. In the feudal culture of India, revenge was the only currency that "honour" accepted. A whole community should not have paid for the vengeful attack on the prime minister, but that is exactly what happened. Thousands of Sikhs were massacred in cities across India. The Congress government failed to protect its citizens; in fact, there is abundant evidence that the complete inaction on the part of the police and military for several days was deliberate. In some instances, the police, instead of protecting people, turned complicit marauders and killers themselves. Suddenly thrust into leadership, Rajiv Gandhi added fuel to the fires of hate and violence against Sikhs by declaring, "When a big tree falls it is only natural that the earth trembles." In the moment of that utterance, Rajiv dwarfed himself.

It was lust for power that begat the Dharm Yudh Morcha, the Bhindranwale phenomenon, and Operation Blue Star. All of that led to Indira's death and the massacre of Sikhs that followed — thousands of people who had had no role in any of this. The corrupt elements of the regime did not lift a finger for several days to stop the massacre. Earlier, Indira allowed the crisis at the Harimandir to get out of hand. She may have been the iron lady of India, but she proved less than farsighted in the way she handled the intransigent Bhindranwale, a dangerous creation of her own Machiavellian underlings. Her lasting legacy in most Sikh minds would be that she attacked the Harimandir complex and damaged the Akal Takhat. There could be no moral equivalence between Bhindranwale's actions and that of the government of India. Bhindranwale was responsible for making the Harimandir a base of his often violent campaign. But he was a small, non-state actor not accountable to anyone. The defence of India as a united, secular country warranted a more nuanced and sophisticated response.

I had criticized the Indira regime for the way it had mishandled Bhindranwale, and publicly condemned both the killing of Indira and the massacre of the Sikhs. To highlight our disgust at the violence in India, a group of us organized a candlelight vigil on the steps of the Vancouver Art Gallery to mourn the victims. As some friends gathered at our home and readied to leave for the vigil, San Minhas, a dear friend, called and asked us to wait at home for him. When he arrived, he told us he had heard rumours that someone was planning to make an attempt on my life that evening. I was concerned but not deterred.

There were about a hundred people assembled on the art gallery steps. They were brave to be there in the face of intimidation and threats. But when we held a moment of silence in memory of all the victims of violence, Manmohan Singh and his associates from the Sikh Students' Federation disrupted it by singing. That was their way of saying they were not sorry for Indira's assassination, and how dare we mourn her death along with all the others. As we concluded the event, the Federation men tried to walk toward me, but they were prevented by friends of mine who encircled them.

All of my statements, with the exception of my Punjabi columns in *Canada Darpan*, were made to the mainstream media. Most separatists at the time were not well versed in English, and they were easily misled by the erroneous reporting of my comments and positions in the Punjabi media. Tara Hayer was the master of misquotation and distortion. He derided me as "Ujjal Gandhi" in an attempt to tag me with Indira and Rajiv Gandhi's name. I accepted the name Gandhi as a badge of honour, since I stood for the non-violence espoused by the other, more important Gandhi, my idol the Mahatma. But for Tara and other separatists, I became Enemy Number One. For many months, his paper wasted as much ink on denouncing me as a "traitor" as he lavished on praising the "living martyr" and eventual Air India terrorist Talwinder Parmar and others of his ilk.

By now, there were several outfits drumming up separatist fervour among Sikhs in the world, including the Babbar Khalsa of Talwinder Parmar, the International Sikh Youth Federation, the Sikh Students' Federation and the World Sikh Organization (WSO). The WSO had been founded at a gathering of several hundred Sikhs from the U.S. and Canada held at Madison Square Garden in New York City in the immediate aftermath of Operation Blue Star. There Ajaib Singh Bagri, in a fiery and vengeful speech, said, "I give you my most solemn assurance, until we kill fifty thousand Hindus, we will not rest!"

Jaswant Singh Bhullar, a retired Indian Army major-general who had moved to the U.S., became secretary-general of the separatist WSO. Bhullar attended a meeting at the Khalsa Diwan Society temple in Abbotsford in the fall of 1984. The television news showed him being saluted by many young Sikhs in army fatigues on the grounds of the temple. Clearly, the message was that Sikhs abroad were being given military training. I spoke out against such outrageous militarizing of peace-loving Canadians. I also criticized the federal government for allowing the likes of Bhullar into Canada. The government of Canada did not give a hoot about our community, I charged. Around the same time, there were news stories about angry separatists taking combat training in the Lower Mainland of B.C. in preparation for inciting violence in India or starting a guerrilla campaign for the dismemberment of India, with the hope of separating Punjab from the country to establish Khalistan.

The torrent of threats against my life and the lives of my family members continued unabated. I continued to insist on my right to free speech, my right to live harmoniously with others in peace, and my commitment to secular values.

One late evening, Bhaji and my brother-in-law Harpartap Sahi came to our home. My family and I needed to leave for the night, they said, because someone had passed on information about a "credible threat" about to be made on my life. I agreed to leave under duress; if I had stayed, I would have been up arguing with them all night, because they refused to leave unless I did. Rami and I bundled up our sleeping young sons and sought refuge at a relative's home, leaving our own home uninhabited. I remained awake all night, thinking about the twists and turns life was taking.

On another occasion, half a dozen relatives crowded into my law office, including Papa, Bhaji, Masarji Dhillon, Harpartap's father and several in-laws of Bhaji's. Those present were worried about my safety, and they attempted to persuade me to keep quiet in the future. No one could have any doubts about my views by now; there was no need to say anything more, they argued. Bhaji's brother-in-law Harchand Grewal, an old Communist Party of India (Marxist) supporter, compared the prevailing winds in the community to a potent storm that could uproot big trees. Perhaps in reaction to Harchand's attempt to use fear as a silencer to protect me from harm, I told them only trees with deep roots could survive a storm of that magnitude. I refused to live in fear of my own voice.

OUR FAMILY CONTINUED TO live as normally as possible; under the circumstances, it was not an easy task. Whenever we needed a quick jug of milk or some additional veggies, we would send Pavel or Aseem to the nearby Punjabi Market. One day Pavel said he did not want to go. "They all stare at me," he told his mother. Everyone knew he was our son; for some he might have been an object of hatred, for others of admiration or simply curiosity. As an eleven-year-old, he was spooked. Despite our efforts to shield our kids, they were exposed to the good, the bad and the ugly of their father's fight and its consequences. It was difficult for kids who were born and raised in Canada and preoccupied more with Saturday night hockey, collecting the hockey cards of their favourite players and reading comics.

Pavel started detesting being in public with men who wore turbans. He did not relish being picked up from school by Rami's bearded and turbaned brother, his own uncle, because he could not explain to his peers that his uncle was a decent human being and different from the small minority of wildly angry protestors in front of the Indian Consulate that they'd seen on television. At home, Pavel was loved by these bearded and turbaned men, and he loved and respected them in return. The situation made no sense to him.

Pavel's plight brought me face to face with the dirty secret of most small ethnic, religious, linguistic or cultural minorities: they can suffocate their members anytime they wish. For first-generation immigrants, even though you may live in an open, liberal and democratic society, the remnants of the despotism of feudal lords in the faraway lands you left lie just beneath the surface. That hidden streak of feudal intolerance is an ugly reality that surfaces when some minorities are confronted by existential questions. This is the tyranny of tribalism,

30

of which our Canadian politicians are either ignorant or to which they remain deliberately blind. They continue on their merry way like ostriches, hoping that these problems will simply sort themselves out.

The ostrich approach may have worked in an age when immigrants from vastly different cultural backgrounds did not arrive in such large numbers. Today, the self-sufficient islands of distinction created by various groups continue to grow in our midst. The ease of communication in our satellited and internetted world makes it more difficult for immigrants to free themselves from the events and prejudices of their motherlands. Over time, these ghettos of "ideas and cultures" become self-reproducing; they can never be the building blocks of a harmonious, secular, diverse and cohesive society. Governments and politicians must ensure that sufficient resources and programs are in place to integrate people into the larger society, not just in terms of jobs and housing but also in political, civic and social ways. Leaving the process to osmosis will have serious, even dangerous, results.

In late 1984, I hoped the next few months would bring relative calming of the tensions in the Indian community in Canada. We were the helpless victims of the anger felt at Delhi and the neglect of a major ethnic and religious community by the mainstream political leadership in Canada. Many people shared my concern that, once isolated, Indians in Canada would form a ghetto easily controlled by the extremists. I spoke to several politicians; many of them supported my views, but none, at the time, felt the need to speak up. The silence of Canadian politicians was pure platinum for the radical fanatics in securing the silence of those who disagreed. The extremists used threats and intimidation, and we in the Indian community were left to fend for ourselves. The war raging within the community pricked neither the peace nor the consciences of the slumbering politicians.

The tumult of thundering slogans appeared to dim. After months of tension and turmoil, the holiday season brought some cheer into our existence. Rami, always the anchor, made sure there was some order in our lives.

I'd still been receiving anonymous threats. They came in spurts.

There were some written threats, shoved through the mail slot at home or at the office. Some came via mail. Ugly messages were left on our answering machine at home. The threats were too numerous to recount, but I remember some of them clearly. "We have killed the bitch ... now it is your turn to die": I took this call the night demonstrators in the Punjabi Market celebrated Indira Gandhi's assassination.

The chant "Ujjal is a Hindu lover ... a Hindu lover ... a Hindu lover. One day soon he will be dead" was followed by the mimicked sounds of gunshots.

"We are going to kidnap your children. We will teach you a lesson, you traitor bastard."

"Stop speaking against Sikhs. If you don't, you will soon be no more."

"You are going to be killed. Your house will be burned to the ground with your sons in it."

A note addressed to Rami was shoved through our mail slot at home while I was appearing live on a national talk show: "You get him to shut up. We know how to shut him up."

In our three-storey home, Rami and I slept on the middle floor, and our sons on the top one. They had been instructed what to do in the case of a fire. A sturdy rope had been tied to one of the three single beds in their room in case they needed to slide down the outside walls of the house. They were aware of the general threats of harm against me, and they slept with baseball bats for that reason, though we had never told them explicitly about the threats to kill or kidnap them. I dropped the boys at school every morning and Rami was always there to pick them up. One day Rami waited outside the school, but our sons were no-shows. Worried, she called me at the law office. I was ready to call the police to report them missing. At that very moment she called back to say the boys had been at the library. They had told Rami about it the day before, but she had forgotten.

Despite the threats, I was determined not to be afraid or to act that way. I never felt hate for haters, only frustration at my own inability to reach them with my message. Steeped in anger, they were lost to the world. Had the great Nanak himself reappeared at that time to talk sense to them, they would have branded him a heretic.

The failure of any public figures to denounce their tactics emboldened these merchants of fear. It did not seem to matter that some brown lawyer and activist was battling the forces of repression and intimidation. The Vancouver Police Department's South Vancouver Community Liaison Team was in close touch with us, and we got to know them well. At one point the police suggested that I carry a gun; under the circumstances, they said, obtaining a licence would be pro forma. I rejected the idea. My friend Ravi Hira took me to Kaban Protective Services on Nanaimo Street, where I did consider buying a bulletproof vest. In the end I rejected that idea too. My whole being rebelled at the mere thought of giving in to fear.

Friday, February 8, 1985, was a morning like any other. I made lunch for the children. Rami had already fed them breakfast. She left for work earlier than I did. I dropped the boys at school, and the law office was busy as usual. Meb and I had five staff, so it was a lively place. I had a five-day personal injury trial scheduled to begin the following week in the Supreme Court of British Columbia; between seeing clients, I prepared for the trial. Sometime during the day, a man called our office and asked the receptionist what time I would be leaving. Upon being told 5:00 PM, he hung up. I thought someone had probably wanted to come and see me. That was not uncommon; some immigrants had not yet figured out that they needed to make an appointment, and many clients simply dropped by my office. I accommodated them whenever I could.

I packed two briefcases full of work for the weekend. Dave Barrett, Mike Harcourt, Wally Oppal and a couple of other friends were invited for dinner the following evening. Since my press conference in August of the previous year, I had spoken privately with them and many others. But fate would deny me the chance to welcome a former and future premier along with a future Attorney General to my home. I was about to confront its more ominous plans for me.

I left my office via the stairs at the north end of the building that led to the parking lot. From our office windows looking west, we could see our cars, but the stairs were poorly lit. Walking down those stairs I never felt the door would open to light.

It was dark out. Parking lots are never places that warm hearts, but this one was at least outdoors, and it rarely felt lifeless, since kids played in the alley after school. Across the alley were homes peopled by ordinary folks. I walked the width of the lot to my second-hand orange Renault Le Car. Unfortunately, Khalistanis had turned orange from the colour of sacrifice, of detachment from greed and fear, into a symbol of terror, fear and the intent to dismember India. I put my two briefcases on the ground and was fumbling in my pockets for the car keys when I heard footsteps running toward me. I wasn't alarmed. I assumed it was a child playing in the alley. But then I heard the footsteps stop near me. I turned my head and saw a tall, large, bearded man standing next to me with his hands raised over his head. In them, he clutched a thick iron bar.

The man pummelled my skull several times in quick succession. Instinctively, I put up my right hand to protect myself; it too got pummelled. I heard yelling, and then Meb was running toward us, his briefcase raised like a weapon. The man paused, tilting his head, and in that moment I picked up one of my briefcases and lunged at the man. He turned and ran into the alley, turning to look back as he escaped. I ran behind him for a few steps, until Meb stopped me. There was a doctor in the same building as our law office, and Meb walked me there. As I lay on the doctor's table, a threat from the day before, left in Punjabi on our home answering machine, flashed through my mind: *"Jay toon bakvaas bund naa kita aseen tenun sodh diangay"* — If you do not shut up, we will straighten you out.

Rami was unpacking the groceries she had brought home for dinner when the phone rang. It was Meb telling her I was hurt. She immediately called Bhaji. When she arrived, I was sitting up on the edge of the doctor's table. She remembers me with bloodied head, face and clothes, telling her, "I am okay." Doctor Tam had cleaned and iced me as much as he could before the ambulance arrived to take Rami and me to Vancouver General Hospital.

I was wheeled into emergency, where a doctor stitched up my head wounds. He told me I was lucky to be alive. It took eighty-four stitches to sew my skull up. The gashes from the iron bar had formed deep Xs and Ys on my skull. If they had been any deeper, the doctor said, they would have threatened the integrity of my brain. Many of the cuts required two layers of stitches to close.

The number eighty-four had a special meaning. All of this had started in 1984, with the Indian Army's entry into the Golden Temple. In addition, eighty-four is symbolic of an important belief among both Hindus and Sikhs: after death, one is usually reborn as a human only after spending eighty-four *lacs* (8.4 million) lives moving through the other species. If one has lived an honest life as a human, however, one can bypass this cycle of eighty-four, as it is called, and be reborn immediately as a human being on this earth. My near-death experience imparted to me a renewed sense of life's purpose.

Rami showed no fear at the hospital. She has always been unflinching in her support of my right to say my piece, even when she has disagreed with the tenor or tone of my public utterances.

With my head stitched up, I waited. I would be able to go home once they had attended to my badly fractured hand, I thought. No bastard was going to hospitalize me. Defiance filled my heart. But soon I received the bad news. My hand needed surgery, and there were no operating theatres available. In addition, because of the trauma to my head, they felt it prudent to observe me in the hospital for at least twenty-four hours. I was wheeled to a bed in a ward.

The *Vancouver Sun* found out I was in hospital. I spoke to reporter Dave Margoshes, and the story spread. The hospital receptionist told Rami they'd had scores of calls to the switchboard asking after me. CBC TV and BCTV wanted to interview me, but the VGH administration would not allow cameras in to accompany the reporters. When a hospital manager came to my bed to explain their rationale, I told Rami I would walk outside to see the reporters. When the hospital manager forbade that, I asked Rami to get me a wheelchair. The manager relented and allowed both the reporters and the cameras in to do their job. The TV interviews received nationwide coverage. Lying in my hospital bed with a bandaged head and right hand, I told the reporters, "My life is not more important than the principles I stand for." A bit pompous in hindsight, perhaps, but absolutely true.

After a couple of days, I came home from the hospital. My sons didn't fuss over me, but our dog Smokey was more expressive. He was visibly happy to see me alive. When Rami had returned home from the hospital that first night with my bloodied clothes in a plastic bag, Smokey had gone berserk, wildly sniffing my clothes and then sniffing around the house. It took some time for him to calm down.

Shortly after the murderous attack on me, the police installed an alarm at our home that would alert them to any intruder immediately. One evening the five of us were at home, visiting with a couple of friends, when someone knocked on the front and the back doors at the same time. We were startled to see two police officers from the Community Liaison Team barging in, guns drawn. That happened one other time, too. Somehow, we had inadvertently set off the alarm ourselves.

For the first few weeks after I got back from the hospital, we had scores of visitors wishing us well and offering support. Some came to say they would no longer support the extremists. Others telephoned with their good wishes, not wanting to be seen walking up or down the steps to our home.

Vancouver mayor Mike Harcourt publicly condemned the attack on me. Ian Waddell, a friend and a member of Parliament in the riding of Vancouver-Kingsway at the time, made a statement in my support in the House of Commons in Ottawa. Vancouver South MLA Russ Fraser denounced the attack in the provincial legislature in Victoria. I was grateful for their public support and their counsel. In a community where first-generation immigrants far outnumbered those born or raised here, the reaffirmation of my right to speak within Canada's legal framework and in accordance with Canadian mores and values was helpful and heartening.

Rami took some time off work to deal with the increased traffic at home and the needs of our sons. Incensed friends organized a meeting at David Thompson Secondary School to condemn the attack. But on the day of the meeting, some members of the Hardial Bains outfit stood at the entrance to the school shouting slogans sympathetic to the extremists; they called Bhindranwale their blood brother. We learned that the auditorium had been occupied several hours earlier by people bussed in from the many temples controlled by the separatists; a Sikh employee of the Vancouver School Board had been coerced into handing over keys to the school. The scheduled speakers, including City of Vancouver alderman Harry Rankin and Art Kube, president of the B.C. Federation of Labour, huddled with Rami and me and the organizers in the foyer. Kube had tried to take control of the stage, but the fanatic occupiers raised a ruckus. Harry Rankin told the disruptors he refused to speak to a crowd that had clearly been emptied out of temples and bussed to the venue. I was angry that a chance to publicly defy the suppressors of free speech had been denied us. For the hard-core disruptors and intimidators, the only apt comparison in history was Hitler's brown shirts.

The next day, several organizations, including the Forum for Communal Harmony and Hari Sharma's Indian People's Association in North America (IPANA), held a press conference to support my freedom of expression. They condemned the actions of the disruptors at David Thompson Secondary School. But many of the organizers did not agree with my firm stand on terrorism, and they did not want to condemn the extremism associated with the separatist Khalistanis or the idea of Khalistan itself. Their view that "this too shall pass" enabled them to live zombie-like through our long night of terror. I was thankful they at least awoke twice during that night: once to condemn the violence against Sikhs in India following Indira's killing, and the second time in my case, purely on the issue of freedom of speech.

The police had assigned a detective to investigate the attack on me. He didn't impress me as knowing what he was doing, though he told me he was studying to finish his law degree. The police had no leads as of yet, and I had not recognized my attacker, though I could not get two of his physical attributes out of my mind. While he'd stood in front of me, he had looked at me with his head tilted as if he could only see through one eye. And his movements had reminded me of Popeye the Sailor Man; his waist seemed to do the walking.

A few days following the attack, my friend Gurnam Uppal heard Jaspal Atwal, a co-worker, claim in the Silvertree sawmill lunchroom that he had visited me to ask about my health: the words Atwal used were "*Main ohdi Khabar lan gia see,*" literally meaning "I went to ask about his well-being." That particular Punjabi expression could have been legitimately construed to mean he had been over to beat me up. I still had the recording of the anonymous threat left on our answering machine the night before the attack. When I replayed the message for Gurnam, he was shocked. The voice belonged to Atwal, he confirmed. Atwal had had a close-trimmed beard until recently, Gurnam said, but he was now clean-shaven. When I passed this information onto the detective in charge, he arranged for me to watch the workers arriving for the afternoon shift at the mill as they walked inside from the parking lot. Many workers came and went, and then suddenly a dark, tall, beardless man emerged from a car. He walked along doing a Popeye the Sailor Man shuffle.

Atwal was charged with the attack, and the trial took place several months later, resulting in an acquittal. Austin Cullen, the associate chief justice who then headed the prosecutions in Vancouver, had called me in before the trial to determine whether I really wanted to proceed with charges against Atwal. I was shocked. Later I learned the Crown's case was weak because of the ID process, and also that Cullen had wanted me to consider that in the event of an acquittal I would have one more confirmed enemy on the loose.

Sure enough, the judge ruled that my identification of Atwal in a police line-up was tainted because I had already spotted him at the mill. I myself had seen no point in that police line-up, since I was already 100 per cent certain that Atwal had been the perpetrator. Why the police and the Crown did not choose to rely on the other convincing evidence against Atwal was beyond me. He admitted during the trial that he had been in the vicinity of my office, but he said he had gone to see an accountant and was not the one who had brandished the iron bar. The Crown's case was further weakened at trial by the alibi testimony of Harjit Sull, an RCMP officer who told the court that in the days leading up to the assault, Atwal had been beardless, even though Gurnam, who worked with Atwal, remembered seeing him that day with his beard still intact. Sull also testified to Atwal's good character.

In November 1985, Atwal was acquitted of the charges arising from his brutal attack on me in February of that year. He would tell me in the years to come that he knew who my attacker was. I advised him to go to the police with the information, but of course that never happened. Nor did he ever confess to the attack on me. Contrary to Atwal's claim that he was not a member of any Sikh activist group, he was in fact an active hatchet- and trigger-man for the International Sikh Youth Federation. In 1986, Atwal shot and injured a visiting Punjabi cabinet minister, Malkiat Singh Sidhu, on Vancouver Island, for which he went on to receive a twenty-year sentence.

One day years later, when I was B.C.'s Attorney General, I would spot the VPD detective who'd been assigned to my case standing next to a limousine in downtown Vancouver, dressed in a driver's uniform. We smiled at each other, and I left him waiting for his fare.

Recovering from my injuries took longer than I had expected. My right hand needed massage and physiotherapy. Over a span of several weeks, it became functional, though my fingers have never gone back to their natural state. My head was a different story. Over the next several months, I began to suffer headaches starting just above the ears. The doctors discovered that my temporomandibular joint had been damaged; the hammering of the iron bar had impacted it into misalignment. So, in my forties, I wore dental braces to realign my TMJ. I had a lot of explaining to do, lest anyone thought this a cosmetic project for beautifying my smile.

Surviving an assassination attempt fortifies the soul. The attack banished any doubts I might still have been harbouring about the path of peace I had chosen and my determination to speak out. Silencing my conscience would truly have meant choosing death.

I HAD NEVER WRITTEN TO elected officials about **31**
the turmoil in Canada's Indian community. Operation Blue
Star had happened in another country, another civilization.
But the upheaval in cities like Vancouver and Toronto was Canadian;
the intimidators and the extremists were Canadian; and those threatened and assaulted were Canadian too. In my heart of hearts I hoped
the politicians were paying attention, even though I said publicly
that they didn't care. Finally, the urging of Gurcharan Rampuri and
Darshan Gill prevailed, and in April 1985 I wrote to Prime Minister
Brian Mulroney and others in power both federally and provincially.
I warned them that the violence in the community was a serious
concern and could lead to murders. Some replied, but many didn't,
including the Prime Minister's Office.

Multiculturalism is a double-edged sword. During the crisis in
the Indian community, both edges were dangerous. Multiculturalism
served as a cover for government neglect in matters of culture and religion; claiming they did not know the mores and values of the Indian
community gave them an excuse for their inaction. On the other hand,
the Indian community could keep politicians at bay simply by arguing
that the community was entitled to a different standard of behaviour
because of different beliefs and interests. The public good and social
solidarity receded into lesser significance. Multiculturalism, intended
as a force for good, had become a perfect weapon for self-imposed and
reinforced exclusion.

Defending the "honour of a religion" through violence is believed
by some to bring glory in the hereafter. It has always been a bone
of contention with me that those who are ready to die or kill in the
name of religion for glory in the hereafter usually do not lift a finger

to alleviate pain or poverty or feed the starving here and now on earth. That is true of all fanatical campaigns; they represent zeal gone berserk.

I issued the Khalistanis a public challenge: if the support among the Sikhs for Khalistan was as near-unanimous as they claimed, they should call a meeting solely in its support outside of a temple setting. If more than five hundred people attended, I would admit to being wrong in my contention. Not one but two such meetings were held, and neither of them registered more than two hundred attendees. The first was on the anniversary of Operation Blue Star in June 1985 in Queen Elizabeth Park in Vancouver, and the other sometime later at the Pacific National Exhibition grounds. My challenge stung them; they had taken the bait and were humiliated. That was the last time anybody ever claimed significant support for Khalistan, a pipe dream supported by a lunatic fringe.

In the meantime, Tara Hayer continued his tirade of hate in the *Indo-Canadian Times*. He was unrelenting in his vicious and demeaning attacks upon my character, my integrity and my family, including my then long-dead father, who had been Tara's teacher and for whom Tara had previously professed admiration. He distorted beyond recognition every word I uttered or wrote. He published defamatory rubbish written about me by other people. Finally, I'd had enough: I filed a lawsuit for defamation against him and his paper. The writ was issued in the late spring of 1985. It took over 150 pages of English translation to capture all the offending material. Tara found out about the writ before it was served upon him and had a mutual friend call me. I was extremely angry, and not in a mood to forgive. But sometime after the bombing of Air India, my counsel, David Roberts, urged me to abandon the suit. Litigation launched in anger only served to dignify the offender, and Tara had sunk to depths beyond redemption. I stopped the proceeding in its tracks, taking no further steps.

THE FIGHT AGAINST extremism had taken a toll on our lives. Rami and I felt it might be redemptive for the family to visit India. The heat of the Indian summer would be intense in July and August, but that was better than the hate in Vancouver. At the end of May, we booked flights from Vancouver to Delhi via Montreal and London.

As the day of our departure drew nearer, however, we started to have second thoughts about the wisdom of taking young kids from the moderate temperature of a Vancouver summer to the heat of the plains of northern India. I remembered that July in India had rains, too, and that the heat and the humidity made one hunger and beg for a cool breeze. It was not just the weather that was on my mind. It was also the security and safety of my family. We had taken whatever steps we could to keep our forthcoming trip a secret. Our flights were booked on Air India for June 23 via Montreal under the names of U. Singh and R. Kaur, to avoid the use of "Ujjal" or "Dosanjh." I had heard rumours of various people asking Sikhs to boycott Air India, since it was India's national carrier. I did not particularly like the service aboard Air India, remembering our terrible experience in 1977. I had decided to fly Air India solely as a gesture of defiance against the boycotters. I had no inkling then that it was Talwinder Parmar and his associates who had warned temple audiences a couple of weeks prior to the bombing not to travel by Air India. But a few days before June 23, we cancelled our reservations and made plans instead to drive across Canada in the three weeks I had set aside in my law office calendar for the trip.

On an exceptionally beautiful morning on June 23, we awoke in Vancouver to news of death and destruction. Air India Flight 182 from Montreal, destined for Delhi via London, had disintegrated at an altitude of thirty thousand feet, two hundred miles off the Irish coast. Rami and I went numb. We were sure this was sheer coincidence. Surely the extremists would not have designed their most evil deed around me, a small fry in the scheme of things. Their target was India, the idea of India as pluralistic, secular and united. Then again, killing two birds with one stone would not have hurt the effort. In Canada,

I was excoriated as an arch enemy, as if I was the only thing that stood between the extremists and their pipe dream of Khalistan. They had bitterly denounced me as a traitor to their "holy" crusade. The fact that we had avoided being killed in the Air India bombing just by chance was something Rami and I have, to this point, shared only with close friends. We did not want to go public at the time of the tragedy, which took so many lives and affected hundreds if not thousands of people across the globe.

The bombing was the work of the Vancouver-based Sikh extremist organization Babbar Khalsa. For months, it had been under surveillance by the Canadian Security Intelligence Agency, but the new and quite anemic CSIS dropped the ball days before the tragedy. Despite CSIS agents following some of the actors at the core of this conspiracy to a location near Duncan on Vancouver Island and hearing an obvious explosion, CSIS decided to discontinue the surveillance. The 329 men, women and children on board Air India 182 paid with their lives for this colossal blunder. At Narita Airport outside of Tokyo, two CP Air baggage handlers died and four others were injured in a lesser-known explosion on the ground. Not only did CSIS bungle the surveillance; they also destroyed several hundred hours of valuable wiretaps, depriving investigators and prosecutors of material that might have sent Ripudaman Malik, Ajaib Bagri and possibly others away for life behind bars for their gruesome deeds. How could CSIS investigators have ignored the test blast in the woods outside of Duncan? Did they think the two terrorists had trekked to the secluded woods simply to smoke hashish? Since the terrorists were Indian, had the CSIS bunglers been duped into believing it was some kind of traditional Indian ceremony the duo was engaged in?

It was almost impossible to believe we were living through such terrible times on Canadian soil. It was even harder to believe that the police and politicians in Canada were oblivious to the terror all around us.

The first Air India–related raids by the RCMP occurred on November 6, 1985. The residences of Talwinder Parmar, Inderjit Singh

Reyat, Hardial Johal, Surjan Gill and Manmohan Singh were targeted. Johal, a Vancouver School Board janitor, had been an NDP member. When I learned that they were suspects in the Air India mass murder, my stomach churned with revulsion. Immediately after the raids, from the police holding cells, I received calls from both Johal and Gill. Each of them wanted to retain me as legal counsel. Defending clients charged with murder was not my specialty, I told them. Each of them said I could retain any senior criminal defence lawyer I wanted as my co-counsel; money would be no object. They were scared and desperate, and it was obvious they wanted to inoculate themselves against accusations of terrorism by retaining me, someone who had spoken out so strongly against terrorists. I politely turned them down, rattling off the names of a few eminent defence counsels.

This book is not the place to delve into the sordid saga of the failure of the Canadian government to care for and protect its own citizens. But I can't forget how lonely we felt fighting the terrorists in our midst. On the night of 329 passengers, most of them Canadian, perishing in the Irish Sea, Brian Mulroney telephoned Rajiv Gandhi to express sorrow for the "Indian" tragedy. The tragedy was Canadian. Until 9/11, the world's largest incident of aviation terror was the bombing of Air India Flight 182, which had originated on and been masterminded from Canadian soil. The perpetrators were Canadian. The victims were Canadian. However, most of the victims were not white but brown. They were of Indian ancestry, not European. I do not believe Mulroney is a racist. I do not believe for a moment he would have been intentionally insensitive to the memory of the lost Canadians or to the feelings of the victims' families. But his response to this horrible incident was the usual response of the Canadian establishment of the day: This Golden Temple thing in India has some people in Canada worked up. The brown guys are hurting brown guys; it is really an Indian problem; the problem will go away in time, so let us not lose sleep over it. Then Air India Flight 182 went down.

The police, for their part, didn't understand the language or the culture of the terrorists. They did not have sufficient numbers of adequately trained investigators to deal with what the government ignorantly considered an island unto itself. They did not have many informants or sources who could help their investigators. It was deeply ironic, then, that any information I passed on to the police or CSIS to ensure my own safety and that of my family's was considered, I learned, to be coming from an "informant." I had always thought informants provided information for money or favours, and I received neither, in addition to almost being killed.

The extremists felt a sense of impunity; they had been emboldened by the lacklustre efforts of the local law enforcement apparatus to apprehend the attackers of Gurcharan Rampuri or the firebombers who targeted Darshan Gill's home. There were numerous cases of beatings and threats where the culprits remained untouched by the law. In the case of my attack, the Crown had been prepared to drop the charges. Under circumstances like these, it was not surprising the extremists felt invulnerable.

A COUPLE OF DAYS AFTER what the *Globe and Mail* called "Black Sunday," Rami and I packed for our family's trip across Canada. As we were loading our stuff into the van, a Vancouver Police Department car pulled up. On some of their wiretaps, the police had heard chatter about killing me. It would be wise to get out of town for a few days as they worked on it, I was told. The officer stuck around until we had finished packing our Vanagon, and soon we were on the Trans-Canada Highway, heading east. We were travelling away from danger, from the fortress of hatred and violence that the Lower Mainland had become.

As the van took us past Abbotsford and on toward the town of Hope, the mountains and the flora on and around them reminded me of the beautiful world we lived in. In the last eighteen months, the only peaks and valleys I'd been aware of were the joys and sorrows of my public and personal life. As we drove, hope began to slowly creep back into my heart: hope for personal tranquility and collective peace.

Seeing the rail tracks alongside the highway sent me straight into imagining Canada's history: the Aboriginal cultures, songs and gestures that must have greeted the Europeans; the Europeans' subjugation of the first Canadians; the waves of immigrants who followed; the chiselling of roads and routes out of the mountains to connect the east with the west; the sweat and blood of each generation who had built this society, sometimes at the expense of their lives. Each bend in the road evoked a milestone, and the trip lent itself to ready reflection.

We stopped off for a night in Prince George to visit with Rami's cousin and his two sons. Our next stop was Calgary, to see a friend in whose basement lived a man named Harry Sohal, whom I had not met before. Harry had saved a recent *Globe and Mail* editorial for me;

he must have known from his landlord we were going to be visiting. The editorial referred to my travails regarding extremism and my urging of Sikhs and other Canadians to speak up. "[Dosanjh] is a credit to his country," the editorial said. "But he needs reinforcements." In its appeal, the *Globe* quoted Edmund Burke: "When bad men combine, the good must associate, else they will fall one by one." Harry Sohal was active on the political scene, which led him to become an MLA several years later. Sadly, shortly after getting elected, he suffered a massive heart attack and died at a young age.

The trip provided time for Rami and me to be with our sons, uninterrupted by the media, my law practice or Rami's teaching. We made overnight stops in Regina, Saskatoon, Winnipeg, Toronto, Ottawa, Montreal, Washington, D.C., and New York. In Toronto, we stayed with my sister Nimmy, and the boys enjoyed being tourists at the CN Tower. In Ottawa, Parliament was not in session, so we had freer access to the House of Commons and the red chamber of the Senate. Of special interest to me, both as a lawyer and as a parent, was the Supreme Court of Canada. The Court was not in session, but our guide allowed us to stand in front of the bench behind which the justices usually sat hearing cases as long as we didn't take pictures. I was so thankful. Prime ministers and cabinets come and go, but guarantors like Parliament and the Supreme Court stand ever on guard for our rights.

In New York City, we took in an exhibition of Indian cultural artifacts at the Metropolitan Museum of Art. It brought alive ancient Indian life for our sons. Like all parents, we worried about our sons' understanding of our ancestral history and culture. On our first trip to India in 1977, Rami and I had brought home a seventeen-volume set called *A Treasury of Indian Illustrated Classics by Amar Chitra Katha, Sketches of Eternal Stories,* which was in comic book form; our sons had enjoyed them. We also visited Times Square and travelled to the top of the now-destroyed World Trade Center. It was a curious twist that in our trip away from terrorism in the wake of the Air India bombing, my family would visit the site that sixteen years later would become a place of pilgrimage for millions determined to wipe out the scourge of terror in the world.

In Washington, D.C., the Smithsonian National Air and Space Museum captivated the boys. We walked around the White House and visited the spot where Martin Luther King had stood to deliver his great "I Have A Dream" speech. From a street vendor, Pavel bought a poster featuring King that would adorn his rooms for years.

As we drove back to Vancouver, I reflected on what awaited me there. I was in a fight with both the extremists and those who lacked the courage to condemn them. Some criticized me in order to avoid being targeted, threatened or killed themselves. For them, there was no distinction between peace and violence. Cowardice always found a way to sound brave without offending those perpetuating evil. A moral blindness gave false equivalency to good and evil, the democrat and the dictator, the suppressed and the suppressor. The extremists had no dearth of apologists, most of whom styled themselves as "objective" observers. In Punjab, however, there had emerged a ray of hope. Sant Harchand Singh Longowal and Rajiv Gandhi had signed an accord that provided a possible pathway for progress.

Rami and I decided to return to India in December 1985, since I wished to see for myself the aftermath of Operation Blue Star, the Gandhi assassination and the massacres of Sikhs. We flew to Delhi separately to avoid the possibility of us both losing our lives in an accident or a man-made disaster. It was the thought of our sons that made us do that. Rami made the trip first, with me following the next day.

In Delhi and throughout Punjab I travelled incognito. Early in our trip, we were warned that Jaspal Atwal had returned to India and was tailing me, so we took extra precautions, such as not taking the same cab or tuk-tuk every day and getting the cab to drop us a slight distance away from our destination. I needed some security, but who would supply it: the government of India, which had issued a visa to my potential killer for the same period I was going to be in India? I'd learned about Atwal's presence in Delhi only by accident, when I met a government intelligence sleuth at a friend's residence. Atwal had been inquiring about my whereabouts, the man told me. I had no doubt it was to attend to his unfinished business. It would certainly not be to beg for forgiveness. Rami and I decided that being constantly on the move, in disguise, was our best security. The *pharen* I had bought in Kashmir during our 1977 trip and the accompanying Kashmiri cap became my armour, and we never told the passengers we sat next to on buses and trains who we really were.

Ever since the attack, I had become more aware of the sound of footsteps; the footsteps I had assumed belonged to some innocent child playing in the alley had almost killed me. Now, any time my ears picked up the sound of steps, my head turned automatically to see where they were coming from. I longed for my pre-assault brain, which had considered such sounds as safe and normal. I looked into men's eyes as they boarded the buses, and searched the faces of male passengers as they sat next to me on the trains. And in India in 1985, those close to me weren't the only threats. A gunshot could come from a distance. Life was cheap. It had been so before Operation Blue Star, and it became even more so in the aftermath.

During our time in Delhi, I met with senior journalists from the many English dailies, including the *Indian Express* and the *Times of India*. My remarks were fairly well publicized. I made it my mission to explain that the vast majority of Canadian Sikhs were peaceful and did not support the dismemberment of India, since the Indian media were under the impression that the opposite was true. Meeting the renowned writer Khushwant Singh was a delight. I had corresponded with him in the aftermath of Operation Blue Star, and he was kind enough to devote one of his famous syndicated columns to our plight in Canada and my visit to India. In Chandigarh, I looked up Khushwant's son Rahul Singh, who was the resident editor of the national *Indian Express* there. Khushwant died recently after a lifetime of superb and fearless writing. When I heard the news, I remembered one of my several visits to his home. It had been a December evening. Khushwant received visitors most evenings, but on that one evening nobody else had shown up yet. He opened the bottle of J&B Scotch I had brought him, and with drinks in hand we chatted for a while. Then he proudly showed me a part of his large library that had not been visible from the room we'd been in. Every book had a story attached about how it had come into his possession: a purchase from somewhere; a gift from another writer, a politician or a friend. I felt almost as if I were a child travelling in the world of letters with an elder. It was a brief, memorable glimpse of his long and fearless life.

In Delhi Rami and I met with a group of young men and women working with the Sikh children who'd been displaced or orphaned by the anti-Sikh riots there. We recognized the inherent diversity of India in that group; the Hindu, Sikh and Muslim students, male and female, were genuinely committed to righting the terrible wrongs of November 1984. At the camp they took us to, girls and boys, turbaned and turbanless, played and studied in friendly surroundings under the watchful, compassionate attention of student volunteers. Rami's eyes grew moist, and at that moment I would have happily died in exchange for a magic wand to end evil and suffering in the world. I dared not ask the children what they had witnessed in 1984. I remembered the horrible TV footage of burning, looting, maiming and butchering. But the children's resilience and determined smiles hid their inner pain.

I was anxious to get to Punjab, the once proud and fabled land of five rivers, now of only two. The year 1947 had been as cruel to Punjab as it had been to Bengal. Both provinces had been bisected in the partitioned India. But politics had future designs on Punjab, which was destined to be divided again. In 1966, the states of Haryana and Himachal were carved out of it. What now goes by the name of Indian Punjab is a mere sliver of a state compared to the Punjab before partition.

Jalandhar, the vernacular press capital of Punjab, was our first destination. I had been corresponding with Jagjit Singh Anand, the editor of the left-leaning Punjabi daily *Nawan Zamana*, and with Vijay Chopra, son of late Lala Jagat Narain, who was head of the Hind Samachar group of newspapers. Chopra's publications had the largest circulation of any in North India, and both men had published my correspondence and statements.

Next we were off to Amritsar, the home of the Harimandir. Our friends the Kandharis had now established their business in Surat as well; they felt the need for a foothold elsewhere, in case the turmoil in Punjab made their lives impossible. I was saddened, but I couldn't argue with their fears.

Rami and I paid our respects at the Golden Temple. Bhindranwale and Mrs. Gandhi were no more, and Longowal, a man of peace, had been felled by an assassin's bullets in August 1985, shortly after signing the Punjab accord with Prime Minister Rajiv Gandhi. I would have relished the chance to speak to each of them again — Longowal especially, but Mrs. Gandhi and even Bhindranwale, too. The Harimandir itself was defiantly tranquil, its embrace open for every seeker of peace. The throngs of pilgrims exuded reverence.

India overwhelms with its omnipresent religiosity, seen in the hundreds of thousands of holy sites and the billion salutations exchanged daily among Indians. It is there in the *mandirs, masjids,* gurdwaras and *girjas* found everywhere, in the mausoleums and *samadhs,* in the *sadhus, pirs* and *devis.* Most homes have a special place or a corner where families sit and pray, with or without holy books, with or without objects of worship. Even on the tin and cardboard walls of *jhuggies,* slums, covered by plastic and jute rags to keep out the elements, religious deities and symbols occupy a place of pride and respect. Sadly, such intense and ubiquitous religiosity has not resulted in a just society.

On our way back from Amritsar, we took the train to Goraya, an industrial town on the Grand Trunk Road just a few miles from Dosanjh. It took us a couple of hours to reach our destination, and we struck up a conversation with a turbaned Sikh merchant on his way to Bombay. We talked about the plight of people in India, the state of the economy and, toward the end of our journey, the impact of the recent turmoil on the people of Punjab. The man asked me where I lived. It turned out that he had friends in Greater Vancouver, some of whom I knew. Our exchange was frank, and as Rami and I rose to disembark at Goraya, I told the Sikh man my name and asked him his. As he heard my name and surveyed my *pharen* and cap, he muttered something about security. He had read about the assault upon me, he said, and other press reports about Canada.

In the rickshaw, Rami was angry with me for telling the man my name. We were on our way to visit Balwinder, her old student. Not a soul in the world knew where we were going. We surprised even Balwinder with our arrival.

WHEN CHACHAJI WAS ALIVE, I had always rushed to our village to see him before doing anything else. The village still pulled me on this visit, but it was not the pull of a father waiting for a son. This was only my second visit to Dosanjh since Chachaji's death in 1980.

No one lived any longer in our dilapidated building at the *khooh*. Like pilgrims to a temple, Rami and I opened up the three decaying houses and dusted off the old framed photos of our elders. I stood for a few moments in silence, thinking about where life had taken me so far and where it might lead next. Then we padlocked the houses to be opened again by the next pilgrim cousin or sibling. That is the fate of homes whose inhabitants desert them for greener pastures in far-away lands. If homes could write letters, those who desert them would receive countless missives. I can hear the song of the land even as it urges us to return.

In January 1986, at the tail end of our trip, we met some wonderful historic figures at a memorable dinner in Delhi held by V.D. Chopra, editor of the daily *Patriot*. Among those present were P.N. Haksar, a one-time advisor and principal secretary to Mrs. Gandhi, and Aruna Asaf Ali, a key figure of the independence movement. Born Aruna Ganguly, she had married Asaf Ali, a prominent freedom fighter, and had gone on to participate in the Salt March as well as the Quit India Movement of 1942. During the Quit India Movement, Aruna Asaf Ali became an icon for Indian youth when she defiantly unfurled the tri-colour at the Gowalia Tank Maidan in Bombay, symbolizing Indian aspirations for immediate independence from the British.

Haksar, a brilliant lawyer and political thinker, had parted ways with Mrs. Gandhi in 1973 in disagreements over the direction in which she was steering the country. His worst fears came true when she declared emergency rule in 1975, curtailing civil liberties and jailing her critics and opponents. Chopra himself was active in Left politics in India. The presence at the dinner of Muneeza Hashmi, the daughter of the great poet of the subcontinent, Faiz Ahmed Faiz, was a treat and a reminder that across the border from Indian Punjab and West Bengal lived our kith and kin.

The dinner conversation continued into the early hours of the morning. It centred on whether faith had anything to do with the survival of democracy in a particular society. An Indian professor of sociology from Britain expressed pessimism about the prospects of democracy in many Muslim countries. Haksar put forth the opinion that India, itself a largely religious country, remained robustly democratic, with the exception of the short interlude of Indira Gandhi's emergency rule, which had been opposed by most Indians. He felt India's democratic and political heritage of the freedom movement had helped in that regard. He pointed out that Christianity, too, had known its share of butchers and dictators, not just in ancient times but also in the recent past, with Hitler and Mussolini.

Darbara Singh, who had resigned as chief minister of Punjab due to the murders and violence before Operation Blue Star, had subsequently been elected to the Rajya Sabha, India's upper house of Parliament. Darbara had not attended Chopra's dinner, since he was not feeling well, so I arranged to meet him at his home. His residence, like the residences of most politicians in those days, was a fortress. After expressing condolence for the passing of Chachaji, who had been his friend, and asking briefly about the situation in the diaspora, Darbara talked for close to three hours. He was distressed at not having been consulted by the government before or after Operation Blue Star. According to him, it had been the president of India, Gyani Zail Singh, who had manipulated the scene until the operation commenced. In the internecine war among Punjabi politicians, Mrs. Gandhi had been ill-briefed about the situation at the Harimandir and the fallout of the different choices that faced her in June 1984, Darbara said.

On our way out of India, a Sikh in an orange turban greeted and embraced me at the terminal. He had met me on a visit to Canada, and as soon as he embraced me, I recognized him. In those days an orange turban could mean fanaticism, but he was a supporter of the Communist Party of India; an Indian first, and only then a Sikh in an orange turban with a flowing beard. An ancient and complex civilization, India resists any attempt to enclose it in rigid constructs, frames or formulas.

33 BACK IN CANADA, both governments and enforcement agencies had become more aware of the level of intimidation and violence imposed by a tiny but vocal minority of Khalistanis on the Indian community. In response to my appeals for police and political leaders to do more, B.C.'s Attorney General, Brian Smith, had asked the police to be more vigilant in protecting Indo-Canadians. But the *Vancouver Province*, in uncaring sarcasm, stated: "Canadian authorities have been accused of being lax in the past about the potential of terrorism. Ujjal Dosanjh, who is described as a Sikh moderate, says the authorities should be more concerned about the source of the problem and not just the potential backlash. How?... Should we do things to zero in on the source that we wouldn't do to other citizens? Are we prepared to become a less open society in order to do that? How much do Canadians expect the rights and freedoms of all to be compromised to deal with what in true perspective may be a very small minority of dangerous activists?"

On the night of January 5, 1986, the day the *Province* editorial appeared, I was a guest on a nationally broadcast talk show on radio network CKO. I made the point I had repeated ad infinitum, that a few bad actors were giving a black eye to the entire Sikh community.

Those bad actors were listening in, and Rami called the police in the middle of the show to ensure that I was driven home safely. While the show was being broadcast, a note on lined paper had been pushed through our mail slot at home. Rami had been alerted to it by a noise at the door, and as she looked outside, she saw that the gate was ajar and a late-model American car was pulling away. The note on a lined piece of paper read: "We know how to shut him up. You tell him."

I did not need a lecture on civil liberties from the *Province*. I was disappointed that the amnesia that had afflicted the political class had also dulled the newspaper's ability to understand the pain and anguish of our community. Our chief criticism was that the authorities had not taken seriously the turmoil and violence unleashed by this "very small minority of dangerous activists." We had often said that because Air India was not Air Canada and most of the victims of the terrorism were brown, authorities had not done "things to zero in on the source" of the violence as they would have done had the victims been white. We were not asking for any special or draconian measures. We were simply asking to be protected like other Canadians.

But the policing community seemed to be getting the message. Two dozen troublemakers had been charged in less than a month with various offences related to violence by separatist Sikhs. That May, while the Punjabi cabinet minister Malkiat Singh Sidhu was on Vancouver Island attending a wedding and visiting his extended family, he was ambushed and shot several times. He survived. The shooter was none other than the man acquitted of the charges arising from the attempt to assassinate me: Jaspal Atwal, with three other accomplices, had done this dastardly deed. In 1987, Atwal and the others would be convicted on several charges, including attempted murder, and sentenced to twenty years in prison.

I decided to not run in the B.C. election in 1986. I was exhausted from constantly battling the extremists, though by now there was strong public support against terror among Canadians from all walks and all ethnic communities. Rami had stood by me like a rock, as had a network of activist friends and supporters. An electoral contest thrust upon my family at that time would have overwhelmed my young sons, and the constituencies in southeast Vancouver did not seem winnable. Dave Barrett had been around as leader of the NDP for a long time, and something in me felt British Columbians would not throw out the Bill Bennett government after the success of Expo 86. Rami continued teaching ESL at Vancouver Community College and hers was the steady paycheque in the family. Mine depended on the efforts I put into law, and over the past three years, my passion for peace had claimed a disproportionate share of my attention and energy.

My law practice grew tremendously once I began to focus on it. In a precedent-setting case, I successfully argued that when a husband was convicted of assaulting his wife, she should be able to sue for civil damages, including aggravated damages. The award of $7,500 was relatively small but extremely satisfying. Rami had trained me well in defending women's equality and dignity. One took these kinds of cases to court not for the fees involved, because often plaintiffs had no money, but for the principle of the thing.

Some of our friends, including Darshan Gill, Sushma Dutta, and Gurcharan Rampuri, helped us set up the Komagata Maru Foundation of Canada to commemorate the seventy-fifth anniversary of the 1914 turning away of the ship full of Indians wishing to land in Canada. With funding from the federal government, we made a documentary, *Komagata Maru: A Voyage of Shattered Dreams* — but not without a lot of fuss from federal officials evidently under pressure from Sikh separatists who had influence in the highest echelons of the bureaucracy. Since the passengers on the ship had been mainly Sikhs, the separatists wanted us to treat it as a Sikh voyage. Since their battle to enter Canada and stay had no religious underpinnings, we insisted the voyage was a secular venture for a better life in Canada; the religious affiliations of the passengers did not matter at all. Our efforts to keep the *Komagata Maru* plaque installed by the City of Vancouver secular was obstructed by officials and their Sikh separatist friends, joined by the likes of Hari Sharma. Things had gotten so bad that Khalistanis and the Left now sang from the same song sheet.

In 1987, to coincide with a Commonwealth Conference in Vancouver that Rajiv Gandhi was scheduled to attend, the Indian People's Association in North America sponsored an Islamist Indian MP of the Janata Party named Syed Shahabuddin to attend a counter-conference to which many Sikh separatist outfits were enthusiastically invited. I wrote the leader of the Janata Party, Chandra Shekhar, former prime minister of India, an open letter, and Shahabuddin was stopped from attending the counter-conference. The extreme Left can rather easily hitch its wagon to the extreme right's goals. In the case of Khalistan, the Left's rigid "Marxist" formulation of a nation and its right to self-determination played into the hands of religious exclusivists and extremists. The Left's original support of the Muslims' right to Pakistan in the 1940s showed ultimate ignorance and was an insult to Marx, who had famously branded religion the opiate of the masses.

The 1985 takeover of the David Thompson auditorium by extremists had given all Khalistani organizations a bloody nose in terms of public opinion. To refurbish their reputations, the extremists held a public meeting to show that the community was not troubled by their activities: there was complete harmony in the community, they claimed, and no one advocated or supported violence. Two representatives, one "Hindu" and the other "Muslim," addressed the meeting, along with many others, at a high school auditorium in Vancouver. I did not attend, but I heard later that I had been branded a heretic from the stage. Jaspal Atwal, who was under active criminal investigation at the time, was honoured at the meeting for allegedly wrestling with and apprehending a thief in an alley in Vancouver's Downtown Eastside. But things for extremists pretending to be saints were never going to be the same. The CBC had started following some of these characters, and in a story some months earlier, Gillian Findlay had isolated six or seven thugs of the extremist fringe and followed their participation in various violent demonstrations and activities. The tide had begun to turn in favour of moderation.

One federal politician was finally courageous enough to take a stand. Foreign affairs minister Joe Clark spoke with a clarity and conviction never before seen in a Canadian politician on the issue of Khalistani extremism when he stated in 1988 that the activities of a small group of Sikhs constituted the most serious internal security threat the country faced. The government of India had expressed concerns to Canada regarding the violent activities of Khalistanis in Canada, and Clark slammed three groups with large bases in

B.C.: Babbar Khalsa, the International Sikh Youth Federation and the World Sikh Organization. Clark was both praised and ridiculed for his comments. One of those critical of him was New Democrat MP Svend Robinson; Robinson was a well-respected politician, but in this instance he was totally off the mark. His was a typical knee-jerk opposition response; because Indians had faced discrimination in Canada and suffered tragedies such as the *Komagata Maru*, some mainstream politicians turned misty-eyed at the thought of having to confront evil in the ranks of the minorities. I responded to the criticism in May 1988 in a letter to the *Vancouver Sun*. "Clark had never blamed all Sikhs for the violence and the security threat; only a minority among us. By defending this dangerous minority among the Sikhs his critics elevated them to the leadership of the entire community. The critics made it look as if this violent minority represented us all." Subsequently, Clark quashed a refugee claim for Santokh Singh Bagga, who had been an associate of Talwinder Parmar. I was clear in my letter that Clark was right to do what he did: "For anyone to say that... attacking the organizations that support terrorism, either directly or indirectly, is attacking the Sikh community is ignorant. It is appallingly dumb."

On the Air India front, it was revealed in mid-July 1988 that while their co-conspirator Inderjit Singh Reyat was fighting extradition from the U.K., Parmar and Ajaib Bagri had slipped out of Canada and into Pakistan. That could not have been accomplished without the implicit support of the Inter-Services Intelligence (ISI) of Pakistan, and the U.S. surely knew what the ISI was up to; the U.S. had spent billions of dollars on aid to Pakistan, of which the Pakistan military was the largest recipient. The Taliban had not yet come back to haunt the West, though that would change after 9/11. But 9/11 was still thirteen years away, thirteen more years in which India and the Sikhs would suffer the evil of Pakistan-sponsored and -financed cross-border terror in Punjab while the U.S. turned a blind eye.

FISSURES HAD BEGUN TO APPEAR among B.C.'s Khalistani extremists in 1986. The differences did not arise out of ideological quarrels; to start with, they were all about money. Tara Hayer's *Indo-Canadian Times* was the mouthpiece for their extremist activities. The *Times* was like a paper of record for terrorists; Tara had rejoiced over Indira Gandhi's murder and the Air India bombing. He had made light of the beating of poet Gurcharan Rampuri and the brutal attempt on my life. But when Parmar and his close associates did not pay for a book they had had Tara print for them, his support for Parmar cooled. The debt ran to several thousand dollars.

An attempted bomb attack on Tara's offices at the *Times* in 1986 had been the result of an internecine struggle for supremacy among the terrorists. It may also have been that they knew about Tara having overheard a Bagri confession related to the Air India bombing in 1985 in London; he was no enemy of terrorism at the time, but he had since fallen out with one group of them over money. The attack could also have been an act of revenge by someone within or outside of the extremist groups whose daughter, sister, wife or mother Tara had brutally insulted or dishonoured in his paper. His published attacks on the female relatives of his enemies were well known. He was an Indian feudal misogynist who often chose to impugn his male enemies vicariously in this way.

When Tara was shot in August 1988 by seventeen-year-old Harkirat Singh Bagga, both strands in his world of terrorism came together. Harkirat was the son of Santokh Singh Bagga, who had been ordered deported by Joe Clark a few months before. It was quite well known in the community that Santokh Bagga was in the Parmar camp that owed money to Tara, and Tara had been writing vicious attacks on Bagga Sr. in his paper, including a pornographic description of Bagga's wife, Harkirat's mother. Harkirat may have been abetted in his attack by Parmar, but Harkirat may have had his own reasons: avenging his mother's dishonour by Tara. Nothing justifies violence, but it is always important to identify the motives. Tara survived the shooting, but he was partially paralyzed. Harkirat received a fourteen-year sentence for the crime.

Tara never stopped supporting terror and violence in India for the cause of Khalistan, but in Canada, he was now accorded "saint of peace" status by the mainstream media. Non-Punjabi-speaking journalists had difficulty following the tortured contours of Tara's output. His basic stance never really changed, and his language was no less vituperative after he was shot. Venom still permeated his writing. As a journalist and a citizen, Tara had the right to express himself. But he was in the vanguard of brutalizing the Indian community while most mainstream journalists ambled along in a deep slumber.

In a way, I too am responsible for the continued misunderstanding of Tara's role by the Canadian mainstream. The day he was shot in 1988, Rami and I had plans to take our sons to the U.S. for a visit. As the news of the shooting broke, I knew the media would ask me to comment. George Garrett, the veteran CKNW radio reporter, was the first to call, just as we were about to leave for Seattle. I spoke to him on the record, condemning the attack and adding that I was not surprised because "Those who live by the sword die by the sword" and "you reap what you sow." On my way to Seattle I heard George give what was perhaps the only balanced report of the attempted assassination.

The national CBC program *The Journal,* hosted by Barbara Frum, had also called. They wanted me in the studio at 6:00 PM to appear on the show, but Rami read me the riot act, and I told *The Journal* to find someone else. Upon my return, I discovered Tara had been turned overnight into a lifelong votary of peace. *Vancouver Sun* journalist Kim Bolan, who had been reporting on the Indo-Canadian community since 1986, had been interviewed by *The Journal* in my stead, and she had presented Tara as peaceful compared to the Talwinder Parmars of the world, completely disregarding Tara's role in the promotion and glorification of hate and violence in Canada and India. With that, the die was cast. How did one argue that a journalist who had been shot should not be honoured once he had been deified in editorials written by the likes of Keith Spicer, formerly Canada's first commissioner of official languages and then editor of the *Ottawa Citizen*? I did not even attempt a correction of the record. Tara had almost died in the shooting, and criticizing him would have come across as insensitive. He was no longer relevant to the struggle, and in his paralyzed state he now symbolized how violence and hate maimed people. Only Punjabi speakers knew full well that he had been the victim of his own success as a tribune of terror.

ABOVE: *My running mate,
Joyce Whitman, and me
visiting Chinatown with
Bill Yee, then a Vancouver
city councillor, during the
1983 election campaign.
We lost to the Socred
candidates in our riding
of Vancouver South.*

OPPOSITE: *NDP MLA
Emery Barnes and me
at a Vancouver South
fundraiser in 1983.*

*Rami and me at home in
February 1985, a few days
after the brutal extremist
attack on me. My head
covering hides the eighty-
four stitches it took to
close my skull wounds.*

276

OPPOSITE: *Celebrating my first election victory with supporters at Heritage Hall, Vancouver, on October 17, 1991. I become the new MLA for Vancouver South that evening.*

ABOVE: *Sitting in my usual seat in my old grade eight classroom in Dosanjh Kalan during a trip to India in 1998.*

Being sworn in as government services minister by B.C.'s Lieutenant Governor David Lam on April 10, 1995. Photo © Jeff Barber

282

OPPOSITE: *Just before my swearing-in as premier: my side of the family at Government House with Lieutenant Governor Garde Gardom and Helen Gardom.*

Posing with Rami's side of the family at Government House just before my swearing-in as premier.

ABOVE: *Traditional Indian music was played for the first time at Government House in Victoria during my swearing-in as premier: Paramjit Singh Vasir on tabla and Devinder Singh Hundal on sitar and other instruments.*

TOP LEFT: *Rami and me with Pakistan's former premier Benazir Bhutto during her visit to Vancouver in 2001.*

TOP CENTRE: *Visiting the legendary Indian writer Khushwant Singh and a friend at his home in New Delhi in 2000.*

TOP RIGHT: *Rami and me at Vancouver's Gay Pride Parade in August 2000. I was proud to be the first Canadian premier to participate in a Gay Pride march. Photo © P.K. Tam*

BOTTOM LEFT: *Rami and I were received in Bollywood by several prominent actors and the chief minister of Maharashtra during our trip to India in 2000.* FROM LEFT: *Amrish Puri; Shatrughan Sinha; Chief Minister Vilasrao Deshmukh; and the host for the event, Sunil Dutt.*

ABOVE: *Speaking to the media on April 18, 2001, at Government House in Victoria. I had just met with the Lieutenant Governor to formally announce a provincial election to be held on May 16.*

OPPOSITE: *A scene outside my Vancouver-Kensington campaign office during the 2001 election campaign.*

The 2001 campaign tour bus.

ABOVE: *Pavel, Aseem, me and Rami with Beverley McLachlin, Chief Justice of the Supreme Court of Canada, at 24 Sussex Drive, Ottawa, in 2004. I had just been sworn in as the federal minister of health.*

Rami and me with Prime Minister Paul Martin at the Gandhi Mausoleum in Delhi in December 2005. Photo © Dave Chan

OPPOSITE: *Attending a 2005 meeting in Winnipeg as federal health minister with the president of the Treasury Board, Reg Alcock, and Prime Minister Paul Martin. Photo © Brigitte Bouvier*

Conferring with the prime
minister in New Delhi, 2005.
Photo © Dave Chan

During our trip to Delhi in 2005,
Prime Minister Paul Martin and
I visited Sonia Gandhi, president
of India's Congress party, at her
home. Photo © Dave Chan

PART 6

ELECTORAL

POLITICS

From the Backbench to the Cabinet

34 OUR LAW PRACTICE WAS doing well, but I felt we needed to make some changes to take it to the next level. When I broached the subject with Meb, it was clear from our conversation that restructuring was not going to work. For me, that meant our partnership had come to an end. Meb reacted with shock, and I understood. Through the thick and thin of the last ten eventful years, we had become good friends. He'd held down the proverbial fort at the practice while I ran for the legislature of B.C. in 1979 and 1983. Above all, he had saved my life by bursting onto the scene and scaring away my attacker on that fateful day in February 1985. Having done a lot of trial work, including family law, I could only console him by saying, "Even an average Canadian marriage lasts only about ten years." Meb and I reached an amicable arrangement and professionally parted ways. I then established my own firm, Dosanjh & Company, retaining the offices on Victoria Drive.

Rami, our sons and I were still living in the old three-storey home we had bought in 1983. When our neighbours to the west told us about a house across the street that was about to be listed for sale, we were interested. The elderly woman who had lived there had died, and one day I spotted her son in the front yard consulting a real estate agent. Once the realtor had left, I spoke to the son directly, and later he and I struck a deal over the phone. Only when the bank needed an inked contract a couple of months later did we write up a bare-bones deal on a plain piece of paper and sign it to complete the formalities. Throughout all this, an election was the furthest thing from our thoughts. But one late-spring weekend afternoon of 1989, the unforeseen once again came to my door.

I had been lounging and enjoying my time with my family when there was a knock on the door. I opened it, and in came a dear friend who had just attended a semi-public outreach event at the Punjabi Market for Mike Harcourt and the NDP. Mike, an old friend from his mayoralty days, had become the leader of the B.C. party. That afternoon, I learned he had been accompanied by Moe Sihota, who had been elected as the MLA for one of the ridings in Victoria. Bernie Simpson, a contender for the NDP nomination in Vancouver-Fraserview, had also been there.

Bill Vander Zalm's Socreds were not doing too well. The party had been in power in B.C. since 1953, except for the three years of Dave Barrett's NDP government. The NDP felt that power was within their reach in the next election and Harcourt's moderate image was a big help. The public also seemed to be in the mood for change.

My friend had wondered why I, a two-time NDP candidate, long-time human rights activist and an active member of the party who lived only a block and a half from the venue, was not at the meeting. He asked around, and he summed up for me in his own words what he had learned: "Ujjal is a spent force. He is disliked by Sikhs. If he is seen with the NDP or runs as a candidate, the party stands to lose ten seats." People had been selectively invited to the meeting, and I obviously had not made the cut.

I enjoyed my friend's visit. My insides were numb with hurt, but I didn't want him to know that. Politics is lonely, and one's pain can't be shared with too many. But I minded very much being left off the guest list of a party to which I had given twenty years of my life, and for a meeting of brown people in my own backyard to boot.

The next couple of days were difficult. I feared I might be dead politically. I didn't buy the truth of what my friend had heard. It was an argument made by those who disagreed with my staunch opposition to the extremists and accepted by those who did not know better or care to find out for themselves. But if the perception of my political demise was allowed to persist unchallenged, it would mean the end of my ability to make even a small difference in the world, even though my passion for social justice remained undimmed. Who would pay any attention to the musings of a has-been? The only way to vanquish the myth of my political impotence was to challenge it directly, and that was the course I settled on. I had not talked to Rami or the boys yet. So far I had persuaded only myself.

My family was not happy to hear of my decision. Rami said she would not help me gain the nomination. Pavel said he thought I had grown out of politics. If not, he said, I should. Politicians didn't make much money; how was I going to finance his and his brothers' education? I assured them they would get help to go to university, though beyond that they would be on their own. I was aware of the poor immigrant phenomenon: parents who tried to live out their own dreams vicariously through their children could find themselves staring into the abyss of depression if the children did not live up to their expectations. I did not want to be a victim of this syndrome, I told Rami and the boys. If I did not follow my heart, I might look back in my later years to see emptiness and regret what could have been. I felt guilty as hell telling my children they were not my only concern. Umber already complained that we drove rickety old cars. The reminder that I had ridden a bike to college and studied by a kerosene lamp had little effect.

A membership drive was a must if I was to make a run for the nomination, and I wanted an east side riding. The only one available was Vancouver-Kensington, and I was considering that when I happened to run into Glen Clark at a funeral service at the temple on No. 5 Road in Richmond. Clark suggested I consider running for the legislature and mentioned Fraserview. I knew that riding was already hotly contested, however, and I told him I did not want a riding with such overtly active religious institutions. Ross Street Temple was a hotbed of Khalistani activists at the time, and it allowed extremists to preach from the stage. Clark thought for a moment, and then suggested the new riding of Vancouver-Kensington, which he said was more like his own working-class Vancouver East, and a stronger NDP prospect. I had already been thinking of Vancouver-Kensington myself. It would definitely be in the winning column if the NDP got a majority.

I approached Bruce Farmer and Malcolm Jones, prominent NDP members who lived in the Vancouver-Kensington area. Jones had been asked by the party to organize the founding meeting to elect the riding's first executive. In keeping with his role, he was civil and friendly to me, but not necessarily encouraging. Bruce Farmer was frank: according to him, I didn't have a chance of winning the nomination. After losing in 1979 and 1983, I had skipped the 1986 campaign. That my friend Mike Harcourt was the party's leader was no help, since Mike had been persuaded I was bad news for the NDP's fortunes. Many activists in the riding had settled on Adrienne Peacock, a bright college instructor and a committed green NDPer. In addition, though my battle with extremism had won mainstream praise, people worried that most Sikhs would not vote for the NDP if I ran as a candidate.

I started visiting homes in Vancouver-Kensington and signing people up in as low-key a manner as possible. But a sign-up campaign, by its very nature, can't remain secret for long. Pretty soon the extremist camp was prowling my neighbourhood, trolling for NDP memberships to oppose my candidacy even though it had yet to be declared. Their campaign against me was a wake-up call to Rami and me. Immigrant communities have long used the tools available to them to settle scores on issues from faraway homelands. The difference in this case was that the actions of Khalistani extremists hurt us in Canada, and they were showing no signs of letting up. Despite it all, I handed in about seven hundred new members.

The Vancouver-Kensington founding meeting was set for November 13, 1989, at Killarney Secondary School. We organized our volunteers to get the voters out. Rami and my campaign team had prepared a slate of candidates for various executive positions, headed by Malcolm Jones and including Bruce Farmer and Adrienne Peacock. Peacock had not signed up any members, and in the race for the executive between my team and my opponents, she agreed to run with us. No matter who won the executive, she could still run to be nominated as a candidate for the election. The other camp, supported by the Khalistanis, had not submitted any memberships, so we were left to wonder about their game plan.

That became clear as the evening started. The opposing slate had ostensibly been put together by Andy Admi, a realtor, and Gurdeep Atwal, a community counsellor working with the Immigrant Services Centre, whose board had at one time been headed by Moe Sihota's businessman friend Herb Dhaliwal. Some of Herb's business associates and relatives were visibly active in the overflow crowd that evening. In 1984, Herb had asked me to stop speaking against the "Sikh community." I was sure he meant the Khalistanis. Anyone who was anybody in the ranks of the extremists in the Lower Mainland was also present that evening. It turned out that the other camp had brought a briefcase full of membership applications signed by prospective members. Even though the forms had not been submitted to or registered with the party office as yet, it was argued that people who had filled out forms should have the right to vote that evening.

There were so many people present at the meeting that our slate ran out of leaflets. I headed off to my law office to make more copies. Rami was worried about my security; it was dark out and my car was parked a couple of blocks away. But having weathered the blows of the enemy's iron, I felt impervious to any threats. When I got back, the chair was trying in vain to call the meeting to order. A bunch of Khalistani extremists whose mugs had become infamous over the years, courtesy of the television screens, had boarded the stage. In the melee, the extremists grabbed the mike. Rami, flanked by her brothers Jasbir and Harwant and her brother-in-law, Mani's husband Ginny, walked over and grabbed it back. Unable to properly conduct an election under the circumstances, however, the chair adjourned the meeting. Glen Clark, the evening's invited guest speaker, called the whole scene "awful."

The debacle at Killarney was the deliberate handiwork of the extremists, who would have lost a fair fight that evening. The fact that the completed membership forms had ended up at the meeting without enough bodies to go with them suggested that the forms may have been filled out in a hurry in a basement somewhere using a couple of phones and a list of friends, family and acquaintances. That has happened in many campaigns on behalf of all parties over the years.

Clearly, the extremists had disrupted the Killarney meeting to ensure that their "briefcase" members would be able to vote at a rescheduled meeting. The executive of the NDP would need to rule on that, so all the declared candidates were invited to make submissions to them. My position was clear: the briefcase members would not have been eligible to vote at the meeting at Killarney, and the disrupters of that meeting should not benefit from their criminal conduct. The new members should not be allowed to vote at a reconvened meeting, either. All but one member of the executive disagreed, however, and the executive ruled that the unregistered members would be allowed to register and then to vote at a new meeting on December 4. Forces bigger than the soft-spoken and utterly without influence Gurdeep Atwal were obviously at work. With the executive of the party lining up against my position, Herb Dhaliwal's relatives and friends arrayed against me, and Moe Sihota calling people in the riding in an attempt to influence the outcome of both the founding and candidate selection meetings, I was getting a good sense of the sheer depth and breadth of the party's "fear" of the "politically dead" Ujjal.

Once the date for the reconvened meeting was announced, a tsunami of hateful propaganda flooded the Punjabi community. The attacks on me were orchestrated, and some of my supporters were annoyed at my silence. The constituency I needed to focus on, however, was not the public, but the members of the NDP in Vancouver-Kensington, who would elect the executive for the riding. They needed to hear that I had not given up after the organizational fiasco of the Killarney meeting and the irrational decision by the party executive to allow questionable, perhaps illegitimate member-ships to stand. I was even more resolute to send a message to the NDP that secular and principled politics still resonated within the Indo-Canadian community; the community was not a ghetto held hostage by extremists.

The venue for the rescheduled founding meeting was John Oliver High School in South Vancouver. The party made appropriate security and balloting arrangements in advance, and NDP heavyweights were present to lend the occasion the importance it deserved. Rami had successfully insisted on a process whereby ballots were scrutinized as they were cast, to ensure there was no hanky-panky.

Riding members were issued ballots in the foyer to take with them into the auditorium. There were quite a few orange turbans in the crowd. Volunteers from both camps distributed candidate pins and information about the respective slates. Many members I knew to be our supporters had donned the rival badges, and as they passed me they either shook my hand or winked at me with a smile. Extremism is a frightening phenomenon. After the Killarney debacle, a couple of members of our slate had had second thoughts about running with us or running at all; we'd had to shore them up and reassure them they were safe. The counting took several hours, but our slate won overwhelmingly. Thunderous cheers went up, piercing the palpable tension in the auditorium.

Outside the auditorium, the extremists vowed loudly that I would never be allowed to cross the ocean to reach Victoria as an MLA. Our slate retreated to my small home, where we partied late into the evening with our new executive and our friends and supporters, including Kashmir Dhaliwal, Amrik Sangha and Kuldip Thandi. The place was standing-room-only. Our victory was bigger than just winning the nomination for me to be a candidate for the legislature of B.C. For the first time in Canada, we had successfully confronted separatists, extremists and the politicians who used them as attack dogs. The people celebrating that night were vindicated in their belief in a more wholesome citizenship than one defined by a particular religion, caste or colour.

The new executive set to work and scheduled the nomination meeting for Sunday, January 7, 1990. I remained in close touch with our volunteers and members, who were extremely loyal to what I stood for. The ballot was their secret weapon, and they were determined to use it to send a message.

Before the founding meeting, I had telephoned Sharon Olsen, a friend and one-time assistant to MP Ian Waddell, to ask her to join our executive slate. When Sharon later surfaced as an aspirant for the nomination herself, I realized why she had tried to dissuade me from running in the first place. She had told me on the phone that because the riding was 35 per cent Chinese, it would be better to have a white candidate; the Chinese people wouldn't vote for an Indian, she said. That was the first time I had heard it implied that Chinese Canadians were racists, and I didn't buy it. I believed if I acquitted myself properly in the public domain, people would accept me as one of them, a Canadian above all else.

Olsen, Admi and Atwal all contested the nomination against me. Once the speeches were over, the counting began. It went relatively quickly. I won, receiving over two hundred votes, with Olson a distant second.

During the lead-up to the nomination, Moe Sihota had made calls in the riding on Olsen's behalf; I was told this by several reliable sources and was not convinced when Sihota's father called to assure me it was not the case. I have never understood the antipathy Sihota felt for me. When he brought in Stan Persky to contest the 1979 nomination against me, I had never met the man. In the B.C. legislature in 1989, when Sihota asked for Premier Vander Zalm's response to the Indo-Canadian community's request for a commemorative plaque for the *Komagata Maru*, Vander Zalm had unfairly accused him of abusing his position and heritage for partisan purposes. A few days later, Sihota, in a gratuitous dig at me, suggested that my role in fighting the extremists was akin to Vander Zalm's criticism of him. His comment was reported in a scarcely read Khalistani rag. When I wrote him asking for an apology, he did not respond. I sent Glen Clark and Darlene Marzari a translation of Moe's words, along with a copy of my letter, and I mentioned to Clark that he might warn Sihota that I would consider suing if he did not apologize. Shortly after that, Sihota called me, minimizing his remarks. Darshan Gill was only too pleased to publish Moe's written apology in *Canada Darpan*.

35 WENDY JANG, TOMMY TAO and a few other activists helped me pick a name for myself using Chinese characters that meant "new ambition"/"new determination," and we printed an introductory trilingual leaflet containing English, Cantonese and a smattering of Punjabi. With those in hand, we started a door-to-door canvass of the riding. Most often I was lucky enough to have a female Cantonese speaker accompany me; Mike Harcourt was well-liked by the city's Chinese Canadians from his mayoralty days, which helped. The reception we got only improved when Vander Zalm resigned in the heat of the Fantasy Gardens conflict-of-interest scandal and was replaced by Rita Johnston after a bruising internal fight among the Socreds. At the doorstep, we sensed a deep yearning for change.

South Asians made up only 4 per cent of the Kensington population. Volunteers called people to identify supporters and possible sign locations. The telephone lines at my law office became a regular phone bank, and Rami had her steady hand in most of the organizing. I took weekend trips to other B.C. cities to raise money. In Williams Lake, veteran councillor Gurbax Saini led the effort; in Quesnel it was Councillor Gordy Sangha; in Kelowna, Chanchal Bal; and in Prince George, Piara Beesla. Money was collected in Toronto by my family and friends too. We held a fundraiser at the Croatian Cultural Centre, and along with the usual suspects, MLA Emery Barnes, Dave Barrett, MP Ian Waddell and legendary city councillor Harry Rankin attended the event. Amrik Sangha by himself brought in close to $3,000, more than a sixteenth of the total needed to run my campaign.

I took every speaking and campaigning opportunity that arose. I wrote guest columns in local community papers and attended coffee parties in various neighbourhoods. The door-to-door canvassing was constant.

The writ was dropped on September 19 for the polling to take place on October 17. Malcolm Jones, Bruce Farmer and Rami rented an office, prepared a rough budget and gathered staff and stuff for the campaign. The telephones were in by the time Barry Salmon, the campaign manager arranged by the party, arrived. Barry was an NDP activist and official from Atlantic Canada who came highly recommended. We hit it off right away. A short, stocky man dressed in a trench coat and cowboy boots, Barry took immediate charge of things, moving the furniture around to put his own chair and table in a commanding place in the office. From then on, I did what I was told to do and went where I was told to go. Barry and I both knew our roles.

Because I was not an incumbent with a high profile, it was important for me to do lots of media to create a buzz around our campaign. I did not speak Cantonese, which was a terrible weakness of my campaign. I did my best on Chinese Canadian media and panels while feeling outgunned linguistically by the Socred candidate, Gim Huey. In an all-party event at the well-known Pink Pearl restaurant sponsored by S.U.C.C.E.S.S., the non-profit serving newcomers to Canada, I was the chief debater on the NDP's behalf. At the end, many in the audience congratulated me for what they said was a good performance.

By happenstance, the riding's only all-candidates meeting was scheduled for the same evening as the leaders' TV debate. Despite that, there was a large turnout to watch Gim Huey, Liberal Ted Olynyk, John O'Flynn of the Family Coalition Party and I slug it out for an hour and a half.

When I got back to our campaign office following the all-candidates meeting, the leaders' debate was still underway. The magic moment of that debate, though, had already come and gone. I watched replays of it during the post-debate discussions. During an awkwardly garrulous exchange between Mike Harcourt and Rita Johnston, Gordon Wilson, the leader of the B.C. Liberal party, had intervened, saying, "...here's a classic example of why nothing ever gets done in the province of British Columbia." The clip, which was played over and over again in the media for the next few days, catapulted Wilson and the B.C. Liberals to top of the public opinion polls. A new player had arrived in B.C. politics. We put our heads down and redoubled our efforts to ensure a win in our riding.

On election night, as the polls closed, I waited in our campaign office watching the results come in. By about nine o'clock, it became clear that the NDP was winning in both Vancouver-Kensington and the province. As Barry Salmon drove me to the Heritage Hall on Main Street for the victory party, it dawned on me that my life was entering a new stage. I was now the elected representative for a constituency whose population was 50 per cent visible minority: 35 per cent Chinese, 5 per cent Indian and 10 per cent others, including Filipinos — a real United Nations. I had worked so hard to get elected, only to feel nervous about whether I would be able to do justice to the responsibility.

I was not the first MLA of colour to be elected to the B.C. legislature. Frank Calder, Emery Barnes and Rosemary Brown had preceded me. I was not even the first Indian or South Asian to be elected to the B.C. assembly. Moe Sihota was. But the hall went wild as we entered. The two hundred or so people gathered there had helped elect me, and it was their victory too. I had been a public entity for a long time. Now I was officially a public person. If in the past my foibles had ever been ignored, from now on they wouldn't be.

THE SOCREDS had been left with only seven MLAS. The Liberals had elected seventeen under Gordon Wilson, and the NDP formed government with fifty-one members in the House. The immediate task for Mike Harcourt was the selection of his first cabinet. While the bureaucracy and the political apparatchiks planned the swearing-in, most of us cooled our heels near our telephones just in case the premier-elect came calling. No call came through for me, though there had been some speculation I could be the dark horse for the coveted post of

Attorney General. I'd known in my heart the chance was remote, and I didn't lose any sleep about being passed over.

Harcourt's swearing-in was a mammoth celebration at the University of Victoria. The victory was sweet after sixteen years of the NDP looking in from the opposition benches. Rami and I attended the swearing-in, and when the cabinet left to attend to their new ministerial duties, we headed back to Vancouver. In a parliamentary democracy, backbenchers are usually called upon to support the work of the cabinet or given special assignments. Some of what they are asked to do is important, such as recommending solutions to issues faced by governments, and some of it is requested just to keep them busy.

I entered the Parliament Buildings in Victoria for the first time as an MLA on a sunny morning. I paused near the fountain in the foreground of the building and I stood there for a long time, watching the building as if it were talking to me. The legislature's exquisite stained glass windows added to the building's intricate architecture. It radiated majesty and power. As I entered the building, I thought of the ancestors on whose shoulders I rode as an elected member of the legislature.

In India, many people use their first and last names only, particularly if, like me, they have several names. In Canada, many of my compatriots from Punjab simply added the middle name "Singh" in referring to me, without determining whether that actually completed my name. It did not. Feeling that our names sounded a bit "old," Chachaji had added "Dev" before "Singh" to Bhaji's and my names as we sat for the grade eight Middle Standard external examinations in Punjab. So my full name was Ujjal Dev Singh Dosanjh, and I was Ujjal Dosanjh to the world.

Self-identification is a right we all enjoy in a democratic society. Or so I had thought until the self-styled religious police of the eighties, led by Tara Hayer, started a denunciation parade against me, mocking the chosen parts of my full name and going so far as to imply that I concealed my Sikh origins by not using "Singh" and that I hid "Dev" because I didn't want people to know I was really a Hindu. In response, I started referring to the first Sikh Guru Nanak by his full name, the one under which he founded Sikhism: Guru Nanak Dev. While it is more common among Hindus, "Dev" is part of many Sikh names. In 1991, Vancouver journalist Belle Puri, herself a proud Canadian of Indian heritage, asked me on camera, as a newly elected MLA, how I identified myself. I replied, "I am a Canadian by citizenship. I am an Indian by heritage. I am a Punjabi by mother tongue. And if at all it is important for someone to know, I was born and raised in a Sikh family."

The first meeting of the NDP caucus was in a committee room on the second floor. Because of the size of our caucus, we would soon be given a newer and bigger room in which to meet. But on that day, as we crowded into the room, Moe, Harry Lali and I happened to enter together. Moe Sihota cracked, "Here comes the Punjabi mafia," prompting laughter from those behind the gathered mikes and cameras.

Once the House was recalled, I took my turn to speak during the debate on the Speech from the Throne. Rereading that speech recently, I remembered what a voracious reader I had been before embracing the busy life of an elected politician. At the time, I could quote Ralph Waldo Emerson and John Kenneth Galbraith in the same breath.

Mike Harcourt asked me to represent him in Vancouver on many fronts. I became his permanent representative on issues in the Downtown Eastside, including addiction, public safety and affordable housing. The problems in this neighbourhood were intractable and complex. Yet workers like the inimitable John Turvey, who had founded and ran the needle exchange program, were icons of hope and determination. A recovered addict himself, Turvey was aggressive to the point of being rude in his devotion to the cause of saving lives by reducing infections and overdoses. It took me some time to realize that a true activist needs to speak truth to power, even if the truth is bitter. I had been an activist for farm, domestic and janitorial workers' rights, but I was unschooled in the advocacy required in the alleys and streets of the Downtown Eastside.

Early after the election, a multi-party members' committee on the Constitution was established to prepare B.C.'s position on the controversial but not yet dead Meech Lake Accord. I was one of several committee members who travelled in the dead of winter to twenty-two full-day hearings all over B.C. and then made recommendations to Moe Sihota, who had been named minister of constitutional affairs.

I soon learned that being excluded from the cabinet was a blessing in disguise. It gave me time to learn the ropes as a new MLA, reorganize my law practice and spend more time with my family. There was a lot to learn too about the way the legislature functioned and the dos and don'ts of conduct in the House. Regular government caucus meetings gave us an opportunity to find out what the cabinet had been up to, though caucus was not always informed beforehand about forthcoming announcements; sometimes we learned about cabinet and government goings-on at the same time the public did. My constituency work was steady, helping people with issues ranging from Workers' Compensation Board cases and landlord/tenant complaints to welfare claims.

I had also become involved in the Chinese head tax issue. The head tax had been levied in 1885 by the federal government to discourage immigration from China. At the urging of the province of B.C., in an environment of racist paranoia about immigrants taking away jobs, the Canadian government had obliged the politicians and the labour leaders of the day. Under the new legislation, any Chinese immigrant to Canada was charged fifty dollars as the price of entry. Eventually, the tax was hiked to a prohibitive $500 per person. Before being abolished in 1923, the head tax brought $23 million to the federal coffers. In my first speech in the House, I referred to the notice of motion I had placed before the House early in the initial sitting of the new legislature, expressing the hope that the House would support my appeal to the federal government to correct this historical injustice and provide a reasonable redress.

On May 22, 1992, almost 107 years after B.C. had successfully sought the imposition of the head tax, my motion for redress was unanimously passed by the B.C. legislature. The issue had earlier been raised in the House of Commons by Vancouver East MP Margaret Mitchell, and several years later, when I was a federal opposition MP, the government of Stephen Harper would issue an apology and provide a token payment to those who had paid the head tax or their surviving spouses.

In its dying days, the unpopular Socred regime had promised to put to referendum the question of whether or not British Columbians should have access to the tools of recall and initiative, essentially allowing them the power to vote between elections to remove elected officials and to compel legislative initiatives upon the government. The question had appeared on the ballot during the October 1991 election, and the overwhelming majority of the voters had voted in favour. Mike Harcourt now asked me to chair an all-party committee of the legislature to study the issue, hold public hearings and report within a year on how the government should enshrine in law the will of the people.

To ensure that everyone had a say, the committee held hearings across the province starting in the fall of 1992. In November 1994, after extensive deliberations, we reported our findings and made recommendations.

On the face of it, implementing recall and initiative seemed an easy question. But the process is essentially alien to a parliamentary form of government. We were asked to graft tools suited to a U.S. style of government onto our own system. The challenge was to implement these tools in a way that would not destabilize future governments and would continue to protect vulnerable minorities from the whims of the majority. The process took time, and the media generally pushed the cynical line that we were the committee of delay. The headline of one of Vaughn Palmer's several columns in the *Vancouver Sun* said it all: "Victoria hems, haws and won't recall." The *Vancouver Province* ran a story with the headline "MLAs stack deck to avoid recalls." But in the end, a *Vancouver Sun* editorial captured the essence of our report in a supportive commentary and concluded: "The safeguards recommended by the committee should be built into the legislation; otherwise, this experiment in grassroots power is sure to be abused and in time to self destruct." The Recall and Initiative Act of B.C. has stringent but achievable thresholds, making individual MLAs more accountable without destroying the inherent stability of our system of government. It was debated and passed in the spring session and enacted in February 1995.

Since then, the legislation has functioned the way it was intended to, avoiding partisan campaigns to refight elections or policy questions. In the case of a former Liberal MLA for Parksville-Qualicum, Paul Reitsma, the mere existence of the legislation proved effective. Elected in 1996, Reitsma was discovered in early 1998 to have sent letters to a Parksville newspaper under assumed names attacking his opponents and praising himself. Reitsma was expelled from the B.C. Liberal opposition caucus, but despite numerous calls for his resignation, he sat as an independent until June 1998, when a petition for his recall appeared to have enough signatures to trigger the recall process. Rather than become the first B.C. politician to be recalled under the new legislation, Reitsma resigned.

36 DURING THE FIRST TWO YEARS of the NDP government under Mike Harcourt, the environment became a particular focus of concern, with recurring blockades against forestry propelling the issue to the cabinet table. A new Commission on Resources and Environment (CORE) was asked to make recommendations on land-use planning in four areas of the province. One area under its consideration was Vancouver Island's Clayoquot Sound, the focal point of the "war in the woods" that had erupted between environmentalists and logging interests under the previous government. While the CORE consultations were underway in March 1993, some three hundred demonstrators forced their way past the main entrance of the legislative buildings in Victoria into the rotunda. The slogan-chanting crowd pushed on toward the doors to the chamber, and in the ensuing melee some personnel of the legislature were injured. Calm finally reigned, but I found it ironic that, as a left-wing government contemplating changes to the province's Forest Practices Code, we faced some of the most serious disruptions in B.C. history.

I've since learned that in politics it is often one's own friends who create unanticipated crises and challenges. Activists have their own mandates and causes they are genuinely committed to. Even the most well-intentioned governments and like-minded activists are often at odds, since the government has an obligation to govern for all and activists have specific causes to pursue. As such, compromises are temporary and conflict permanent, regardless of the government's political stripe.

In the spring session of 1993, amendments to the province's human rights legislation were introduced. The amendments were aimed at ensuring any communication not intended to be private did not discriminate against or promote hatred of a person, group or class of persons. The amendments were fairly broad, aimed at protecting minority groups and individuals such as gays, lesbians and people of colour. The Liberal opposition, however, excoriated us for what they regarded as excessive limits on freedom of expression. The day of the second reading I was in Vancouver for a prearranged day off when I got a call from the premier's office; I was asked to return to the legislature in time to address the amendments that afternoon. There was nothing special in the remarks I made, though. I was still a practising member of the bar, so my intervention was mainly a legal analysis of the existing legislation and of why the proposed amendments were both legally and socially appropriate. What made my short speech stick in my memory was a comment afterwards from John Heaney, a one-time NDP deputy minister, who said he thought he'd been listening to "our Attorney General" two years before my appointment to that position actually happened. The amendments passed.

It was a busy two years in Victoria. Along with much other legislation, our government also drafted and passed the Freedom of Information and Protection of Privacy Act under the leadership of Attorney General Colin Gabelmann. I sat on the committee that reviewed the draft legislation before it was introduced in the House. My legal training and experience did not make the draft any easier to digest, though; that was the fault of neither the drafters nor those who briefed us. The complex but important legislation for the first time threw open government records to the public while also protecting privacy.

Backbenchers were also assigned to sit on various all-party committees of the legislature. The NDP backbench itself was divided into two caucus committees: one focussed on social issues and the other dealt with economic issues. Activists, community organizations and various experts sought to make representations to the appropriate committee on government policy. Based on these submissions and the research made available to us, the committees made recommendations to the government. Not too often, however, did we see caucus committees' concerns reflected in active government legislation or policy agendas. The Harcourt government tried its best to make the lives of the NDP backbenchers more productive and interesting, but that could not overcome the reality that the cabinet and the premier were the government.

Over time, fellow backbenchers Gretchen Brewin, Mike Farnworth, Sue Hammell and I, with Leonard Krog occasionally joining us, evolved into what we called the Tea Caucus. We met in the dining room of the legislature after Question Period, often joking about our "state of respectable insignificance," a Latin expression I had come across in my reading. Over the years I have spoken to many backbenchers from other parliamentary democracies, and the feeling is quite common.

The most important role backbenchers play is that of supporting the government in the House. Despite Pierre Trudeau's famous remark about backbench MPs being "nobodies" beyond the parliamentary precinct, there can be no government without them. But party discipline and the desire to eventually get into cabinet do encourage backbenchers to toe the party line. Quite often, the mavericks among them are those who have abandoned any dreams of a cabinet position or have realized they are never going to make it. Being freed from the clutches of cabinet ambition can be empowering for a backbencher. In the dying days of an unpopular government facing sure defeat, backbenchers may decide there is nothing to lose by rebelling against the leader or the party.

Policy and legislative initiatives were brought before caucus after the cabinet-caucus joint committee had reviewed them, so that the members could raise any concerns they might have. Because the caucus did not have access to the same level of information or to the briefings at the disposal of cabinet, the discussions could be perfunctory. But on environmental, forestry and budgetary initiatives, the debate was often heated. The Harcourt government had inherited the "war in the woods" from the Socreds, but the intensity of that war and the divide between the urban South of the province on the one hand and the Interior and the North on the other was clearly evident in our caucus.

The House was about to rise for the summer in 1993 when Harcourt invited me to dinner at a hotel close to the legislature. I was intrigued. This was the first such invitation from him in the over two years since our election. When I got to the hotel, Joy MacPhail, the caucus chair, was there as well. There had been rumours about an impending cabinet shuffle, and Harcourt was clearly weighing his options. From what he said, the dinner was ostensibly meant to thank Joy and me: Joy for managing the caucus through some difficult times and me for standing in for Mike in and around Vancouver. But if our conversation that night was a job interview of sorts, I obviously did not fit Harcourt's immediate plans. On September 15, 1993, Joy MacPhail was sworn in as the minister of social services in a shuffle that saw thirteen ministries change hands and three ministers fired.

With the shuffle, Harcourt sought to change the message people were getting from our then-unpopular government. In a major speech, he attacked the welfare "varmints" he said were plaguing the province, pledging to "clear the cheats and the deadbeats off the welfare rolls." The province's welfare rules were tightened, with the corresponding implementation of the B.C. Benefit, a monthly payment to the working poor to supplement their employment earnings. Both NDP activists and social justice advocates were highly critical, though Harcourt got a positive response from the public at large. MacPhail's presence in the cabinet helped to assuage the left wing. At the time, she lived with Ken Georgetti, president of the B.C. Federation of Labour. Harcourt was not considered to be close to labour interests, and as the joke went, Georgetti had become a permanent but invisible member of the Harcourt cabinet even before MacPhail was inducted.

Being left out of the cabinet during the fall shuffle forced me to reconsider my long-term plans. I had been content to be left out in October 1991, when I was a new MLA needing to learn the ropes. But now I had two years of experience under my belt. I had headed the committee on recall and initiative and been part of the members' committee on the Constitution. In my riding and around Vancouver I had met with many individuals and groups, both individually and on Harcourt's behalf. And of course I had sat through many a Question Period, witnessing and enjoying the exchanges. I needed to do more. I felt I was underutilized, and I was financially much poorer than I would have been as a private lawyer.

I spent several days considering my options, and then made an appointment to see Harcourt at the cabinet offices in Vancouver. The House did not sit in the fall, so MLAs did not have to be in Victoria. The cabinet met on Wednesdays, and the rest of the time the premier and his ministers were in various parts of the province on government business or in their ministerial offices or ridings. As I drove downtown on the appointed day, I reviewed in my mind what I was planning to say to Harcourt. The sun was shining brightly, and the softer edges of life appeared to have hardened. It was the steeling of my heart. I had never asked anyone for favours, and I was not going to ask for one now. I was not meeting Harcourt to ask if he would put me in cabinet. He had made his decision, and it was time I conveyed him mine.

In his office, I found the same friendly Harcourt I had known for the better part of my Canadian life. He greeted me with a welcoming smile. We sat across from one another at a small coffee table, chatting as we looked out at the sparkling sea and the mountains in the distance. I was sure he had guessed why I was there. Despite understanding the difficult decisions he faced choosing a cabinet, I said, I was extremely disappointed at not being included. He reviewed what he had had to contend with, but I stood firm. From then on, I told him, I would not be doing any events for him or the government. I would faithfully do my constituency work; as a backbencher, I would support the work of government and complete my committee assignments. Finally, I told him I would not run in the next election if at the time of its call I was still not in cabinet in a meaningful role. I was not angry with him, I told Harcourt, but I was not prepared to spend the years to come as I had spent the last two. We parted with a mutual understanding of each other's constraints and imperatives.

Since Joy MacPhail's elevation to cabinet, the position of caucus chair had stood vacant. Without much forethought I had extended support to my friend Leonard Krog in his bid for the position. But being left out of the cabinet had changed much for me: I wanted to make as much of a contribution in my elected public life as possible, since I might not be running again. When a couple of caucus colleagues approached me about running for the caucus chair, I was extremely reluctant, because I had already promised Krog my support. Krog was gracious and suggested I should run regardless. The caucus's vote went in my favour.

I chaired the caucus for the next twenty months. When the House sat, the caucus met every day. Out of session, caucus meetings were held approximately monthly, in different parts of the province. As chair I made some changes. I put a time limit on the ministers' presentations on policy or legislation, to ensure there was ample time left for questions from the backbenchers. Quite often ministers brought in bureaucrats to make their presentations, but as chair I made sure civil servants took up the time of the caucus only if the minister concerned deemed it absolutely necessary for them to be there. We were more interested in hearing the political rationale for policy changes from the ministers themselves, since they would be fronting the campaign to sell the changes to the public. I also began the practice of setting aside ten minutes at the end of every meeting for members who had questions for the cabinet members on any subject. I felt that if the ministers could answer the opposition benches during Question Period, they should easily be able to answer friendly questions in the privacy of the caucus room.

As the NDP was veering right with Harcourt's "varmints, welfare cheats and deadbeats" speech, the B.C. Liberals experienced a scandal of their own. Judi Tyabji, a descendant of the great Indian patriot Badruddin Tyabji, had been made the Liberal house leader by Gordon Wilson, and there were rumours of dissension in their ranks. A four-page letter found its way into the media, confirming that despite their public denial, Wilson and Tyabji were having an extramarital affair. Sex and politics are a toxic mix; in the otherwise sombre surroundings of the legislative precinct, the combination can make for salacious gossip. The fact that Wilson and Tyabji had not been forthright from the beginning destroyed any chance of Wilson remaining the leader of the Liberals. Other forces were at play to end his tenure as well. The then Vancouver mayor Gordon Campbell, who had the backing of business groups in the Lower Mainland, was set on wresting control of the B.C. Liberals. In the leadership review that followed, Wilson lost to Campbell. Wilson and Tyabji formed a new party, the Progressive Democratic Alliance, and followed up by making their marital alliance official.

The most amusing part of the Tyabji-Wilson scandal was the lawsuit Tyabji launched in an attempt to stem the widespread publication of a love letter she'd written; she argued that she held the copyright on it, as it was intended only for Wilson's eyes. The copyright argument was novel but silly in the heartlessness of the political arena.

At the end of 1993 I decided to visit India for a change of scenery. I hadn't been there since January 1986, and I eagerly soaked up the sights, sounds and smells. I was concerned about my security but Punjab had recently elected a secular government, and I felt I was safe as long as I travelled discreetly. Old journalist friends were anxious for my take on the situation in Canada, as was I for their assessment of the state of India.

I attended a seminar in Chandigarh on "The Identity Crisis among the NRIS" — non-resident Indians abroad — where I was presenting a talk. There I bumped into my Canadian writer friend Ajmer Rode and I asked him to join me and others on the dais. From the questions, it appeared the audience members were most worried about the "loss of culture" for NRIS; I felt that would inevitably change, I said, and there was nothing wrong with natural evolution. People seemed oblivious to the cultural and ethical rot setting in in Punjab and in India, the country as a whole, as well. When one of the attendees, sporting stubble and sitting next to a man with a saffron turban, asked a question about the extremists in Canada, I suggested we look forward to more important struggles in India, like the need for food, shelter, equality and social justice. The man smiled, and thus began my enduring friendship with the well-known journalist Baljit Balli.

Punjab appeared to be on the mend after years of terrorism, but not without the terrible blemish of terrorists and innocents alike being killed in all-too-frequent "fake encounters" — episodes in which deliberate killings were staged to appear as acts of self-defence. I voiced concerns about these to Beant Singh, then the chief minister of Punjab, at a breakfast he hosted for me. Beant and the Punjab Police had been credited with stemming the tide of terrorism but not without using the horrible tactics of false accusations and fake encounters. And acts of brutality were by no means reserved for suspected terrorists. The day of the breakfast, some women from a "lower" caste who'd been accused of theft had had the word *chor*, thief, etched with knives on their foreheads by police. I raised it with Beant, and I was shocked at his response: he found the story a reason for mirth. Just eighteen months after our breakfast in Chandigarh, Beant Singh was killed by a suicide bomber.

PARTY ACTIVISTS from different ethnic groups had been asking the Canadian government to expand the list of examinable languages for university entrance to include Punjabi, Mandarin and Japanese. I had spoken in the legislature early in 1994 on the matter, urging my government colleagues to support the initiative, and Harcourt announced the change that summer at the Chinese Cultural Centre in Vancouver. Of course the change would help cement NDP support in the affected communities, but it was also the right thing to do, given the evolving demographic reality of Canada and the economic shifts in the world.

Harcourt's cabinet shuffle was also bearing some fruit. His approval rating rose as did support for the party. Our agenda was full of new labour legislation, and over fifty other bills passed. The caucus pursued the City of Vancouver for information involving city contracts given to a developer, Jim Moodie, a friend of Gordon Campbell, during Campbell's mayoralty days. The City played hardball, delaying the information by arguing that it would cost the City too much to provide it and that Moodie had received city contracts under Harcourt too.

The B.C. government's gaming policy was under review, and there was a lot of opposition to a proposed casino for the downtown

Vancouver waterfront. We were also contemplating expanding charity casinos and introducing electronic bingo and video terminals to them. Tom Perry, one of my most honourable and ethical colleagues (and who had been shuffled out of cabinet the previous year), was vehemently opposed to the for-profit, Las Vegas–style casino being promoted by Ken Georgetti and the B.C. Federation of Labour. I too felt a waterfront Vegas-style casino would be a huge mistake. Regardless of the jobs it might create, it was bound to have negative impacts, including an increase in organized crime and a siphoning of money from programs supporting poor people and from arts, cultural and social organizations dependent on charity gaming. NDP MLA Bernie Simpson had already gone public with his opposition to it. Tom and I penned a joint letter that received fairly wide publicity. The premier's office was not very happy with us, and neither was Georgetti, who was a director of the union fund–backed VLC Properties, which had partnered with Mirage Resorts' Steve Wynn for the proposed waterfront casino.

The gaming hot potato was made even hotter by the fact that some in the aboriginal community wanted to operate for-profit casinos on reserves, ostensibly for economic development. The cabinet was particularly concerned that the aboriginal view of sovereignty might be leveraged to expand gaming onto reserves without government input or control. To forestall that eventuality, some cabinet members were ready to allow casinos on reserves with stringent conditions. In October, Harcourt rejected the waterfront casino idea but allowed the expansion of charity gaming, including adding electronic bingo and video terminals.

Into the relative quiet of my backbencher's life in the summer of 1994 came two envelopes carrying hate mail addressed to me at home. One of them incoherently referred to the murder of a politician in India. It could have been the work of a deranged lunatic or some organized hate group; it was hard to discern much from the hateful scribble. If it hadn't been for the experience of the iron bar on my skull, I would have ignored the hate mail completely. The police did get involved, and happily nothing untoward happened.

I HAD NO PLANS FOR travel abroad in the fall of 1994
until I was approached by the B.C. trade office to accompany
Moe Sihota and Bernie Simpson on a trade mission to India.
I spent three weeks in Delhi, Chandigarh and Punjab, travelling with
the trade delegation and on my own. We met with then finance minister Manmohan Singh, who would become India's prime minister in
2004, the first Sikh to hold the office. I also met with veteran journalist
Khushwant Singh, who had become a friend on my 1985 trip to India
and had featured me in one of his syndicated columns. He and I shared
our concerns about the deteriorating state of civil liberties and human
rights in India.

At a briefing specially organized by India's Ministry of Home
Affairs, Sihota, Simpson and I were given information about the numbers of detainees in Indian prisons and the extent of the security
threat India faced. I already knew much of what we were being told.
For instance, despite the persistent problems in Punjab and Kashmir,
there were actually more people in detention under anti-terrorism laws
in the state of Gujarat. Why were people languishing in jails without
charges or trials? I asked. Why were so-called fake encounters still taking place, with people who were uncharged and untried being killed
by the police in cold blood? My anger found its expression in lawyer-
like questions that were met with bureaucratic gobbledygook laden
with euphemisms and buzzwords. I did not buy the Home Ministry's
rationale for such massive denial of basic rights to Indians.

One evening I spoke at the theatre in Chandigarh named after
the late Nobel Laureate Rabindranath Tagore. Marriages to NRIs was
the issue. Many male Indian immigrants to countries such as Canada,
the U.S. and the U.K. returned to India to get married, but after the

wedding and consummation, the grooms left and would not sponsor their wives to join them abroad. That was the basic problem, with many variations. On the flip side, some of the men and women sponsored as spouses in countries like Canada never intended to stay married to their sponsors, simply melting into the rest of society directly from the airport or after a short cohabitation with the sponsoring spouse. Both deceitful sponsors and those merely posing as brides or grooms are despicable. But people willing to marry anyone in exchange for a plane ride to a "foreign heaven" are not free from blame. My remarks that night at the Tagore Theatre must have irked those who had come for a more sympathetic hearing.

A CONTINUING SAGA, that of the Nanaimo Commonwealth Holding Society, returned in May 1992 to haunt Harcourt, even though he'd had nothing to do with the debacle. The Society and three other groups with ties to the party had been controlled by Dave Stupich, a veteran NDP MLA, minister and MP who was an accountant by profession. Set up in the 1950s, the Society raised money from charity bingos, and now there were accusations that the money had been funnelled to the party rather than to charitable causes. Harcourt had never been involved with the Society himself. But realizing that the scandal wasn't going away, he asked forensic accountant Ron Parks to audit the books and prepare a report.

We headed into the 1995 spring session hoping that the Parks report, due sometime in March or April, would clear the party of wrongdoing and put an end to the constant scandal mongering. However, Harcourt's approval rating was sliding. It took a major hit when a televised "town hall" forum meant to set the stage before tabling the budget turned into an unmitigated disaster. CKNW's Victoria bureau chief, Kim Emerson, added to the government's woes by making a so-called citizen's complaint alleging favouritism by Harcourt in awarding Ron Johnson's NOW Communications the NDP's advertising contracts. Until Harcourt was cleared by the B.C. Conflict of Interest Commissioner Ted Hughes and the Auditor General, George Morfitt, there was a media feeding frenzy. The budget debate got lost in the din around the Emerson complaint and allegations that government services minister Robin Blencoe had sexually harassed three women who worked for him. Blencoe was fired.

Perched on the backbench, I watched all of this unfolding. Then a couple of days after Blencoe's removal from cabinet and caucus, Harcourt's chief of staff, Chris Chilton, told me to be ready to be sworn in to replace Blencoe. My first question was whether David Lam, B.C.'s first lieutenant governor of colour, would be around to administer the oath. Lam was nearing the end of his extended term, but I was delighted to hear that he would remain in office until April 21. I was scheduled to take the oath of cabinet on Monday, April 10.

I spent the weekend mowing the lawn and cleaning up the backyard. My son Umber would travel with us to Victoria, but Pavel and Aseem were in the middle of term-end papers and exams. None of my sons has ever been much impressed with the world of politics, perhaps because they have experienced so much of the attendant nastiness. Rami and I prepared ourselves for a life together that was going to be even busier than before.

On Monday morning I flew to Victoria by Helijet. Our extended family and friends travelled with Umber and Rami by ferry. At the office of the government services minister, Deputy Minister Maureen Nicholls gave me a crash course in what was about to happen at Government House. Nicholls would prove a good teacher, and she kept me from making many a rookie mistake as minister in the months to come.

Lam administered the requisite oaths, and before I signed the register he warmly shook my hand and whispered, "I have read your name often in the Chinese papers. Until today, I thought you were Chinese." Obviously my adopted Chinese name had worked that wonder! Jokingly, I said I was a quarter Chinese, since my grandfather had worked in Shanghai as a security guard, moonlighted as a wrestler there and travelled to Hong Kong to play soccer.

Formalities over, it was time for the media scrum. The reporters zeroed in on my ethnicity. I guess they assumed "whites" had no ethnicity, since nobody had ever asked a white rookie minister whether his or her induction into cabinet meant "a greater role for multicultur-alism on the government agenda," as David Hogben of the *Vancouver Sun* phrased the question. "Can we get beyond colour to the real issues facing British Columbians?" I replied. According to Hogben's later story, my response indicated impatience with reporters. Darn right it did. I am impatient with anyone who pigeonholes people based on gender, ethnicity, sexual orientation, religion or any other distinct-ive quality. Multiculturalism pushed to the ultimate breeds isolation. Assimilationists aren't the only enemies of true diversity.

During my first Question Period after being sworn in, I got a question from the well-known, bright and likeable Liberal MLA David Mitchell. "When is the minister going to answer a question on video lottery terminals?" Mitchell said, to which I responded, "As soon as the honourable member asks one." The House on both sides roared with laughter. In my heart, I thanked Mitchell for not asking me a real question that day. I wouldn't have had an answer.

The government had asked my former law school professor Bill Black to do a review of B.C.'s human rights legislation and make rec-ommendations for strengthening it. Activists welcomed the move. Bill Bennett's government had disbanded the Human Rights Commission and the Labour Department's Human Rights Branch, and Bill Black had been a member of the Commission when it was scrapped. As gov-ernment services minister, I used recommendations from Black's report to shepherd expanded legislation through the House.

The gaming issue posed some difficulty. There had been some negotiations with aboriginal leaders; despite Harcourt's clear policy enunciation in October 1994, some chiefs were insisting on what to me looked like Vegas-style casinos and video lottery terminals. Cabinet was divided on whether or not to end the negotiations, but I argued for a quick termination. Eventually I got the go-ahead since there was no chance of us finding an acceptable resolution. I called a few chiefs to let them know about the decision before I announced it to the press. I addressed the notion of a sovereign right to gaming by saying,

"It's never been the intention of this province to treat gaming as an aboriginal right." To those who raised the possibility of violence by native groups or the setting up of illegal casinos on reserves, my answer was even simpler. I expected them to obey the laws of B.C., I said, as well as the Criminal Code of Canada. Keith Baldrey of BCTV led the evening news with the line "There is a new sheriff in town," emphasizing the toughness of my stance. I had thought I was simply being firm and clear. That is perception for you.

In the bigger picture, things for the government as a whole were not going too well. Ron Parks forwarded his forensic report on the Nanaimo Commonwealth Holding Society to Elizabeth Cull, the NDP minister of finance. Just as Cull was about to share the report with cabinet and release it publicly, the Ministry of the Attorney General under Colin Gabelmann forbade her from doing so; the ministry asked for and received all copies Cull had in her possession. Through no fault of Cull's, or of anyone else in cabinet, the report was being withheld for legitimate reasons: to protect a criminal investigation that was underway. The call for a public inquiry persisted, and we were unable to change the channel, no matter what Harcourt or the government did.

My last event as minister of government services turned out to be the opening of the Western Canada Summer Games in Abbotsford on August 15, 1995. I did the honours alongside Lieutenant Governor Garde Gardom, and when I got back to Vancouver, Rami told me that Mike Harcourt had been looking for me and wanted me to call him back. It was about 10:00 PM by then. We had a friend waiting to be picked up at the airport, and I was hungry. I ate my food in the car as Rami drove. Harcourt's call might be bad news, and bad news could wait, I said to Rami.

It was close to midnight by the time I called the Premier. He was making another small cabinet shuffle, he told me. He talked about his long-term plans and how what he was doing would help prepare us for re-election. He concluded our conversation by saying, "All right, Mr. Attorney General." I was in total disbelief, and Rami and I stayed up talking for a long time.

I didn't need to be sworn in as AG, since I was already in cabinet. It was simply my ministerial designation that would change. I attended the cabinet meeting the next day in Victoria as B.C.'s Attorney General, with additional responsibilities for multiculturalism, human rights and immigration. The ministry encompassed the Solicitor General and the Attorney General, as well as the Liquor Control Board. Colin Gabelmann took over government services, and the mini-shuffle brought Moe Sihota back into cabinet as environment minister, a move that earned a lot of negative media coverage for the premier and the government. In my case, Nathan Smith of the Trial Lawyers Association told the media he welcomed my appointment, while my favourite lefty, Harry Rankin, said he had been disappointed by my remarks about being tough on serious crime. The *Province*'s editorial was less than charitable to all three of us, saying about me, "we're less than overwhelmed; Dosanjh's recent flip-flop on gambling and shepherding of the fraudulent recall law was hardly the stuff of a dynamic leader." (Surely, after the HST drama in B.C., no one believes that the recall and initiative law was fraudulent any longer.)

After the scrum with Harcourt, Maureen Maloney, the deputy minister, and Stephen Owen, the deputy Attorney General, took me on a tour of the ministry offices. As the visit ended, I prepared to take my leave, but Maureen said they had something very important to brief me on. It was the troubling occupation at Gustafsen Lake.

Apparently the situation had been simmering since June 13, when a rancher in the area gave aboriginal campers an eviction notice because they had cut trees and built fences on his land. On several occasions, starting on June 14, forestry workers, an aboriginal ranch hand and aboriginal fishing officers had been shot at. On July 31, several shots from a high-powered rifle had been fired from the woods at a nearby house; one of the bullets had hit the roof and then entered the house.

The aboriginal occupiers had been camping on the site for a sun dance ceremony for a few summers with the rancher's permission. Now they were claiming that it was their traditional territory and that the title to it hadn't been the B.C. government's to transfer to anyone, including the current owner, Lyle James. The occupiers appeared to be armed, and obviously some of them were willing to shoot. The Cariboo Tribal Council and the Alkali Lake band did not support the outlaw campers of Gustafsen, I learned during the briefing.

Another pressing situation also needed attention. The Gitksan band had blockaded a road near Smithers, affecting forestry contractors and a sheep-grazing business. The band alleged the government had not consulted it before permitting tree cutting and road building in the area. The government was seeking an injunction, and I was anxious to issue a press release explaining our position. A staffer in government communications kept arguing with me about the wording of the press release, however; she didn't understand the urgency for the government to reassure British Columbians that we cared about the situation. When Harcourt walked into the office, I took him aside and shared my concern about unelected twenty-somethings telling ministers how to do their jobs. He told me that as AG I should do what I felt was right, and after that the press release went quickly and as I wanted it. What we were doing proactively in regard to the Gitksan blockade would be in the news cycle all through my first weekend as AG, with various quotes from me: "Blockades or other acts that inconvenience the public and interrupt lawful businesses are not acceptable... The Criminal Code of Canada applies to every inch of B.C.... Any activity that defies the law is to be taken serious note of... We will resolve land claims at the negotiating table... It is very clear in my mind there will be no negotiations on land claims until the blockades are down." The message was loud and clear, and that was the last time anyone interfered with the communications from my office.

38 A MERE THIRTY-SIX HOURS after I had become AG, Harcourt called to see how I was doing; he had heard that the RCMP was calling a press conference regarding Gustafsen Lake. My office also suggested that I learn how to use my new cell phone, since the Mounties might be calling me on it.

Gustafsen Lake was not just any blockade. A group of about fifteen militants, heavily armed, were patrolling the contested area in masks and combat fatigues. TV images of the Oka standoff — the barricades, the death of a police officer, and the siege by the Quebec provincial police and the Canadian Army — were still fresh in my mind. On Saturday morning, on my way to the Ross Street Temple for a friend's personal function, my cell phone rang. I had not yet mastered the not-so-new technology, and the call was cut off. I quickly pulled the car to the side of the road and read the phone manual, learning the basic functions in a couple of minutes. The phone did not ring again, however, until I was ensconced in the temple in the middle of prayers. Surely it couldn't be God answering my prayers, I thought. It wasn't. It was the RCMP, wanting to brief me about the press conference that had just finished. I rushed from the temple to hear about these temporal problems, leaving the matters of God to those on the inside.

Nothing prepares you for a situation like the Gustafsen Lake blockade. I was mindful of the mess that Canada had made of aboriginal peoples' lives. But I also knew that blockades and violence were wrong; too often, there were unintended victims. In this case, the local aboriginal people were victims too. They did not like the actions of the militant campers one bit. No civilized society can allow itself or its institutions to be terrorized by any individual or group. That conviction underpinned and informed my approach to the Gustafsen occupation. Giving in to those who were illegally occupying private lands and shooting at police and fisheries officers would never be an option, but we needed to do everything possible to end the siege peacefully. On several occasions I reminded those who wanted quick action that we were British Columbia, Canada, not Waco, Texas. The RCMP would decide on the most opportune moment and the best means to vacate the camp. Their limit and mine was that militants were to surrender unconditionally. The Crown would not negotiate land claims or legal due process at the point of a gun. We did not rule out the use of necessary force to end the occupation; on the contrary, I stated clearly that, as a last resort, the use of force was an option. I understood civil disobedience. Protesting with AK-47s was not civil but criminal.

The RCMP confirmed that one of its officers had been shot at the day before as he scouted the aboriginal camp. William Ignace, an occupier going by the name Wolverine, pledged that he and the other campers would leave only in body bags. Tensions mounted. I made a personal plea to the armed protestors to lay down their arms and move off the ranch. The next day, Assembly of First Nations leader Ovide Mercredi arrived in an effort to broker a deal. That same day, two people fired a score of shots at an RCMP officer from what looked like assault rifles. The lawyer for the occupiers, Bruce Clark, claimed that the armed campers were within their rights to occupy the land and kept encouraging them not to leave. Ignace himself demanded diplomatic immunity and/or a meeting with the Privy Council and Canada's Governor General, Roméo LeBlanc. I rejected all of that without talking to the feds. The demands were absurd.

On Friday, August 25, a shot was fired again, piercing the air just as *Vancouver Province* staff reporter Barbara McLintock drove up to the RCMP blockade near the camp. By Sunday, August 27, Mercredi had failed to make a deal with the aboriginal occupiers. There were suggestions floating around that the ranch could be put on the table in land claims negotiations, or that immunity from prosecution could be considered for those who peacefully surrendered. I rejected both possibilities. I had already said that this outlaw camp had nothing to do with land claims; it had everything to do with the campers' illegal occupation of the land, the weapons in their possession and the crimes they were committing. I was in constant touch with the RCMP and my deputies. I was accessible to the media 24/7. I was on the evening news, night after night, assuring everyone that the RCMP would not move precipitously but that ultimately they would have to act.

On August 27, two RCMP officers were shot at just outside the camp when they were backing up their vehicle. They encountered crossfire from semi-automatic weapons that knocked out windows, blew out tires and pierced the body of their truck. The officers ran to get help from other officers. The police were convinced that the officers survived only because of their bulletproof vests. I was shocked, as I indicated then:

"We have bent over backwards to solve this peacefully . . . I am shocked these rebels have not heeded the advice of the national leader of the Assembly of First Nations [and have] not heeded the appeal made some days ago that they surrender . . . They have not heeded the RCMP appeal, and that can't be allowed to go on . . . My immediate objective is to see that the law of Canada is enforced . . . We have given peace a chance. It is also appropriate that we give law and order a chance . . . There is a public safety issue at hand, and there is the safety of the RCMP personnel . . . The RCMP have the mandate to dislodge these individuals, to end the illegal occupation and eliminate any danger to public safety . . . The shooting crystallizes in everyone's mind that this issue is a law enforcement issue and has nothing to do with aboriginal land claims."

Once again, I made an appeal to the campers: there was still time for a peaceful solution if they surrendered. On Friday, September 1, the Gitksan blockade was ordered down.

The radio-phones of the campers at Gustafsen Lake had been disconnected. Lawyer Clark had not been allowed into the camp. On Wednesday, August 30, the RCMP relented and established a radio-phone link for Clark so he could help end the standoff. It was the police's view that Clark had softened his hard-line position, and if he could help end the occupation peacefully, they were not going to turn his offer down, despite his outlandish claims and allegations and the disbarment proceedings underway against him in Ontario. If anyone could bring the rebels out peacefully, Clark could, the RCMP thought, but in the end they were wrong. When Clark emerged from the camp he had in his possession an affidavit from the rebels full of false allegations about the police firing the first shots at them and statements that the standoff was part of the genocide of aboriginal people. Clark's proposed solution was that the federal justice minister and I consent to the rebels' petition to the Queen for an international tribunal to rule on the claims made by the rebels regarding Gustafsen. Once there was confirmation of our consent, the rebels would leave peacefully.

I was incensed by Clark's actions, and my comments to the press summed up my determination:

"We shall not bargain in the course of a serious criminal investigation ... and approach either the Queen or anyone else ... We don't run messages for people with AK-47s ... who shoot police officers ... What we are dealing with here is an illegal, armed occupation of private property, where threats of violence and actual violence [are] being used to impede a very serious criminal investigation ... We shall not participate in what is a criminal extortion of the administration of justice."

Ovide Mercredi's pleas to the rebels had fallen on deaf ears, and he unleashed his anger on the police for pushing ahead with their strategic plans. Mercredi felt that was what had precipitated the last bout of shooting, but I totally disagreed with him. Clark, meanwhile, flew to London, England, to present his case to the Privy Council and the Queen.

At some point in the preceding days, the camp had been encircled by the RCMP to ensure there was no infiltration of weapons or trouble makers. Armoured personnel carriers had been brought in to use defensively and were taken past police barricades. I reiterated the non-negotiable conditions for ending the standoff: 1. No immunity from prosecution for those in the camp; 2. No negotiations about who owned the land that was being occupied; 3. No international tribunal to look at the rebels' claims. Shuswap elders spent hours over the next couple of days talking to the rebels, without much positive movement, and the public was becoming impatient. Within government, and unknown to me at the time, there was concern that the standoff could explode into more violence, ending in fatalities or serious injuries. That was bound to make "heroes" of the rebels, and such an outcome would make it more difficult for the moderate aboriginal leadership to negotiate land claims or to speak on behalf of their people with any degree of credibility. On September 6, aboriginal claims to land in and around Ipperwash Provincial Park in Ontario erupted into violence between police and the protestors, resulting in the death of an aboriginal Canadian. The fear in everyone's minds was real, and it kept me up at night too.

Five days after the fatal violence at Ipperwash, a rebel truck at Gustafsen was incapacitated by remote control as it crossed the security perimeter established by the police. The truck's occupants abandoned it and ran. The police discontinued their pursuit when the fleeing rebels started firing at them, but they found an AK-47 and a hunting rifle in the abandoned truck. Subsequently, a couple of people voluntarily came out of the camp, one of them a woman occupant who was initially thought to have been killed in the truck. She had sustained an injury to her arm and was being cared for by the rebels, who had rejected the RCMP's offer to help with her treatment. Those in charge of the camp had no regard for the law or for peace, and they had even less regard for human life; they shot at the police and had said they were prepared to come out in body bags. Despite our determination to see a peaceful end to the standoff, the gunfire after the rebels abandoned their truck dimmed the chances of a peaceful resolution, and I said as much to the press.

The knee-jerk reaction by some to the RCMP profiling a number of the rebels for the media, along with divulging their criminal records, baffled me. Convictions happened in open courts, and it was important for people to know something about the cast of characters we were dealing with. Ordinary political protestors do not carry AK-47s or shoot at police officers. The legitimate leaders of the area, such as Chief Agnes Snow, would never have picked up a gun and pointed it at a police officer.

Bruce Clark returned to the camp to see his clients, but his demand to enter was rejected. Aboriginal negotiator Marlowe Sam had persuaded five of the renegades to come out by now. The rest of the occupiers made new demands for international observers and buffer zones between themselves and the RCMP, and the demand for the Queen to intervene was raised again. My simple answer was no. Bruce Clark appeared in the Supreme Court of Canada to argue that Canadian courts have no jurisdiction in aboriginal matters. The chief justice dismissed his argument as preposterous. The occupiers who had surrendered told Clark they no longer needed his services.

By September 17, nine people had left the camp, and twelve or so remained inside. Percy Rosette indicated they were prepared to leave if John Stevens of Alberta, a spiritual guru of theirs, told them to do so. Stevens went into the camp, and after about four hours the rebels were on their way out, peacefully escorted by the same RCMP officers that some of them had been shooting at. Only in a democracy, a free society under the rule of law, could this scene have been possible. Neither indecent haste to resolve the situation nor unreasonable delay would have served peace in the long run.

The standoff at Gustafsen Lake was the largest police operation in the history of Canada, involving over four hundred officers from all over the country and armoured personnel carriers on loan from the army. Politics was the furthest thing from my mind as I dealt with the Gustafsen occupation. Premier Harcourt and the cabinet did not interfere or ask for reports on the situation. Harcourt always ended our conversations on the situation by saying, "You are the AG."

I had been asked throughout the occupation by the B.C. Liberals and the media why I was not going to the site of the standoff to see for myself what was happening. However, I did not want to grandstand or to interfere with the work of the RCMP. I was the AG, not just any minister. To maintain the utmost public confidence, law enforcement must not meet even the shadow of politics. As Ovide Mercredi was trying to negotiate an end to the standoff, he had placed a call to me. Edward John of the B.C. First Nations Summit was also on the line. The conversation started off civilly, with me explaining why I could not meet with Mercredi or anyone else to negotiate in the middle of a standoff. Mercredi persisted with his demand. When I remained firm in my position, he lost his temper and called me "an Indian agent of old." Deeply hurt by his colonial and racist reference, I politely ended the conversation. John most likely understood the limitations and the imperatives of my job, but Mercredi must have taken my refusal hard, since over the next few days he repeatedly asked "white leaders" to get involved. His repeated request for "white leaders" depressed me. I was an Indian, of the type Columbus was trying to find when he encountered Mercredi's ancestors in North America.

I was also puzzled by the B.C. Liberals' questioning of the cost of the standoff to the B.C. treasury. An editorial in the *Province* on September 19 summed up my view: "Despite pressure for police to move in, they played the waiting game, and no lives were lost. If it costs us millions, the tradeoff is worth it."

The potential for loss of life became starkly obvious to me during my visit with the media to the epicentre of the vacated rebel camp. The police showed us bunkers, foxholes and a fire pit in which they found the charred remains of an AK-47, a Lee-Enfield rifle and an FN assault rifle. Behind a cabin, hidden at the foot of a tree, police had found a cache of weapons, including a potent pipe bomb, a bow, a dozen rifles and nearly a thousand rounds of ammunition. Had we failed to reach a peaceful end to the standoff, the cost in lives lost and in poisoned relations between aboriginals and non-aboriginals would have been immeasurable. History would not have forgiven us.

Calls for an inquiry into the standoff came from different quarters. I made clear that as long as I had anything to do with it, the only inquiry into the standoff would be via the criminal proceedings arising out of Gustafsen Lake. Some were anxious to see a silver lining in the crisis, saying it had brought attention to the aboriginal push for sovereignty. But I did not believe the standoff had anything to do with either land claims or sun dance spirituality. Spirituality in the heart and an AK-47 in the hands don't go together.

There was much speculation in the press about the political consequences of the standoff at Gustafsen Lake. Norman Ruff, a political science professor at the University of Victoria, was interviewed by the *Vancouver Sun*, which reported that "Ruff said the NDP has quickly transformed anxieties over aboriginal issues from a political liability into an asset, partly due to the patient but firm stance taken by Harcourt's newly appointed attorney-general, Ujjal Dosanjh." The article went on to quote Ruff as saying, "One of the best things that has happened to the NDP is Ujjal Dosanjh."

"Dosanjh's recent handling of Gustafsen Lake will doubtless close [the] gap" in the polls between the B.C. Liberals and the NDP, wrote Malcolm Parry in the *Vancouver Sun*. Rafe Mair, in the *Vancouver Courier*, said, "It only remains to be seen how much damage Gabelmann and Harcourt have done to their re-election chances and how much repair work Dosanjh has been able to accomplish."

ELECTION SPECULATION was rampant, and Harcourt considered dropping the writ as our poll numbers rebounded. We had taken a beating in the early spring due to the unfounded allegations of government contracts to NOW Communications, even though Harcourt had been cleared by the Conflict of Interest Commissioner's investigation. Then, in May, Moe Sihota had to resign from cabinet due to his censure by the Law Society for professional misconduct. But by early October our numbers had bounced back into respectable territory. It was time to think about hitting the hustings, given that our mandate had only a year to go.

But the Parks report, made public on October 13 following an RCMP raid on the offices of the NDP, doomed any chance of a quick trip to the polls. Though no member of the government, including Harcourt, was implicated in the report, as an indictment of the party it was devastating.

The Parks report established clear financial links between the party and the Nanaimo Commonwealth Holding Society. Parks also found that, unknown to Harcourt, the party had secretly returned over $60,000 in an attempt to sever all ties with the society. But the party had not directly repaid the funds to the NCHS. It had given the money to Democrat Publications Inc., the publisher of the party's newspaper, which in turn had forwarded it to the society. Obviously, the aim had been to put some distance between the party and the society, which was embarrassing for Harcourt and the government.

As caucus chair, I had sat on the provincial executive of the NDP for eighteen months. During that time, the party had taken the position that the caucus chair should not be involved in any deliberations regarding the NCHS. I was Attorney General when the Parks report was released, and as such I was criticized by some for willful blindness on the issue during my stint as caucus chair. I accepted the criticism in the sense that I had agreed with the party that the NCHS was a party and not a caucus matter.

As if the government's woes weren't bad enough, the way we had managed the Gustafsen Lake standoff was seen by the media as proof that Harcourt was "weak" compared to my tough stance as AG, despite the fact he had strongly supported me throughout the crisis. Sadly, the Parks report would prematurely end his premiership.

In his autobiography, *Mike Harcourt: A Measure of Defiance*, Harcourt reveals that after reading the Parks report, he made up his mind to retire from politics but decided to give himself thirty days to help the party recover. A wholesale resignation of the party executive might have saved the day for Harcourt, but they refused to do it. In his book, he says it was the demand by the labour wing of the party and the B.C. Federation of Labour leadership that he "had to go" that led him to make his decision public.

What transpired behind the scenes tells a different story. Years after the fact, Chris Chilton told me that for most of April 1995, Moe Sihota had been asking Chilton, then Harcourt's chief of staff, to arrange a meeting with Harcourt for Sihota, Glen Clark, Dan Miller and Joy MacPhail without Chilton being present. Chilton refused, realizing what the four were up to. One day when Harcourt was alone in the legislative dining room, Sihota obtained from him the promise of such a meeting. A push was on to get rid of Harcourt, and for it to succeed, his most trusted advisor, Chilton, would have to go first. On the appointed day, Sihota, Clark, Miller, Elizabeth Cull, Andrew Petter and Joy MacPhail met with Harcourt, telling him Chilton had to go. After the fateful meeting ended, Chilton walked into Harcourt's office. Somewhat apologetically, Harcourt explained to Chris the gist of the gang of six's message. Joy MacPhail, who was still there, blurted, "Sorry, Chris, nothing personal." Of course, it was all political. Chilton took the bullet for his boss, who was the real target, and resigned in May 1995. Thus was set the stage for Harcourt's eventual ouster.

39 THE CAMPAIGN TO replace Mike Harcourt became official the moment he resigned, with Glen Clark as the odds-on favourite to replace him. The party set the leadership convention for mid-February 1996. In media speculation about who would run, I was usually mentioned as a credible contender. Some, such as *Vancouver Sun* columnist Trevor Lautens, thought I should be the party's choice. But I had not been in cabinet long, and I had no ties to the labour movement. Clark had not formally announced his intentions, but I realized most of my cabinet colleagues would support him if he ran. Dan Miller, the only other credible contender, bowed out in Clark's favour. After some thought, I declared my support for Clark too. He had been good to me during my difficult days of fighting the extremists, and it was he who had encouraged me to run in 1991. It wasn't a difficult decision.

Harcourt's resignation gave the party a ten-point boost in popularity. Clark's election as leader in February 1996, being more of a coronation, added to the party's fortunes. Clark called an election, setting a date of May 28, and his team ran a sophisticated campaign, including campaign commitments on crime prevention to help inoculate us against the usual accusations of the NDP being soft on crime. In the run-up to the election, Clark pledged the formation of an unsolved-homicide squad to investigate over four hundred unsolved murders; the purchase of a new gene-sequencing machine to speed up the investigations; the establishment of the first forensic dentistry lab in Canada; the establishment of a provincial prostitution unit to apprehend and prosecute johns; a hate crimes unit; a program for youth involvement in crime prevention; one hundred new police officers across the province; and $5 million for victim assistance and services.

We won the election, and Clark asked me to remain the AG. Even when he suggested during a later cabinet shuffle that I take over a cabinet position with more social heft, such as minister of health, I told him my preference was to serve as Attorney General.

For the next three years, I enjoyed my job. It had its share of ups and downs, but I got a great deal of satisfaction from dealing with justice and public safety. The independence of the AG's role also suited me, though I knew the respect the public showed was for the office, and not necessarily for me, its temporary occupant.

I have always considered myself an activist first and a politician second. From implementing extensive restorative justice to investigating the use of the unjustifiable "homosexual panic defence," as AG I took on many causes and issues. My deputy Attorney General, Maureen Maloney, and I had a running list of issues we were dealing with. Most of them were initiatives we were able to see through to completion. The unsolved homicides squad was established, and we turned up the heat on unauthorized lottery ticket resellers, who were victimizing unsuspecting seniors.

B.C.'s Coordinated Law Enforcement Unit had been in place since the seventies, and it had lost its vigour. In its place we established the Organized Crime Agency of B.C. It was headed by Bev Busson, who went on to become the first woman deputy commissioner of the RCMP.

Along with a push for the diversion of non-violent offenders away from the courts and into the community, I liked the idea of drug and community courts that could deal with chronic offenders and send them to available resources and treatment under strict monitoring. I approved a drug court that materialized several years later.

The AG could not interfere in criminal prosecutions, but whenever I felt an appeal was warranted, my direction to the prosecutors for an appeal was published in the *BC Gazette*. One of the cases in which I directed an appeal to the Supreme Court of Canada involved Bert Stone, who had killed his wife, Donna Stone, by stabbing her over forty times. Stone argued that his wife had nagged him, and the jury relied on the defence of provocation to convict him of the lesser offence of manslaughter. Stone had been sentenced to four years in prison. I wanted to send a message to British Columbians that violence against women would be pursued to the bitter end, and when I was told the established law indicated against an appeal, I ordered an appeal anyway. For the first time in years, I gowned up, and I made the preliminary opening argument myself before the Supreme Court of Canada. I was only the third AG nationally to appear before the Supreme Court, and perhaps the first-ever in a criminal case. AG prosecutors ably made the rest of the argument. The Supreme Court turned down the appeal, which was not surprising; there had been only an extremely remote chance of it succeeding. Regardless, the point had been made.

Violence against women is an entrenched problem, not conducive to easy solutions, and that was made terribly obvious by the murder in Vernon of Rajwar Gakhal and several members of her family by her estranged husband Mark Chahal. The AG's ministry made many changes following the inquiries and investigation into the Vernon tragedy, and we continued to work hard on the issue, as did women's groups. B.C. became the first province to allow oral victim presentations in parole hearings, a step later adopted by the federal government.

More than any of my counterparts in other provinces, as AG I prodded the federal government to change and strengthen laws, including in the areas of stalking. I was the first AG, and B.C. the first jurisdiction in Canada, to propose a violent sex offender registry as an added tool to protect the public. It came about a few years after my term as AG. I also asked so often for federal action on enhancing the Criminal Code that federal justice minister Anne McLellan gave me a good-natured scolding for it. Later on, she would become a good friend and colleague.

A hate crimes unit was also established, with dedicated police officers and a crown prosecutor. Hate crimes pose their own investigative challenges, and the request had been spearheaded by the Jewish community in and around Vancouver. We also succeeded in getting legislation passed to ensure the annual proclamation of Holocaust

Memorial Day in B.C. As the work of the hate crimes unit proceeded, it became clear that the hate provisions of the Criminal Code were not sufficient. I asked that they be broadened to include simple possession of hate literature for the purpose of distribution, though the B.C. Civil Liberties Association and its president John Dixon disagreed with me. Different responsibilities lead to different views. The BCCLA's duty was to protect free speech and civil liberties; mine was to balance that duty of the Crown with its obligation to enhance public safety and prevent hate from being spread.

An issue that dogs any B.C. government did not spare us: fugitives from other provinces who had fled to ours to avoid facing summary offences and sometimes more serious charges. We started the process of identifying the fugitives and purchasing them one-way bus tickets. It was hard to measure our success, but we did make other provinces aware of the need to give the warrants issued by their courts some teeth. I also blame the B.C. weather and our generosity as a society for the number of people flocking here; may those two things never change, except for the better.

The AG's ministry acted against the illegal poker clubs in Vancouver's Chinatown, despite the cries about our "cultural insensitivity"; the evidence suggested the clubs were essentially crime dens. Sexual predators targeting children were also targeted. We created a provincial prostitution unit of the police, engaged designated Crown prosecutors to prosecute johns and child traffickers, and lobbied Ottawa for changes to the Criminal Code in that area too. We also shepherded through the legislative assembly a new police-complaints regime headed by civilians for municipal police forces other than the RCMP. We were interested in subjecting the RCMP in our province to a similar civilian disciplinary regime, but there were jurisdictional hurdles, as well as the RCMP's general reluctance. That posed a problem, since the RCMP was also the provincial police force. B.C. was and still is the single largest user of the RCMP, with over a third of the force working in and for B.C.

There has been a reluctance among various police departments and mayors in the Lower Mainland to adopt regional policing. This misguided resistance is reinforced by the fact some of the large municipalities, such as Surrey and Richmond, are policed by the RCMP. Regional policing in the Lower Mainland is long overdue, but it won't happen until the B.C. government legislates it. Difficult though that may be, it is the right thing to do. During my time in office, we pushed to have coordinated, multi-force units such as the one we'd established to deal with gangs.

Under my watch as AG we amended family law to provide relief for same-sex couples in the areas of child maintenance, custody and spousal support, creating a level playing field. These amendments were the first of their kind in North America, and we ushered in another North American first: the extending of survivor pension benefits to gay and lesbian couples within the B.C. public service. Throughout this precedent-setting work on gay and lesbian equality, I was ably assisted by my colleague Tim Stevenson and a confident and savvy political assistant, Rachel Notley, who would lead the NDP to a landslide victory in Alberta in 2015.

Our work on these issues, particularly with regard to pensions, caused uproar in religious circles. I was condemned by the Catholic Archbishop of Vancouver, Adam Exner, and the moderate president of the Guru Nanak Sikh Gurdwara in Surrey, Balwant Gill. Exner inadvertently helped me a great deal by arguing that in principle he was not opposed to what we had done; it was only that he wanted pension rights extended to other persons such as parents or siblings in long-dependent relationships. Of course, this was not the first time in history that progress had rubbed religion the wrong way. Organized religion usually fossilizes over time into a set of outmoded restrictions and prohibitions. With pride, I walked in the Gay Pride Parade: the first AG in Canada to do so. I continued that tradition and became the first-ever Canadian premier to march for gay pride in 2000.

Equality in general was of particular concern to me. Belonging to a visible ethnic minority, I was acutely aware of the plight of aboriginal people in Canada and of the fact that in our midst, including in some immigrant communities such as the Indo-Canadian community, there were islands of prejudice against aboriginals. I always made a point of speaking about true equality, in particular mentioning aboriginal and gay and lesbian equality. Despite my strong advocacy, there was never any backlash against my views in the larger society or in minority communities. That taught me a very important lesson: Canadians do not punish politicians for their views on the kind of society we need to build, as long as the dreams and aspirations espoused are genuine. It should concern us when politicians busy themselves singing the undue praises of different cultures in Canada rather than talking about what makes one a good Canadian in deed and word. Their vacuous platitudes simply mask the rarely articulated but widely held view of cultural equivalence. Their mistaken belief that one culture or tradition is necessarily as good as any other takes away the need for change to enhance political and social integration, social solidarity and social cohesion.

During the 1996 election campaign, the issue had been raised that the $2,000 personal property exemption under B.C.'s bankruptcy laws was woefully inadequate. I had called the low exemption ludicrous. Doug Wellbanks, my old friend from my Langara and SFU days, now worked in the consumer affairs section of the AG ministry, and after our re-election, his nudging kept the issue in my mind. We expanded the limits despite much lobbying by the debt industry against the change. Some bureaucrats did not like the idea either, though the only reason I could identify for that was bureaucratitis, a condition that causes ministry officials who have been around a long time to believe it is their job to protect the status quo.

Not all of the decisions I made as Attorney General look good in hindsight. Our decision not to ban the use of mobile phones while driving was clearly wrong, as was an early decision to oppose a safe injection site in Vancouver. But I was always willing to change my views when I heard more convincing arguments. By the end of my time in B.C. politics, I would be in favour of safe injection sites and of decriminalizing marijuana, and I would know that mobile phones in the hands of drivers are killers.

Some politicians do not understand that laws must apply across the board unless we want checkerboard jurisdictions. The colourful mayor of Surrey, Doug McCallum, had decided he would not allow photo radar vans operated by a provincial unit in his municipality, and he threatened to have the vans towed away. A police officer in one photo radar unit read McCallum the riot act and threatened to arrest anyone seen blocking the unit's work. In another example, some municipalities started issuing lower fines than the provincial ones via municipal tickets. In the race to please their municipal masters, the affected cops forgot that unless the violations were entered into the provincial database, corrective actions would never be initiated.

The historic Nisga'a Agreement, concluded outside of the regular treaty process, signalled the completion of a quarter-century of negotiations. The initialling ceremony took place in New Aiyansh on August 4, 1998. Liberal leader Gordon Campbell had sought a referendum before any agreement was signed, but we were opposed to any such referendum, particularly one to decide on the rights of minorities who had had few rights so far. We were also making preparations for a lawsuit to recover damages from tobacco companies. I visited Seattle to watch the launch of Washington State's own legal case and New York to meet with individuals who might be able to help us put together our soon-to-be launched legal action, another first in Canada. We made key allies during our fight, including AG Christine Gregoire of Washington State; Bennett LeBow of Liggett Tobacco, the first tobacco company CEO to admit that cigarettes are addictive and deadly; and AG Mike Moore of Mississippi, a pioneer in suing Big Tobacco. The B.C. government launched the suit on November 12, 1998, and as of this writing it is still wending its way through the courts.

Often an issue arises that proves the old axiom that the law is an ass. An example that transpired during my time as AG didn't concern law but policy. For the first time, it was announced that B.C. liquor laws prohibited the Armistice Day "dawn patrol," a celebration by war veterans that included a 7:00 AM drink to toast fallen comrades. As far as I could see, this required only a simple policy change at the level of permit issuance. I intervened to reverse the situation, and the vets commemorating the World War One pilots' practice of having nerve-calming liquor shots when returning from early-morning flights were able to do so again on November 11, 1996, at 7:00 AM sharp.

Some issues are also never-ending. In my secular life, the violence associated with Sikh issues has been one such constant. In January 1997, I was in India on a trade mission when tempers at one of the Surrey Sikh temples flared over an edict from Amritsar that people eating in temples should sit on the floor and not, as was the longstanding Canadian practice, on chairs at tables. I felt handicapped in my response, sitting far away in India, but I did speak to my ministry and then to the media on more than one occasion. I was shocked to see some of the bad actors from the August 1985 attack on the Indian Consul's home in Vancouver resurface in this latest melee, but by the time I returned to Vancouver, tempers had cooled. To my pleasant surprise, the acerbic Mike Smyth of the *Vancouver Province* had something nice to say about my response. In a column headlined "Sad deja vu for Dosanjh," Smyth concluded that my commitment to peaceful co-existence and non-violence arguably made me the best minister in Clark's cabinet.

On November 18, 1998, Tara Singh Hayer was shot and killed at his Surrey home while getting out of his car. No one was ever convicted of the crime, but it is most likely that he was killed by the Air India terrorists or at their behest. In 1985, Tara had overheard a self-incriminating statement made by Ajaib Bagri in London, England, to Tarsem Purewal, Tara's mentor in merchandising hate and extremism. Purewal himself was killed in 1986. It took Tara ten years to tell the RCMP what he had overheard. Parmar had been killed in India in 1992, and with Tara's death, his statement to the RCMP would no longer be admissible as evidence.

My AG stint had more ups than downs, but downs there definitely were. Nothing saves one from the fiscal constraints of government, and I had to close courthouses (though a lot fewer than I was asked to), reduce staff and raise probate fees.

The crime rate in B.C., including violent crime, had been falling for several years. However, "if it bleeds it leads" remained the principle for news outlets, and people walked away from their TVs and radios believing the world contained nothing but crime; little wonder that the general public's call for tougher sentences continued. It was difficult in that climate to deal with B.C. Supreme Court Justice Duncan Shaw's judgement in the child pornography case of R. v. Sharpe. In his ruling, Shaw declared that the portions of the Criminal Code pertaining to the possession of child pornography were unconstitutional. The public and some legislators criticized the judge, and Shaw received some death threats. I was clear about the public's right to criticize decisions, but I condemned the threats, arguing that our judiciary must be able to make decisions in absolute independence, guided only by law and without fear. I was direct with legislators, too, reminding them they had the right to change the law but not criticize the judge. That important principle sometimes gets lost in the din of politics.

A point needs to be made about the legitimate public hunger for improvements to our laws and lives. As I learned in my years in cabinet, even if you can't change many things at once, people will be happy if they see you at least asking the questions that are on their minds. Laws change slowly. But if people see you as an advocate, rather than someone who defends the status quo, they will consider you the embodiment of their hopes and aspirations. That is as it should be. Otherwise, why be in politics?

One of my distinct privileges as AG was to recommend provincial court appointments from a list approved by the judicial council and the bar to cabinet. Our government remained firm throughout my tenure about appointing 50 per cent women. We also appointed properly qualified and recommended aboriginal, minority, and openly gay and lesbian judges. None of these were token appointments. Whether we like it or not, all of us are "in politics." By our actions or omissions, we all make a difference.

IN FEBRUARY 1999, an issue emerged regarding an online accusation made by Gillian Guess, posted in violation of court orders, that as AG I was in conflict of interest because Paul Gill, brother of the notorious gangster Peter Gill, was a friend of mine. I had known Paul since his high school days, when he'd volunteered on my first election campaign in 1979. I did not know Peter.

Peter Gill and five others, including Bindy Johal, Sun News Lal and Rajinder Benji, had been tried and acquitted of several serious criminal charges in 1995. Guess had been one of the jurors, and it was alleged by the Crown, in laying obstruction of justice charges against her following the acquittal, that during the trial and afterwards she had had a sexual relationship with Peter. I had been advised of this fact in late 1995, as the police began to close in on her. My name had apparently come up in a taped conversation when Guess was haranguing Peter to ask his brother, Paul, to get the police to lay off her. From that moment until the time I was out of the provincial political arena, Paul and I kept an absolute distance from one another. At no time earlier had he ever spoken to me about his brother Peter or Gillian Guess; the first time I heard her name was when my deputies sat me down and told me about what the police had picked up in the wiretap chatter.

I immediately contacted Ted Hughes and asked him to rule on the matter. After doing his due diligence, including talking to me and my deputies, he cleared me of any real or apparent conflict of interest. Just to be on the safe side, Josiah Wood, a former court of appeal judge who had been appointed by the deputy Attorney General to deal with matters relating to the Guess prosecution, was asked by the assistant deputy minister for criminal justice to look into the extent of my relationship with Paul Gill, and he too found no evidence of any wrongdoing. Guess had been charged and convicted of obstruction of justice in June 1998. She was appealing the decision against her, and she had tried to make hay with the spurious allegations against me.

I WAS MADE acutely aware of Vancouver's missing women, most of them aboriginal, in the early spring of 1999. I was troubled by both the reality and the perception that police were not doing enough. The offer of a reward for information was being demanded by activists such as Maggie de Vries, whose sister was one of the missing women, and as AG I was anxious to provide the money for that through a 70/30 split with the City of Vancouver. The demand had become more pronounced after the government posted a reward of $100,000 for information leading to arrest and conviction in connection with a series of armed robberies of people's garages; it was only natural for the missing women's advocates to feel that property was receiving more governmental attention than the plight of the missing women. The City and the Vancouver Police Department were reluctant about the idea of a reward in this instance, but the Police Board came around to my view and requested the AG's assistance. Vancouver mayor Philip Owen and I announced the award at a press conference at Vancouver police headquarters that included John Walsh, the host of the TV show *America's Most Wanted,* and for the first time the issue received the national and international attention it deserved.

The eventual arrest and conviction of serial killer Robert Pickton vindicated the long struggle of the advocates and relatives of the missing women, but we still have not learned enough. Year after year, the demand for a national public inquiry into the more than five hundred missing and murdered aboriginal women across the country has fallen on deaf ears. I cannot imagine that the Canadian government would have ignored the call for a national public inquiry related to five hundred white or affluent women who had gone missing. Is it because these women happen to be mainly aboriginal and poor that the government has failed for so long to move on this issue? This is a recurring theme and question in Canadian history. As I write this, newly elected PM Justin Trudeau has promised that an inquiry will finally be opened; we can only hope that this is the beginning of real change.

THE LANDMARK Nisga'a Treaty, negotiated over many long years, was signed, sealed and delivered to the legislature on May 27, 1999, late in Glen Clark's mandate. As we approached the debate in the House, Liberal leader Gordon Campbell rose to ask questions about the constitutionality of the treaty. I was armed with a legal opinion from Peter Hogg, the foremost constitutional scholar in Canada. Campbell asked me questions for the duration of Question Period, to which I provided robust answers. What happened once that fifteen minutes of mud-wrestling was over remains etched in my memory. Campbell sat in his seat staring at me, uttering the word "disgrace" several times. He appeared stung by what had just transpired.

The Nisga'a Treaty was the result of Nisga'a people negotiating for over two decades with the B.C. and federal governments. It ushered in a new era of equality and sovereignty for the Nisga'a Nation in the Canadian federation. It was the first modern treaty in B.C., and I was proud to have been a part of it.

40 SPECULATION THAT the gang of six — Miller, Sihota, MacPhail, Clark, Petter and Cull — had pushed Harcourt out was always denied vehemently by the group. Now the gang of five was in control, with Clark in the premier's chair. I was always seen as a member of the outer cabinet, but that was a comfortable place to be for an AG. I was part of the government, yet seen by the public to be apart from it. This distance from the core of government soon became a blessing critical to maintaining the integrity of the AG's office. The period from March 2, 1999, when the RCMP raided Glen Clark's home, until Clark's resignation on August 21 was a tension-ridden time.

On the morning of March 2, the *Victoria Times Colonist* ran a story headlined "I am not quitting, says premier" on its front page. The story speculated about Clark's possible departure before the next election because of our government's dismal standing in the polls. The story about Clark came out of the blue, and I do not believe the *Times Colonist* had any inkling of what was coming that evening. I certainly didn't. But the story unwittingly portended a bombshell that would shake our government to its foundations: the evening RCMP raid on the premier's home.

As the raid was in progress, I received a call from Ernie Quantz, the assistant deputy minister responsible for criminal prosecutions, who informed me that the raid was underway. I was told the basic facts — Clark was under police investigation regarding a possible conflict of interest regarding a casino licence application — and informed of Martin Taylor's appointment as special prosecutor by the deputy AG dating back to January 15. Quantz's call to me had been approved by Taylor himself.

Legislation regarding the special prosecutor had evolved as a result of the Bud Smith scandal of the 1980s and the subsequent inquiry. Bud Smith, then Social Credit Attorney General, had been recorded on his car radio-phone asking a journalist for media advice and also referring inappropriately to a breach of trust case in which he had intervened; he was forced to resign as a result. Special prosecutors were appointed in politically sensitive cases where there might be a perception that regular prosecutors would be under pressure to act a certain way. It was Martin Taylor's brief to advise and assist the police in their investigation in the Clark matter and to decide upon any charges to be laid. Sometime before I became AG, the RCMP had agreed to a protocol mandating them to advise the AG, and through him or her the premier, if any member of the legislature was under criminal investigation. If a special prosecutor for the case had already been appointed, the responsibility to advise the AG would fall to the special prosecutor, as it had in this case.

An initial police investigation is usually undertaken as a prelude to a possible formal criminal investigation. That distinction is always important. I was subsequently told by Quantz that the premier had been advised on March 3 that police were conducting a preliminary investigation that involved him. To ensure the integrity of the investigation, the special prosecutor's advice to me was not to speak with the premier about the raid or the steps that might follow.

The casino licence application in question involved a company in which contractor Dimitrios Pilarinos, a friend and neighbour of Clark's, was a principal. Local authorities had decisively rejected the North Burnaby Inn as a casino site for the licence Pilarinos's company sought. Then, in December 1997, Mike Farnworth, the minister responsible for gaming, announced that the North Burnaby Inn had been given approval in principle for a casino licence. After the raid on his home, Clark made a brief statement about the matter, in which he alluded to specific instructions he had given his staff to ensure his insulation from any decisions regarding the North Burnaby Inn, due to his friendship with Pilarinos. Those instructions would later turn out to be in the form of a forged and backdated memo to file by Adrian Dix, then principal secretary to the premier.

All hell broke loose, and there were calls for Clark to step down. He vowed to fight on to prove his innocence. The newspapers and other media started digging up stuff on Pilarinos and his associates, including allegations that he was trying to peddle his "closeness" to Clark. Even before the raid, the NDP had only 21 per cent of voter support B.C.-wide. Our popularity was now in free fall. Most members of the caucus wanted to give Clark time to clear himself, and he hunkered down for the long haul. Farnworth, returning from a trip to Peru, said he alone had made the decision to approve the North Burnaby Inn for the casino licence. Nonetheless, there was intense speculation about potential replacements for Clark. My name was mentioned, along with those of MacPhail and Gordon Wilson, who was by now a cabinet colleague, having disbanded his own Progressive Democratic Alliance and crossed the floor to join the NDP. But premiership was the furthest thing from my mind. We had a crisis to get through, and I had perhaps the most difficult task: that of maintaining my independence as AG and doing the right thing in the crazy environment following the raid.

On March 8, for the first time since the raid, Clark was scheduled to meet with the caucus. The meeting started with some formalities, but as the premier rose to speak, I realized that caucus members needed to be absolutely free to speak. I felt uncomfortable sitting there in my independent role, so I decided to leave the meeting. On the way out, I explained my reasoning to the waiting media. The old adage of justice being done and being seen to be done applied *mutatis mutandis* to the role of the AG. My departure was meant to ensure that my independence remained intact and was seen to remain intact. Some members of the caucus had not liked me leaving the meeting through the front door, but many of them had never understood the AG's independent role.

I attempted to carry on with my duties, but it was difficult in the intense aftermath of the raid. In a move that added fuel to the burning fires, the NDP provincial office mass-mailed a fundraising letter to members, implying a conspiracy in the raid on Clark's home and indicating that the RCMP had violated the premier's rights, alluding to the fact that the media had been tipped off about the raid and so appeared on the scene. The implication was an improper one for the party to advance: the RCMP had acted pursuant to warrants issued by the courts, and they had already said publicly that they were investigating to determine if and how news of the raid had been leaked to the media. I had not been advised of or shown the letter in advance, and I made it clear the letter was unacceptable coming from a governing or any political party. Adding insult to injury, Harry Lali, the minister of transportation, had made comments to the Merritt Herald about "a conspiracy . . . between the RCMP, BCTV and the provincial Liberals." On my way into the caucus meeting, I had let it be known that it was inappropriate for ministers of the Crown or elected officials to criticize the judiciary or law enforcement agencies directly or indirectly. I had already reprimanded Lali for wearing a lapel button that read "www.RCMP.TVforBC.com." Lali persisted in his stupidity for another day, subsequently apologizing for misspeaking and using "intemperate" language. I didn't expect Clark to fire him, though in Clark's position, I would have done so when Lali first refused to apologize. I was not making any friends in my independent role so far.

On April 7, the premier briefed the caucus in my absence. I had been told Clark's lawyer, David Gibbons, would also be present. Over the next few days, details emerged about a hunting knife Clark had given Pilarinos. Around the same time, a judicial summary of the contents of the RCMP's search warrant was made available to Clark and Pilarinos's lawyers on the condition they not share it with their clients. The situation was getting murkier by the moment. By now it was widely known that at least a month after public submission by Pilarinos of his application for a casino licence, Clark had authorized Pilarinos to take out a building permit to build a deck on Clark's home. The construction was completed, and a final inspection was done on

July 14, 1998. The casino application went before cabinet on July 29. The optics looked bad.

By early May 1999, the near-extinction of the NDP was predicted in the next election, whenever that might be. I was busy dealing with changes the federal government had made to strengthen police and prosecutors' hands in dealing with youth sexual exploitation. I put the brakes on photo radar expansion and ordered a review of the practice. After being briefed about the continuing RCMP investigation of the Air India bombing, Maureen Maloney and I went to Ottawa to meet with the minister of justice, Anne McLellan, and the solicitor general, Lawrence MacAulay. The meeting had a positive outcome: we secured some additional funding for the Air India investigation and prosecution.

At the regularly scheduled NDP convention in June, Glen Clark tried to rally the troops, exhorting us all to "go back to our values." In the shadow of the Casinogate investigation, it was a hard message to sell, though we all hoped things would turn around once the raid issue resolved itself. But our fate, particularly that of Clark, was in the special prosecutor's hands. The tension continued, and among friends in the caucus, discussions took place over a friendly pint or two in a neighbourhood pub or a shared scotch. Were we worried about the future of the government? Yes. Were we worried about Clark's fate? Darn right we were. Clark being cleared would have been the best outcome, regardless of whether he resigned or stayed. But that could take a long time, and time was running out for the party. Many of us, including Joy MacPhail, Corky Evans and me, privately shared the view that it would be prudent and best for the party if Clark were to resign.

At one point, Clark had refused to answer questions from the police. I spoke to him about it in the presence of Maureen Maloney so there would be a witness to our exchange. I advised Clark that in their investigation of his actions, the police represented the Crown, as did he in his capacity as premier. It was in his capacity as premier that police were investigating his actions, and as an element of the

Crown, he had an ethical and legal obligation to aid others, including the police. As long as he was premier, he could not refuse to answer the police's questions, I told Clark. If he insisted on his right to silence, he would have to resign. I gave Mike Farnworth the same advice. In his ministerial capacity, Farnworth was representing the Crown, and as such he could not refuse to answer questions from the Crown, in this case the police.

One day in mid-July, one of my favourite British Columbians, Dave Barrett, showed up unannounced at my office at the legislature in Victoria. I was busy with some guests in my own room. I couldn't kick them out, but I didn't want a party elder to have to wait any longer than necessary so I took Barrett into my ministerial assistant's office, which happened to be empty. I invited him to sit down, but he refused, launching into a tirade accusing me of undermining Clark. He must have rehearsed his attack; it was fast and furious. It was true I had remarked at a caucus meeting that Clark should consider the good of the party, as had some others. I had done nothing underhanded, and I had maintained caucus confidentiality and solidarity. Ministers are chosen by premiers and prime ministers to give them frank advice, and I had simply and respectfully done my job. By doing so, I had apparently invited Barrett's wrath.

My meeting with Barrett was short and swift. He left the office, and I returned to the chambers. The nature of the meeting subsequently leaked out, but it didn't happen from my end. I didn't understand the motive behind the Clark camp's release of this information or for their leak of the fact that Moe Sihota had also unsuccessfully tried to speak with me subsequent to my brief exchange with Barrett. When I learned of the leak, I worried about the possible undermining of my independent role as AG. Concerned about that, and angered by a not-so-veiled threat Barrett had made, I told the media: "It was a very short meeting. I heard what he had to say, but he also heard what I had to say. We had a very frank exchange of views... but no one, and that includes Mr. Barrett, has ever attempted to speak to me about my role as the Attorney General... I want to put that to rest... I also have a political role [but] I keep those two separate." What I told the media was true, but there was more. I did not want to stoke the fires of division in the ranks at the time. The situation was bad enough without me doing that. But Barrett had been vicious and downright mean. His threat to me had been, "If I hear you undermining Clark I shall smash your political career to smithereens. You will never again amount to anything in politics in B.C." For effect, he had liberally peppered his threat with expletives as well. I told Barrett I would do what I felt was appropriate, acutely mindful of my independent role as Attorney General.

I was hurt by Barrett's visit, but his threat did not hit home as he intended. Politics was not my career. I could say goodbye to the legislature any day, as I had once told Harcourt, and hang out my shingle as a lawyer once again. That has given me a freedom in politics that others may not have had. I was wedded to my integrity and my passion for social justice during my time in politics, not to power for power's sake. I knew elected office was always temporary, and I was always ready to quit.

Shortly after Barrett's visit, the government held a caucus meeting at a conference centre in Sidney. Billed as a retreat to discuss the summer and fall agenda, it was a session for ministers and MLAs alike to put their views on the table. Joy MacPhail, Corky Evans, Sue Hammell, Cathy McGregor and I, along with several others from the caucus, asked Clark to do the right thing for the party. When I spoke, I did not ask him to leave; I truly believed he should hang on until his name was cleared if he felt that was in the best interests of the party. For me as AG, asking him point blank to leave at that moment would have been improper.

Clark indicated that he would stay and fight: he and his supporters were adopting a scorched-earth policy. MacPhail resigned from her post as finance minister the next day, and the premier's parliamentary secretary, Graeme Bowbrick, followed suit. Sue Hammell tendered her resignation next. I had no prior inkling of these resignations, though others may have had. Norman Ruff of the University of Victoria speculated in the media that if I resigned next it would be fatal to Clark. But to do so would have politicized my office; my independent role as AG had vested in me special knowledge of facts that others did not have. As a result people would have read more into my resignation than simply the act of a disenchanted leadership aspirant. (Though at that point I was, while certainly disenchanted, not yet an aspirant.) Former ministers Bill Barlee and Elizabeth Cull added their voices to the call for Clark to step down, and some elders of the party, including former AG Alex Macdonald, joined the chorus. The B.C. Federation of Labour echoed the call without putting a date on when they wanted to see Clark's exit.

While I was gone on a human rights trip to Guatemala, a cabinet shuffle brought Moe Sihota back into cabinet after his third departure. Jimmy Doyle and former minister Joan Smallwood (who had once been fired by Harcourt) were sworn in. The media was divided on the impact of the shuffle. Some thought Clark had outmanoeuvred his opposition, while others saw it as a temporary reprieve. I was in the latter camp. The disenchantment in the ranks was too deep to be silenced by a minor shuffle.

The court had fixed August 13, 1999, as the date to hear arguments from lawyers, including some representing media outlets on how much could be made public regarding the Clark/Casinogate matter. As the court finished its deliberations, I went into a prescheduled meeting with special prosecutor Martin Taylor and my officials, including Maureen Maloney and Ernie Quantz. Since I had just returned from a conference in Alaska that had brought together the western AGs from Canada and the U.S., this was the earliest date on which our meeting could be held. At the meeting, Taylor walked us through the allegations and the evidence against Clark. Charges against Clark would likely proceed, he told us; this was no longer a preliminary police investigation. The meeting ended with Taylor reversing his earlier advice, which had barred me from speaking either publicly or to Clark himself. I left the meeting believing that Taylor had made up his mind to eventually charge Clark.

I COULD FIND NO precedent in Canadian history where an Attorney General had been faced with what was now in naked terms, and as seen by Clark supporters, the taking down of a premier. Under normal circumstances, the premier would have resigned on March 3, when he was informed about the preliminary police investigation. But our system of special prosecutors, designed to ensure the independence of the criminal investigations of political persons, had an unintended effect in this case. Because of the special prosecutor's original instructions, I had not been able to share with the public or with Clark what Clark and I both knew: that he was under criminal investigation. That had provided Clark with a shield from resignation even though his ability to do his job stood compromised.

After my meeting with Taylor, I consulted with Maureen Maloney and others, including some prominent B.C. figures, in confidence, to seek their advice on the way forward. It was something that had never been done in Canada: to go as AG to a premier with the fact of a criminal investigation and advise him or her that it was untenable and improper to remain in office. I believed then, and still do, that the unprecedented situation was the result of Clark hanging on to his premiership rather than resigning upon first being told he was under criminal investigation.

In the twenty-four hours following the meeting with Taylor in my Hornby Street offices, I came close to resigning rather than being the bearer of bad news. Had I resigned, however, my successor would have had to perform the same unenviable task during his or her first hours on the job. Even the straight-shooter Maureen Maloney reaffirmed my conviction about what I had to do. I decided to live up to my independent role as the AG and inform the premier.

AFTER A SLEEPLESS NIGHT ON August 13 and an anxious morning on the 14, I asked my deputy, Maureen Maloney, to let the premier's office know that I would like to see him. My office received no response for the next twenty-four hours. Eventually, I had my office connect with Clark's deputy, Doug McArthur. When Doug and I spoke, he told me the premier was vacationing in eastern Canada. A meeting date was fixed for the time of Clark's return.

41

The premier and I met on August 17 at the cabinet offices in Canada Place, Vancouver. It was a beautiful sunny day, but I was feeling anything but sunny. I felt the load of the world on my shoulders. In a rare action for me, I had jotted down some notes in advance regarding the exact legal expressions I wanted to use in my conversation with Clark. I was ushered into his office. With only the two of us in the room, we shook hands and sat down. I believed the premier knew why I was there. Both the AG ministry's lawyers and his knew that the court was soon going to make public the affidavits and the attachments that had formed the basis of the search warrants in the first place. In his office, I formally advised the premier of the fact of the criminal investigation and the fact that I had been now freed by the special prosecutor to inform him about it. I affirmed for him the fact that I had known about the preliminary investigation as of March 2 and that he had known about it as of March 3. I advised him that, under the circumstances, it was improper and untenable for him to remain the premier. I told him that advice was coming from me as the AG because constitutionally we had no other mechanism to deal with a premier under criminal investigation. An ordinary cabinet minister would have been given those orders by the premier.

In this case I could only give Clark the advice to resign, not order him to do so. Should he choose to disregard my advice, I would have no option but to resign myself. I told him the matter was serious and warranted action on his part sooner rather than later. I advised him that the criminal investigation was going to be made public soon. I told him I was there to advise and inform him and to answer any questions. He had none, but simply repeated his public position that he had done nothing wrong. Our meeting was over.

Unexpectedly, it also became my responsibility to ensure that the public was informed of the fact of the Clark criminal probe. In my discussions with Maloney, I had been advised that since the criminal investigation had moved beyond the exploratory phase, police would make public the fact of the premier's investigation once the court threw open the allegations in the search warrants through releasing affidavits that had so far been sealed. I took that to mean that from the point of view of the investigation, police felt that was the appropriate moment for public disclosure of the Clark probe. As AG, I should not pre-empt the RCMP, since that might jeopardize or prejudice their work.

But on the day before the scheduled unsealing of the search warrants by the court, the RCMP developed cold feet. On August 19, 1999, Maloney passed on to me the RCMP's assertion it was against their policy to state publicly that any particular person was under criminal investigation. According to RCMP/government protocol, I was told, their only agreement with government was to inform the AG and/or the government if any government members were under criminal investigation. I could not be angry with the RCMP for their decision, except that I now owed Clark the courtesy of advising him of the moment of public disclosure regarding the criminal investigation. The court disclosures would provide more grist for the speculation mill, but on their own they would not confirm or clear the question about whether Clark was under criminal investigation or not. The public needed to know about the investigation before the court released the documents on the afternoon of August 20.

With very little time on my hands, I once again had to find the premier. I started searching for him on the afternoon of August 19 to let him know I would make public the fact of the criminal probe against him on or before the morning of August 20, unsealing or no unsealing of the search warrants by the court. Clark had had at least forty-eight hours after our meeting of August 17 to resign. During that time he had neither resigned nor made the fact of the criminal investigation public. He obviously had no intention of doing either. My office and I left messages for him and his deputy, but we had no luck in contacting him. It had never been difficult for me to talk to any premier, including Clark, before the Casinogate saga began. Now, for the second time in a week, I was being ignored, and for obvious reasons.

After more calls to his office and an irate message from me left for Clark and his deputy, I finally heard from the premier. It was mid-morning on August 20, and I had already been inundated with requests from media who had been rerouted to me because the RCMP was refusing to answer questions about the Clark criminal probe. The RCMP had the option of silence, but I did not. I was the Attorney General, and it was my duty to advise the public. Before doing that, it was only fair to inform Clark.

During our phone conversation, I told Clark of my plan to go public with the information. I also let him know I was being hounded by the media. His response was not one I had ever expected from a premier. I was dumbstruck to hear him say: "Why don't you go away for a week, and they will lay off you?" I told him that was not an option, and neither was silence.

Following my conversation with Clark, I called the caucus chair. He happened to be on a conference call with the caucus and put me on the speaker phone. I informed the caucus that it was my obligation to advise the public about the Clark criminal investigation. The debate got heated, involving the usual suspects, and I was accused of being blinded by my leadership ambitions. Little did they know how hard making the decision had been. I advised them again that I had no option but to make the matter public; the Attorney General couldn't share the information with the premier and the caucus while leaving the public in the dark. If Clark didn't resign, I would have to go, but to shrink from my duty for fear of doing my job would have been cowardice.

Instead of a formal press conference, I arranged to be available in my office for the media. I read a brief prepared statement and answered almost no questions. I had done my duty as the AG, and in the process had won more enemies in the NDP. For losing friends in the party, I was on a clear winning streak.

WITH THE PUBLIC confirmation that Clark was under criminal investigation, the excrement hit the fan. I was accused by some of illegitimately hiding the information during the months since March 2. Others accused me of being in indecent haste to tell the public and take the premier down. One member of caucus, speaking to the press on condition of anonymity, called it the "first non-violent political assassination in the history of this country." For another, my actions amounted to "turning the knife." For still another, my disclosure amounted to "shooting a bullet" at the premier. All of the accusations were hurtful, and none of them were true. I had simply done my job as the Attorney General. People were lashing out at the messenger, and it angered me. The critics who cloaked themselves in anonymity when speaking to the media angered me even more. "I have always believed my colleagues, all of them, have the moral courage and integrity sufficient enough to append their names to any comments they make," I told reporters. I also let it be known that the anonymous critics were "ethically challenged." The partisans had lost sight of the fact that we had been elected to clean up Bill Vander Zalm's unethical mess. Our government stood to set a new low in ethical standards for premiers under active criminal investigation, and I wanted no part of that.

It is not my objective here to argue for or against the charges that were eventually laid against Clark, only to lay bare the difficult processes and principles behind the events. Pundits and politicians are quick with ready-made opinions, and only some do the necessary homework to ensure their opinions are based on facts. The Attorney General's role is perhaps the least understood role in government at the best of times. In complex situations such as the Clark probe, it becomes even more difficult to comprehend.

My actions were publicly defended by Alex Macdonald, who had served, in the Barrett era, as the first NDP Attorney General. Former Socred AG Allan Williams publicly endorsed my approach, as did Stephen Owen, who had conducted an inquiry and recommended the special prosecutor approach after the Bud Smith fiasco. In addition, there was a lot of editorial support for the correctness and ethical nature of my actions. My heart and soul were at peace.

Glen Clark resigned on the evening of August 21, and Dan Miller took over as interim premier. During his short and difficult tenure, Miller did a very good job of keeping the various NDP factions from destroying themselves and the party. In September, a Pollara poll indicated that I was the pick of over 30 per cent of British Columbians as the next NDP premier, followed by Gordon Wilson at 23 per cent, MacPhail at 14 per cent and Nelson Riis at 10 per cent. The poll put the party at 16 per cent. The other 31 per cent were undecided or "didn't know." Hypothetically, with me as leader, support for the NDP rose to 30 per cent; with Wilson as leader it was 28 per cent. Either way, the Liberals remained at 53 per cent — a near-wipeout of the NDP. An Angus Reid survey also showed me to be the public's favourite among the potential contenders for the NDP leadership. My approval would compare favourably with Gordon Campbell's even into the dog days of the 2001 election campaign. But that would not translate into support for the party. At least in the short run, the NDP had been damaged beyond repair.

I thought my years in politics had given me the ability not to worry about idiots, but I found out I was not as thick-skinned as I assumed. As soon as Glen Clark resigned, his supporters started spreading the lie that I had been signing up members across B.C. since the spring of 1998. They repeated the falsehood enough that it bothered me. I had

signed up some people in my riding in 1998 to bring my own membership to a respectable level; nothing more. But it suited his supporters to
spread such mythical nonsense, since their man Wilson needed time to
get to know the party before a leadership convention. The party executive realized the need for an early convention, but at the Prince George
provincial council meeting in September 1999, Wilsonites argued for
a later convention to be held in the new year. The purported members
I had signed up were one reason given for the delay. Other spurious
arguments included fall sports events such as the Grey Cup. Some
council members misunderstood my role in Clark's resignation, and
the Wilsonites gleefully played on that. Without that misrepresenta-
tion and the late convention date of February 2000, their man would
not have had a chance.

I had not decided for sure that I was going to run, particularly
if it meant living through a mass membership campaign. Clark, who
stayed on as MLA for Vancouver-Kingsway while the investigation
continued, was in Wilson's camp. Sihota and Lali were already court-
ing support from the fundamentalist leadership at the Khalsa Schools
and various temples, and memberships were being signed up in droves.
Sihota even made the rounds of the Sikh temples urging people to sign
up in support of him. Existing party members all knew he was supporting Wilson.

Another rumour making the rounds was that if I became leader,
the Wilsonites might join with Gordon Campbell to defeat a Dosanjh-
led government in the legislature. Former Clark aide David Schreck was
worried enough about that claim to go public, and the *Times Colonist*
declared, "Clark on warpath against Dosanjh and MacPhail." On the
bright side, Cathy McGregor had arrived at the council meeting clutching a poll of Prince George residents that placed me ahead of every
other potential candidate.

In September, a day or so after the Prince George meeting, Gordon
Wilson and Education Minister Paul Ramsey swapped portfolios.
Wilson had been minister of finance for only two months, and this
would be his third cabinet portfolio since joining the NDP in January.

But Premier Miller wanted his minister of finance to be neutral and to just manage the department; the swap out of that portfolio freed up Wilson to run for the leadership.

I was upset by the attacks on my integrity, but friends encouraged me to run, and Dennis McGann set up a website, www.ujjal.net, as a component of the larger "Run Ujjal Run" campaign started by some of my supporters. David Schreck offered to help. To help overcome my resistance, my supporters enlisted my biggest booster, Rami, as an ally. She was as ambivalent as I about the wisdom of running for leadership, but she never doubted for a moment our ability to win if I contested.

My supporters asked Rami to keep me at home during the September 25 – 26 weekend. Cabinet and caucus colleagues John Cashore, Tim Stevenson, Sue Hammell and Cathy McGregor showed up at our house, along with others. There were about thirty people in all, including B.C. Teachers' Federation president Alice McQuade, United Church of Canada moderator Bob Smith and Susan O'Donnell of the B.C. Human Rights Coalition. It was gratifying to witness colleagues with such faith in me, and also a burden: if I failed, I would dash their hopes. But I was touched, and I promised to give running for the leadership serious consideration.

Over the next couple of days, I shared my angst with my closest friends. The accusations of being a political assassin were hurtful, and I realized that if I won the contest, Wilson and his toxic crew would be part of the baggage I would have to deal with. In many ways, the NDP leadership at that juncture seemed nothing more than a crown of thorns. A cartoon of me in the *Province* by Bob Krieger with the caption "And if I run, I risk winning" captured the essence of my inner struggle. My public musings about not being inclined to run even ended up on the front page of the *Vancouver Sun*.

Sue Hammell and her spouse John Pollard invited Rami and me to their home in Surrey for a visit. I was there to confirm with Sue my overwhelming desire to not run. I hated the sniping in the party, I told them, and I wanted no part of it. As we chatted, I recalled someone saying that not running was perhaps my way of proving to the world that Clark had gone down for his own sins, whatever they may have been, not because of my hunger for power. That rang true to me, and I suddenly became aware of the major source of my inner struggle.

I continued my duties as AG, making announcements and following up on the important issues, be it preventing the exploitation of children or seeking funding from the feds for housing recently arrived boat people from China for the duration of their refugee determination process. We took steps to protect child witnesses by enhancing technology, as well as providing a safe environment in the courthouse or in remote locations for them to testify. During this time I also announced a new resource guide to combat racism in schools.

Svend Robinson, who had been considering a run for the leadership, announced he had decided against it. Gordon Wilson became the focus of some controversy surrounding a debt owed to a widowed friend as well as information in his biography that others alleged was untrue. With that, his poll numbers began to decline. Even his staunchest supporter, Moe Sihota, appeared to have cooled.

By mid-October the race had its first declared contestant: Corky Evans. The sniping against me had not let up. I knew it was designed to knock me off my game. I was still undecided about running, but our membership sign-up was in full swing, and we had identified key supporters in all regions and constituencies. The basic team was in place and met regularly at our home.

Shortly after Evans entered the race, Joy MacPhail declared her candidacy. She had some impressive supporters, including Doug McArthur, Bill Tieleman, Margaret Birrell, Elizabeth Cull and Sheila Fruman. Graeme Bowbrick from the caucus and Ken Georgetti and some others from labour were in her camp. But MacPhail, ever the capable and feisty scrapper, was surprisingly slow off the mark. With Wilson hobbled by the debt allegations, Sihota set his sights on our interim premier and led the move to a "draft Miller" campaign. Miller nipped it in the bud.

I was concerned that some of those who were unscrupulously signing up Indo-Canadians would eventually try to hide their sins by blaming me. I attempted to deal with the membership issue before it arose by making a public appeal that members should be enrolled in a manner respectful of the rules and the history of the party. I also made a public appeal to my supporters to be cautious in the way we signed up members. Moe Sihota surprised everyone by arguing that I should withdraw all of my new memberships, saying, "I don't think one ethnic group should be the sole determinant of the outcome of the leadership race." Moderates in the community were angered by his remarks, and he was forced to retract them, eventually admitting that he himself had signed up quite a few members in the Indo-Canadian community. Vaughn Palmer covered the story for the *Vancouver Sun*, writing, "[T]his latest twist is the most ridiculous yet — a prominent Indo-Canadian politician associating himself with a plot to exclude thousands of Indo-Canadians from a role in his own political party." Nonetheless, both Sihota and Lali kept up the façade of wanting to run for the leadership themselves, hoping to attract more members to the Wilson camp. I continued to speak to MLAS, ministers and other activists to seek their support. I felt it was only fair and proper that I ask Sihota and Lali for their support, too, despite their dislike of me.

Something else happened in the last half of October that would contribute to my future decision never to run for the federal NDP. Alexa McDonough, the national NDP leader, had been calling for a public inquiry into what had transpired at Gustafsen Lake. In sync with McDonough's demands, the little-known B.C. chapter of the New Democratic Party's socialist caucus passed a resolution asking for a public inquiry and an investigation specifically into my role in the standoff. I found the federal NDP's position on Gustafsen hollow and morally bankrupt. The federal party was not an organization worthy of my allegiance or commitment.

Sihota seemed obsessed with ensuring I did not win the provincial leadership. A *Vancouver Province* cartoon by Dan Murphy amusingly captured the situation with a caption that read "Most compelling reason to believe Ujjal Dosanjh would be a great premier — Moe Sihota hates the idea." By now, Joy MacPhail was also crying foul about my membership drive. She wanted a meeting of various camps to discuss the issue, but my campaign and I were doing nothing wrong. I wanted no part of such a meeting, and it didn't happen.

The media was being fed false analysis by my opponents. Some had branded me "Saint Ujjal," arguing that I had avoided the big political mess by using the "Attorney General Defence." They argued I would not be able to take the heat of the race or of the larger, more political office of premier. They had somehow forgotten my no-nonsense stand on the Gustafsen Lake standoff and the difficult decision I had made in fingering the sitting premier of my own party. I had courted and defied dangers in all of my political and personal life.

Two things happened that helped me make the decision to run. One was a Mark Trend poll that put Gordon Campbell and me in a dead heat at 28 per cent on the question of who would make the best premier, with Wilson and MacPhail trailing at 12 per cent and 9 per cent respectively. "His rivals can joke all they like about 'Saint Ujjal,'" Vaughn Palmer wrote, but the numbers "amounted to a personal tribute" to me. A McIntyre & Mustel poll found that almost half of British Columbians would consider voting NDP if the party chose an effective leader; 46 per cent considered me very effective or somewhat effective, with MacPhail and Wilson trailing at 27 and 24 per cent respectively.

The other deciding factor was a conversation I had with Darshan Gill. Darshan was aware of my reluctance to run, but he was of the view that I must run for reasons of the party and the province. He also articulated one additional reason I had not thought of. No one knew when a person of colour would next be as well positioned to make a run for the premiership of any province, he said. "Destiny or a confluence of events has placed you in these circumstances where all the stars are now aligned for a successful candidacy. Do it not for yourself but for opening the doors for future generations, for busting the barriers, real or imagined," he argued forcefully.

I made my announcement on November 7. John Cashore had agreed to chair my campaign. David Schreck led on the press contact front, and Sandra Huston signed on to manage the campaign.

I had prepared a speech with the assistance of former Harcourt advisor Chris Chilton and Dennis McGann of NOW Communications. Until then, I could have counted on my fingertips the number of speeches I had made from a prepared text, but this was an important speech. It needed to chart a path distinct from the situation with Clark and set me apart from other declared and potential candidates.

My speech acknowledged some of the mistakes our government had made, like the fast ferries and a centralized government run from the premier's office. I promised to get back to a cabinet-run government and not to pick unnecessary fights with Ottawa, like those over the now-expropriated Canadian Forces torpedo test range at Nanoose Bay and the stalled Vancouver convention centre. And I argued for putting our financial house in order.

Seventeen sitting or former MLAs and cabinet ministers, including six current ministers, were on stage behind me at the announcement at Robson Square. It was gratifying to have that impressive support behind me, with other supporters and activists crowding in to create an overflow crowd. A kid from a dusty Indian village was making a bid to lead the government of the third-largest province in Canada, and he was the odds-on favourite to succeed.

After I had announced my leadership ambitions, some aboriginal leaders spoke about a campaign to "tarnish me" because of the Gustafsen Lake standoff and other blockades. The leader of the Green Party of Canada called for a public inquiry into Gustafsen. The Liberals called for me to step down as Attorney General for the duration of the race, but Dan Miller reminded them that both Pierre Trudeau, federally, and Brian Smith, provincially, had run for the leadership of their respective parties while serving as Attorney General.

Another unexpected situation arose. Some months earlier, Gurnam Uppal had asked me for the names of some prominent criminal defence lawyers in connection with drunk driving charges against his cousin Balwant Gill, the president of the Guru Nanak Sikh Gurdwara in Surrey. I rattled off the names of some lawyers I had high regard for, including Ravi Hira, Richard Peck and David Gibbons. I did not call any of them, but the instant I offered the names I realized that in doing so while in office as Attorney General, I had made a mistake. I immediately informed my office, and the criminal justice branch appointed a special prosecutor to prosecute the case against Gill. But to create the whiff of a scandal, someone in the know from the Clark camp told the media about my conversation with Gurnam Uppal. I admitted my error and it was a one-day story.

As interim premier, Dan Miller, along with Finance Minister Paul Ramsey, tightened the fiscal reins. One of the decisions emanating from the tightening was the cabinet rejection of a Clark-era welfare measure costing $35 million. The measure allowed welfare recipients to earn $100 a month in outside income before facing clawbacks on their social assistance payments. I supported Miller in this decision, arguing that any new spending should await the new premier. But a revolt in the caucus led by Clark forced Miller to reverse course. Jenny Kwan, who many years later led the ouster of Carole James from the NDP leadership, was prominent in the revolt against Miller, as were Erda Walsh and Steve Orcherton. I believe I was their intended target, but they didn't care if Miller suffered a black eye in the process. Wilson declared his intention to run for the leadership on live radio with Rafe Mair on CKNW.

During the first week of December, a conference of the country's justice ministers and AGs took place in Vancouver. British Columbia had led the fight on harsher sentences for stalking and criminal harassment, and the federal minister, Anne McLellan, was urged by all provinces to raise the age of consent.

In the middle of the conference, another allegation against me by the Wilson camp surfaced. This time, they were accusing my campaign of signing up "bogus" members. I was sickened by it, but there was no way of knowing who had actually signed up the members in question. Their names didn't appear on the list of members my campaign had signed up or submitted to the party office. In one case, a family who told news outlets that my supporters had signed them up without them knowing about it were later seen at a delegate selection meeting wearing Gordon Wilson buttons. They had obviously lied to the media.

Similar allegations were made the following week about new members claiming they had been drafted without their knowledge. These and subsequent, equally baseless allegations were used to support a resolution before the provincial council by supporters of Evans, MacPhail and Wilson that party membership be retroactively cut off as of September 1999, the date of the Prince George council meeting. At that very meeting Wilson, Sihota and others had specifically argued for a February 2000 convention date in order to have time to sign up more memberships. Now they sought a reversal of the clock to September 1999. Council rejected the resolution. The truth of it was that my campaign had simply out-organized those of the other contenders.

The NDP had arranged a tour of the debating candidates that would start in Vancouver on December 9 and end in Victoria on January 17. In the middle of the divisive dirty-tricks campaign aimed at me came the first all-candidates debate on December 9 at Sir Charles Tupper Secondary School in Vancouver. I was disheartened by the mudslinging, and in a foul mood I threw away the written remarks agreed upon by my campaign team and adlibbed a lacklustre performance. I knew I had bombed, and there was no excuse for it. Evans shone, and MacPhail and Wilson did well too.

In the debates to come, I followed my script and did not feign oratorical brilliance. My initial stupidity and the bad press that followed had hurt my camp, but my performance improved, and I fared well at all other stops across the province. Of course, none among us had Evans's folksy charm, but whenever journalists referred to my low-key style, I countered by saying, "I have been the cool Attorney General for a hot province; I can be the cool premier for a hot province," stealing a Harcourt line.

On Boxing Day, a fire bomb went off at my constituency office on Victoria Drive in Vancouver. A Molotov cocktail had been thrown through the window, and it burned hot enough to melt a computer hard drive and a keyboard. The tenants upstairs, luckily, were safe. I hadn't been aware of any threats, but I discovered that, ending several weeks earlier, police had driven by my home for seventy-four days, several times a day, checking our doors and windows. The fire bomb may have been an attempt to destroy computer records in the hopes of damaging my leadership campaign, except that my campaign had nothing to do with the constituency office. I had no reason to believe I was personally targeted, but I couldn't be certain. Perhaps the device was meant to unnerve me and knock me off my stride. If so, it didn't work.

At a meeting in Vancouver early on in the campaign, even before I had declared my candidacy, my close supporters and I had discussed the possibility of signing up members and transferring them into two or three key ridings in the Lower Mainland for ease of organizing. Our perfectly legal plan was leaked to party headquarters overnight, and the party declared by a directive that memberships could not be transferred from riding to riding. That meant in ridings with small memberships, even a small number of committed members could tip the balance in delegate selection. We asked Kashmir Dhaliwal, Gurbax Saini and others to find us anchors and group leaders across the province and we picked up a large number of extra delegates in many ridings as a result. A device designed to constrain my campaign had actually ended up helping it.

The attacks upon me by the other camps, most viciously the Wilsonites, continued. The gap between Wilson and me narrowed, but my numbers were still much ahead of the others. Lali, Helmut Giesbrecht and Erda Walsh publicly declared their support for Wilson, followed by Sihota. All of this set the stage for Dave Barrett to appear at the legislature in Victoria to endorse Wilson. It was clear the Clark-Barrett forces were together in opposing my candidacy.

Around this time, my campaign scored its first big win from the ranks of labour unions: the United Food and Commercial Workers Union, a large private-sector union with several dozen delegates, endorsed me. So far labour had stayed on the sidelines, though. Wilson was rumoured to have the bulk of labour support. Eventually, I won the support of the Canadian Auto Workers Union and some others, while the International Woodworkers of America backed Wilson. The United Steelworkers were with MacPhail.

In early January 2000, the Wilson camp released what could only be termed a rogue poll that concluded that only Wilson could save the NDP and beat Gordon Campbell in a landslide. Vaughn Palmer, writing in the *Vancouver Sun*, called the poll "worthless." In fact, Wilson's numbers had suffered a significant decline, and in December Mark Trend's polling numbers had indicated a three-to-one edge for me over Wilson. According to Mark Trend, even against Campbell I was considered a better bet to protect education and healthcare, and I led by ten points on the question of "being honest and having integrity."

The leadership debates around the province were attracting only a few die-hard partisans. In Cranbrook, for example, a large town in Wilson-backer Erda Walsh's riding, the debate drew less than three dozen people. The Vancouver, Victoria, Surrey and Kelowna crowds were the largest and most enthusiastic. In early January, at the end of the debate in Kelowna, Joy MacPhail told me she was ready to quit the race and throw her support behind me.

Shortly after MacPhail's withdrawal, trade union activist Len Werden entered the race as a stalking horse for Wilson, to bring home some union support. In the middle of all this, allegations of violations of the Election Act by Wilson's former party, the Progressive Democratic Alliance, surfaced. The AG's ministry appointed a special prosecutor, which I learned about only from a public comment by the RCMP.

After Barrett's declaration of support for Wilson, Mike Harcourt threw his support behind me. He came out swinging, defending my handling of the Clark probe. Former AG Colin Gabelmann also joined the ranks of my supporters, which soon included ministers Joan Smallwood and Penny Priddy. Sue Hammell was already a committed supporter.

The first weekend of voting went well, with my campaign winning all twenty-four delegate spots in Burnaby-Edmonds, eleven of twelve in Surrey-Whalley and over 90 per cent in other ridings. In terms of delegates, Corky Evans was gaining ground, Wilson was fading. As the Wilson camp sensed the approaching defeat, their allegations of improper sign-ups by my camp became more desperate, though again there was no evidence linking my supporters to that or to the allegation that there were many B.C. Liberals on the NDP membership list. We were picking up delegates all over the province, and with union support we were on track to win on the first ballot.

Although I was accused of being an "ethnic" candidate, our slates were always a mix of veteran NDP men and women and new recruits. For example, in Surrey Green Timbers, our slate was only half Indo-Canadian, while what the media called the "Sihota-Wilson-Lali" slate was entirely Indo-Canadian, with Wilson's campaign literature, under Sihota's name, appealing to "my nation" to support Wilson. A technical error on my team's part was used by Wilsonites in Glen Clark's Kingsway riding to disqualify our slate. Wilson swept all those delegates. We won all the delegates from Vancouver-Fraserview, Surrey-Newton, Delta North and Mission-Kent, but a lot of dirty tricks were still being played to derail my campaign. A woman named Harjinder Kaur Shergill was a case in point: she had been signed up and had alleged in a Vancouver Television interview in January 2000 that my campaign had put her on the membership list in Vancouver-Fraserview unbeknownst to her. Then, at the Vancouver-Fraserview delegate selection meeting, she voted wearing a Wilson badge. When reporter Kim Bolan recognized her from the VTV interview and asked her about it, Shergill said that at the time of the interview she had forgotten that she had earlier signed the membership forms. The sign-up mess wasn't of my making, but it definitely hurt me.

Increasingly desperate to hurt our campaign, Gordon Wilson tried to muddy the waters by reviving the call for an inquiry into the Gustafsen Lake standoff and alleged that federal Liberal supporters were also supporting me. An anomaly of B.C. was that a disproportionately high percentage of federal Liberal supporters voted NDP provincially, while many supporters of the provincial NDP voted Liberal federally. Many truths became casualties in Wilson's rush to score political points.

PART 7

SERVING

AS

PREMIER

42 AMID ALL THE FINGER-POINTING and dirty tricks came the news that the legendary Rosemary Brown was going to endorse me. Brown was the first black woman ever to be elected to the B.C. legislature, and her endorsement at this juncture, along with the string of victories in delegate selection meetings, buoyed my campaign. A McIntyre & Mustel poll, released on the eve of the all-candidates debate at the leadership convention, showed that 39 per cent of B.C. residents would support the NDP if it were led by me.

By now, I had the support of the vast majority of the cabinet ministers and MLAS, as well as that of several former MLAS and ministers and of NDP MPs Libby Davies and Svend Robinson. A large chunk of the union delegates were also supporting our campaign. My Friday night debate performance at the convention was not bad, except for a hoarse throat I had developed. The RCMP had provided me with security cover, I assumed out of an abundance of caution.

My Saturday speech had been well rehearsed. There would be no adlibbing this time, and we candidates would also have the benefit of a teleprompter, my first time using one. My speech wove together the personal and the historical, emotion and economics, politics and social justice. My staff, volunteers and advisors had all done their work. Now it would be my turn to honour their work and cement our delegate support.

Len Werden, who had given up his leadership bid, had surprisingly lent his support to Evans. He had essentially no delegates, other than a lone MLA, but his move to Evans made it clear the Barrett-Clark faction had figured out Wilson had no chance of beating me. To keep his campaign intact, Wilson denied he was about to fold in Evans's favour.

Mike Harcourt had put his heart and soul into my campaign. In one of his interviews from the floor of the convention, he fingered Sihota as the person responsible for the massive sign-up. "Ujjal got a bum rap in all of this," Harcourt said, "and frankly it happened because Moe Sihota decided that's what he was going to do ... Anybody but Ujjal. So he and people around him took over that council meeting [in September 1999, the meeting at which the convention date had been set] and delayed the leadership, and then [Sihota] went out and started to sign up bulk memberships. So what's Ujjal going to do? Say, 'Gee, that's unfair' and lose, or fight fire with fire? So he fought fire with fire, and he did it far more successfully." Harcourt conceded there had been pressure for him to resign the premiership from what he called the labour wing of the party: Clark and Sihota. He was now chairing my transition team, and we were on the cusp of victory.

The Saturday of the convention, there was an impressive show of my campaign's orange "U! for Ujjal" signs on the floor. We had had a lot of financial and moral support from Indo-Canadians across Canada. The close leadership race had even been news in India and in the Indian diaspora in North America, Europe, the Middle East, Australia and New Zealand. I had received requests for interviews from all over the world. But winning the B.C. leadership had of course remained our focus.

The day began with Ken Georgetti recommending a change of rules for future conventions, to avoid the kinds of allegations that had surfaced during this race. Dan Miller followed with a plea for party unity. Werden had dropped out following some clandestine discussions between the Evans and Wilson camps to assess their combined support. The discussions between them continued amid denials as the candidate speeches got underway.

Surprisingly, Wilson's speech did not shine, as would have been expected from an accomplished orator. He spent time distancing himself from his past; that was odd, because in the earlier stages of his campaign, he had prided himself as "having been there" and therefore having a good read on the B.C. Liberals. Corky Evans, usually a great orator, dampened his own supporters' enthusiasm by asking them to not interrupt too much with clapping, in case he ran out of time. When I got the two-minute signal, I went straight to the last few paragraphs of hard copy in front of me and, luckily, delivered my final points seamlessly. It was all done except for the balloting and counting that would happen the next day.

If there was any hope of stopping me, it had to be on the first ballot. We knew Wilson would drop out; the only question was timing. The strategy of my opponents would continue to be "anybody but Ujjal." The balloting was only hours away, but we could not afford to sleep, lest we slipped up. While I rested, my team made calls late into the evening to ensure we would have every delegate present and delivered to the balloting booths in the morning. The team had been loyal and committed, and they did an exceptional job of organizing on the ground.

On Sunday morning, we heard that Wilson was going to quit and support Evans. He had spoken to his delegates as early as 7:30 AM, we learned. The floor was opened to the delegates at 8:15, and shortly after 8:30 Evans and Wilson emerged from a meeting with the Wilsonites wearing Evans's badges. The B.C. Government Employees' Union, the largest public-sector union, announced for Evans shortly after the International Woodworkers of America, with a substantial block of delegates, threw its support behind me.

With the camps now clearly defined, we got ready for the balloting, which began shortly after ten. Pavel, Aseem and Umber were with Rami and me that morning, as was customary, though I worried about the emotional stress on my sons. As on all other political occasions, I was there voluntarily. My family were in it for their love of me.

We took our seats at the Vancouver-Kensington table in the arena as the count got underway. Supporters and friends from the floor came by in a steady stream to shake hands and reassure me that we were winning. I was fairly optimistic, but in a convention where every delegate is a free agent, the outcome is never guaranteed. So when the officials climbed to the podium, our hearts were pounding. Paul Gill was one of them, and he told me afterwards that when it was clear to the counters I had won, he asked the others to allow him to announce the numbers. Of 1,318 ballots cast, I had secured 769 and carried the convention. The floor erupted into cheers, and the animosity of the campaign evaporated, albeit temporarily.

My family and I were ushered onto the stage. Evans, Miller, MacPhail, Wilson and others were up there with us to convey a sense of unity. After Evans declared the election unanimous, I promised the convention that we would provide a government British Columbians could trust, with putting the province's financial house in order as a priority. I did not talk about winning the next election; cleansing and rehabilitating the party as a credible entity was more important than anything else. After my short speech, we met with friends and well-wishers, and I made the rounds of the news outlets reporting from the convention floor. It was a strange feeling having won the crown but knowing the road ahead was not going to be easy.

Outside we could hear the *dhol*, the Indian drum, and the shouts of bhangra music in full swing. I never learned who had arranged for the drummers to be there, but it was a touching Indian finale to a historic convention. The celebrations spilled over into a full-blown party at the Fraserview Hall in southeast Vancouver. The ever-gracious Baldev Khanna opened up the hall to close to a thousand people that night, and the party lingered into the wee hours of the morning. My elderly Biraji was there. All his life he had counselled me to study and work hard lest I remain second fiddle to the important and the powerful. He was happy that evening.

My leadership win was news all over the world. Headlines from North America to Europe, the Middle East, the Asia Pacific and Australia hailed the victory. In India, I was hailed with great joy as a "son of the soil" who had succeeded abroad, indeed the first to achieve a premiership, one of the highest political offices in the West. The celebration was wonderful, but the task at hand was putting together a cabinet and then governing British Columbia in a way that would earn back the trust of our citizens.

THE MEDIA PREDICTED an early election, and they speculated endlessly about the so-called "inner circle" and the possible "ins and outs" of my cabinet. One thing they all agreed on was that Moe Sihota, who had almost popped a blood vessel in his hysterical speech nominating Wilson, deserved to be out. I had made no such decision. Our government had been battered and we were hurting badly from the self-inflicted wounds of fighting the federal government, Washington and Alaska on the Canada-U.S. Pacific Salmon Treaty and the torpedo testing at Nanoose Bay. We needed to cool the rhetoric and bring in a budget and a throne speech before the end of March. With barely a month to go, we needed to get moving. A new McIntyre & Mustel poll that showed 39 per cent of B.C. voters were inclined toward us prompted the *Province* to editorialize: "The NDP isn't the only party badly in need of a new leader."

As preparations got underway for my swearing-in at Government House, I was briefed about the budgetary situation facing the province. It wasn't pretty. With a debt of $1.8 million, the party coffers were empty too. The caucus was feeling tired and bruised, and on the national front, our relationship with the Chrétien government lay in tatters.

I had decided the oath should be taken at Government House to eliminate the extra expense of having it done close to my riding. As we travelled to Victoria for the swearing-in, the *Vancouver Sun* published an article outlining the major court losses our government had suffered during my time as AG, including the case of Bert Stone, in which I had personally argued before the Supreme Court of Canada. We'd also had countless wins, but they didn't count for a media bent upon creating hooks for stories. Another story reminded readers that the Glen Clark probe was set to close in two months.

Once we arrived at Government House, the official photographs were taken, including some with my extended family on both Rami's and my side. Then it was time to be piped into the hall and onto the stage. The multi-coloured crowd was a sight to behold for its historic significance. Skin pigmentation matters when it represents the distance from exclusion to inclusion. People's smiles and tears of joy were the acknowledgement of this milestone. The journey from peasant to premier was momentous for a man whose forebears on the *Komagata Maru* had been turned away from Canada under the shadow of guns.

The celebrated classical sitar player Devinder Singh Hundal, accompanied by tabla player Paramjit Singh Vasir, was asked to play before and after the oath ceremony. For the first time ever at the swearing-in of a premier in Canada, Indian classical music was played and pakoras were served at Government House. "A touch of India as Dosanjh sworn in," wrote the *Province*. A colour photograph of the turbaned Hundal and Vasir adorned the space above the story. It was a joyous day, but now it was time to get down to work.

43 AS ONE OF MY FIRST orders of business as premier, I hired competent Chris Chilton as my chief of staff; he hired Sandra Huston as his deputy. Former provincial secretary Hans Brown and former MLA and economist David Schreck were taken on as special advisors. I refused to speculate on the budget until it was presented, since I did not want to tie Finance Minister Paul Ramsey's hands. Going into cabinet formation, he was the only one who would stay in his portfolio.

Chris Chilton, Hans Brown and I met at the Vancouver cabinet offices, using an easel loaded with paper to write out possible names and positions. As our discussions continued and the lists developed, a consensus emerged to exclude Moe Sihota from cabinet. Sihota was not kept out because of his speech at the convention or because he opposed me. But if there was anyone who epitomized Glen Clark and his style of politics, it was Sihota, who had had three previous excursions from the cabinet to the backbench for reasons that were well known. To induct him would have sent a message to the citizens of B.C. that the government had not learned anything.

Sihota was not happy to hear the news, but the other decisions were easy. Dan Miller stayed on as both minister of energy and mines and minister responsible for northern development, portfolios he had carried while he was interim premier. Joy MacPhail was selected to be deputy premier, with responsibility for labour and B.C. Ferries. Andrew Petter was the natural choice for Attorney General. Sue Hammell was back in as minister responsible for the public service, and Gretchen Brewin, who had earlier resigned from the speakership, now became minister for children and families.

I thought Tim Stevenson, who had been deputy speaker, should be allowed to stand on behalf of our caucus as speaker. Sihota also lobbied like crazy for the job. The caucus chose Bill Hartley in the end.

We decided that the fast ferries would be sold as soon as possible. The Auditor General had already investigated what went wrong, obviating the need for an inquiry. Our case on the Pacific Salmon Treaty was withdrawn, ending the bitter federal-provincial fight. The House was recalled for March 15, with the throne speech to be followed by the budget. In the next McIntyre & Mustel poll, our numbers moved to 25 per cent support, but the Liberals were way ahead.

The NDP had had a premier who hung on far too long, almost fatally wounding the party. Now the party was on life support, and it showed not much sign of recovery, no matter what we did. The way Clark loyalists continued to behave in Victoria and controversies surrounding Gordon Wilson's extravagant flying habits added to our misery. These antics affirmed in the public's mind the claim of our opponents that ours was not a new or different government.

The Throne Speech highlighted new budget transparency legislation to be introduced and the beginnings of universal child care, with a promise for before- and after-school care. We promised modest tax cuts for all but weighted them in favour of low- and middle-income families. We promised to increase to 12 per cent the protected land mass in the province. Reaction to the speech was mixed. The budget we presented was fiscally conservative but socially progressive, ensuring healthcare and education got the needed resources.

Our daycare plan came in for criticism I felt was ideologically inclined rather than fair or rational. The media coverage was as expected: cynical and not too kind. In the meantime, the fact that we could not find a press secretary went public. It was embarrassing but true; with the short time we had left to govern, and the uncertainty regarding the election timing, there were bound to be few takers. But we soon hired Shari Graydon, a media critic and former Canadian president of Media Watch, and her experience and knowledge helped me greatly throughout my time as premier.

A serious labour situation was brewing, too. About twenty thousand school support workers in forty school districts, including special needs assistants, janitors, and clerical and maintenance workers represented by the Canadian Union of Public Employees (CUPE), were about to go on strike. I urged the parties to settle, but to no avail. The strike came upon us, and we needed to act.

On Monday, March 28, Irene Holden and Vince Ready were appointed as industrial inquiry commissioners, to report to me by Saturday noon. If there was no settlement, I made it clear I was prepared to look at other options to get children back in school — some of them were set to begin writing exams, and I wanted to ensure they didn't lose their year — and families back to their routines by April 3. When there was no deal, the government passed a law to send the support workers back to work. MLAS Erda Walsh, Glen Clark and Steve Orcherton skipped the vote. Orcherton, then our deputy whip, not only missed the vote but did so after speaking against it in the House, in the process breaching caucus confidentiality by mentioning the reluctance of other members to support the legislation. There were calls for Orcherton's head.

I couldn't understand Clark wanting to avoid such a vote except to create trouble for me. In his time, he had legislated an end to a school strike and had also outlawed public-sector strikes for the duration of the election he called in 1996. Moe Sihota, who was now reluctant to send CUPE back to work, had enthusiastically voted for both of the Clark initiatives. The situation provided more fodder for the media about divisions within the caucus. Jim Sinclair of the B.C. Federation of Labour was unhappy with the legislation, and so was the Hospital Employees' Union, which accused us of creating a "Bob Rae style of relationship between Victoria and the public sector unions." There was talk of open rebellion by the new "six pack": Clark, Sihota, Orcherton, Walsh, Helmut Giesbrecht and Dennis Streifel. But NDP whip Gerard Janssen made sure Clark was there to vote on the supply bill on the night of March 29, when it counted. So the talk of threats to our stability was overblown. I knew no NDP MLA would dare bring down our own government.

The back-to-work legislation had a lingering effect on my relationship with the party and the labour movement. I found the resentment hypocritical; the party had been through back-to-work legislation several times during its reign in B.C. but was now acting noxiously sanctimonious. I had simply followed the precedents established by previous NDP regimes. Through three separate bills in 1974 and 1975, Dave Barrett had sent fifty thousand forestry, pulp and other sundry workers, construction industry workers and firefighters back to work. Harcourt had sent the Vancouver teachers back to work in 1993. In 1996, as noted, Glen Clark had legislated an end to a school strike and had legislatively banned strikes in the health and education sectors before calling an election.

Now, however, the NDP provincial executive and the provincial council of the party passed motions condemning my legislation. The party, it seemed, had decided to abandon its own premier and government. Three hundred members of CUPE walked out of the B.C. Federation of Labour's convention when I went to address it. By this time, I felt totally abandoned by both the party and the labour movement. Of course I had friends in the NDP and in labour who stood with me. But the public display of disloyalty by the provincial council and the provincial executive in condemning the back-to-work legislation amounted to a condemnation of me. Where had this commitment to labour piety and trade union sacrosanctity been in 1974, '75, '93 and '96?

I sensed a similar detachment from reality within the party on the balanced budget law we had introduced. I had advised the provincial council that the legislation was coming, and the beating we had taken on the fiscal front had left us with no option but to act. It was not about winning the next election, which we were sure to lose anyway. Our problem was deeper than that: no one believed the NDP anymore on fiscal issues, and rampant public cynicism was the price we were paying for our past sins. The Budget Transparency and Accountability Act was about sowing the seeds of credibility for the party in the future beyond the next election. The caucus was on board in general terms, and Sihota had offered to help achieve consensus. But Adrian Dix, former chief of staff to Clark, wrote a brutal critique of the principle of it. Presumably he thought the NDP governments of Saskatchewan and Manitoba, which had already passed similar legislation, were unprincipled too. In any case, I had decided to push ahead with the measure no matter what the opposition to it internally. The NDP was at 16 per cent in the polls, with the Liberals at 57 per cent. My own performance rating was 64 per cent, versus Campbell's 53 per cent. On the question of who would make the best premier, I was at 40 per cent for Campbell's 38 per cent. The party needed to be where I was, but so far we had failed because of the real and perceived disconnect between me and Clark's supporters, including most of the labour aristocracy.

On June 27, the caucus committee's final report on the balanced budget bill was discussed in caucus. As we exited the meeting, the media told me there were NDP MLAs who had declared they would vote against the bill. To call the dissidents' bluff, I declared the vote on the bill to be a confidence measure: vote for the bill or face an election none of us was ready for. The bill passed. The 1999–2000 budget came in with a small surplus, and the 2000–2001 year would end with a surplus of over a billion dollars. Both surpluses were certified as such by the Auditor General. Commentators accepted the numbers as legitimate, but they were in agreement that it might be too late for our government to realize any electoral returns for the achievement.

EARLIER THAT SPRING, I had flown to Ottawa to repair our frayed relations with the Chrétien government. I met with various ministers, including Finance Minister Paul Martin and Environment Minister David Anderson, as well as the B.C. Liberal senators. I had lunch with federal fisheries minister Herb Dhaliwal, and I met the prime minister in his office in the precinct. It was a very cordial meeting; I needed to rebuild B.C.'s relationship with the feds and Chrétien needed an ally in his forthcoming discussions with the provinces on health. I did not like the fact that Ontario, under Mike Harris, was spending millions of dollars to bash the Chrétien government on health funding and transfers. That was no way to build a better nation, I felt; provincial and federal leaders must be nation builders first and foremost, of course without the provinces abandoning their just share of the national pie. It was my view, shared by the PM, that a first ministers' conference would be more useful once the premiers had arrived at a consensus on sorely needed health reforms.

A short time later, I took a similar fence-mending and relationship-building trip to Olympia to meet with the state of Washington's governor, Gary Locke. Locke later paid me a return visit in Vancouver. Locke was a second-generation Chinese American, and he and I shared family stories along with discussing state-province relations.

During the second week of April, a trial had begun of a case known as Friesen v. Hammell that targeted several MLAs including Sue Hammell, Glen Clark and Elizabeth Cull, as well as the NDP as a whole. The suit alleged that the budget introduced just before the 1996 election was fraudulent, since the finance minister appointed after the election had announced upon a review that the budget wouldn't be balanced. David Stockell, a B.C. Liberal supporter from Kelowna, founded an organization called Help Eradicate Lying Politicians (HELP) and commenced the action. The second element of the Liberal attack was a series of recall campaigns, including one against Paul Ramsey. In the end, both initiatives failed, but they battered our credibility in the process. The Liberal strategy had been the very effective political equivalent of water torture.

In the middle of everything, Moe Sihota dropped the political bombshell that he was considering a run for the federal Liberals in the upcoming election because he liked their "new focus on social policy." Celso Boscariol, the former president of the B.C. wing of the federal Liberals, denied any knowledge of this and rejected outright a bid to run for the federal Liberals by someone who had been, as the *Vancouver Sun* reported him saying, "bounced from cabinet so many times in disgrace." The *Sun* then quoted Boscariol directly:

"His thinking is fatuous ... this idea is not on." Herb Dhaliwal was also quick to distance himself from Sihota's claim, denying that "any discussions had taken place." The *Vancouver Sun* reported that the federal Liberals it contacted had laughed at the idea of recruiting Sihota, and then cringed.

Glen Clark continued to make mischief. One day he was questioning my support of the Chrétien government's request that provinces have a plan to reform healthcare before seeking more federal money, and the next he was introducing a private member's bill to allow pets in rental accommodation. He seemed to be lashing out in anger at losing power, and none of it did the party's reputation any good.

AROUND THE SAME TIME, I had some unwelcome surprises on the personal front. My son Aseem had been at the University of Windsor attending law school and was set to graduate. On the last day of the school year, he headed out with some classmates to a bar popular with Americans. When a friend of his, Sunny Parhar, was sucker-punched by an American rowdy looking for a fight, Aseem went over to ask what was going on. The bar's bouncer asked them, not the American rowdy, to leave. When they asked him why, the bouncer told them these Americans were the owner's favourites. The bouncer failed to add the fact that the Americans were white, too. Aseem and several friends decided to leave.

As Aseem exited the front door, he was thrown against the exterior wall of the joint by the same American rowdy and his friends. He extricated himself and joined Parhar and the others in walking away. They had only gone a few steps when they realized that their friend Harv was missing. When they looked back and saw a group of men beating someone, they ran back, worried the victim was Harv. It was, and when they tried to get him out of there, they were attacked by the rowdies. Unknown to Aseem and Parhar, plainclothes police had arrived to deal with the fracas, and I am sure it was not coincidence that the police targeted the young brown men. While Aseem's shirt was pulled over his head, he let go a punch that hit a plainclothes police officer, who hit him back. Parhar came to his aid, and they were both arrested. The white guys who had started it all were let go.

When I first heard the news, I was in a concert hall in Vancouver listening to the famous Indian classical singer Jagjit Singh. I stepped out to take a call from a close friend of Aseem's who had been with

44

him at the bar. Shortly afterwards, Jagjit asked me to come up on stage and join him in singing a couple of lines of a Punjabi folk song, which I did. I smiled on stage, but I was hurting inside. I was angry at the racism of the Windsor police. Other law students who had witnessed the events had tried to tell police officers, both on the scene and at the police station, that they had arrested the wrong chaps. Some of the students would later speak to the media, too, alleging racism by the police. "They arrested the brown guys and the white guys walked away," said Sarah Rimmington, a fellow law student. "When the police arrived, they immediately went after the two... East Indian law students [and] let the white Americans run away," Laura Olsthoorn, another law student, told reporters. Aseem and Sunny Parhar were not drunk, the police admitted. So why, out of all those involved in the "large disturbance," were they the ones who were arrested? I could not demand answers then. But answers were needed. The whole thing stank to high heaven. Later, a police spokesman would make the lame excuse that there were not enough cops on the scene to arrest everyone responsible. I learned this kind of thing happened in Windsor all the time, particularly at certain bars.

Aseem had been scheduled to start his articles at Ravi Hira's Vancouver law firm. He retained Windsor lawyer Pat Ducharme to defend him, with Ravi as co-counsel. Rami and I accompanied him on his first appearance in court in Windsor on May 8. As I entered the courtroom that morning, I remembered something I had said to Aseem years earlier: "If you do something wrong, do not expect me to come to your aid." Not long after I'd told him that, he and his cousin were attacked at Vancouver's famed annual fireworks festival. Their attackers were thugs who had gone to the event carrying socks filled with stones to have some fun at someone else's expense. Luckily, a black American sailor came to their aid. Aseem called from the hospital, where he was being cleaned up and bandaged, and spoke to Rami. I refused to speak to him or to go with Rami to the hospital, because I mistakenly believed Aseem had been at fault. I apologized when I learned the truth, and it taught me a lesson. Even if it had been Aseem's fault, I should have been there, first to comfort him in his pain, and then to counsel him.

Both Aseem and Parhar were acquitted by the court in Windsor. While one could argue that the ordeal likely made them better lawyers and better human beings, it certainly rendered their wallets empty, since Aseem paid part of his legal costs from his articling salary. The day after he was charged, his mug adorned the front page of the *Vancouver Province*. After his acquittal, he turned to me with that front page in hand and said: "I couldn't have bought this with a million bucks." He was obviously trying to make light of his ordeal by alluding to the wide publicity's benefit to his legal career. But what cost the true heartache?

AROUND THE TIME THAT Aseem was charged in Windsor, I attended a wedding reception on a Saturday evening at the Hellenic Community Centre in Vancouver. I was there very briefly; I arrived just after 10:00 PM and left before 11:00 PM. Shortly after I left the hall, a murder took place about two blocks away.

The murder was in the news, and so was the fact that I had been at the nearby hall earlier. One news channel alleged there had been gangsters at the wedding as it screened a shot of Aseem and me walking together in Windsor. It was despicable. The next morning, I had to answer media questions about whether I had known the victim, who was wrongly alleged to be a cousin of the late gangster Bindy Johal. No, I had not known the victim, I told reporters; I hoped they didn't expect me to know 250,000 Indo-Canadians personally. On Monday afternoon, the press gallery members in Victoria cornered me as I was about to enter the caucus room. I patiently answered the same question. As I emerged from the caucus room an hour later, the same question was asked for the third time. I lost my cool, and when I spotted a reporter from the TV channel that had run the shot of Aseem and me, I told him angrily he should assess his channel's ethics. I also pointed out to the assembled journalists that they would not have asked that question of a Barrett, a Bennett or a Clark, let alone asking it three times, if one of those men happened to be at a reception and a murder took place two blocks away. For God's sake, I said, we lived in a society where some people lived next door to each other for decades without knowing each other's names. Some journalists took issue with what I said, and Vaughn Palmer accused me in his column of being prickly. I didn't care. I was being subjected to implicit assumptions, and I wasn't going to take it any more.

Luckily, there were moments of joy during this period too. The Nisga'a Treaty, which I had defended in debates and a clause-by-clause examination in the House, came into effect on May 12, 2000, exactly thirty-two years to the day I had landed in Canada. Freed from the shackles of the Indian Act, more than 5,500 Nisga'a became truly equal Canadians. Both as a premier and as a human being, it was a moment to behold. In another happy moment, Prime Minister Chrétien and I unveiled a plaque at a ceremony designating the Clayoquot Sound United Nations Biosphere Reserve.

AS THE FALL OF 2000 came around, it was time to ask those caucus members who would not be running in 2001 to declare that fact. Miller, Petter and several others came forward, so none of them remained in my shuffled cabinet. I was castigated by some for not leaving experienced ministers in their portfolios, but if I had let them remain, I'm sure the same critics would have said it was the wrong thing to do. I brought in Tim Stevenson, the first openly gay person to be in any cabinet in Canada, to handle employment and investment. In an unorthodox move, I made Chief Ed John of the Tl'azt'en Nation the minister of children and families. The Liberals criticized the appointment, as did some aboriginal leaders. But I felt it was important to have John in that ministry, since a disproportionate number of children in care belonged to the aboriginal communities, and he had pledged to run for the NDP in the next election. John was only the second aboriginal British Columbian to be named to a B.C. cabinet; in Dave Barrett's government, Frank Calder had been a minister without portfolio. This latter fact had not escaped John. Later, at a birthday celebration, he reminded me, "It took one Indian to make another a real minister in B.C."

At the time of the cabinet shuffle, the Burnt Church crisis, a dispute between the Mi'kmaq people and non-aboriginal fisheries, was continuing to unfold in New Brunswick. I attended a meeting of aboriginal leaders at which Chief Bill Wilson remarked to me, "Fisheries Minister Dhaliwal is making a mess out of the Burnt Church situation. You, from the Punjab, as premier of the province of British Columbia, are doing your best in what perhaps may be a losing cause. It struck me on my way up here to the meeting after sharing a lunch with another successful person from the Punjab — and Mr. Premier, please do not take this as a racial comment, for it is not intended as such — that I believe we are being governed by the wrong kind of Indians." I laughed, as did others.

Fazil Milhar of the *Vancouver Sun* either heard or was told of Wilson's remarks, and he wrote a piece in the paper criticizing Wilson as being racist. I was shocked; Wilson's comments had been anything but. In a letter to the editor, Wilson ably defended himself. "I went on to make other comments about the powerlessness of aboriginal people. The premier responded in what I considered to be a brilliant rejoinder, 'Well Bill, as one Indian to another . . .' This kind of exchange to me is how we must solve our problems . . . If I were a racist, I would have to be opposed to my own cause. The reductio ad absurdum of Mr. Milhar's argument is that I do not like coloured people regardless of where they originated. How stupid. Should I try to change my colour and just pretend as he and others seem so ready to do?" My sentiments exactly — but brilliantly phrased by the inimitable Wilson.

THE PREVIOUS SUMMER, I had attended the Western premiers' conference. I was anxious for us to make in our communiqué a reference as a group to the creeping privatization of Canada's healthcare, but unity on the health file eluded us. A couple of months later, at a Canadian premiers' conference in Winnipeg chaired by fellow NDP premier Gary Doer, the same problem arose. Ontario and Alberta refused to agree to a reform package for healthcare or even to a reference in our communiqué to our concern about the creeping privatization. Saskatchewan's Roy Romanow and Newfoundland's Brian Tobin agreed with the B.C. position that, with or without Quebec, we should have a reform package for health. Quebec could use the same principles and craft its own plan, as it did in most things. The discussion heated up, and at one point, with Ontario's Mike Harris out of the room, we persuaded Ralph Klein to go along with us. Harris rushed back into the room yelling, "I don't give a shit what B.C. wants!" Romanow gave in to the inevitable a few hours earlier than I did. He was a veteran of these battles and knew how far one could push. I was still new and learning. I was disappointed, but it was a lesson for me in the difficulty of achieving consensus in the federation.

A few weeks later, the premiers met with Prime Minister Chrétien to try to get more money from Ottawa with a view to reform healthcare. Ontario and Quebec had been erecting major roadblocks, but the night before the meeting, Chrétien wined and dined us at 24 Sussex Drive, and by the end of the evening it seemed we had the makings of a deal. Klein, being close to both Mike Harris and to Quebec's Lucien Bouchard, may have played a role behind the scenes. The next morning at the formal meeting, however, as the text of the agreement we'd worked up was brought before us, Bouchard worried out loud that some elements of the deal could be seen as giving away "exclusive provincial jurisdiction" over health. Remembering the famous notwithstanding clause of the Canadian Constitution, I suggested the addition of a clause specifying that nothing in the agreement would "derogate from the respective governments' jurisdictions." Ralph Klein dubbed it the "Dosanjh clause." Klein was a tough negotiator, and someone with a mean streak, but he was always ready to make a deal in the national interest, despite his occasional declarations bordering on Alberta separatism.

With the federal money B.C. would receive over the next five years, it was our government's plan to lay the foundation for more robust public healthcare and to establish a publicly subsidized child-care system. We had already made a good beginning on the latter front with before- and after-school care, and around this time it became clear that the province's financial fiscal situation was finally on the mend, with a credible framework in place, one balanced budget under our belts and another in the works. That earned us praise from some commentators, and some even suggested we were on the right track for rebuilding the party.

But as we were beginning the long road to recovery of both the party and our government's fortunes, we were jolted by the resignation of the perpetually unhappy MLA Rick Kasper in order to sit as an independent. Kasper had not got his way on the issue of the ferry serving his riding or on his demand for CAT scan equipment for his riding. His riding executive had also been taken over by other elements in the party. A second blow to the party came in October when conflict of interest charges were laid against Glen Clark. That ensured we would have the issue hanging over our heads during the upcoming election.

The federal election loss of NDP MP Nelson Riis in Kamloops in November seemed a warning of the fate awaiting us at the polls in B.C. The federal NDP kept its other two seats in B.C., but the party's share of the vote had fallen from 18 per cent in 1997 to 12 per cent in 2000. What would happen on the provincial level remained to be seen. Gordon Campbell's only strong point remained the public's dislike of the NDP, but would Vaughn Palmer's description of me — as the "right guy, wrong party" — stick?

45   RAMI AND I NEEDED TO GET AWAY from B.C., at least for a little while, and when the government of India invited me as a state guest, as did the government of Punjab, I bought tickets for us and our son Umber. No civil servants accompanied us on our trip, though I invited my friend Ramesh Singal, who worked for the NDP at the time, to come along to assist me at his own expense. Singal corresponded with India and Punjab on my behalf and as a courtesy kept Peter Sutherland, the Canadian High Commissioner in India, informed of our plans. The Punjab government was desirous of enhancing trade and exchanges with B.C., and to that end I asked government bureaucrats to draft a memorandum of understanding to be signed during my visit.

In Delhi, Peter Sutherland, Rami and I met with the Indian prime minister Atal Bihari Vajpai. A poet and a scholar, Vajpai was a soft-spoken man, and on political stages and in Parliament he shone as an orator. He and I chatted mostly in English, exchanging a few words of Hindi as well. His Hindi of course was impeccable, though mine was more the Hindustani of Bollywood movies. It was the first time since the nuclear tests carried out by India many years earlier that any Canadian High Commissioner to the country had met with a federal minister, let alone the prime minister, so Peter Sutherland was very happy. Over the next few days, he was able to meet more federal ministers and the chief ministers of the states I visited.

We flew to Hyderabad, known in the cyber age as Cyberabad, where we toured the high-tech IT centre and met with the governor of Andhra. The governor's mansion, an ancient structure decorated with classical Indian artifacts, could have been from the Middle Ages.

The aspect of our visit that brought it into the present was the articulate woman governor of the state.

Our next stop was Mumbai, which had shed its British colonial name of Bombay in 1995. Sunil Dutt, a prominent screen actor from the sixties and seventies who was now a member of the Indian Parliament, hosted a dinner for us at a local hotel. Mumbai is the home of the famed Bollywood, and many prominent members of the film world were there, dressed in their best and sparkling no less than they had in the scores of movies I had watched them in. Shatrughan Sinha was seated on one side of me and the chief minister of Maharashtra, Vilasrao Deshmukh, on the other. At one point during the festivities, while Deshmukh was speaking, Sinha told me that even Bill Clinton had not been honoured with this kind of sit-down dinner. Whether that was true or not, I was touched and overwhelmed by the affection I was shown.

While we were in Mumbai, Deshmukh invited me to a luncheon with his cabinet in attendance. Rami and I also called on the governor, P.C. Alexander, whom we had first met in January 1984 when he was Indira Gandhi's principal secretary. At a function presided over by veteran Indian politician and deputy prime minister of India L.K. Advani, the World Punjabi Organisation in New Delhi had honoured me as Man of the Millennium. At a function hosted by the same organization in Mumbai, I was seated next to Ramanand Sagar, a prominent Punjabi and a much-celebrated director, producer and writer in Bollywood. Unknown to me, Sagar had written a letter congratulating me upon becoming premier, and he told me he had been hurt by the automated and electronically signed reply he had received from my office in return. I apologized profusely. All my life I have admired people like Sagar who were uprooted during the partition of India. He came from Peshawar, now in Pakistan, but as an adopted child of poor parents he made a life for himself in India, remaining true to the ideal of a secular India despite suffering personally the ravages of hate and faith-fuelled partition. After hearing the story of his life, I was left in tears.

The newspapers and TV channels in India were full of coverage of my visit. My home state of Punjab was the last state I visited, but not the least. The Punjabi celebrations started at the Delhi railway station as I boarded the train, though I noticed a lot more police around me there than I had seen in other places. Rami, Umber and I were seated in a compartment reserved for us, along with some security personnel and our Canadian friends Amrik Sangha and Kashmir Dhaliwal, who were travelling with us for the Punjab portion of the trip. Indian friends like Vikramjit Sahney had joined us in Delhi, too. Vikramjit, a Delhi businessman active in the World Punjabi Organisation, was known for his flair for throwing huge parties — and for singing. For most of our train journey to Amritsar, Vikramjit entertained the group with Punjabi and Hindi songs.

At the Amritsar railway station, hundreds of people had gathered on the platform to cheer our arrival. Again, I noticed lots of police present, but that was probably due more to the presence of the chief minister of Punjab, Parkash Singh Badal, who was there to greet us. On the campus of Guru Nanak Dev University, where we were to stay the night, Badal and I had a long conversation about our respective governments.

The government of Punjab held several events at which we were honoured. Bhangra dancers and politicians mingled at a large dinner with over a thousand people in attendance. The chief minister of Haryana, Om Prakash Chautala, wined and dined our group at another large dinner where Badal also joined us. I especially enjoyed the special convocation at Guru Nanak Dev University, and not just because I was receiving an honorary degree. The event prompted me to make a joke about my less-than-distinguished university career in India, but it also allowed me to pay tribute to the many immigrants from India who had departed for other lands. The pain of separation from one's native land drove my remarks as I dedicated my degree to all the Indians who had left Indian shores over the centuries, beginning with the indentured labourers to the West Indies and Fiji. As I was speaking, the memory of me crying my eyes out as I boarded the train from Phagwara to Delhi on my way to England was so strong that my eyes welled up. I was quite unashamed of the depth of my emotions.

We had had discussions with the Badal government about travel before we left Canada, and because of shortness of time, they had suggested I go by helicopter to Dosanjh Kalan. Apparently the road to my ancestral village was not navigable by car, due to huge potholes. I urged them to fill and pave the road, but they told me it was not possible to do that quickly. When my staff told them I would rather walk if the people in my village could not drive that road, the road got paved. So I did travel by helicopter from Amritsar to Dosanjh, and for the first time ever, I saw parts of Punjab from the air. The fields, crops and pathways looked magical from there, though the roads and the few trees left on their margins reminded me of the continuing neglect the state, as well as the country, had suffered. Repeated promises by the chief ministers to turn Punjab into a prosperous and developed "California" had not materialized. But it was not my place to assign blame or find fault, certainly not one who had deserted India to become the premier of a province in a faraway country.

The helicopter landed on the ground of my old high school. Students and teachers had lined up to greet me, delighting me with their hugs and cheers. I drove to my ancestral home, where the villagers had gathered for tea and sweets. There were smiles all around.

ONE OF THE MOST memorable events of our trip was our visit to the Women's College in Sidhwan, the oldest women's school in rural Punjab. It predated the girl's high school in my village, which was started in 1914. Both of us spoke, but Rami's was the better speech. The students were smart and fearless. Both of us encouraged them to be assertive and inquisitive as well. They laughed, perhaps in disbelief, when I urged them never to look down or bow in so-called respect when talking to anyone, young or old, powerful or weak. Quite often, the behaviour we demand of young people engenders timidity and subservience, leading to an irrational fear of authority. But a robust liberal democracy can't exist without people asking tough questions of those in power. One young woman assured me afterwards that she would no longer shy away from looking people straight in the eye when she spoke to them.

I knew security, needed or not, was often deployed in India to project power and status, but I was uncomfortable with the number of security personnel and vehicles assigned to us. As we'd been driven from Chandigarh to Dosanjh, I had spotted police at T-junctions and crossroads all the way to my village. While we were travelling from Sur Singh, near Amritsar, back to Chandigarh, I spotted a sugarcane juice stall on the roadside and asked our driver to stop. The entire security contingent came to a halt as well, encircling the stall and literally shooing the curious away. I had to intervene to stop security personnel from pushing people around. Some of those gathered noticed that, and they asked me why Indian politicians couldn't be more like their Canadian counterparts. The security had created a distance between us and the people. It troubled me. It was most unnecessary. But although the excessive security was troubling and the Mercedes following us were embarrassingly ostentatious, there was nothing I could do about it. I was a guest of the government of India.

Toward the end of our trip, a huge function was held on the Dosanjh Kalan school grounds. Chief Minister Badal attended and gave some money to the village to honour my visit. The more than forty thousand people who attended had come from all over Punjab to see this now-grown man from B.C. who had once walked the dusty roads of these villages. I was overwhelmed by their affection.

At the Delhi airport, Indian government diplomats assisted me with a speedy check-in. Rami and Umber had stayed behind to travel separately. I was assigned an aisle seat in the last row on the huge plane, and I fell asleep even before the plane took off, to be awakened only when we landed at Heathrow. My trip to India had been very busy, but I arrived back in Vancouver feeling rested and ready to resume the tough task of governing B.C.

BACK IN VICTORIA, a poll greeted me. Our numbers had gone up to 27 per cent, but the Liberals were at almost double that. Facing a wipeout, we set to work on a strategy to highlight what our NDP government stood for at that moment in the history of the province. We had balanced the budget. We had increased funding for child care, bringing subsidized day care to eighty-five thousand spaces from the previous sixty-seven thousand. We had created new parks to achieve a goal of 12 per cent of B.C. as parkland. Post-secondary tuition had been frozen and would see a reduction of 5 per cent in the 2001–02 budget. We had provided more money for health.

46

But in the middle of our campaign to win over the parts of our base that were drifting to the Greens or even to the Liberals, two bomb-shells left us badly bruised once again. The Carrier Lumber case had been wending its way through the courts for years. After the Harcourt government cancelled a timber licence for Carrier Lumber of Prince George, the company sued. The case was decided against the govern-ment in the B.C. Supreme Court in July 1999, with the court finding that the government had wrongly cancelled the licence and deliber-ately withheld documents from the company. As AG, I had received advice from my ministry that there were legitimate grounds of appeal, but when the government found more documents that had not been produced before the court, we decided to abandon the appeal and seek mediation. The media now pounced on me, asking whether I had read the case in July 1999 before ordering an appeal. In a rare moment of anger, I stupidly said I had not read the original judgement. In fact, I had read parts of it, reproduced and attached to the advice I had received from the ministry, but the proverbial shit hit the fan.

I made a bad situation worse. Following that, I apologized to the family that owned Carrier Lumber for the harm done to them by our governments, and the family was gracious enough to accept the apology in the spirit in which it was made.

The other question that bedevilled us was what to do about the grizzly bear hunt: ban it or not? The question was bound to cause division within the caucus, and it did. Upon considering all the scientific evidence, we decided to impose a moratorium on the hunt. Andrew Petter, Ian Waddell and several others supported the decision. The announcement, set to be made on February 8, 2001, was leaked to the press a day early, and as we got ready to start the press conference, we heard that Harry Lali had resigned from the cabinet, in a move timed to do maximum damage to the government. David Schreck's departure from the cabinet some days earlier had been even more disconcerting, since he had served as a bright and committed special advisor. His decision had come as a surprise to me, too.

A trip to China as part of Team Canada was a respite from the political environment in B.C. and it allowed time for reflection. Jean Chrétien led the team in meetings with Premier Zhou Rongji and President Jiang Zemin. The tremendous focus and drive of China's leadership was evident in the conversations we had with them. We visited several cities, including Beijing, Shanghai and Hong Kong, and the terracotta museum in the city of Xi'an impressed me; looking at the hundreds of warriors, I could relate them to the scale of progress China was making now. The trip inspired me in another way, too: our government needed to break free of the rut we were in and to do something bold. We decided I would do a televised address on February 28 upon my return.

Gordon Campbell was offering dramatic tax cuts if the Liberals formed government. We needed to provide an alternative vision, and we settled on modest tax cuts along with more money for healthcare and services that met people's needs. We recalled the legislature to present a projected balanced budget for 2001 – 02, boosted healthcare funding, and reduced tuition fees by 5 per cent while budgeting for five thousand more post-secondary spaces. The legislature amended the Human Rights Code to outlaw gender-based discrimination related to wages, to ensure equal pay for work of equal value. A new law was also passed to protect citizens from lawsuits designed to discourage public participation in controversial issues. In addition, we attempted to draw out the divisions within the Liberal ranks and get the party to take what for them might be uncomfortable positions in response to controversial motions in the House. It may have seemed desperate for us to do so, but we were searching for something that might resonate beyond the 15 to 20 per cent of voters who were already supporting us. In the end nothing worked.

On April 4, the government signed an agreement with environmentalists, loggers and eight coastal First Nations to protect the area known as the Great Bear Rainforest. The agreement was hailed by all three groups. The B.C. Federation of Labour did not approve, but those supporting the initiative had worked on it since 1997. I wanted to ensure their hard work was rewarded.

It was time to drop the writ. I wanted to call the election for May 15 but since that was the 2001 national Census day, we decided on May 16 instead. Rami, our sons and I once again rode together to Government House. I knew in my heart that it was for the last time. Not that I did not believe in miracles, but I was also a realist. The life had been sucked out of the party by years of internal wrangling and scandals. People were mad at us and ready to vote us into oblivion. Dropping the writ, I likened our chances in the election to the story of David and Goliath, casting myself as the underdog. Back at the legislature, staff and local activists gave us a send-off to Vancouver by emblazing our campaign bus with the words "Ujjal Dosanjh Premier." I had already seen the campaign signs with that inscription in bold lettering and "Today's New Democrats" inscribed in small type at the bottom. I didn't particularly like the highlighting of my name; it smacked of ego. But because of my favourable public approval numbers, I deferred to the pollsters and strategists who said it was good for the party.

An evening event in my riding nominated me the day we dropped the writ. Our next event, the following morning, drew more journalists than supporters, and that set the stage for additional campaign blunders in the coming days. The harder we tried, the more mistakes we made. One day my campaign bus took a wrong turn and got lost on the way to Simon Fraser University. Another day, campaigning in Coquitlam with media in tow, my handlers and I walked over to a bar and grill to speak to the customers. The owners locked the door as they saw us approaching. Most days a middle-finger salute greeted our bus as we drove from place to place. The public's fatigue with the past few years hovered over our every move.

The *Vancouver Sun* did profiles of both Gordon Campbell and me. The one about me was published first. While it was not badly written, the advance promo for it was misleading, an example of fear-mongering at its worst.

My profile was to be published on April 21. The first promo ad for it appeared on April 19: a quarter-page featuring my 1964 Indian passport photo, in which I was wearing a turban, captioned "Unrecognizable: The Strange Story Behind The Premier. From Communist radical to disciple of Gandhi to premier of British Columbia, Ujjal Dosanjh's political evolution has been a long and storied tale." The accompanying text continued, "In a special profile in Saturday's *Mix* section, the *Vancouver Sun* will take you deep into the premier's past. You'll be surprised at what you read." The April 20 promo used the same turbaned head shot of me and the same caption. On April 21, the front-page lead-in to the profile used the same photo again, this time accompanied by the words "The Other Ujjal" and "What you don't know about B.C.'s premier." I am proud of my heritage, and I had provided the photo of my younger self to the journalist. But the story itself revealed nothing not already known about me, and I found the *Sun's* sensational packaging of it despicable. The paper's promos for the Campbell profile took no such approach.

DURING THE TELEVISED leaders' debate, I was relentless in attacking Campbell and the Liberals, though the format did not allow for any formal exchanges between us. I was pleased with my performance, and our numbers stabilized. A *Vancouver Sun* caption under my photo on May 2 captured the growing shift in mood: "Premier Ujjal Dosanjh starts to breathe life into his election campaign with an animated speech to supporters in Duncan." But the same day, Vaughn Palmer revealed that on the eve of the election, Gordon Wilson, as minister of forestry, had written a letter committing taxpayers to purchase two forest tenures from Doman Industries at a price that could exceed $30 million. At our midday event, that was all the media wanted addressed. The deal had been made, under my watch, but it had not been approved by cabinet or my office. I ignored calls for Wilson to be fired from cabinet. When Paul Ramsey took the file over from Wilson and told Doman there was no deal, Doman sued the government. Our rebounding numbers went into free fall.

In my own riding, I was losing badly, and there were only two seats left in the province that seemed possibilities for us: Joy MacPhail's Vancouver East and Jenny Kwan's Vancouver-Mount Pleasant. Even they were no longer sure wins. Facing that hard reality, we decided to ask voters to keep at least some of us in the legislature. Hans Brown, always creative, came up with the line exhorting voters not to elect seventy-nine Gordon Campbells. On May 7, I pleaded with British Columbians, "I accept that I will not form another NDP government... We need to have an effective opposition... The issue is who will hold Gordon Campbell accountable."

Many have since argued we should have soldiered on, pretending we could still win. But the NDP's problem was that nobody believed us anymore. If we had continued on false bravado, the two seats we did win on election night would have gone Liberal too, as overnight tracking showed us. We rescued the party from total oblivion by our late-in-the-game change of strategy, and we had given B.C. good government in our last year and a half at the helm, planting the seeds of a future recovery. •

I had made up my mind to resign on election night as part of my concession speech. At the Vancouver Renaissance Hotel, Rami, our sons and I walked into a room full of tears and disappointment. My heart ached as I looked into hundreds of moist eyes. We had let them down, and I felt responsible. That night, no excuses would have lessened my burden. I congratulated Campbell, but I also cautioned that "the joy of victory precedes the challenges of governing." I was reminded of that years later, when he resigned in disgrace during his third term due to his mishandling of the harmonized sales tax.

PART 8

FROM THE FEDERAL SCENE TO THE FUTURE

47

MY SPEECH at the provincial council a few days later was my last contact with the provincial NDP. No one from the provincial wing got in touch with me after that; as far as the party was concerned, I had ceased to exist. I had no desire to interfere in party affairs, and I allowed my membership in the NDP to lapse.

I presented Campbell with the transition books in the presence of media a couple of weeks after the election. During the last days of our government, I had threatened to sue him for defamation regarding comments he'd made about the Carrier case. By the time I handed him the transition books, I had realized I needed to make a clean break from the pettiness of politics. From the moment the RCMP raided the Clark residence, B.C. politics had been unpleasant, particularly within the NDP. Campbell had bigger things to worry about, and I wanted no part of any continuing nastiness. All that remained was for me to take my records and personal belongings home.

After the election loss, I received a call from Prime Minister Jean Chrétien, expressing sympathy and saying if I ever needed anything I should call. I thanked him for his call, which ended with his saying, "I am your friend." I appreciated the prime ministerial gesture. Perhaps the little guy from Shawinigan saw something of himself in the peasant from a dusty village in the Punjab. There was no such call from the leader of the federal NDP, Alexa McDonough, perhaps a sign of things to come.

My toiling day and night as an elected representative had meant that a lot of things on the home front were left wanting my attention. Now, for the first time in over two decades, I did not have to attend scores of public, social or political events. I could sit back, reflect and then embark on the rest of my life. Rami was teaching. Pavel was articling in Vancouver. Aseem was practising law and trying to revive my once-thriving law practice. Umber was figuring out what he would do after finishing his undergraduate degree from UBC. I was now at home every day, walking our dog Rasha and trying to learn some Indian cooking. I was already good at cleaning the house, doing dishes and making dough for chapatis.

For the first time in ten years, I had unencumbered hours in which to resume my reading. Books have been permanent companions throughout my life, particularly books about the history and politics of India, and of course about Mahatma Gandhi. Because I left India as a youngster, books have helped fill the void of a life unlived in its dusty villages and teeming cities. I started building a small library soon after my family bought our first home in Vancouver, using concrete blocks and planed pieces of wood from the green chain at Burke Lumber. Books nurture the mind, and as pieces of art for the home, they are second to none.

Now, with my time once again my own, I suddenly had the urge to read the Indian classics *The Ramayana* and *The Mahabharata*, and I read more Mahatma Gandhi as well. I also wrote a thirty-thousand-word manuscript on what I believed ailed India at the time. The boys and I painted the exterior of the house, and I tried to bring under some semblance of control the overgrown bushes and wild blackberry on the slope in our backyard. Both Pavel and Aseem got married that summer, and our two new daughters-in-law, Shauna and Boby, joined the family. We had never been rich. My sons had been put through five university degrees among the three of them, and Umber had one more to go. To pay for the weddings, we cashed in some life insurance policies.

During the months following our election defeat, I was reminded of what I had always known: real friends can be counted on one's fingertips. The previously unending phone calls mercifully ended, and the seekers of power melted away. My liberation from the pretenders to friendship was exhilarating.

In the spring of 2002, I joined Aseem at the law practice. Soon after, Pavel joined us, and we moved offices. The business was on its way back up. It also allowed me to spend time with my sons, and most evenings, as the boys worked, I would sip some good scotch and read before hitching a ride home with one of them.

The media came knocking often asking me to comment on politics. I always refused to oblige. As far as I was concerned, I was through with electoral politics. I followed politics as a concerned citizen, but I was no longer consumed by it. I did have the odd prominent visitor. One day Jack Layton visited my office, urging me to run federally for the NDP. We chatted for about an hour. He was full of energy and enthusiasm, but I had no desire at the time to run again for public office and certainly not for the federal NDP, whose attitude toward the events at Gustafsen Lake had alienated me so deeply.

In January 2003, the government of India decided to honour ten members of the Indian diaspora in Delhi. The event was to mark January 9, the date in 1915 on which Mahatma Gandhi had returned to India from South Africa to participate in and eventually lead the Indian freedom movement. I was among the honourees, and Rami and I, along with Aseem and Boby, decided to make the trip. The other honourees included Prime Minister Anerood Jugnauth of Mauritius and former Commonwealth Secretary Sridath Ramphal.

Sitar maestro Ravi Shankar and sarod maestro Alla Rakha entertained us in a hall temporarily renamed Komagata Maru. The two maestros had teamed up for the first time in their long and illustrious musical lives to commemorate the return of the Mahatma. We were called to the stage one at a time to be honoured by the prime minister. People walked in slow, measured steps, in accordance with the extreme formality of upper-class Indians, a relic of the British colonial past. When my turn came, I ran the twenty yards up onto the stage. The audience broke into smiles and laughter, and Prime Minister Vajpayee laughed heartily himself.

One day after I had returned to Canada, Herb Dhaliwal called on behalf of Prime Minister Chrétien. Chrétien wanted to appoint me the consul general for Canada in Chandigarh, Dhaliwal told me.

I considered the offer. I would enjoy being a consul general, I thought, but I cherished my ability to speak freely about the rampant corruption in India. As a diplomat, one loses the unbridled freedoms one exercises daily as a public commentator. I also worried about the negative consequences of being a consul general in India, more so in Chandigarh. Most Indo-Canadians and most residents of North India would come to know about my appointment, and many would expect favours a consul general could not deliver — being issued a visitor's visa, for instance. That could lead to the perception in people's minds that perhaps I was on the take. It takes only a nanosecond to besmirch a reputation built over a lifetime of blood, sweat and tears, and I didn't want to risk it. I respectfully declined the Chrétien offer with thanks.

I spent a lot of time thinking about the decades gone by. As an activist turned elected politician, I had traversed the intensely unpredictable world of politics. In politics, it is impossible to make everyone happy. All you can do is what your gut tells you is the right thing, remaining true to the principles and sense of idealism that first led you into the public arena. After getting elected in 1991, I had quickly realized the limits of power in government. The financial resources are always limited, and in established democracies the room to manoeuvre is narrow. Political conventions and cultures are usually well entrenched, making radical change impossible. Social justice must be married to fiscal responsibility. To idealists unschooled in the realities of governing, incremental change often feels like selling out. But in government, you have to make choices. You have to say no even to some of your pet projects and committed supporters. Saying no had been the most difficult thing for me to learn. I had spent my first three campaigns assuring people that if they voted for the NDP, it would be heaven. Actually, being in government was a sobering experience, and not one I anticipated repeating. But a chain of events was about to pull me back into the electoral arena.

The 2003 federal Liberal leadership campaign was in full swing. Chrétien had announced he would step down after losing the full support of his caucus, and Finance Minister Paul Martin was considered his likely successor. I had met Martin several times, in both a professional and a personal capacity, and one day he called me to see whether I could provide some help to one of his B.C. supporters, Barjinder

Sandhu, who was also working to secure the Liberal nomination in one of the Surrey ridings. I knew Barjinder, who was related to our extended family, and I agreed to assist behind the scenes with strategic advice. Because of the large number of crossover voters in B.C. between the provincial NDP and the federal Liberals, it was inevitable that he'd be approaching provincial NDP supporters. However, I did not see that as an issue; I was no longer a member of the NDP, and I had had no further contact with anyone in its ranks. Martin thanked me and suggested we meet next time he was in Vancouver.

A few months before the federal election in 2004, Martin, now Canada's prime minister, invited me to meet at a hotel in downtown Vancouver. He was alone in the room, and he opened a bottle of single malt scotch and poured us drinks as we settled into our conversation. I had gone into the meeting thinking Martin just wanted to reconnect, but a few minutes into it he asked if I would be open to running under his leadership as a federal Liberal candidate. He assured me that, as part of his team, I could look forward to playing a meaningful role in his government. I was floored, and my mind was churning. I had given up the thought of ever running for any election again. I had already turned down Jack Layton's proposal that I run for the federal NDP. Could I consider running for the federal Liberals? Should I even ponder that question? I promised to think about it and to speak with Martin later.

I thought hard about the idea of running under the federal Liberal banner. The Liberal party of Sir Wilfrid Laurier, Lester Pearson and Pierre Trudeau had been socially progressive. Liberal governments had helped to establish Tommy Douglas's Medicare Canada-wide, as well as the Unemployment Insurance program and the Canada Pension Plan. In a sense, the B.C. NDP was its provincial equivalent. The B.C. Liberals were a collection of old Reformers, Socreds and Conservatives with a smattering of federal Liberals thrown in. The provincial party had no legal or other official relationship with the federal Liberals. Gordon Campbell was more of a Conservative, in the old Socred tradition.

After thinking it through, I did not foresee any philosophical challenges to joining the federal Liberals. But I realized that joining them would mean angering the cultists in the NDP. All political parties have cultists; for them, the party is God. If I were to run for the Liberals federally, my punishment would be condemnation, excommunication and derision. I also worried about losing some good friends; they might not want to publicly associate with an apostate. But I never, ever had much time for cultists and zealots, and I believed that most of the people who had voted for me provincially would vote for me as a federal Liberal. Another former NDP premier, Bob Rae of Ontario, had formally quit the NDP some years earlier, and would successfully run as a federal Liberal in 2006.

The idea of abandoning my sons' law practice also bothered me. I enjoyed working with them, and I thought they could use my presence in the office for at least the next couple of years. In the traditional part of my Indian mind, I expected to be a provider for them not only through their education but for as long as I lived. My Canadian side knew that children needed to grow up to be independent and self-reliant, and that my sons would do well whether I was with them or not. Still, I was reassured when senior trial lawyer Art Vertlieb, who had heard I was considering going federal with the Liberals but was hesitant because of my sons' nascent practice, offered to give up his own practice to join my sons. Their partnership went on to last almost ten very fruitful years.

I knew Martin had been talking to many prominent British Columbians about joining his team. Those who had agreed to join him included Canfor CEO David Emerson, IWA union veteran Dave Haggard and Shirley Chan, an activist who had worked with and for Mike Harcourt over the years. I spoke to many NDP friends about my possible decision. Quite a few saw no problem with it, though some of course disagreed vehemently. Finally, though I knew my decision to join the federal Liberals would not be universally liked, I came to the conclusion that I was ready to re-enter the political arena. Usually one searches for an opportunity to serve one's country, but in my case the opportunity had found me.

In February 2004, the Auditor General had issued a report on the federal government's sponsorship program in Quebec. A program designed to raise awareness in Quebec about the role and contributions of the federal government had been abused to line the pockets of some bureaucrats and Liberal political operatives. The day following the report's release, Prime Minister Paul Martin had announced a judicial inquiry into the matter to be headed by Justice John Gomery. What came to be called the sponsorship scandal had already taken its toll on federal Liberal fortunes, and by the time I made my decision the federal Liberals were at 35 per cent in the national polls, heading for at best a minority government and at worst a defeat at the polls. I wanted to do what I could to bolster the only party that had a chance of defeating the Conservatives in the election to come. I spent the next several weeks organizing my affairs before the news went public.

Martin was in Vancouver for the announcement on the morning of April 1, 2004. In joining the Liberal party, I would be appointed as the candidate for Vancouver South, the riding vacated by the retiring Herb Dhaliwal. I did not expect the executive of the party in Vancouver South to take kindly to my appointment, at least at first, but I was prepared to do the work of winning them over. The appointment of candidates, as opposed to a nomination race, legitimately irks many. But I do not subscribe to the view that appointments must never be made. In exceptional circumstances, when time is tight and a party is attempting to broaden its base and renew its ranks and skills before an election, I believe there ought to be power vested in the party's leader to appoint people as candidates where necessary. The media was mixed on the announcement of my candidacy. I was criticized for "quitting" the NDP by some and praised for stepping onto the federal scene by others. I was secure in my decision. The B.C. NDP had quit on me.

At the party level, Gordon Campbell commented that my federal Liberal candidacy "puts the lie to the idea that the B.C. Liberals and the federal Liberals are connected. We are not." His comment was helpful, since he made it clear I was certainly not joining the B.C. Liberal party. NDP hardliners were naturally nastier. Joy MacPhail wondered out loud, in a biblical vein, whether I had received my "thirty pieces of silver." Paul Ramsey, on the other hand, in a column entitled "Political crossovers in B.C.," argued that my federal Liberal candidacy "reinforces the overlap between support for the provincial NDP and federal Liberals. Except for the high profile of the individual involved, the crossover is nothing new or startling. In 2005 [the then-upcoming provincial election] lots of federal Liberal supporters will make the same choice — in reverse — that Mr. Dosanjh made and will support the provincial NDP." Now, after the 2015 federal election has brought us another Trudeau government, the newly defeated long-time NDP MP Peter Stoffer is arguing that provincial wings of the party should have no legal relationship with the federal wing. That has been my own opinion for a long time; I was never active in the federal NDP. Had there been no relationship between the federal and provincial wings of the party in 2004, my joining the federal Liberals would have been the non-issue I believed it to be.

Firm in the conviction that I had done the right thing, I spoke to some local federal Liberals and started building a team to win the riding. I brought in people who had been defeated by the riding's current inexperienced executive, and many of my non-ideological NDP supporters joined my new team as well.

Former Saskatchewan premier Roy Romanow, in his royal commission report on health, had asked for more funding for and reforms in healthcare. Paul Martin had promised to substantially act on those recommendations, and I highlighted that promise during the pre-election period. Candidates Chris Axworthy, Dave Haggard and I also attended a presser in support of Liberal candidate Richard Mahoney, who was running against the iconic Ed Broadbent in the Ottawa Centre riding. I expressed then what I still believed: on the federal level, a "vote for the NDP is a vote for the Conservatives."

We opened our campaign office in Vancouver South during the second week of May. The election was called on May 23 for June 28, a thirty-five-day campaign. Door-to-door canvassing and telephone calls to households formed the bulk of our activity. The reaction was good at the doorstep. People still remembered me, and while there was some criticism of my jump to the Liberals, we were able to raise a lot of money. Anne McLellan, the deputy prime minister, attended a fundraiser in Vancouver that raised $120,000, and donations rolled into the office from all over Canada.

The Liberals did something during the 2004 campaign that no other party had ever done: we released a specific platform focussed on our commitments for British Columbia. Martin visited B.C. a couple of times during the campaign, and one of his national announcements about funding for seniors was made in my riding, with me in attendance. The party ran ads in B.C. featuring me and the other new recruits.

As usual, Rami had been less than enthusiastic about my decision to run. She believed politics to be a thankless job. But once the decision was made, she put her heart and soul into the campaign. She had taken early retirement from teaching, and she was at the campaign office every day, recruiting volunteers, assisting the staff and helping to manage the campaign overall.

With about ten days to go, the party's numbers began to improve. According to one journalist, Martin had finally "found his groove." On the last day of campaigning, he dipped his feet into the Atlantic early in the morning and made several campaign stops on his way to the west, reaching Vancouver International Airport late that night. After he had dipped his feet into the Pacific Ocean, a boisterous crowd of supporters and candidates greeted him at the south terminal. In his final rallying speech, he made an effective last pitch for the election of a Liberal government.

My campaign had lots of volunteers on election day, and we pulled every vote we could. Vancouver South was followed nationally by all the major networks, with a little platform set up in my office for cameras. Because of the blackout on results from the rest of the country until the close of B.C. polls at 8:00 PM, the public did not know what was happening. But the scrutineers' information collated by party headquarters indicated we were in minority government territory, and by evening's end that was confirmed. I won my own riding handily, with 44.5 per cent of the vote. I had embarked on a new phase of my political career.

ABOUT A WEEK LATER, the Prime Minister's Office advised me to make travel arrangements to Ottawa for June 17 and 18. I assumed a cabinet post was in the offering, and I was tipped off by Senator Jack Austin, who would become my cabinet colleague as leader of the Senate, that I was about to get a social portfolio of great importance to the country. Rami and my sons and daughters-in-law travelled with me for the swearing-in. It was only my third time in the nation's capital. As I waited for a call from the PM, we walked around Parliament Hill and its environs, acquainting ourselves with the place where I would spend most of the next seven years. It felt strange to think I was on the cusp of becoming a member of Canada's cabinet and the Queen's Privy Council.

During our first visit to Ottawa, the statue of Thomas D'Arcy McGee on the Hill had captured my imagination. An Irish immigrant, a member of Parliament and a father of Canadian Confederation, he was assassinated in 1868 by a supporter of the Irish Fenian movement because he'd urged Irish Canadians to not bring the hatreds of the old world to the new. I did feel a certain kinship with him, but only as a much lesser mortal.

My cell phone rang, and it was Martin. He asked where I was, and upon hearing we were in front of a restaurant, deciding to eat, he said, "Tell them the food better be good and neat, or you will have the restaurant condemned." That was his way of telling me I would be the next minister of health for the country. It would be a difficult portfolio. Not much could be done without the cooperation of the provinces, and during the election, Martin had promised a healthcare "fix for a generation."

The swearing-in was sombre and short. The PMO had told us Martin wanted certain ministers to be highlighted. I was among them, due to my new portfolio; the government was heading into open negotiations on a ten-year federal-provincial agreement that would be negotiated at a monumental healthcare summit in full view of the TV cameras. I spoke briefly, promising to work to stem the tide of creeping privatization in healthcare. The Canada Health Act, the strongest mechanism attached to healthcare and brought in by Pierre Trudeau, was being violated with impunity by some provinces. Under the guise of innovation, some premiers were pushing privatization as a panacea for the health of Canadians.

Perhaps I sounded more strident and unilateralist than I intended; the chief editorialist at *La Presse*, André Pratte, later wrote that I had "sent shivers down the Quebec federalists' spines by stating, in effect, that since healthcare is a national concern, it has become a national responsibility." What I had actually said was that the Canada Health Act was the law; the shivering wasn't my fault. Journalists reminded Canadians of my unsuccessful fight in 2000 to have the final communiqué from the premiers' annual conference acknowledge the problem of privatization making inroads into our healthcare. Some writers put my latest mention of the issue down to my principles; others, to my mule-headedness.

Perhaps those in the latter group were correct. A few days after taking over Health Canada, I attended a meeting of the provincial and territorial health ministers. I went into the meeting planning to deliver the federal message and then leave. I had prepared some remarks, and foolishly I stuck to them, rather than asking those assembled what they thought were the problems facing us and what solutions they proposed. I did not make any friends that day, and by the time the meeting ended I had realized my mistake. Ontario's George Smitherman, who had chaired the meeting, took me aside before we spoke to the press. I needed to work with the group, he said; they were colleagues with a different perspective, not enemies. (I learned my lesson — so much so that in the run-up to the 2006 election, I was invited by the provincial and territorial health ministers to share the stage with them at a good-news announcement about the progress made since the 2004 accord.)

We needed staff around me quickly, since the healthcare summit was upon us. We settled on Robert Fry as chief of staff, and he helped me hire a smart and loyal crew of others. The meeting with the premiers was preceded by — a historic first — a meeting with the aboriginal leadership, since health on reserves was a federal responsibility. It was a public acknowledgement of a nation-to-nation relationship with them and produced a package of funding initiatives. Negotiations were tough during the summit, though I was able to meet with many of the premiers one on one. One morning I was invited to the PM's residence at 24 Sussex Drive to strategize with him before speaking to the media. Martin was very helpful all along the way. I had done reasonably well during the negotiations, except on one occasion when I'd been addressing a media scrum. Halfway through the scrum, I realized I did not have all the necessary information, and the questioning got completely out of control. It was the only black eye I ever suffered at the hands of the media during my political life. It could have been avoided, and it was embarrassing.

But there was no time to shed tears. I had been pilloried by many right-wing commentators because of my remarks about creeping privatization. I wanted tight strings attached to the flow of federal money to the provinces. That did not happen. Nonetheless, the accord was reached, and it was celebrated for flowing $42 billion over the next ten years to the provinces and territories in exchange for them setting benchmarks, reducing wait times, enhancing the availability of equipment, doctors and nurses, and reporting to the residents of their own jurisdictions. I had wanted those reports to be sent to Ottawa, too, but the provinces balked at that, Quebec most vehemently. Nor did the provinces get everything they wanted. The premiers' demand for a national pharmacare plan was very attractive, but it could not be entertained without a common drug formulary and the bulk purchasing of drugs, as well as some federal control over the cost-drivers that were mostly in the hands of the premiers. We did, however, set up a group to pursue a pharmacare proposal that included catastrophic drug coverage for rare drugs and disorders.

I learned one thing from sitting around the federal cabinet table that I would never have learned otherwise: the Canadian federation is very fragile. It is constantly being challenged, and often weakened, by Quebec's sovereignty by stealth. On any issue that involved national programs or national standards, an inordinate amount of time was spent allaying the fears of the soft federalists. Sovereigntists and separatists didn't need to be at the federal table; their concerns were expressed through the fears and timidity of the soft federalists at the table instead. The robust federalism of Pierre Trudeau was, by then, and continues to be, a thing of the past. Perhaps I felt this more than any of my colleagues in cabinet, since health was both federal and provincial. The federal government of the time shied away from picking a fight with the so-called federalists of Jean Charest's Quebec government. Separatists had frightened them into acquiescence. Who needed another referendum, when incremental separatism was so successful? The political class in Ottawa had been numbed by fear. The same holds true today. For instance, the provinces are obliged by the Canada Health Act to provide some annual health information to Ottawa, yet it has been eons since Quebec provided that information to the feds.

As federal health minister, I had a fair amount of freedom to pursue issues. Control from the centre was almost nonexistent except when it came to obtaining more money. One of my first initiatives was to reverse the earlier policy of not compensating Hepatitis C victims of tainted blood from the pre-1986 period. Bureaucrats explained to me why this couldn't be done, but I asked them to make it happen. In the end, I was able to win over Martin, and the government extended support and compensation to those previously excluded.

We undertook many other health initiatives as well, from strengthening Canadian and world pandemic preparedness to opening up many decision-making processes. We protected the supply of prescription drugs for Canadians by stemming the rising internet sales of drugs from Canada into the U.S. I believed it was as unethical for Canadian doctors to sign prescriptions for U.S. patients they had never met as it was for pharmacists to fill them. Premier Gary Doer of Manitoba saw my campaign as an attack on free enterprise and took a cheap shot at me about that. I took a trip to Washington, D.C., to speak to several senators about the issue. Some U.S. states had threatened to throw their doors open to internet drug sales from Canada, because of our relatively low prices and the low Canadian dollar. I urged them to reconsider, since it would undermine the Canadian drug supply. When I was invited to Harvard Medical School to speak on the state of healthcare in Canada, I warned the overflow crowd of students that Canada couldn't be a drugstore for the U.S., since that would undermine the supply for our own needs and threaten our controlled pricing regime. I was impressed by the interest in the issue I encountered south of the border.

Severe Acute Respiratory Syndrome (SARS) and Avian Flu awoke the world to the need for an enhanced network of international cooperation. During my time as health minister, Canada took the lead on this. I visited the United Nations in New York to speak on the issue together with former media mogul Ted Turner, who co-chaired the Nuclear Threat Initiative (NTI) with U.S. Senator Sam Nunn. The NTI had invested in a Canadian project for detecting bioterrorism and epidemics called the Global Public Health Intelligence Network. In Washington, D.C., I met with Mike Leavitt, secretary of health for President Bush, to talk specifically about pandemic preparedness, and I made a trip to China to see what that country was doing on the same front. In November 2005, I hosted a G20 Conference in Ottawa attended by the Chinese health minister, the U.S.'s Leavitt and many others from across the globe, including the director of the World Health Organization, Dr. Lee Jong-wook.

At the end of 2004, the world witnessed one of the worst disasters in living memory when a tsunami hit Indonesia and Sri Lanka. Prime Minister Martin had been set to visit India, and I was to accompany him. Martin tasked a cabinet committee, of which I was a member, to monitor the aftermath of the disaster and formulate Canada's response. The committee suggested that the Disaster Assistance and Response

Team (DART) be deployed. I left ahead of Martin to assess the situation in Sri Lanka, meet with our High Commissioner there and prepare for a visit by the PM to Colombo arriving just in advance of DART. I met with Sri Lankan officials and surveyed the utter devastation. People's homes were flattened, washed away or waterlogged. I travelled on to Delhi to meet Martin. I briefed him about the situation in Sri Lanka, describing in detail the devastation and Canada's work on the ground so far.

The plan for me to accompany him back to Colombo shortened Martin's stay in Delhi, during which we met with a diminutive Sonia Gandhi, who was accompanied by Foreign Minister Natwar Singh. A lunch followed with Prime Minister Manmohan Singh. He and Martin sat across from each other at an inordinately wide table, which made it impossible for them to converse with each other. It was left to me to keep India's prime minister busy, flanked as I was by him and Montek Ahluwalia, the vice-president of the now-defunct Planning Commission of India.

The Liberal budget was introduced in the House of Commons by Finance Minister Ralph Goodale on February 23, 2005. Jack Layton dubbed it the first federal NDP budget, since it had been crafted by our government with a view to winning the NDP's support for its passage. Despite the NDP's support, however, the margin for the budget to pass was razor-thin, and as the budget vote on May 19 loomed, defeat stared our government in the face. Martin worked on cementing as much support as he could from former Liberals now sitting as independents like Carolyn Parrish and David Kilgour. In mid-May, Magna International auto-parts heiress Belinda Stronach had crossed the floor and gone straight into Martin's cabinet from the Conservatives, changing the balance of power in the House in favour of our government. MP Chuck Cadman, representing Surrey North, was now sitting as an independent after having lost the Conservative nomination. Cadman's son's death in a random street attack by other teens had turned Cadman into a thoughtful activist for reforming the justice system. He and I had developed a good relationship during my time as B.C.'s Attorney General and premier, and Paul Martin asked me to see if Cadman would be open to a meeting with him about the forthcoming budget vote. I met him at his Surrey home; he and his wife Dona kindly received Rami and me. I knew Cadman had been ill, and the ravages of cancer were clearly visible. Despite that, he agreed to meet with Martin in Ottawa.

I was present at their meeting in Ottawa, as was Dona Cadman. The meeting lasted about half an hour, during which Martin made the case for Cadman's support in the budget vote. Cadman listened intently. He refused to say what he would do, but he did advise Martin that he had been talking to constituents who were supportive of the budget and of the need for the government to continue. No promises were sought or made at the meeting by either man.

During the lead-up to the budget vote, while I was in Vancouver for the weekend, I received a call late one evening from Bob Cheema, a friend of Conservative MP Gurmant Grewal's. Cheema wanted to come and see me. It was urgent, he said. When he arrived at my home, he spent about an hour telling me that Grewal wanted to cross the floor and that he wanted to meet me to discuss it. I agreed to speak to the prime minister about it once I got back to Ottawa. The next morning, I got a call from Sudesh Kalia, another friend of Grewal's, who also wanted to see me before I left for Ottawa that afternoon. I had known Kalia from the early seventies, so I agreed. We met at my constituency office on Fraser Street, and he drove me to the airport. Kalia's message was the same as Cheema's, though he told me he hadn't known about Cheema's visit the previous night. My response to Kalia was also the same: I told him I would speak to the PM about it.

Back in Ottawa, I talked to Martin's chief of staff Tim Murphy, who spoke to the prime minister. I could meet with Grewal, Martin said, on the condition no promises were made. My meeting with Grewal took place at my apartment the evening after the Cadman-Martin meeting. I had my brief from Martin: no promises were to be made or sought. Grewal told me that both he and his wife, Conservative MP Nina Grewal, wanted to cross the floor. In return, Grewal wanted a cabinet berth for himself and a Senate seat or appointment to the

United Nations for his wife. I told him clearly that Martin's instructions were for me to make no promises.

As we talked for over an hour, Grewal looked distinctly uncomfortable, often fiddling with his left wrist using his right hand. At one point he went into the bathroom and came out clutching his left wrist. I thought nothing of it at the time. As our meeting ended, Grewal was clearly unhappy, but he promised to get back to me the next day.

The next day, Grewal phoned and said he wanted to meet with Tim Murphy. The three of us met in my office in the Confederation Building on the Hill. Again, no promises were made. Murphy wanted to give Grewal some hope for the future, though he and I privately shared the view that Grewal was not cabinet material; nor was Nina Grewal suited for either of the posts her husband had mentioned. Grewal heard us out, and later that day he talked to Murphy again.

On the evening of May 18 — the day before the budget vote — Grewal released a tape of his conversation with Murphy and told the media he also had four hours of recorded conversations with Murphy and me. I now understood his clutching of his left wrist and his uncomfortable demeanour during the meeting at my apartment. In his comments to the media, Grewal claimed that I had first approached him. I immediately called Sudesh Kalia, who volunteered to speak to the media and tell them the truth. He did so, also giving the media a record of the number of times Grewal had called Kalia to ask him to speak to me. Since Kalia confirmed as well that Grewal had initiated the conversation about the rewards he wanted for himself and Nina in exchange for switching parties, we had an independent witness that Grewal was lying.

The next day, May 19, the atmosphere in the House was electric. The Grewal tapes story had led the news that morning and the night before. Stronach's defection was still reverberating. Still, the most important order of business for the government was to win the budget vote. Chuck Cadman was the last to stand and vote on the budget, and he voted in favour. That made it a tie vote, forcing the speaker to cast the deciding vote for the survival of the government.

GREWAL FINALLY RELEASED more tapes on May 31, and even then they were not released in their entirety. I listened to the released tapes at the Liberal party headquarters in Ottawa alongside Ken Polk, my brilliant communications director. As I listened to the tapes, I was shocked to find the sentence structure of my comments altered. For example, in one instance where I remembered distinctly telling Grewal "Cabinet can't be ..." the tape had been doctored to make me say "Cabinet can be ..." Polk and I came back to my office and drafted a statement to be released to the press that evening. Martin's deputy chief of staff Scott Reid felt the controversy would blow over in a couple of days if we did nothing, but I was seething: at stake were my integrity and my reputation.

Polk released our prepared statement to the press about 9:00 PM. We awoke the next morning to confirmation from CFRA radio in Ottawa that the tapes had been doctored. The station had asked both an in-house audio engineer and an outside audio expert to examine the tapes, and both had come to the same conclusion. Within the next couple of days, a forensic audio engineer who examined the tapes for CBC News and Canada's leading sound analyst, Stevan Pausak, who did the same for the Canadian Press, both found that the tapes had been "crudely" edited and that "something was amiss." Ravi Hira stick-handled the RCMP and the parliamentary ethics commissioner's probes. The parliamentary ethics commissioner, Bernard Shapiro, issued a report that was sharply critical of Grewal, calling his actions "extremely inappropriate." The report found no evidence that I had offered any specific rewards or inducements to Grewal. When Conservative MP John Reynolds complained to the Law Society of British Columbia about my involvement in the tapes affair in another attempt to smear my name, the society dismissed the complaint, stating, "In [our] view the conversation amounted to an unsuccessful effort by Mr. Grewal to extract promises of specific rewards." Grewal declined to run again for election in 2006.

49 IN JUNE 2005, the debate on public and private healthcare became heated again. The Canadian Medical Association had argued for parallel private insurance for healthcare services in Ontario. On June 9, the Supreme Court ruled in the case of Chaoulli v. Quebec that health insurance legislation in Quebec, which prohibited private medical insurance, violated the Quebec Charter of Human Rights and Freedoms, particularly with regard to long wait times. A minority of judges held that the legislation also violated the Canadian Charter of Rights and Freedoms. Since wait times were one of the focal points of the 2004 federal health accord, the issue disappeared for the moment.

The Canada Health Act is in essence our charter of public healthcare in Canada, and during my time as minister of health I vigorously championed its enforcement. I had been working with the provinces and the territories to strengthen healthcare. The largest amount of federal money during any ten-year period had been promised to the provinces to enhance delivery and shorten wait times for certain medical procedures. The Conservatives and the Bloc Québécois were pushing for an election as soon as possible, and support for our government was down across the country. Wanting to capitalize on the Chaoulli decision and the continued fallout from the Gomery report on the sponsorship program, NDP leader Jack Layton threatened to bring the government down on a non-confidence motion.

Layton wrote me a letter asking the government to impose conditions on federal transfers that would prevent the provinces from using the money to subsidize the private sector; to put restrictions on doctors who practised in both the private and public sectors; and to require the provinces to report back on where federal money was spent.

I responded in writing, outlining for Layton our commitment to directing the provinces to use any new healthcare funding for the public system to ensure that doctors who practised in both the public and private sector not be allowed to undermine the public system. Layton, however, was not really serious about healthcare. He was more interested in forcing an election. On November 28, the Martin government was defeated. Layton had chosen to support the Bloc Québécois and the Conservatives in defeating a government that had made healthcare one of its top priorities.

Martin dropped the writ, fixing January 23, 2006, as polling day. At the beginning of the long campaign, the Liberal party was ahead by about five points. The Gomery report had concluded that Martin had no part in the sponsorship scandal. But when the central campaign of the Liberal party slowed down for Christmas, the Conservatives continued to announce elements of their platform, gaining the lead in the polls. The Liberals responded with hard-hitting ads that some thought were negative. I was featured in a few of them, while David Emerson and I teamed up in another.

Toward the end of December, the government was hit with a leaked RCMP letter confirming that Finance Minister Ralph Goodale and the Ministry of Finance were under investigation regarding the possible leak in November of a budgetary tax proposal about income trusts. It was reported that Goodale's name was specifically included in the letter at the insistence of RCMP commissioner Giuliano Zaccardelli. Although in the end the Martin government, including Goodale, was cleared of any wrongdoing, the damage had been done. Prior to the leak of the RCMP letter, we had been detecting upward movement in our numbers, but the leak reaffirmed in the minds of the electorate the corruption the sponsorship scandal had exposed. Campaigning door to door in my constituency, I now heard some desire for change.

It was highly unusual for the commissioner of the RCMP to confirm an investigation into a ministry or a minister in the middle of an election. In my opinion, Zaccardelli's letter was at best puzzling and at worst a hatchet job. The RCMP's normal practice, particularly in sensitive cases, was to review the facts and the readily available evidence to determine if an investigation was warranted. Even then, the organization had the discretion not to make the fact of an investigation public unless they were sure charges would follow. It didn't appear they had used any such caution in this case. And what was the rush for Zaccardelli to approve the highly questionable modus operandi? In my view it amounted to the RCMP having a hand in defeating the government.

By the end of the evening on January 23, the Martin government was no more. We retained the Liberal seats in Vancouver, and in B.C. overall we did well. My margin of victory was larger in 2006 than it had been in 2004. But some of my comments that night betrayed the anger I felt. Knowing it was the health file that Layton had used to break with us disappointed me. Our Liberal government had done a very good job on health, providing unparalleled resources. I knew that the Conservatives, under Stephen Harper, did not believe in federal leadership on health, nor would they put any additional money into it. Politics is full of irony and unintended consequences. Canada would now pay for the unintended consequence of Layton's "progressive" politics and live under a right-wing government.

One of the Liberal seats in B.C. was David Emerson's Vancouver-Kingsway. A couple of days after the election, I attended a Chinese New Year function in Vancouver's Chinatown. The speeches had finished by the time Emerson showed up. Someone from his staff told me Emerson had been in Ottawa on a pressing matter, though I knew there was nothing earth-shaking happening in the capital that would require the presence of a former cabinet minister in a newly defeated government. Emerson wished everyone a very happy new year and then extended greetings on behalf of the prime minister elect in the spirit of the season. But his trip to Ottawa and his greetings on behalf, not of Parliament, but of the PM elect, set off the alarm bells in my head. I said nothing to anyone. On the day of the swearing-in of Harper's cabinet, I watched the proceedings live on TV. When I caught a glimpse of Emerson exiting a limousine outside Rideau Hall, my suspicions were confirmed. I was critical of his move, as were his constituents. Emerson was a former industry executive who, I felt, believed himself "born to rule"; perhaps harshly, I said as much publicly.

Paul Martin had resigned the night of the election, and Bill Graham, former external affairs minister, had taken over as acting leader. Now in opposition, I was appointed defence critic, which was important since our Afghan mission was soon to expand. Not long after becoming prime minister, Harper militarized the language of Canada's foreign policy and travelled to Afghanistan, where his speech proclaiming "You cannot lead from the bleachers... cutting and running is not my way" mimicked Churchill's "never surrender" speech grotesquely. This was no Second World War, not even close. The situation was serious, but we were not fighting another country, only the defeated remnants of its rag-tag military, who had run and hidden among the populace. They were dangerous, as was their ideology, and it was important to stabilize Afghanistan, if that could be accomplished. Others of the bygone era had tried, however — not just once, but several times. None had succeeded. Nor would we, I feared. My apprehension was well founded. Canadians have now left Afghanistan, as we knew we would, and in the process our brave soldiers have lost lives and limbs. Taliban violence is on the increase again. In view of the uncertain future Afghanistan faces, Harper's initial assurances ring even more hollow.

THE LIBERAL PARTY plunged into a leadership campaign to replace Paul Martin. I had many calls from people across the country who asked if I would consider running. But despite my somewhat inconsistent efforts at learning the language since becoming an MP, I did not speak French. Some friends and supporters argued that shouldn't matter, since I knew Hindi and Punjabi and understood most spoken Urdu. But none of those was one of Canada's official languages. An officially bilingual leader of a federal party is not mandated by law, but knowing both official languages in all their nuances is fundamental to successful leadership on the federal level. I decided to support Bob Rae instead.

Rae had become a member of the Liberal party in 2006, and I felt his political leadership skills, honed by a lifetime of public service, would inspire Canadians and bring them together. Although Michael Ignatieff was well known as a public intellectual, I did not believe he had what it would take to re-energize the party.

A December leadership convention meant a long campaign, and it became nasty. On behalf of Rae, I spoke to several Liberals. Two of them wanted a commitment by Rae on the sunset clause in the post-9/11 anti-terrorism law passed by the Chrétien government. I told them Rae would do what was in the national interest when the clause came up for review, but that wasn't good enough for them. Khalistani elements in the party also accused Rae of being anti-Sikh because he had prepared a report for the federal government on the Air India disaster. Khalistanis, who have found their way into all federal parties, have never accepted that Sikh terrorists downed the Air India plane, and in this case they spread rumours and misinformation about Rae and his supposed bias. Islamists, not to be left behind, also had advocates on the floor of the convention; they focussed on the fact that Rae's wife, Arlene Perly Rae, was a Jew and supposedly a supporter of "Zionist" Israel. Since Rae's ancestors too had been Jews, he could not be trusted, declared the Islamists. Tamil separatists also had unreasonable demands and promises they wanted to extract before their sizeable contingent would support Rae. I was disgusted as I witnessed all of this. We have learned little about how terrorism creeps into our lives, and we wake up only when things blow up in our faces.

Several candidates dropped out after the first ballot. Others, including former education minister Gerrard Kennedy, who was supported by Justin Trudeau, dropped out after the second. Some of Kennedy's support had come, as outlined by Tarek Fatah in the *Globe and Mail*, from Islamist and Khalistani groups. I do not believe Kennedy was aware of that: many mainstream politicians aren't aware of the intricacies of the internal politics of many ethnic communities.

I approached Kennedy's B.C. organizer, Bruce Young, to see if Kennedy's support could come to Rae, but Young told me they had a pact with Stéphane Dion: the first of the two to fall off the ballot would support the other. In the third round of voting, Rae trailed Ignatieff and Dion. Dion won on the final ballot. Kennedy's defeated network of 2006 would fold itself into the frontline of Trudeau's 2013 leadership campaign.

The Liberal party lost more seats in the 2008 election. On election night I won by a mere thirty-three votes, reduced to twenty in a judicial recount. I worked very hard for the next three years in both Ottawa and Vancouver, but with a dismal performance by our leader in the 2011 election, the Liberals were relegated to third-party status in the House of Commons. Jack Layton's charm and optimism had turned Quebec's disenchantment with the Bloc Québécois to the NDP's advantage. It was a known fact that Jack was seriously ill, but despite that he persisted in a gruelling campaign. I lost my seat by about 1,500 votes. I had decided going into the election that win, lose or draw, 2011 was going to be my last election. I had had enough of the weekly flights to and from Ottawa, and I was impatient to do something else. Now, the rest of my life beckoned.

50

A VARIATION ON THE common Indian expression *"Mullan de daur maseet taeen,"* which roughly translates as "An imam's ultimate refuge is the mosque," sums up my relationship with the world: India is my *maseet*. I have lived as a global citizen, but India has been my *mandir*, my *masjid* and my *girja*: my temple, my mosque and my church. It has been, too, my gurdwara, my synagogue and my pagoda. Canada has helped shape me; India is in my soul. Canada has been my abode, providing me with physical comforts and the arena for being an active citizen. India has been my spiritual refuge and my sanctuary. Physically, and in the incessant wanderings of the mind, I have returned to it time and again.

Most immigrants do not admit to living this divided experience. Our lack of candour about our schizophrenic souls is rooted in our fear of being branded disloyal to our adopted lands. I believe Canada, however, is mature enough to withstand the acknowledgement of the duality of immigrant lives. It can only make for a healthier democracy.

Several decades ago, I adopted Gandhi's creed of achieving change through non-violence as my own. As I ponder the journey ahead, far from India's partition and the midnight of my birth, there is no avoiding that the world is full of violence. In many parts of the globe, people are being butchered in the name of religion, nationalism and ethnic differences. Whole populations are migrating to Europe for economic reasons or to save themselves from being shot, beheaded or raped in the numerous conflicts in the Middle East and Africa. The reception in Europe for those fleeing mayhem and murder is at times ugly, as is the brutal discrimination faced by the world's Roma populations. The U.S. faces a similar crisis with migrants from Mexico and other parts of South America fleeing poverty and violence, in some cases that of the drug cartels. Parents and children take the huge risk of being killed en route to their dreamed destinations because they know the deathly dangers of staying. Building walls around rich and peaceful countries won't keep desperate people away. The only lasting solution is to build a peaceful world.

Human beings are naturally protective of the peace and prosperity within their own countries. A very small number of immigrants and refugees, or their sons and daughters, sometimes threaten the peace of their "host" societies. But regardless of whether the affluent societies of western Europe, Australia, New Zealand and North America like it or not, the pressure to accept the millions of people on the move will only mount as the bloody conflicts continue. Refugees will rightly argue that if the West becomes involved to the extent of bombing groups like ISIS, it must also do much more on the humanitarian front by helping to resettle those forced to flee, be they poverty-driven or refugees under the Geneva Convention. With the pressures of population, poverty and violence compounded by looming environmental catastrophes, the traditional borders of nation states are bound to crumble. If humanity isn't going to drown in the chaos of its own creation, the leading nations of the world will have to create a new world order, which may involve fewer international boundaries.

In my birthplace, the land of Mahatma, the forces of the religious right are ascendant, wreaking havoc on the foundational secularism of India's independence movement. I have never professed religion to be my business except when it invades secular spaces established for the benefit of all. Extremists the world over — the enemies of freedom — would like to erase both the modern and the secular from our lives. Born and bred in secular India, and having lived in secular Britain and Canada, I cherish everyone's freedom to be what they want to be and to believe what they choose to believe.

I have always been concerned about the ubiquitous financial, moral and ethical corruption in India, and my concern has often landed me in trouble with the rulers there. Corruption's almost complete stranglehold threatens the future of the country while the ruling elite remain in deep slumber, pretending that the trickle of economic development that escapes corruption's clutches will make the country great. It will not. Just as more education in India has not meant less corruption, more economic development won't result in greater honesty and integrity unless India experiences a cultural revolution of values and ethics. The inequalities of caste, poverty and gender also continue to bedevil India. Two books published in 1990, V.S. Naipaul's *India: A Million Mutinies Now* and Arthur Bonner's *Averting the Apocalypse,* sum up the ongoing turmoil. A million mutinies, both noble and evil, are boiling in India's bosom. Unless corruption is confronted, evil tamed, and the yearning for good liberated, an apocalypse will be impossible to avert. It will destroy India and its soul.

On the international level, the world today is missing big aspirational pushes and inspiring leaders. Perhaps I have been spoiled. During my childhood, I witnessed giants like Dr. Saifuddin Kitchlew of the Indian freedom movement take their place in history and even met some of them. As a teenager, I was mesmerized by the likes of Nehru and John F. Kennedy. I closely followed Martin Luther King and Robert Kennedy as they wrestled with difficult issues and transformative ideas. I landed in Canada during the time of Pierre Trudeau, one of our great prime ministers. Great leaders with great ideas are now sadly absent from the world stage.

The last few years have allowed me time for reflection. Writing this autobiography has served as a bridge between the life gone by and what lies ahead. Now that the often mundane demands of elected life no longer claim my energies, I am free to follow my heart. And in my continuing ambition that equality and social justice be realized, it is toward India, the land of my ancestors, that my heart leads me.

This book almost didn't get written. Many friends felt I had a story to tell. I resisted. Then family and friends pushed, shamed and cajoled me to begin. The thought that my grandchildren Solaina, Alexie, Suhani, Iyla, Mila and Damon might be curious enough one day to know more about their grandfather (Baba) kept me going as they kept me entertained, asking "are we in the story yet?" I could write a whole book on how it all came to happen and about the men, women, friends and family that helped along the way; but I won't.

This book is as much, if not more, my life partner Rami's as it is mine. She has been there for and with me in life, and she insisted that I write it myself; no ghost-written autobiography for her husband, she said. A conversation of long ago with my friend Sudhir Handa reminded me why it had to get done, and his continuing interest and support helped move the Journey forward. My friend Ravi Hira, generous to the core with more than just legal advice and moral support, has kept me humble and grounded.

Courtesy of the Laurier Institution's Farid Rohani, I was lucky to have Julia Inglefeld from Germany intern with me for over three months in the summer of 2014 to organize the clippings and documents from the last forty-five years of my life; she is now doing her graduate work in the U.S.

I didn't consult with any authors or editors while completing my manuscript. Viren Joshi, a dear friend, was the only one, other than Rami of course, to read my draft as it progressed. He must have laboured through my meanderings, but all I ever heard from him was praise and encouragement.

Scott McIntyre — of the old Douglas & McIntyre — a well-known elder of the publishing world in western Canada, was the third person to see the finished first draft of the manuscript. He was kind enough to go through it and say "there is a very good book in it." He helped me discover and connect with Figure 1. The publisher Chris Labonté of Figure 1 was my first and main contact throughout. From the moment we spoke, I knew my Journey and I were in extremely talented hands.

The immensely experienced editor Barbara Pulling moulded my wordy wanderings and helped reshape and meld them into a cohesive whole.

As Melanie Little copy edited the Journey, she patiently taught me the Word editing functions to help do it. Lana Okerlund read the proofs like a breeze. Natalie Olsen has beautifully designed the book.

My friends Amrik Sangha and Sukhwant Tethi were there with their standing offers of whatever I needed done.

Managing editor Lara Smith brought and kept it all together throughout for the Journey to be in the readers' hands.

Clark, Joe, 271–72, 273

Clark government: and 1996 election, 334–35; appointment of, 334; cabinet shuffle, 353; calls for Clark to resign, 352–53; Casinogate, 346–51, 353, 354, 355–59, 391; and labour issues, 380, 381; resignation of, 359. *See also* Clark, Glen

Clayoquot Sound, 308, 388

Communist Party of India, 51, 205

Congress party (India), 36, 51, 171, 174–75, 227

Connaught Place, Delhi, 71–72

Cosmic Crayon Company, 95–97

CSIS (Canadian Security Intelligence Agency), 256, 258

Cull, Elizabeth, 321, 333, 353, 362, 383

Cullen, Austin, 251

D

Dada (paternal grandfather (Harnam)), 4

Dadi (paternal grandmother (Bishan Kaur)), 4

Dalits, 80

D'Arcy, Thomas, 413

Davies, Libby, 372

daycare, *see* child care

Delhi, India, 71–72, 181, 213, 223, 262–63, 265–66

Desai, Moraji, 171

Deshmukh, Vilasrao, 393

Des Pardes (newspaper), 101, 104, 204

Dhahan, Nashatter, 156

Dhaliwal, Herb, 296, 382, 384, 406, 410

Dhaliwal, Kashmir, 298, 368, 394

Dharm Yudh Morcha, 210–11, 222, 224, 228–29, 240. *See also* Bhindranwale, Jarnail Singh; Sikh extremists

Dhillon, Daljit, 160

Dhillon, Gurdev, 118

Dhillon, Manjit (Masarji (uncle)): introduction to, 118–19; and altercation at Ross Street Temple, 131; and Daljit's charges against Ujjal, 160, 161; help from on arrival in Vancouver, 119, 120, 122, 123; and Tommy Douglas, 127; and Ujjal's safety, 242

Dhillon, Ram Singh, 127

Dion, Stéphane, 427

Dix, Adrian, 194, 348, 382

Doman Industries, 401

Dosanjh, Amar Singh, 174–75

Dosanjh, Aseem (son): arrest in Windsor, 385–86, 387; attack at fireworks festival, 386–87; birth of, 157; childhood burns, 166–67; endearment term for, 182; at Golden Temple,

217, 221; law career of, 404–5; marriage of, 405; and parents' trip to India, 170, 190; photographs of, *115, 288*; and politics, 319, 374; and tensions within Sikh community, 243; trip to India, 214, 221

Dosanjh, Balbir Singh, 42

Dosanjh, Bhagwan Singh, 49

Dosanjh, Hargurdeep "Chand," 61

Dosanjh, Kamal (Bhaji (brother)): and Bachint Kaur, 3; and Chachaji's poor health, 201; childhood of, 31, 41–42, 47; and death of mother, 28; education of, 9, 33, 36, 52; at lumber mill, 123; marriage of, 124; photographs of, *106, 107, 108*; and threats against Ujjal, 242; and Ujjal leaving for England, 60–61, 67, 70; in Vancouver, 135

Dosanjh, Pavel (son): birth of, 149; childhood of, 166; endearment term for, 182; law career of, 404; marriage of, 405; Martin Luther King poster, 261; and parents' trip to India, 170, 190; photographs of, *115, 288*; and politics, 294, 319, 374; and tensions within Sikh community, 243; trip to India, 214, 221

Dosanjh, Pritam Singh (Chachaji (father)): and altercation at Ross Street Temple, 130–31; in Canada, 125; courtesy of, and political disagreements, 49; death of, 201; and Dosanjh School, 7, 34, 35, 36; education of, 5, 35–36; family land owned by, 2; and family's education, 7, 9; financial support from Biraji, 82; height of, 4; library of, 39; life of, 4, 34–35; and Muslims, 38; and *naqlaan* incident, 50–51; photographs of, *105, 107, 108, 114, 115*; political involvement of, 36, 37, 38–39, 126, 202; and Rami's father, 145; relationship with Ujjal, 42, 44, 50, 52–53, 54–55, 56, 73–74, 120; in retirement, 162; and superstitions, 8; and Ujjal leaving for England, 60–61, 65, 71, 73–74; and Ujjal's passport, 62; and Ujjal's return trip to India, 174; ventures of, 47–49; visits to Bahowal, 25–26; wedding of, 19–20

Dosanjh, Ujjal: appetite of, 72; on dealing with idiots, 89; on emigration, 170; eyesight of, 44, 64, 93; fiction writing attempt, 226–27; gestures of kindness to, 172; hair cutting by, 73–74, 88; as Indian diaspora honouree, 406; and languages, 39, 227; name of, 129, 303–4; photographs of, *107, 110, 111, 112, 113, 276–82, 284–90*; pride in India, 84; reflections on India, 428, 429–30; stomach problems, 161;

stuttering of, 84. *See also* Dosanjh, Ujjal, as B.C. Attorney General; Dosanjh, Ujjal, in B.C. provincial politics; Dosanjh, Ujjal, childhood and early adulthood; Dosanjh, Ujjal, education; Dosanjh, Ujjal, in England; Dosanjh, Ujjal, family life; Dosanjh, Ujjal, in federal politics; Dosanjh, Ujjal, law career; Dosanjh, Ujjal, political involvement; Dosanjh, Ujjal, and Sikh/Indian politics; Dosanjh, Ujjal, trips to India; Dosanjh, Ujjal, in Vancouver; Dosanjh extended family; Dosanjh government

Dosanjh, Ujjal, as B.C. Attorney General: and Aboriginal rights, 338–39; and Air India investigation, 350; appointment to, 321–22; and Armistice Day "dawn patrol," 340–41; and bankruptcy laws, 339; and Bert Stone case, 335–36, 376; and Carrier Lumber case, 397–98; and Casinogate, 346–47, 348–49, 350–51, 353, 354, 355–59; and child protection, 337, 350, 362; conflict of interest accusation, 343; conflict of interest in Balwant Gill case, 365–66; and drug and community courts, 335; and fugitives, 337; in Gay Pride Parade, 338; and Gitksan First Nation, 323; and GLBT rights, 338; and Gustafsen Lake standoff, 322–23, 324–31, 363, 365; and hate crimes, 336–37; and illegal gambling, 337; and mobile phones and driving, 339; and Nisga'a Agreement, 340, 345; and Organized Crime Agency of B.C., 335; and policing jurisdictional issues, 340, 350; problems facing, 341–42; and prostitution, 337; and provincial court appointments, 342; and racism, 362; reflections on, 335, 346; and regional policing, 337–38; and R. v. Sharpe, 342; and safe injection sites, 339; and Sikh extremists, 341; and tobacco lawsuit, 340; and women, 336, 344, 366

Dosanjh, Ujjal, in B.C. provincial politics: 1979 Vancouver South NDP nomination, 193–95, 197–98; 1979 Vancouver South NDP campaign, 199–200; 1983 Vancouver South campaign, 207–8, 276, 277; and 1986 election, 269; 1991 Vancouver-Kensington NDP nomination, 298–99; 1991 Vancouver-Kensington campaign, 278, 300–302; 2001 election campaign, 286, 287, 399–400, 401–2; as backbencher, 302–3, 305, 309–10, 311–12; as caucus chair, 313, 332; and Chinese head tax, 305–6; Chinese name for, 300;

decision to run for NDP leadership, 361–62, 363–65; as DTES representative, 304; early involvement in, 126, 148; freedom in, 352; and gaming policy, 316, 320–21; hate mail received, 316; and human rights legislation, 309; life after, 404–6; meeting with Barrett, 351–52; molotov cocktail attack, 367–68; in NDP leadership race, 280, 364–70, 372–75; perception of political demise, 293–94; as services minister, 279, 319–20, 321; in Tea Caucus, 310; Vancouver-Kensington NDP executive election, 294–98, 299; Vancouver South NDP riding association, 191–92.
See also Dosanjh, Ujjal, as B.C. Attorney General; Dosanjh government

Dosanjh, Ujjal, childhood and early adulthood: at Billayhana farm, 10–11, 12; buffalo incident, 31; and buffalo milk, 43; cinemas escapade, 54–55; and Connaught Place, Delhi, 71–72; in Dosanjh Kalan, 33–34, 36, 40–41, 47–48; and family approval, 57; and father, 25–26, 42, 50, 52–53, 73–74; field hockey, 41–42; finding own voice, 46; first memory of, 7–8; friends of, 22–23, 66–67; household members, 2–3; journey to live with maternal grandparents, 13–15; mango season, 30–31; with maternal grandparents, 21, 23–24, 25–26, 30, 33; and mother, 26–29; and *naqlaan* incident, 50–51; passport application, 61–62; and poetry, 50, 87; police extortion incident, 53–54; and Punjabi language, 39; rebuilding of family house, 47; *shucker* fire incident, 43; and status-consciousness, 44, 45, 55; toys of, 8, 9; walk home from Phagwara, 63–65; and young women, 46. *See also* Dosanjh, Ujjal, education

Dosanjh, Ujjal, education: application to study in England, 58–61; application to UBC, 148; at Bahowal School, 20, 21–22; composition and thinking ability, 45–46; at Dosanjh School, 33, 36, 43–44; law studies applications, 148–49; law studies at UBC, 156, 157–58; pursuing in England, 93–94, 98, 99; at Ramgarhia College, 52–53, 55–57; at Simon Fraser University, 142, 143–44, 148; typing class at Langara, 226–27; at Vancouver Community College, 128–29, 135; at VCC Langara, 136, 137, 138

Dosanjh, Ujjal, in England: application to study in, 58–61; arrival in, 80–82; caste system in, 100; departure from, 103–4; job at Armco,

99–100; job at Cosmic Crayon Company, 95–97; job at Elstow Abbey Secondary School, 98–99; job at *Mamta Weekly,* 100–101; job with British Rail, 88–89, 91, 93; leaving for and flight to, 68–69, 70–71, 74–77; life in, 98; marriage proposal in, 100; political activities in, 97–98; preparations for, 63, 66, 67, 68, 71; pursuing education in, 93–94; return visit to, 172; settling into, 83–84, 85, 86, 87–88, 90, 91–92, 94, 96–97

Dosanjh, Ujjal, family life: and 1986 election, 269–70; and Bob and Leah Osterhout misunderstandings, 162; and election campaigns, 191; family photos, *282*; financial difficulties, 159, 202; grandparents' involvement, 166–67; holiday across North America, 259–61; holiday to California, 203; housing, 149, 151, 191, 209, 292; marriage dynamics, 157; and Rami pre-wedding, 138–39, 140, 141; and Sikh politics, 243, 244, 245; single parent experience, 226; sons' weddings, 405; wedding of, *112,* 144–47. *See also* Dosanjh, Ujjal, trips to India; Dosanjh extended family; *specific family members*

Dosanjh, Ujjal, in federal politics: 1974 election, 191; 2004 election campaign in Vancouver South, 411–12; 2006 election campaign, 424; 2008 and 2011 elections, 427; assistance to Barjinder Sandhu's nomination, 407–8; decision to run for Liberals, 408–9, 410; as defence critic, 425; and federal NDP, 363, 404, 406; and Grewal tapes, 419–20, 421; as health minister, *288, 289,* 413, 414–17, 422–23, 424; and leadership race to replace Martin, 425–27; reactions to Liberal candidacy, 410–11; swearing-in as MP, 413, 414; trip to India, 417–18. *See also* Martin government

Dosanjh, Ujjal, law career: after 1979 election, 201–2; articling, 164; call to bar, 167; Dosanjh & Company law firm, 292, 409; Dosanjh & Pirani law firm, 192, 270, 292; D&V Janitorial Services case, 165–66; farm worker assault case, 164–65; first day in court, 163–64; with Motiuk, 163, 164, 170, 190, 192; Peltier case, 165; and political involvement, 192; practising in India, 187; pro bono work, 167; and restlessness, 226; return to after provincial politics, 405–6; as trial lawyer, 190

Dosanjh, Ujjal, political involvement: and 1980 Vancouver mayoral election, 202; and Attorney General office, 152; and B.C.

Human Rights Branch, 152; in England, 97–98; legal information radio program, 149–50; life after, 430; and October Crisis, 133–34; offer to be consul general in Chandigarh, 406–7; on party discipline, 202; political development of, 53–54, 127–28, 134, 137, 157, 304, 428–29, 430; reflections on, 407, 428–29; and unionization of farm workers, 153–56. *See also* Dosanjh, Ujjal, as B.C. Attorney General; Dosanjh, Ujjal, in B.C. provincial politics; Dosanjh, Ujjal, in federal politics; Dosanjh, Ujjal, and Sikh/Indian politics; Dosanjh government

Dosanjh, Ujjal, and Sikh/Indian politics: altercation at Ross Street Temple, 130–31, 132–33; column in *Link,* 231, 236–37; false assault charge against, 160–61; and family life, 243, 244, 245; and Foreign Exchange Regulation Act, 208; India Independence Day ceremonies, 233–34; lawsuit against Tara, 254; letters to Canadian politicians on separatists, 253; letter to Indira Gandhi on separatists, 235–36; parking lot attack, 246–52, *277*; political prisoners protests, 129, 224; press conference on separatists, 234–35; against regional prejudices, 122; response to press conference, 236–38; statements on separatists, 151, 229–30, 241–42, 268; support for after parking lot attack, 249–50; threats against for, 240, 242, 244–45, 246, 259, 261–62, 268; vigil for victims of violence after Indira's death, 240–41

Dosanjh, Ujjal, trips to India: 1994 trade mission trip, 317–18; and Air India bombing, 255–56; in Amritsar, 175, 176, 214, 264, 394; as B.C. premier, 392–96; in Bollywood, *284,* 393; cane incident, 187; car accident, 184; at Centaur Hotel, 225–26; and Chachaji's poor health, 201; in Delhi, 181, 213, 262–63, 265–66; in Dosanjh Kalan, 174, 265, *279,* 395, 396; at Durgiana Mandir, 221–22; in Fatehpur Sikir, 180–81, 213–14; as federal MP, *288, 290,* 417–18; first trip back, 170–71, 172–74, 260; fourth trip to, 314–15; in Gaddanian Farm, 185–86; at Gandhi Mausoleum, *288*; at Golden Temple (Harimandir Sahib), 214–17, 221; at Guru Nanak Dev University, 394–95; in Hyderabad, 392–93; for Indian diaspora honour, 406; in Jalandhar, 263; John Borst in, 183–84; in Kashmir, 178–79; in Lucknow, 181; meeting with Bhindranwale, 217–21; meeting with Indira Gandhi, 222–24; meeting with Longowal, 222; in Mumbai (Bombay), 182–83, 393; Rami's family and friends, 175, 176–77, 185, 214; return to Canada after, 188, 190, 225; second trip to, 212–13, 214, 226; in Simla, 186–87; and Taj Mahal, 179–80, 213; third trip to, 261–67, *284–85*; train ride to Bombay, 181–82; train ride to Goraya, 264–65; at Women's College, Sidhwan, 395–96

Dosanjh, Ujjal, in Vancouver: arrival in, 118; back injury, 129, 132, 133, 135, 231–32; first job at lumber mill, 119; houses in, 124, 135, 149; job at Burke Lumber, 123, 129, 149; settling into, 119–20; sponsoring of family to, 125. *See also* Dosanjh, Ujjal, education; Dosanjh, Ujjal, family life; Dosanjh, Ujjal, law career

Dosanjh, Umber (son): after undergraduate degree, 405; birth of, 192; on family's car, 294; photographs of, *115*; and politics, 319, 374; trips to India, 214, 221, 392

Dosanjh & Company law firm, 292, 409

Dosanjh extended family: ancestors of, 2, 6; Billayhana farm, 10–11, 12; children exchanges within, 20; Goraywala farm, 11–12, 33; houses in Vancouver, 124, 135, 149; maternal family, 5; paternal family, 3–4. *See also specific family members*

Dosanjh government: 2001-02 budget, 398–99; achievements of, 397, 398–99; and balanced budget bill, 381–82; cabinet, 378–79; cabinet shuffle, 388–89; and Carrier Lumber case, 397–98; Chief Bill Wilson on, 389; and child care, 379, 390–91, 397; and Chrétien government, 382–83; and Clark, 384; and Clayoquot Sound, 388; and Doman Industries, 401; dropping the writ, 399; and Friesen v. Hammell, 383; in Gay Pride Parade, *285*, 338; and Great Bear Rainforest, 399; and grizzly bear hunt, 398; and healthcare, 389–90; and Human Rights Code, 399; immediate priorities of, 376, 379; and labour issues, 380–81; and Locke administration (WA), 383; and murder case, 387–88; and Nisga'a Agreement, 388; press secretary for, 379; problems facing, 391, 397–98; resignation as premier, 402, 404; swearing-in ceremony, *280, 281, 282, 283,* 376–77; throne speech, 379; trip to China, 398; trip to India, 392–96

Dosanjh Kalan (ancestral village): agriculture in, 6, 9–10, 12, 40–41, 65; canal running through, 68–69; Dosanjh family in, 2, 9;

girls school in, 20; *khooh* in, 33; as parochial, 28; poetry readings in, 50; politics in, 49; return trips to, *114,* 174, 265, *279,* 395, 396

Dosanjh & Pirani law firm, 192, 270, 292

Dosanjh School (Guru Har Rai Khalsa High School), 7, 34, 35, 36, 42, 43–44, 46

Douglas, Tommy, 127

Downtown Eastside, 304

Doyle, Jimmy, 353

drug and community courts, 335

Durgiana Mandir, 64, 221–22

Dutta, Sushma Sardana, 229, 270

Duvall, Jim, 193, 198, 200

D&V Janitorial Services, 165–66

E

East Indian Defence Committee (EIDC), 205–6

East Indians, *see* Indian community, in Canada/ B.C.

East Indian Workers' Association (EIWA), 205–6

economic immigration, 91

education: in India, 44. *See also* Bahowal School; Dosanjh, Ujjal, education; Dosanjh School (Guru Har Rai Khalsa High School)

EIDC (East Indian Defence Committee), 205–6

eighty-four, number, 248

EIWA (East Indian Workers' Association), 205–6

Elstow Abbey Secondary School, 98–99

Emerson, David, 409, 424–25

Emerson, Kim, 318–19

England: in 1960s, 83, 90–91; Indian community in, 84–85, 90–91; Punjabi newspapers in, 101; race relations in, 94, 102, 103. *See also* Dosanjh, Ujjal, in England

environmental issues, 308, 310, 388, 399

Evans, Corky, 352, 362, 367, 370, 372, 373–74

Exner, Adam, 338

F

fake encounters, 177, 315, 317

family life, *see* Dosanjh, Ujjal, family life

Farmer, Bruce, 294–95, 301

farm workers, 152, 153–56, 166

Farnworth, Mike, 310, 347, 348, 350–51

fast ferry scandal, 379

Fatehpur Sikir, India, 180–81, 213–14

field hockey, 42

Findlay, Gillian, 235, 271

First Nations rights, 338–39. *See also* Gitksan First Nation; Gustafsen Lake standoff; Nisga'a Agreement

Sikhs: in Bedford, England, 81; and caste system, 8; children displaced by anti-Sikh riots, 263; Guru Nanak, 6, 37, 69, 134, 146, 304; history of, 6, 16–17, 215, 222. *See also* Indian community, in Canada/B.C.; Ross Street Temple; 2nd Avenue Temple; Sikh extremists

Sikh extremists: overview of, 204, 205, 207; and Akali Dal party, 210–11; apologists for, 261; attempted rehabilitation by, 271; Canadian response to, 244, 246, 257–58, 268–69, 271–72; growth of worldwide, 228–29, 232–33; Khalistan, 18, 122, 204, 206, 213; and *Komagata Maru* commemoration, 270; and Leftists, 270–71; letters to Canadian politicians on, 253; moderate Sikhs against, 238; organizations for, 241; press conference on, 234–35; proving support challenge, 253–54; on Rae, 426; statements against, 241–42, 268; tensions within, 273; and Vancouver-Kensington riding, 295–97, 298. *See also* Air India Flight 182 bombing; Bhindranwale, Jarnail Singh; Dosanjh, Ujjal, and Sikh/Indian politics; Harimandir Sahib (Golden Temple); Hayer, Tara Singh; Parmar, Talwinder Singh

Sikh Students' Federation, 231, 241

Simla, India, 186–87

Simon Fraser University, 142, 143–44, 148

Simpson, Bernie, 293, 316, 317

Sinclair, Jim, 380

Singal, Ramesh, 392

Singh, Babaji Naranjan, 118–19

Singh, Baldev, 37

Singh, Beant (Punjab chief minister), 315

Singh, Bela, 121

Singh, Bhag, 24–25

Singh, Bhola, 3, 4

Singh, Bir, 5, 16, 202

Singh, Budh, 4

Singh, Chacha Chain, 87, 93

Singh, Darbara, 37, 38–39, 211, 266

Singh, Dharam, 60

Singh, Dunna (paternal great-great-grandfather), 3

Singh, Gurdit, 16

Singh, Gyani Zail, 223, 266

Singh, Harbans, 65

Singh, Jagat Jit, 182

Singh, Jagjit, 385–86

Singh, Joginder (Tayaji (uncle)): and ancestral lands, 2, 7; at Billayhana, 10–11; and Biraji's education, 7, 59; and

chai, 11; childhood of, 4, 5; childhood with, 28; as farmer, 5, 36, 40, 52–53; height of, 4; in household, 33; and oxen, 6; photograph of, *108*; and Ujjal's departure for England, 68; and Ujjal's departure for maternal family, 14

Singh, Khushwant, 262–63, *285*, 317

Singh, Makhan, 21

Singh, Manjit, 214

Singh, Manmohan (prime minister), 317, 418

Singh, Manmohan (separatist), 231, 241, 257

Singh, Meehan (Bedford Dalit), 100

Singh, Meehan (godman), 212, 213

Singh, Mewa, 121

Singh, Nand (paternal great-grandfather), 3, 4

Singh, Sabu, 131

Singh, Sewa, 186

Singh, Swaran, 37

Singh, T. Sher, 234

Siripawa, Premchit, 150

Siso Bhenji (cousin), 7, 9, 33, 70–71, 72, *106*, *108*

Smallwood, Joan, 353, 369

Smith, Bob, 361

Smith, Brian, 268, 365

Smith, Bud, 347

Snowdon, 96–97

Social Credit Party (B.C.), 293, 300, 302, 306. *See also* Bennett (Bill) government; Johnston, Rita; Vander Zalm, Bill

Sohal, Harry, 259–60

Somjee, A.H., 143

South Africa, 101

South Asians, *see* Indian community, in Canada/B.C.

space race, 101

special prosecutors, 347, 354

sponsorship scandal, 409–10

Stevenson, Tim, 338, 361, 379, 388

Stockell, David, 383

Stoffer, Peter, 411

Stone, Bert, 335–36, 376

Streifel, Dennis, 380

Stronach, Belinda, 418

sugarcane, 10

Sull, Harjit, 252

Sung, Baba, 6

Sutherland, Peter, 392

Symes, Robert, 96

T

Taeeji, *see* Kaur, Bhagwant (Taeeji (aunt))

Taj Mahal, 179–80, 213

Tao, Tommy, 300